KU-278-621

WITHDRAWN

LIVERPOOL JMU LIBRARY

3 1111 01387 5800

The United States and the Vietnam War

Significant Scholarly Articles

Series Editor

Walter L. Hixson
University of Akron

Routledge
Taylor & Francis Group

Series Contents

1. The Roots of the Vietnam War
2. Military Aspects of the Vietnam Conflict
3. Leadership and Diplomacy in the Vietnam War
4. The Vietnam Antiwar Movement
5. The Lessons and Legacies of the Vietnam War
6. Historical Memory and Representations of the Vietnam War

Military Aspects
of the Vietnam Conflict

Edited with introductions by

Walter L. Hixson
University of Akron

Routledge
Taylor & Francis Group

First published in 2000 by
Garland Publishing, Inc.
Reprinted by Routledge
270 Madison Avenue,
New York, NY 10016

2 Park Square, Milton Park,
Abingdon, Oxon OX14 4RN

Introduction copyright © 2000 Walter L. Hixson. All rights reserved.

Transferred to digital printing 2010.

Library of Congress Cataloging-in-Publication Data

The roots of the Vietnam War / edited with introductions by Walter L. Hixson
    p. cm. — (The United States and the Vietnam War. Significant scholarly
articles ; 1)
    Includes bibliographical references.
    1. Vietnam—Politics and government—1945–1975. 2. Vietnam—Foreign
relations—United States. 3. United States—Foreign relations—Vietnam. 4.
United States—Foreign relations—1945–1989. I. Hixson, Walter L. II. Series.

   DS556.8.R65 2000
   959.704'3—dc21   00-030859

ISBN   978-0-415-88626-0 (POD set)
ISBN   978-0-815-33531-3 (v. 1)
ISBN   978-0-815-33532-0 (v. 2)
ISBN   978-0-815-33533-7 (v. 3)
ISBN   978-0-815-33534-4 (v. 4)
ISBN   978-0-815-33535-1 (v. 5)
ISBN   978-0-815-33536-8 (v. 6)

Contents

vii   Series Introduction

xiii   Volume Introduction

1   Hanoi's Three Decisions and the Escalation of the Vietnam War
King C. Chen

23   Political Polarization in South Vietnam:
U.S. Policy in the Post-Diem Period
George McT. Kahin

51   The Search for the "Breaking Point" in Vietnam:
The Statistics of a Deadly Quarrel
John E. Mueller

75   The Development of the American Theory of Limited War,
1945–63
Michael W. Cannon

109   The Social Incidence of Vietnam Casualties: Social Class or Race?
Gilbert Badillo and G. David Curry

120   Cohesion and Disintegration in the American Army:
An Alternative Perspective
Paul L. Savage and Richard A. Gabriel

157   West Point at War:
Officer Attitudes and the Vietnam War, 1966–1972
James Jay Carafano

168   Patrolling Hill 55: Hard Lessons in Retrospect
Howard A. Christy

177   Paradox of Power: Infiltration, Coastal Surveillance,
and the United States Navy in Vietnam, 1965–68
Clarence E. Wunderlin, Jr.

193   The Significance of Local Communist Forces in Post-Tet Vietnam
Peter Brush

205   The Attack on Cap Mui Lay, Vietnam, July 1968
Faris R. Kirkland

232   Tonnage and Technology: Air Power on the Ho Chi Minh Trail
       Darrel D. Whitcomb

247   The CIA and the "Secret War" in Laos:
       The Battle for Skyline Ridge, 1971–1972
       William M. Leary

260   Fast-Movers and Herbicidal Spraying Southeast Asia
       Richard D. Duckworth

273   Setup: Why and How the U.S. Air Force Lost in Vietnam
       Earl Tilford, Jr.

289   Differing Evaluations of Vietnamization
       Scott Sigmund Gartner

309   People's War in Vietnam
       John M. Gates

329   Acknowledgments

Series Introduction

These six volumes focus on the history and legacies of the Vietnam War on the basis of the best scholarly articles. The six volumes analyze, respectively, the origins of the Indochina wars; military strategy; the role of prominent individuals; the antiwar movement; the lessons of Vietnam; and representations of the war in popular culture. A brief introduction accompanies each volume.

The six volumes address most of the key issues pertaining to the history of the Indochina conflict. The articles, culled from journals published over a span of nearly 50 years, reflect the divergent interpretations of more than 100 authors. The brief narrative history that appears in each volume provides context and a ready resource for the reader. Taken as whole, the series offers a comprehensive source for students, specialists, and the interested public.

* * * * * *

The United States and the Vietnam War:
A Brief Narrative History

The war in Southeast Asia, which claimed millions of Asian and American casualties and left the United States deeply divided, was inextricably linked to the Cold War. Indeed, the Vietnam War, engulfing all of Indochina (comprising Vietnam, Laos, and Cambodia), was the most violent and sustained conflict of the Cold War era.

European colonialism lay at the root of the Vietnam conflict. France established its control over Vietnam in the mid-nineteenth century in a quest for profits and world influence. Resistance evolved until Vietnamese nationalists, led by Ho Chi Minh, pressed for independence in the aftermath of World War I (1914–1918). While France clung to its empire, Ho embraced Marxism-Leninism and built a determined following. Ho's organization, the Vietminh, prepared to assume power after the Second World War, which had left France greatly weakened. Partly based on a racist contempt for the Vietnamese, however, French officials still believed they could reassert control over Indochina.

THE FIRST INDOCHINA WAR (1946–54)

War erupted in 1946 and lasted until Vietnam defeated France at the battle of Dienbienphu in 1954. In the settlement at Geneva ending the First Indochina War, France agreed to withdraw. Ho, supported by the Soviet Union and the People's Republic of China, held power over North Vietnam. The diplomats in Geneva agreed that there would be elections in 1956 to reunify Vietnam as an independent nation. The Cold War, however, intervened. The United States did not sign the Geneva Accords and, though it pledged not to disrupt them, in fact proceeded to undermine the planned elections. Encouraged by Washington, a mandarin elite and former monk, Ngo Dinh Diem, proclaimed the existence of an independent government based in Saigon, "South Vietnam."

The United States, which had funneled millions of dollars into the French war effort, now pledged millions more to Diem's government. Beginning in the late 1950s, a revolutionary movement, the National Liberation Front (NLF) — indigenous to South Vietnam but supported by Ho — launched a guerrilla war against the Saigon regime. Diem's government could overcome neither the rebels nor its own internal enemies. Plagued by the NLF guerrillas, sectarian violence, and his own ineptitude, Diem fell in a U.S.-sanctioned military coup in November 1963. President John F. Kennedy, himself assassinated only three weeks after Diem's murder by the South Vietnamese army, left a legacy of 16,700 U.S. advisors in the country and a commitment to contain communism in Southeast Asia.

JOHNSON TAKES COMMAND

Lyndon Johnson, Kennedy's successor, had no intention of abandoning the effort in Southeast Asia. Johnson recalled how the fallout from the "loss" of China in 1949 had destroyed fellow Democrat Harry S. Truman's presidency. He vowed that no nation would fall to communism on his watch. Yet a succession of military leaders failed to establish a stable government in Saigon. The NLF, meanwhile, continued to gain momentum. Not all of the southern Vietnamese revolutionaries were communists, to be sure, but they opposed the Saigon government as a puppet regime of the United States — a continuation of foreign control that Vietnam had been struggling to overcome since the establishment of French colonialism.

As the southern insurgency gained more and more ground in South Vietnam, Johnson decided that only direct U.S. military intervention could reverse a deteriorating situation that threatened to confront him with the dreaded charge of losing a country to communism. Johnson, who had been awaiting an opportunity to gain broader congressional authority to wage war against the southern insurgents, achieved his aim by misrepresenting a naval clash in the Gulf of Tonkin in August 1964. The subsequent Tonkin Gulf Resolution, passed by both houses of Congress with only two dissenting votes in the Senate, gave Johnson a blank check to take any and all actions he deemed necessary to defend the United States against "aggression." The President immediately launched retaliatory bombing raids against North Vietnam. The southern insurgency, backed by Ho's government in Hanoi, stepped up its resistance in the South and branded the United States the aggressor. The war was on.

In February 1965, using a guerrilla sapper attack on a U.S. base in Pleiku as a pretext to implement a planned escalation, Johnson ordered more retaliatory air strikes that eventually became Rolling Thunder, a regular campaign of aerial bombardment. Soon bombs rained not only on Vietnam, but on guerrilla sanctuaries and supply lines, as well as other communist forces, in neighboring Laos and Cambodia. Both of those nations found themselves sucked into the vortex of war. Washington was fighting an increasingly unlimited "limited war" in Indochina.

THE DEPLOYMENT OF COMBAT TROOPS

U.S. national security elites concluded that the NLF and North Vietnam would abandon their efforts under the weight of the enormous number of casualties that could be inflicted by U.S. firepower. Hence Johnson authorized U.S. combat troops to embark on "search and destroy" missions aimed at finding the guerrillas and killing them. Under this strategy, gauging success depended on the number of enemy dead bodies that could be amassed. In less than a year the United States had dramatically Americanized the Vietnam conflict. Extrication years later would prove to be a far more wrenching ordeal than the original escalation.

For years the United States pummeled Indochina with a total tonnage of bombs that exceeded that expended by all belligerents in all theaters of World War II. Washington also employed Agent Orange and other defoliants — later determined to have caused cancer in thousands of U.S. troops and countless villagers — in an effort to remove natural vegetation which provided the southern rebels with cover. In the face of punishing U.S. military power, the determined Vietnamese continued their struggle and even executed a surprise uprising, the Tet Offensive of January 1968, in an effort to win the war. Launched simultaneously in hundreds of hamlets, towns, and cities across South Vietnam, Tet failed to achieve its ultimate objective of igniting a collapse of the Saigon government. Massive U.S. military might eventually put down the offensive, which caused widespread destruction in an increasingly ugly and inconclusive war. The NLF infrastructure suffered heavy losses, though increasing numbers of North Vietnamese regular army troops entered the southern mountains and jungles to replace them.

It had long since been clear that U.S. bombing could not bring an end to the war. Millions of Americans had erupted in protest, especially in the wake of Tet when the press published reports that Johnson was considering sending 200,000 additional troops to Vietnam. Already more than half a million Americans were fighting in Indochina, with more every year coming home in body bags. The war was proving not only divisive, but alarmingly expensive as well. While the fighting and bombing continued, a defeated LBJ scaled back U.S. involvement, opened neogitations, and abandoned his own plans to seek reelection.

NIXON'S STRATEGY OF EXTRICATION

Most Americans wanted out of Vietnam but did not want to lose a war to a communist government backed by China and the Soviet Union. Richard Nixon, elected President in 1968, promised to achieve an honorable settlement. Nixon began systematically to withdraw U.S. troops, but he authorized the most intense bombing campaign in history while seeking a negotiated settlement.

The antiwar movement, restrained in Nixon's first year, exploded anew in the spring of 1970 when Nixon announced that U.S. troops would fight in Cambodia. At Kent State University in northeast Ohio, National Guard units stunned the nation by opening fire on protesters, killing four students. America was coming apart over the Vietnam War.

Nixon and his chief foreign policy aide, Henry A. Kissinger, finally negotiated a peace settlement in Paris in January 1973. U.S. prisoners of war, some of whom had been detained for almost a decade, returned home, but North Vietnamese troops were allowed to stay in place in South Vietnam. In reality, the Paris agreement offered no solution to the conflict, only an opportunity for America to get out. The Saigon government, headed by Nguyen Van Thieu, bitterly opposed the agreement, fearing accurately that the U.S. pullout would lead to its own rapid demise.

THE COLLAPSE OF SOUTH VIETNAM

That is precisely what happened. Sickened by the long, divisive, and indecisive war, most Americans did not even want to hear the word Vietnam spoken again after the Paris agreement. Congress turned sharply against the war, repealing the Tonkin Gulf Resolution in 1971, cutting off money for bombing, and in 1973 passing the War Powers Act, legislation limiting the President's ability to make war without eventual direct congressional authorization.

With the Nixon administration destroyed by the Watergate scandal, a series of illegalities that forced the President to resign in August 1974, no U.S. response materialized to the final offensive launched by North Vietnam in 1975. North Vietnamese forces steamrolled through cities and the countryside on the way to Saigon, which they captured in April. The South Vietnamese regime, the Achilles heel of the American war effort, collapsed in a heap. Millions of South Vietnamese frantically left the country for the next several years. Many of these "boat people" perished in rickety craft on the high seas or fell prey to pirates. Others languished in refugee camps throughout Southeast Asia. The United States admitted millions of Vietnamese, Cambodians, and Laotian mountain dwellers who had supported U.S. efforts.

While the Hanoi government did not launch a bloodbath, the fanatical communists who took over Cambodia, the Khmer Rouge, engaged in genocide against their own people, killing as many as three million. The communists assumed power in Laos as well, but no other Southeast Asian states adopted communist governments. The much-feared domino effect never transpired. In fact, the communist states turned on one another. By 1969 the Soviet and Chinese communist regimes were on the brink of war — with each other. Ten years later, the communist governments of Vietnam and China fought in a brief but bloody conflict over a Vietnamese attack into Cambodia against the Khmer Rouge.

The consensus in the United States was that the Vietnam War had been a colossal mistake. More than 58,000 Americans, most of them very young men, died in Indochina. Hundreds of thousands more returned home with physical or psychological wounds. The nation as a whole struggled for decades to recover from a foreign policy debacle that, however tragic, had flowed logically from U.S. Cold War perceptions. As for Indochina itself, with millions dead and maimed and ideological divisions still rife, generations would be required to recover from one of the twentieth century's longest and bloodiest wars.

Volume Introduction

More than a mere recounting of battles, military history offers a wide lens for viewing the Vietnam conflict. Among the issues addressed by articles in this volume are strategy, presidential decision-making, the nature of "limited war," the use (and misuse) of air power, and spraying of herbicides to facilitate counterinsurgency warfare. Collectively, these articles flesh out the nature of the Vietnam War, a guerrilla conflict fought in the South by the National Liberation Front (or, perjoratively, the "Vietcong") aided by North Vietnam and its communist allies in China and the Soviet Union. The articles analyze key decisions, such as Lyndon Johnson's escalation of the conflict, as well as the Tet Offensive (1968), a turning point in the war. While the Vietnamese endured a punishing assault, the U.S. public became increasingly disenchanted with the inconclusive conflict.

The reason the United States became directly involved in Vietnam was the mounting success of the guerrilla movement that aimed to topple the U.S.-backed Ngo Dinh Diem government in South Vietnam. King C. Chen's article offers insight into key decisions made in Hanoi to back the NLF guerrillas in the South. Chen argues that those decisions, taken in 1959, 1960, and 1963, came in response to stepped-up efforts by Diem and the United States to destroy revolutionary forces in the South. Ho Chi Minh and his comrades decided, in response, to increase support and infiltration to back their southern comrades. After nearly a generation of armed struggle, Chen concludes, Hanoi's strategy proved successful.

George McT. Kahin's article suggests that the armed conflict that followed Hanoi's stepped-up support for the southern rebels may have been avoided entirely had the United States adopted a different response to the 1963 overthrow and assassination of Diem. Kahin's research reveals that an opportunity existed for a group of South Vietnamese generals, led by Big Minh, to negotiate a neutralist government with the NLF rebels. To prevent precisely that from happening, Washington intervened, overthrew Big Minh, and installed a series of new governments determined to fend off the Hanoi-backed insurgents.

Like John F. Kennedy before him, President Johnson expected to achieve victory through escalation of the U.S. commitment in Vietnam. Surely superior American firepower would subdue a band of lightly armed guerrillas. Except perhaps for its own Confederate states in the Civil War, however, the United States never faced a more determined enemy than the "Vietcong" and their allies in North Vietnam. In

LIVERPOOL JOHN MOORES UNIVERSITY
LEARNING SERVICES

"The Search for the 'Breaking Point' in Vietnam," John E. Mueller concludes that "the military costs accepted by the Communists in Vietnam were virtually unprecedented historically."

Based on history, Mueller argues, it was not unreasonable for Washington officials to conclude that U.S. escalation would force the enemy to confront its "breaking point." The extraordinary resilience and determination of Hanoi and the NLF, however, went a long way toward explaining the ultimate American defeat in Southeast Asia.

As U.S. escalation failed to subdue the NLF, public frustration with "limited war" — first evident during the Korean War (1950–1953) — reemerged in the 1960s. In the nuclear age, of course, unlimited conflict could lead rapidly to the annihilation of tens of millions of people and entire civilizations. Nonetheless, in a nation accustomed to prevailing in war, the notion of a limited, inconclusive conflict did not sit well. Michael Cannon argues, however, in a rich analysis of the development of theory about limited war, that such conflicts possessed positive features. For example, limited war forced policymakers to consider non-military solutions to resolve conflict and encouraged civilian control of the military. Finally, although it may seem all too obvious, the most positive aspect of limited war theory, as applied to Vietnam, is that it helped prevent the conflict from spilling over into a third world war.

Americans grew frustrated not only with the inconclusive struggle in Vietnam, but with the rising numbers of U.S. casualties. Some argued that the selective service system that compelled young men to serve in Vietnam disproportionately tapped people of color and poorer Americans. This was true in the early years of the war, before publicity prompted changes in the composition of the U.S. military forces. In their article, based on quantitative research on Cook County, Illinois, Gilbert Badillo and G. David Curry found that social class, more than race, accounted for the disproportionate casualty burden in Vietnam.

By the late 1960s and early 1970s, popular unrest over the inconclusive war and the draft began to affect the morale and performance of U.S. forces in Vietnam. In an article notable for its stark conclusions, Paul L. Savage and Richard A. Gabriel argue that the disintegration of the U.S. Army in Vietnam in the latter years of the war stemmed from internal factors. Specifically, the rotation of unprecedented numbers of officers, many driven primarily by careerist "ticket punching," undermined cohesion and morale. Unethical and incompetent officers failed to inspire the regular troops, many of whom turned to drugs, whose widespread availability and use "the Army condoned, if only by inaction."

James Jay Carafano, however, offers a useful corrective to the perception of an army in disarray. Carafano's article, based on letters written by officers during the war, shows that the officer corps remained committed to ethical behavior contrary to a "public myth" that incompetence, drug abuse, and fragging (the murder of military commanders by men under their own command) typified the U.S. military. Although the Army did unquestionably begin to unravel late in the war, Carafano insists that traditional values embodied in the motto "duty, honor, country" continued to characterize professional soliders' attitudes despite the shattering experiences of Vietnam.

In a sobering personal account, retired Marine Lieutenant Colonel Howard A. Christy recounts the bitter lessons of "Patrolling Hill 55" during his Vietnam service in the mid-1960s. Christy's article reflects on the difficulties inherent in the U.S. combat mission — difficulties that, in retrospect, suggest the futility of American efforts. Marines were dropped into unsecure landing zones, where they encountered a deadly environment of land mines, snipers, and booby traps. Christy concludes that no military operation can be successful if commanders wantonly disregard the welfare of their soldiers.

While Christy calls into question U.S. combat strategy, Clarence E. Wunderlin Jr., argues in his article that U.S. naval strategy in Vietnam was fatally flawed as well. In "Paradox of Power: Infiltration, Coastal Surveillance, and the United States Navy in Vietnam, 1965–1968," he argues that although earlier implementation of a more effective strategy probably would not have changed the outcome of the war, the Navy nonetheless failed to launch an integrated campaign of interdiction of enemy supply lines along coastline and internal waterways, especially at the Cambodian border in the delta region.

As the war ground on inconclusively, Hanoi and the NLF went for the kill in the 1968 Tet Offensive, which proved to be a turning point in the conflict. U.S. and South Vietnamese forces eventually beat back the carefully planned NLF offensive, after bitter fighting in cities and towns throughout South Vietnam. Tet has been at the center of controversy about the Vietnam War, with some writers insisting that the United States had failed to exploit its victory in the aftermath of the enemy uprising. According to this interpetation, the NLF infrastructure had been destroyed in Tet, offering the United States an opportunity to achieve its goals if only the public had been willing to "stay the course."

In "The Significance of Local Communist Forces in Post-Tet Vietnam," Peter Brush disputes the claim that indigenous forces in the South had been decimated by massive losses during the Tet uprising. Brush argues that, despite its substantial losses, the NLF remained a crucial element in the struggle, though ultimately the southern rebel forces would be rendered insignificant with the North Vietnamese consolidation of power after the 1975 communist victory.

Faris R. Kirkland's article analyzes the only major military operation in Vietnam involving all four U.S. military service branches, a July 1968 asault on North Vietnamese Army installations at Cap Mui Lay. The operation, code named Thor, succeeded, Kirkland argues, in turning back another stage of the 1968 communist offensive and helped create a politcal climate conducive to a bombing halt and the beginning of negotiations for an end to the war.

One of the most significant lessons of the Vietnam War, actually evident from the outcome of previous wars, was that air power alone could not bring victory. Though the United States pummeled Indochina with some eight millions tons of bombs, the campaign ultimately proved futile.

Darrel D. Whitcomb, in "Tonnage and Technology: Air Power on the Ho Chi Minh Trail," explains the reasons for the failure of U.S. air power to interdict resupply along the Trung Son Road (Ho Chi Minh Trail). Hanoi used the series of trails, running north to south but also west to east through Laos and Cambodia, to send personnel, military and medical supplies, and equipment to the southern forces. Through a variety of means, ranging from simple camouflage to death-defying determination, North Vietnamese persistence converted the Ho Chi Minh Trail into the "road to victory."

Although Laos and Cambodia officially remained neutral in the war, the United States pounded both countries with heavy aerial bombardment in an effort to combat Hanoi's exploitation of those nations for sanctuary and supply lines. Despite a formal 1962 agreement on the neutralization of Laos, the small country remained a Cold War battleground. While the highly publicized Vietnam War raged, the CIA conducted a covert air and ground campaign in Laos against the communist Pathet Lao for more than a year. The U.S-backed Lao, Thai, and Hmong forces won some impressive victories — including the 1971–72 Battle for Skyline Ridge, analyzed in this volume by William M. Leary — but ultimately lost the war.

In "Fast-Movers and Herbicidal Spraying Southeast Asia," retired Air Force officer Richard D. Duckworth analyzes a controversial aspect of the U.S. aerial campaign in Vietnam. The spraying of herbicides from 1962–1971 not only proved ecologically devastating but also, Duckworth concludes, failed in its ultimate goal to remove enough vegetation to enable the United States to win the battle of the Ho Chi Minh Trail; that is, to prevent the movement of sufficient personnel and supplies into South Vietnam.

Washington, particularly under President Richard M. Nixon, persisted in efforts to achieve its aims through massive bombing. In "Setup: Why and How the U.S. Air Force Lost in Vietnam," Earl H. Tilford Jr., warns not only of the limitations of air power — which is only one aspect of the "art" of warfare — but of the danger of myths about air power effectiveness. The myth in question in Tilford's study is that Linebacker II, the Nixon administration's "Christmas bombing" of 1972, "won" the Vietnam War at the January 1973 Paris Peace Conference, allowing for U.S. withdrawal.

Nixon's emphasis on air power complemented his "Vietnamization" program, under which the South Vietnamese themselves were to gradually assume responsibility for their own defense. Employing sophisticated quantitative measures, Scott Sigmund Gartner argues in his article that Nixon's Vietnamization strategy changed the nature of the conflict and succeeded in its aim of turning the war over to South Vietnam itself. The problem, of course, in what might be the ultimate epitaph of the war, was that the Saigon government and military were never able to stand on their own.

Following U.S. withdrawal in January 1973, the Hanoi government and its southern allies girded for the final offensive. In "People's War in Vietnam," John M. Gates rejects a popular revisionist argument that the Vietnam War was a conventional war in which an invasion force from the North toppled the South. Gates's evidence demonstrates that the conflict is best understood as a revolutionary war fought by both conventional and unconventional means. The simple fact that the war ended in a conventional offensive, Gates points out, does not justify misrepresenting the entire character of the long revolutionary struggle.

Hanoi's Three Decisions and the Escalation of the Vietnam War

KING C. CHEN

As the Viet Cong and North Vietnamese in 1975 launched their heavy assaults in South Vietnam, the world's attention was attracted once again to the temporarily forgotten but unsettled Vietnam problem. In historical perspective, the renewed fighting in 1974–1975 had a crucial connection with the past. That fighting was simply a continuation of the long-term Vietnam war that had been briefly de-escalated after the 1973 Paris cease-fire accords.

Many books have been published on the roots of the United States role in the expansion of the Vietnam war, but not so much has been written on the origins of the North Vietnamese escalation.[1] Insofar as Hanoi is

[1] Among numerous publications on the origins of the Vietnam war the following are most frequently cited: Department of State, *A Threat to the Peace: North Viet-Nam's Effort to Conquer South Viet-Nam*. Two Parts, Department of State Publication 7308 (Washington, D. C., December 1961); The Senator Gravel Edition, *The Pentagon Papers: The Defense Department History of United States Decision-making on Vietnam*, 4 Vols. (Boston, 1971); Department of Defense, *United States-Vietnam Relations: 1945–1967*, 12 books (Washington, D. C., 1971); Neil Sheehan et al., *The Pentagon Papers*, as published by *The New York Times* (New York, 1971); The Committee for the Study of History of the Viet Nam Workers' Party, *An Outline History of the Viet Nam Workers' Party, 1930–1970* (Hanoi, 1970); Ho Chi Minh, *Against U. S. Aggression for National Salvation* (Hanoi, 1967); Le Duan et al., *South Vietnam: Realities and Prospects*, special issue of *Vietnamese Studies*, nos. 18–19 (Hanoi, 1968); George McT. Kahin and John W. Lewis, *The United States in Vietnam* (New York, 1967);

KING C. CHEN is associate professor of political science at Rutgers University. His books include *Vietnam and China: 1938–1954* and *The Foreign Policy of China*, and he is currently working on a book about China and the Vietnam war.

Political Science Quarterly Volume 90 Number 2 Summer 1975

239

concerned, three major decisions in 1959–1963 had a crucial relationship to the origin and escalation of the war. The first decision of January 1959 approved in principle the resumption of armed revolt by the Communist movement in the South for its own protection against the suppressive measures of the Diem regime; the second decision of September 1960 set the general policy of the "liberation" of the South—i.e., the overthrow of the Diem regime and the establishment of a coalition government favorably disposed toward reunification with Communist North Vietnam; and the third decision of December 1963 adopted a more aggressive, offensive strategy including intensifying the sending of troops and matériel aid to the South. After these decisions were made, Hanoi found it hard to retreat from its commitment to the war. And yet, what was the background of these decisions? How were these decisions made? In other words, did Hanoi initially make these decisions or was she forced into them? And what were the content and context of these decisions? This article is directed to probe these questions. To be sure, it is difficult to apply the decision-making approach to this study because of the lack of data from the decision makers in Hanoi.[2] Yet, public documents, secret papers, and interviews provide us with sufficient information to deal with the subject. And an examination of the issue at this juncture, when the unpopular United States involvement in the war was over but the renewed fighting has rekindled our concern about Vietnam, will enable us to see calmly the nature and origin of the Vietnam war and help us understand the possible development in Indochina.

CAUSES OF THE WAR: TWO OPPOSING VIEWS

There are two major opposing theories on the causes of the Vietnam war. The first is that the war originated from the expansion of commun-

---

Russell H. Fifield, *Americans in Southeast Asia: The Roots of Commitment* (New York, 1973); Chester L. Cooper, *The Lost Crusade: America in Vietnam* (New York, 1970); David Schoenbrun, *Vietnam: How We Got In, How to Get Out* (New York, 1968); Victor Bator, *Vietnam: A Diplomatic Tragedy: The Origins of the United States Involvement* (New York, 1965); Bernard B. Fall, *The Two Viet-Nams: A Political and Military Analysis* (New York, 1964); Jeffrey Race, *War Comes to Long An* (Berkeley, Calif., 1972); Jean Lacouture, *Vietnam: Between Two Truces* (New York, 1966); Robert Scigliano, *South Vietnam: Nation under Stress* (Boston, 1963); Douglas Pike, *Viet Cong* (Cambridge, Mass., 1966); Dennis Warner, *The Last Confucian* (Baltimore, 1964); and Donald S. Zagoria, *Vietnam Triangle: Moscow, Peking, Hanoi* (New York, 1967).

[2] Unlike Glenn D. Paige on Harry Truman's decision on Korea in *The Korean Decision* (New York, 1968), or Townsend Hoopes on Lyndon B. Johnson's decision on de-escalation of the Vietnam war in *The Limits of Intervention* (New York, 1969), the

2

ism from the North to the South. The second asserts that the conflict was caused by United States military intervention and aggression. Despite their different reasonings, they seem to reach a common conclusion—i.e., the war was inevitable.

The first argument is too familiar to dwell on here. But briefly, this view was maintained by Washington and Saigon as well as many other governments and individuals. As the State Department asserted, when the Communists were negotiating with the French in Geneva in 1954, they had already made "plans to take over all of Viet-Nam."[3] A number of party members and guerrilla units were not evacuated from the South to the North after July 1954; they were assigned to stay in the South. Arms and ammunition were cached in secret spots running from Saigon to the jungle areas. The men were instructed to await further orders to renew warfare.[4] Under these circumstances, the outbreak of the war was only a matter of time.

To cope with the Communist expansion, the United States first offered military aid to the French colonialist authorities in Indochina. Then in early 1954, with the Dien Bien Phu crisis, France requested Washington to intervene militarily. This request, after a heated debate among the decision makers, was denied by President Eisenhower due to the lack of support from Congress and the allies.[5] Soon after, the U. S. government turned down a French request to send United States military personnel to train the South Vietnamese army. After the Geneva settlement, however, a compromise between the "hawks" and "doves" was reached: the United States was to start anew to assist non-Communist South Vietnam, and this assistance would include the training and advising of a national army. This compromise was made between the Departments of State and Defense in which "political considerations . . . were allowed to govern."[6] To be sure, such a decision was guided by the containment policy.[7]

outsiders of Hanoi's decision-making circle will probably never have access to significant inside data on Hanoi's decisions on the Vietnam war.

[3] Department of State, *A Threat to the Peace*, Part I, p. 3.

[4] Ibid.

[5] Dwight D. Eisenhower, *Mandate for Change: The White House Years, 1953–1956* (New York, 1963), p. 347.

[6] Department of Defense, *United States-Vietnam Relations, 1945–1967*, Book 2, IV, A. 4., pp. 2.1 and 1–3. For the debate and compromise, see another account by a participant, James M. Gavin, in collaboration with Arthur T. Hadley, *Crisis Now* (New York, 1968), chap. III.

[7] Hans J. Morgenthau, "The Role of the United States in Indochina," in Gene T. Hsiao (ed.), *The Role of External Powers in the Indochina Crisis* (Edwardsville, Ill., 1973), pp. 8–9.

A feeling that American military mentality was superior to that of the French seems to have entered into the minds of the policy makers in Washington at that time. The Defense Department stated:

> The reasons the United States undertook the training of the Vietnamese armed forces had their roots not only in the desire to contain Communism and preserve the freedom of South Vietnam, but also in the U.S. discontent and frustration with French military policy during the Indochina war. A strong desire to *correct French mistakes* generated considerable bureaucratic momentum.[8]

Undoubtedly, this strong "correct-French-mistakes" desire was reinforced by the belief in the capability of American military power. As events turned out, the subsequent United States involvement in Vietnam became a natural development from training and advising to actual fighting. It needed a miracle to reverse the trend in the early 1960s.

The second argument was held by the North Vietnamese, the Viet Cong, together with many other individuals and governments. Hanoi has clearly and repeatedly stated that Vietnam is one nation and that the Vietnamese revolution, in the North and South, is a revolution in two different stages. The completion of it, including national reunification, is the "sacred" mission of the Vietnamese. They will allow no obstacle to stand in their way. To this end, they can use either political or armed struggle, or both. It is only a matter of strategy.[9]

After the Geneva conference in 1954, Hanoi was hopeful about national reunification by peaceful means. But, Hanoi argued, the American intervention prevented this. What the United States wanted in Vietnam was to colonize the country. As Ho Chi Minh denounced the United States in 1950, the American "imperialists" contrived to "kick out" the French colonialists and "occupy" Indochina themselves.[10] Im-

---

[8] Department of Defense, *United States-Vietnam Relations, 1945–1967*, p. 2.1. *(Italics added.)*

[9] "The Path of the Revolution in the South" (*Duong Loi Cach Mang Mien Nam*) was a document of guiding principle for the South in 1956–1959. It was believed to have been written by Le Duan, then secretary of the Nam Bo Regional Committee and a member of the Central Committee. Captured in Long An province in 1957, a copy of it was deposited with the Center for Research Libraries by Jeffrey Race as Race Document 1002. Also consult *Working Paper on the North Vietnamese Role in the War in South Viet-Nam* (hereafter cited as *Working Paper*), Document 301. The text of the *Working Paper* was reproduced in *Viet-Nam Documents and Research Notes*, nos. 36–37 (Saigon, June 1968), and in *Congressional Record*, Vol. 114, Part 10 (May 9, 1968), pp. 12614–12620. "Resolution on South Vietnam" of the Ninth Conference of the Central Committee of the Vietnam Workers' Party, December 1963, in *Viet-Nam Documents and Research Notes*, no. 96 (Saigon, 1971). Le Duan, *The Vietnam Revolution: Fundamental Problems, Essential Tasks* (Hanoi, 1971), pp. 62–82.

[10] Ho Chi Minh's interview with Voice of Vietnam, Vietnam News Agency (hereafter cited as VNA), July 16, 1950.

4

mediately after the French left Indochina, the Americans supported the "reactionary" Diem regime, trained its "puppet" army, and helped murder thousands of Vietnamese patriots—both Communist and non-Communist. To stop the United States intervention and aggression, the Communists were forced to resort to armed resistance. It was, therefore, "the United States policy of intervention and aggression" that began the Vietnam war, Hanoi asserted.[11]

Separately, neither of the above arguments offers a really convincing explanation; but jointly, they provide one. Since the completion of the revolution had been decided as the "sacred" mission of the Communists, a military confrontation with the United States containment policy was a foregone conclusion. Consequently, war became inevitable.

THE SITUATION IN THE SOUTH, 1955–1959

The immediate post-Geneva years were relatively peaceful. North Vietnam was engaged in social and economic reconstruction, China adopted peaceful policies at home and abroad, and the Soviet Union was campaigning for its peaceful coexistence policy. But the United States actively assisted Ngo Dinh Diem. The Diem regime began to build its national army, while it consolidated its political position, improved its economic condition, and above all eliminated a good number of the Communists. This created a growing difficulty for the Communist activities in the South.

Diem began his anti-Communist campaign in mid-1955. In May 1956, his government announced that the campaign in a period of ten months had "entirely destroyed the predominant Communist influence of the previous nine years." More than 94,000 former Communist members had "rallied" to the government and 5613 other cadres had "surrendered" to the government forces.[12] As the time went on, the campaign intensified. In the province of An Xuyen alone, for instance, a five-week campaign which ended in late February 1959 had resulted in the surrender of 8125 Communist agents, and the denunciation of 9800 "other" agents and of 29,978 sympathizers.[13] These official figures must have included all of Diem's political foes, Communist and non-Communist.[14]

The Phu Loi prison incident of December 1958, in which more than

[11] Xuan Thuy's statement at the Paris Peace Talks, VNA (Hanoi), June 24, 1971.
[12] U. S. Operations Mission to Vietnam (USOM), *Saigon Daily News Round-Up*, May 14, 1956, p. 3.
[13] USOM, ibid., February 28, 1959, pp. 4–5.
[14] Consult Pike, *Viet Cong*, p. 59; and Philippe Devillers, "The Struggle for the Unification of Vietnam," *The China Quarterly*, no. 9 (January–March 1962), 12.

twenty Communist detainees were reportedly poisoned, added new fear to the campaign. The drive reached an apex in May 1959 when Diem announced his severe Law 10/59 against both his Communist and non-Communist enemies.[15] It generated increasing discontent with his regime.

The campaign up to mid-1959 had caused the Communists great losses. The party apparatus could no longer function regularly; thousands of party members had surrendered or been captured or killed; and there was no place secure enough for members to stay except in the jungle and remote areas. The Diem regime, as a captured document reported at that time, had "truly and efficiently destroyed" the party.[16] This captured paper was supported by a Hanoi source of 1974. It stated rather frankly:

> The revolutionary movement suffered heavy losses. Hundreds of thousands of cadres and people were arrested or massacred. The self-defence organizations in the countryside were broken up. The armed forces in the resistance bases had to be reduced. In particular, the resistance army of the religious sects dwindled into a mere token force.
>
> Naturally, the more the people's self-defence organizations shrank, the more aggressive the cruel agents in the localities became and the bloodier the crimes they perpetrated. More and more cadres were arrested and many more revolutionary organizations in the villages and hamlets were broken up. The South Vietnamese people call this "the darkest period."[17]

An interview with a former party member of Long An province confirmed this "darkest period" (1958–1959).[18] Another source from Hanoi stated unequivocally that party membership in the South had declined from 15,000 in 1957 to 5000 by mid-1959.[19]

The demand for armed struggle increased daily. Many party members believed that political struggle was no longer applicable. A captured document said that "the majority of the Party members and cadres felt that it was necessary to launch immediately an armed struggle in order to *preserve* the movement and *protect* the forces." But the Nam Bo (south-

---

[15] According to the law, the Diem government had the power to eliminate not only Communist agents but also those who committed crimes "with the aim of sabotage" of the economy and finances of the State, or "of infringing upon the security of the State, or injuring the lives or property of the people." For the text of the law, see Marvin E. Gettleman (ed.), *Viet Nam: History, Documents, and Opinions on a Major World Crisis* (New York, 1965), pp. 256–260.

[16] *Working Paper*, Document 301, p. 9.

[17] Ta Xuan Linh, "How Armed Struggle Began in South Viet Nam," *Viet Nam Courier*, no. 22 (March 1974), 22.

[18] Race, *War Comes to Long An*, p. 99.

[19] *Tinh Hinh Nam Bo Tu Sau Hoa Binh Lap Lai Den Hien Nay* (The Situation in the South from the Restoration of Peace to the Present), p. 26. (A captured document, hereafter cited as *Tinh Hinh Nam Bo*.)

ern part) Regional Committee leadership, which was then in charge of the southern revolution, hesitated. The principal reason was the fear of violating the party line[20]—the line of political struggle set forth by the party.

The friction between the individual members and the party apparatus grew wider. Some members became so angry that they "took weapons the Party had hidden and came out of the jungle to kill the officials who were making trouble for them or their families. . . . Sometimes these individuals were so angry at the Party that they purposely allowed themselves to be captured afterwards—just to spite the Party."[21] Under these circumstances, "responsible elements of the Communist Resistance in Indo-China came to the conclusion that they had to act, whether Hanoi wanted them to or no."[22]

To understand the situation thoroughly, Le Duan reportedly made an extensive trip to the South in late 1958. There is no further information available about his trip or his findings. But undoubtedly, it must have been a combination of Duan's findings and the increasing desire for armed struggle that prompted Hanoi to make a new decision.

HANOI'S FIRST DECISION—JANUARY 1959

The general party line prior to 1959 had guided North Vietnam to engage in economic and social reforms, notably the land reform and the Three-Year Plan. Even after the party activities in the South had suffered severely, Hanoi still hoped to achieve a gradual and peaceful reunification. For instance, the Fourteenth Enlarged Central Committee Conference in November 1958 deliberated mainly on the Three-Year Plan,[23] and in December of that year Pham Van Dong proposed a plan to Ngo Dinh Diem for the normalization of South and North relationships. Even if Dong was playing a game with Diem, the major points proposed were not "militant" nor were they really unfavorable to Diem.[24] In fact, several proposed items, such as no military alliances for either side and trade between the two sides, were among the tentatively agreeable conditions between Hanoi and Saigon in secret negotiations in early 1963 (see discussion below). Internationally, Hanoi endorsed Khrushchev's proposal for the creation of a peace zone in the Pacific area. And in March 1959 *Nhan Dan* praised the Soviet-British talks as an effort to safeguard world

[20] CRIMP Document, in *Working Paper;* also see *Tinh Hinh Nam Bo*, p. 32.
[21] Race, *War Comes to Long An*, pp. 99–100.
[22] Devillers, "Struggle for the Unification of Vietnam," p. 15.
[23] Hanoi Radio, in Vietnamese, December 8, 1958.
[24] Pham Van Dong's note to President Ngo Dinh Diem, dated December 22, 1958, VNA, December 26, 1958.

peace.[25] These domestic and foreign policies explain, at least partially, why Hanoi was late in responding to the demand for armed revolt in the South. But the urgent situation there forced Hanoi to resort to the "people's war."[26]

The first new decision approved the resumption of armed struggle. It was made in principle at the Fifteenth Central Committee Conference in January 1959. But the order (directive) to carry out this decision was not issued until after the Politburo meeting in May 1959.[27] In view of the timing of the directive's issuance, Law 10/59 (May 6, 1959) must have served as the last impetus to the action.

The communiqué of the Fifteenth Central Committee Conference of May 13 (four months after the conference) made no mention of armed revolution.[28] Other sources, however, clearly suggested the date of the first decision on war.

One day after the publication of the communiqué *Nhan Dan* carried the following editorial on how to achieve the Vietnamese reunification:

> Our compatriots in the south will struggle resolutely and persistently against the cruel U.S.-Diem regime, holding aloft the tradition of the (1941) South Vietnam uprising, the (1945) Ba To uprising, and the August (1945) general uprising . . . and other valuable traditions of the workers' movement and of countless legal and semilegal struggles. . . . Our people are determined to struggle with their traditional heroism and by all necessary forms and measures so as to achieve the goal of the revolution.[29]

Clearly, the editorial was disseminating the party's permission of armed uprisings—the first new decision—against the Saigon govern-

---

[25] *Nhan Dan* (People's Daily), March 5, 1959.

[26] P. J. Honey, in *Communism in North Vietnam* (Cambridge, Mass., 1963), p. 67, suggests: "The desperate and increasing food shortage led the DRV leadership to decide —probably at the meeting of the Central Committee of the Lao Dong Party held in May 1959—to change its tactics toward South Vietnam and to revert to the technique of the 'people's war.' " New evidences have proved that the main reason for this change was for the survival of the revolution in the South, not for the food shortage in DRV.

[27] The date of the Fifteenth Central Committee Conference had previously been a confusion. Early sources tend to suggest May 1959 (VNA issued the conference's communiqué on May 13, 1959); but both "The Resolution on South Vietnam" of the Ninth Conference of the Central Committee of December 1963 and *An Outline History of the Viet Nam Workers' Party, 1930–1970* indicate the date was January 1959. It can be established that the conference was held in January 1959 but was not made known until May 1959 when the Politburo decided to issue its armed struggle "directive." I would like to express my thanks to Carlyle A. Thayer for his discussion of the matter with me.

[28] Hanoi Radio, May 13, 1959.

[29] *Nhan Dan*, May 14, 1959.

ment. The so-called tradition of uprisings, "all necessary forms and measures" and "legal and semilegal struggles" indicate that the end justifies the means.

A second source is a captured secret document of the "Resolution on South Vietnam" of the Ninth Central Committee Conference in December 1963. It stated categorically:

> The Resolution of the 15th Central [Committee] Conference (January 1959) and the subsequent Resolution of the Third Party National Congress have clearly set forth policy for the revolution in the South and the struggle guideline designed to win victory.[30]

A third source of evidence is a captured notebook of an unidentified but apparently high-ranking cadre. This secret document, contained in the *Working Paper*, read as follows:

> Since the end of 1959, particularly after the Phu Loi massacre, the situation truly ripened for an armed movement against the enemy. But the leadership of the Nam Bo Regional Committee at that time still hesitated for many reasons, but the principal one was the fear of violating the Party line. *The directive of the Politburo in May 1959 stated that the time had come to push the armed struggle against the enemy.*[31]

Thus it is is obvious that the first decision was made in January 1959, and the resulting directive for armed struggle was issued in May 1959.

Soon after, Hanoi launched a strong propaganda campaign against the United States and Diem (My-Diem). Originally, it was supposed to be a month-long drive (July 1959); it turned out to be a decade-old anti-American movement. According to Hanoi, 4 million people in the North had participated in rallies and demonstrations during the drive from July to November.[32] More significantly, *Hoc Tap* (Studies), on the occasion of the August revolution, carried a forceful editorial calling for the strengthening of the united front in the South, and explaining why and how:

> In view of the present situation in the South, the front must have a minimum platform and rational organizational forms so as to be able to group together different strata of people, including political and religious sects; people's organizations; various nationalities; individuals interested in peaceful reunification, independence, and democracy; and even southern officials opposing Ngo Dinh Diem's subservient policy. We must profit by the experi-

---

[30] The "Resolution on South Vietnam" of the Ninth Conference of the Central Committee of December 1963 in *Viet-Nam Documents and Research Notes*, no. 96, pp. 3 and 41.

[31] *Working Paper*, Document 301. (Italics added.)

[32] VNA, July 19, 1959 and November 27, 1959.

9

ence of the Viet Minh front and the August revolution to unite with every person, win him over to our side, or neutralize him whenever possible.[33]

It went on to say that the front should "allow itself to be led by the workers' party" and "carry out the party's plans." In short, Hanoi wanted the front to have a fresh, vigorous struggle program under the party's command.

THE SECOND DECISION—SEPTEMBER 1960

In the South, the Viet Cong began to increase armed activities in the fall of 1959. A few months later, their activities had become a threat to the life of many local government officials. In late February 1960, for instance, the Viet Cong, grouped in small bands, attacked government offices, personnel, security forces, and schools in Vinh Long, Long An, Kien Hoa, and five other provinces. In April, the clash between the government and Communist forces broke out 126 times throughout South Vietnam.[34] Another report on Long An province offered some specific figures. In 1959 in that province alone, the government lost 21 people (including the killed and kidnapped), the Viet Cong lost 440; the former was approximately 5 percent of the latter. In 1960, the government losses were 175, the Viet Cong 797; the former had increased to 22 percent of the latter.[35]

When men's lust for power is generated mainly by passions and not by reason, they transform "revolutions into dictatorships."[36] This is the evil aspect of human behavior which was reflected in Diem's rule at that time. As of 1960, Diem's repression policies had provoked serious discontent and anger from the non-Communist people. In April of that year, for instance, eighteen non-Communist political leaders (many of whom were Diem's former aides) publicly charged Diem with copying "dictatorial" rule.[37] These eighteen leaders well indicated the national mood of serious dissension.

[33] *Hoc Tap*, editorial, "It Is Necessary to Strengthen and Develop the United People's Front," no. 8, August 1959.

[34] Report in *Hsin-wen T'ien-ti* (Newsdom, Hong Kong), May 21, 1960, pp. 14–16.

[35] Race, *War Comes to Long An*, p. 114.

[36] Hans Morgenthau, *Scientific Man vs. Power Politics* (Chicago, 1946), p. 195.

[37] The eighteen leaders included Dr. Tran Van Do, former foreign minister under Diem, Dr. Phan Huy Quat, former minister of national defense, Tran Van Van, former minister of economy and planning, and seven other former ministers. *The New York Times*, May 1, 1960, p. 1. In March 1960, the Nam-bo Veterans of the Resistance Association also issued a declaration, calling upon the people to put an end to the government's bloody operations and repression in South Vietnam. The declaration might have been the product of a meeting of the Association in following the decision of the Central Committee in 1959.

Accurately reading the political climate in the South, Le Duan, for the first time, strongly asserted in April 1960 that the liberation of South Vietnam was "not only a task of the southern people but also of the entire people, of the South as well as of the North."[38] And in May 1960, Hanoi began to argue that it "was impossible to negotiate peacefully with warmongers."[39] It thus became militant on the South. In July, Pham Van Dong said at the Second National Assembly that the reunification of Vietnam was a "sacred task" of the Vietnamese people.[40] In August, Nguyen Chi Thanh, in applying the experience of the resistance war of 1946–1954 to the situation in 1960, drew a conclusion that the correct way to solve the "contradiction" between the Lao Dong party and its enemies was to use "revolutionary violence."[41]

Against this background, Hanoi made another significant move by convening the Third Party Congress in September 1960.

In retrospect, Hanoi's second decision on the war as made at this Congress was clear: (1) it set a general policy line for consolidation of the North, liberation of the South, and reunification of the nation; (2) it called for the establishment of a united front and a coalition government in South Vietnam; and (3) it urged the application of the August revolution "model" to the South. Of the three, the first was the most important and logical policy. National reunification required the "liberation" of the South which, in turn, depended fundamentally on the success of the socialist construction in the North. Of all the public documents released immediately after the Congress, an article by Minh Tranh was probably the most instructive. It specified "who," "what," "how," and "when" to accomplish the general policy line:

> The problem of the struggle for the unification of the country and that of the revolution in South Vietnam are indivisible. They are closely bound together. . . .
>
> Now, *who* will have to struggle to realize the unification of the country? Since there are two zones, it is natural that the people in both zones must consider this struggle as their own task and responsibility. . . .
>
> To achieve unification of the country, *what* path should the revolution in South Vietnam follow? . . . Everyone is aware that the enemy of unification is nobody but the U.S. imperialists and their agents who are governing South Vietnam. . . . It is obvious that any hopes to turn the present southern regime into a government which would willingly and peacefully discuss with us the

[38] Le Duan, "Leninism and Vietnam's Revolution," *On the Socialist Revolution in Vietnam*, 3 vols. (Hanoi, 1965 and 1967), I, p. 48.
[39] *Nhan Dan*, May 18, 1960.
[40] VNA, July 7, 1960.
[41] Nguyen Chi Thanh, "Our Party Has Skillfully Led the Revolutionary War, the Building of the Army, and the Strengthening of National Defense," *Hoc Tap*, nos. 8 and 9 (August and September 1960).

unification problem are merely utopian. [How?] We should, then, completely destroy the present southern government and set up another one. . . .

One thing is certain . . . [when] the day our southern compatriots succeed in completely liberating themselves from the yoke of the U.S.-Diem clique, a democratic and national concord government will be set up in South Vietnam. Then the possibility of peaceful unification of our country will become a reality.[42]

Hanoi had now moved from a decision advocating a war for self-protection of the Viet Cong to one for the overthrow of Diem and the establishment of a coalition government including Communist elements. To this end, the Congress called for the establishment of a united front which led to the organization of the National Front for Liberation of South Vietnam (NLF) in December 1960.

The connection between the "call" and the "establishment" of the front, however, has become a controversial subject. The State Department asserted that the front was "Hanoi's creation," whereas scholars rebutted it.[43] It seems that Hanoi had played a crucial role in the establishment, a view substantiated by the following two sources.

Apart from *Hoc Tap's* urge for a new program for the front in August 1959, Le Duan made a formal appeal at the Third Congress. He strongly suggested that the Communists

establish a united bloc of workers, peasants and soldiers and to bring into being a broad national united front with the worker-peasant alliances as the basis, directed against the U.S.-Diem clique in South Vietnam.[44]

Another source, a captured document, revealed some precise information. After the front was established, a southern regional committee of the party issued in January 1961 "instructions" to zones 1, 2, 3, and 4 (eastern, central, and western zones of Nam Bo and the Saigon-Cholon zone). It explained that the alliance of the workers and peasants was the basic force composing the front, but that in the situation in the South, these two classes did not have such capability of achieving decisive victories. This "reason prompts the Party to apply the policy of the Front [sic] and to *set up* the People's Front for Liberation of South Vietnam to attract bourgeois intellectual circles which comprise young men and girls and students in the cities, middle and rich peasants in the countryside."[45]

[42] Minh Tranh, "The Revolution in South Vietnam and National Unification," Hanoi Radio, in Vietnamese to South Vietnam, October 19, 1960.

[43] Department of State, *Aggression from the North: The Record of North Viet-Nam's Campaign to Conquer South Viet-Nam* (Washington, D. C., 1965), pp. 2 and 20. For the rebuttal, see Kahin and Lewis, *The United States in Vietnam*, pp. 119–120.

[44] Le Duan's speech at the Third Congress, Hanoi Radio, September 5, 1960.

[45] Department of State, *A Threat to the Peace*, Part II, p. 97; the document's photostatic copy, p. 96.

If Hanoi had played no role in the formation of the front, why did it call for and "set up" the organization? Naturally, the factors for the creation of the front were complicated. But, judging by the available evidence, it is fair to say that Hanoi did not "create" it, but it did take the initiative to urge and set a concrete policy for its establishment.

Hanoi in early 1959 began to nurse its expectation of an "August revolution" in the South. At the Third Congress, General Vo Nguyen Giap praised the August revolution as a "model" of revolution:

> The August general uprisings are a model of successful uprising in a colonial and semi-colonial country and a model of a clever association between political and armed struggles and between the political forces of the masses and the revolutionary armed forces.[46]

Giap implied that the revolutionists should apply this "model" to the South for its liberation. In fact, a second "August revolution" had been a dream of Hanoi's strategists since 1959. To this end, a concrete revolutionary machinery was soon to be established which included in the South a united front, an army, and a Communist party.

THE THIRD DECISION—DECEMBER 1963

Two months after the Third Congress, a coup broke out in Saigon. The incident, albeit abortive, served to indicate the rebellious mood against Diem. One month later, in December 1960, the news media in Saigon and Phnom Penh reported the organization of the NLF. Hanoi Radio did not make such a report until January 29, 1961.[47] Its ten-point program, which was announced by Hanoi in February, emphasized the overthrow of the Diem regime and the establishment of a democratic coalition administration. No socialist item was included.[48] Yet on February 15, the real strength of the NLF, the People's Liberation Armed Forces, was officially established.

In 1961, the Viet Cong scored several victories. The development alarmed Diem who in October of that year called the conflict a "real war"—no longer a guerrilla action. In the same month, General Maxwell D. Taylor, in his capacity as President Kennedy's military advisor, was sent to South Vietnam on a fact-finding mission. As a result, a new assistance program was recommended, including a "U.S. military task force."

---

[46] Giap's report to the Third Congress, Hanoi Radio, September 12, 1960.

[47] In view of the lateness of Hanoi's report on such an important event (one month after the reports from Saigon and Phnom Penh) and in view of Hanoi's capacity and practice in serving as the spokesman for the revolutionary activities in the South, it is fair to say that Hanoi had chosen to delay the report so as to show its "noninvolvement" in the establishment of the front.

[48] Hanoi Radio, February 11, 1961.

In mid-December, two United States military helicopter companies arrived in Saigon, marking the first direct United States military support to Diem. Hanoi must have been very concerned about this new development. To boost morale and show its potential strength, in late December Hanoi invited a strong Chinese military delegation for a visit. It seems that both the United States and North Vietnam had begun to prepare for a future military conflict.

On January 1, 1962, the Vietnam People's Revolutionary party (Dang Nhan Dan Cach Mang Viet Nam) was founded in the South, proclaiming its objectives of independence, freedom, democracy, socialism, and communism. On the United States-Saigon side, in February the United States Military Assistance Advisory Group in Saigon became the more powerful "United States Military Assistance Command, Vietnam." It was actually the headquarters of a military command. Moreover, the United States began to arm the tribesmen and delivered to Saigon more helicopter companies and other military aid. And American helicopters had already engaged in fighting with the Viet Cong.

The year 1963 was punctuated by a series of crises in the South. Diem's repression became intolerable. The people's rebellious mood ran high.[49] At the height of the Buddhist crisis in late August, Ho Chi Minh issued a statement, calling on the people in the South to continue their struggle until complete victory was achieved. On the following day, Mao Tse-tung responded with a statement strongly endorsing Ho's stand. But the overthrow of the Diem regime in late October, for which Hanoi had repeatedly called, was not carried out by the NLF forces, but by Diem's generals with the involvement of the American CIA. The postcoup situation was chaotic and critical. The United States, as Secretary of Defence McNamara reported in December, was now seriously concerned that the "indecisive and drifting" junta regime might go Communist if the situation was not reversed in two or three months.[50]

Against this background, Hanoi convened the Ninth Central Committee Plenum in December 1963. It was an extremely important conference on South Vietnam and on the Sino-Soviet dispute. Of its four signifi-

---

[49] One of the most effective means of Diem's repression was the so-called Can Lao Nhan Vi Cach Mang Dang (Personalism-Labor-Revolutionary party). Led by Ngo Dinh Nhu, Diem's brother, it launched a "three-anti movement"—i.e., anti-Communist, anti-American, and antiweakness. The party's repression policy was often criticized as being Fascist.

[50] Document #61, "Vietnam Situation" from Secretary of Defense Robert S. McNamara to President Johnson, December 21, 1963, in The Pentagon Papers (The New York Times version), pp. 271–274; for the November 1963 coup, see chap. 4 of the book. Another account of the coup was given by Henry Cabot Lodge, The Storm Has Many Eyes—A Personal Narrative (New York, 1973), pp. 205–214.

cant documents available as of early 1975, three public ones were on the dispute, and one, the "Resolution on South Vietnam," was classified "top secret."[51] According to this "secret" document, the ten-day meeting, apart from reaffirming Hanoi's confidence in the struggle and assessing the United States role, made Hanoi's third decision on new strategies and tasks for the war.

Three new strategies and tasks were included: (1) to confine the war within the boundaries of the South, (2) to intensify aid from the North, and (3) to adopt an offensive strategy on both the political and military fronts.

As of December 1963, the United States had not yet bombed the North; but Hanoi saw "the necessity to contain the enemy in the 'special war' and confine this war within South Vietnam." Clearly, it was a strategy of "war in one country." Such confinement later proved to be essential to the survival of North Vietnam. In operation, therefore, Hanoi decided not to openly become involved in the war so as not to provoke the United States to retaliation. Instead, Hanoi decided to act quietly and secretly. And yet the situation in the South, though favorable, still needed a strong push in order to achieve its "liberation." The conference therefore resolved that the North should play a truly active role in the fight by intensifying its aid to the southern insurgents. As the resolution stressed, the leadership should have a strong determination in its support and aid; both *mien* (sides—i.e., South and North) must make "maximum efforts" to defeat the enemy. What kinds of aid were offered to the South? Although the resolution did not specify, the war development later proved the aid to be both manpower and matériel.

The adoption of an *offensive strategy* for the South was probably the most urgent decision at that moment. The same "secret" resolution repeatedly discussed the issue of the "balance of forces" in the world and asserted that the revolution in South Vietnam would inevitably evolve into a "general offensive and uprising." Of all the data available today, the most forcible and revealing argument for such offensive strategy was an article in the January 1964 issue of *Hoc Tap*. It was actually a summary and interpretation of the aforementioned four documents of this conference. It rebutted the idea that an offensive strategy would lead to a major war and denounced the "defensive strategy" of compromise and cooperation with the imperialists as a policy of "abandoning revolution." It went on to say:

Since 1961, U.S. imperialism has launched a "special warfare" against the people in South Vietnam. This is the biggest war now being fought in the world. Such being the case, the people in the South should not pin their hope

[51] See *Viet-Nam Documents and Research Notes*, no. 96.

on the "sincere desire for peace" of the U.S. aggressor, nor should they wait for fifteen or twenty more years for the defeat of the imperialist camp by the socialist camp in their economic competition, before they can bring about a peaceful reunification of Vietnam. On the contrary, they should rise up and integrate their political struggle with armed struggle to uphold their right to existence. The road of struggle now taken by the people in South Vietnam is the only correct road to liberation.[52]

Clearly, the adoption of such offensive strategy was the final outcome of this conference. However, it must be pointed out that in 1963 there were secret contacts between Hanoi and Saigon for an accommodation. Leaders like Ho Chi Minh and Pham Van Dong reportedly still hoped to seek a peaceful settlement first with Diem and then with the post-Diem junta. Western diplomats to Hanoi reported at that time that such a settlement would permit a resumption of South-North trade and mutual visits and would gradually force the departure of American military personnel. Hanoi desired this settlement for three reasons: the economic difficulties in the North, the possibility of a deeper military conflict with the United States, and the strain of the Sino-Soviet rivalry in Vietnam. Immediately after the November 1963 coup, the new minister of security in Saigon said that the junta had learned about Diem's negotiations with Hanoi through the Polish representative on the International Control Commission.[53] In January 1975, this Polish diplomat, Mieczyslaw Maneli, confirmed the report and revealed some details of this unsuccessful development. He said that in the spring of 1963 he was asked secretly by Diem and his brother, Ngo Dinh Nhu, to approach the Hanoi government to explore the possibilities for a peaceful resolution of the struggle. Such a resolution would lead to the withdrawal of American military forces. In the summer of 1963, after long discussions with the North Vietnamese leaders, Hanoi produced plans under which the North and South could gradually develop postal, economic, and cultural relations. Other details were even more important:

> The North would not press for a speedy reunification, but instead a coalition government would be set up in the South. . . . Such a government could be headed by Mr. Diem. . . .
>
> Hanoi had always sought neutralization of the South. As for the North, both Ho Chi Minh and Pham Van Dong were reluctant to accept the label "neutralization," but were eager to accept the idea. North Vietnam would not become an aggressive outpost against other countries, and neither Soviet nor Chinese troops would under any conditions be allowed on Vietnamese soil. . . .

[52] "Balance of Forces and Strategic Offensive," *Hoc Tap*, January 1964; Hanoi Radio, February 11, 1964.
[53] *The New York Times*, November 10, 1963.

What guarantees could be offered to the West that Hanoi would keep its word? . . . The answer was that in case of a United States withdrawal, the North would be prepared to give all kinds of substantial guarantees and American participation in the supervisory process was not excluded.[54]

Several questions would have to be raised. First, what were the objectives of Hanoi and Saigon for reaching such an accommodation? Hanoi, probably under the influence of the 1962 agreement on the neutralization of Laos, seems to have believed that a neutralized South Vietnam would force the United States departure and would eventually work in favor of the Communist desire to take over the country. Meanwhile, Saigon hoped that such a neutralization would at least reduce the threat from the Viet Cong and lead to the withdrawal of United States forces and pressure;[55] such a development would, in consequence, help Diem to continue to stay in power. Second, what caused the breakdown of the secret contacts? They were apparently interrupted by the Buddhist crisis in the summer and cut off by the postcoup junta. Third, did the United States block the possibility of such accommodation? It seems that the United States had at least blocked it by attempting to replace Diem and/or Nhu and by implicitly or explicitly endorsing the November coup of the Saigon generals who firmly rejected the Saigon-Hanoi secret talks.[56]

Consequently, it can be assumed that only after the Saigon junta had rejected in early November Hanoi's attempt to resume secret negotiations had Hanoi made in December her new decision on offensive strategy. It was, therefore, a decision in response to the chaotic situation in the South and the uncompromising position of the junta.

Peking also was concerned about the situation. Peking offered strong, although unspecified, advice of a cautious but flexible strategy of protracted war to the Vietnamese revolutionaries. The advice was carried by an article published both in Chinese and English. The Chinese version appeared in *Jen-min Jih-pao* on July 31, 1963, when the Saigon Buddhist crisis ran high, and the English version appeared in the *Peking Review* on November 15, 1963, when the postcoup situation was critical. A sense of urgency was clearly shown in the article by the repeated use of strong words, such as "must" and "essential," in pointing out how such a war should be fought.

To highlight the significant development of Hanoi's strategies for the

---

[54] Mieczyslaw Maneli, "Vietnam, '63 and Now," *The New York Times*, January 27, 1975, p. 25.

[55] The United States was exercising her influence seeking the removal of Diem and his brother, Ngo Dinh Nhu. See *The Pentagon Papers*, chap. 4; and Lodge, *The Storm Has Many Eyes*, pp. 206–210.

[56] Ibid.; see also *The New York Times*, November 10, 1963.

South from 1959 to 1963, a content analysis of the public documents of the above three meetings (1959, 1960, and 1963) was made. As Table 1 shows, a report and a communiqué of the Central Committee meetings of 1959 and 1960 were also included in order to illustrate the major points of analysis.

The table warrants the following analysis: (1) As stated by the 1963 resolution, the party "set forth the policy" and "directed" the revolution in the South. It began to act at the January 1959 conference, continued at the September 1960 Third Party Congress and other meetings, and finally at the December 1963 Plenum (major policies and themes developed from "national reunification," "smash U.S. imperialism and its lackey," "liberation of the South," to "the North increases aid to the South," and so forth). The policy developed from general to specific. This development unequivocally indicated the consistency of Hanoi's strategies to guide the revolution in the South. (2) The theme on "socialist revolution in the North" developed from ten times (71.4 percent) in 1958, twenty-five times (36.77 percent) in 1960, to three times (7.14 percent) in 1963; and the emphasis on "national reunification" shifted from three times (21.4 percent) in 1958, twelve times (60 percent) in 1959, thirty times (only 44.12 percent) in 1960, and two times (4.76 percent) in 1963. But, Hanoi's urge for the coordination between the "political and military struggles" and preparation for "the general offensive and uprising" advanced from *zero* at the meetings of 1958, 1959, and 1960 to eighteen (42.86 percent) and ten times (23.81 percent) respectively in 1963. Likewise, the party's decision on the intensifying of aid to the South, which included both weaponry and manpower, developed from *zero* at earlier meetings to a new and urgent appeal in 1963 (three times —7.14 percent). This trend shows clearly the growing intensity of Hanoi's involvement in the armed struggle. In sum, this analysis serves to prove that North Vietnam's commitment to the war in 1959–1963 had developed from general guidance to specific assistance, and from political struggle to armed revolt.

CONCLUSION

An examination of Hanoi's three major decisions in 1959–1963 makes the questions raised earlier fairly clear. Hanoi sees the origin of the war in ideological perspective; revolutionary interests are often placed at the apex of policy-making deliberation. The revolution is long and difficult, and the use of peaceful or violent means is only a matter of strategies and tactics. If the peaceful means fail, violence will be employed, and vice versa. The Vietnamese revolution, therefore, is characterized by the long, hard political and military struggles. Hanoi does not regard the

TABLE 1

Frequency of Major Themes of Hanoi's Decisions on South Vietnam, 1958-1963

Major Theme	Report of the 14th Central Committee Meeting, Nov. 1958	Communiqué of the 15th Central Committee Meeting, May 1959	Communiqué of the 18th Central Committee Meeting, July 1960	Resolution of the Third Party Congress, Sept. 1960	Resolution on South Vietnam of the 9th Central Committee Meeting, Dec. 1963
Socialist revolution in the North	10 (71.4%)	2 (10%)		25 (36.77%)	3 (7.14%)
National reunification	3 (21.4%)	12 (60%)	1 (14.3%)	30 (44.12%)	2 (4.76%)
War preparation by U.S.–Diem	1 (7.2%)	2 (10%)			
Terror and massacre of U.S.–Diem		3 (15%)		2 (2.94%)	
To smash U.S. imperialism and its lackey		1 (5%)	1 (14.3%)	4 (5.88%)	1 (2.38%)
Unity of the Socialist camp			4 (57.1%)	3 (4.41%)	
Approval of the communiqué of the Bucharest Conference			1 (14.3%)		
Liberation of the South				4 (5.88%)	
Political struggle coordinates with armed struggle					18 (42.86%)
The party sets forth the policy for, and directs, the revolution in the South					5 (11.91%)
The North should increase aid to the South					3 (7.14%)
To prepare for general offensive and uprising					10 (23.81%)
TOTAL	14 (100%)	20 (100%)	7 (100%)	68 (100%)	42 (100%)

problems of war and peace as two separate, short-term issues as does the United States. They are only two aspects of one issue—the revolution. In this context, Hanoi's "sacred mission" of, and commitment to, the completion of the revolution in the South do serve as a fundamental cause of the origin and escalation of the Vietnam war.

And yet, North Vietnam's main domestic concern in the post-Geneva years was her socioeconomic construction. Her Three-Year and Five-Year Plans were geared to build socialism in the North. Her economic difficulty and political-struggle policy prevented her from taking an initiative to launch a war in the South at that time. It was the growing military campaign of the Diem regime against the Communists with America's support that compelled Hanoi to decide to revert to war. Once the war decision was made, Hanoi found it hard to retreat. Undoubtedly, there were other decisions made by party conferences; but the three discussed were the most important. And these decisions must have been originated and formulated by a few top leaders.

The first decision of January 1959 on the resumption of armed struggle in the South marked a departure from the party line of political struggle established after 1954. This decision was made originally for self-preservation rather than "aggression." The second decision of September 1960 resolved to liberate the South in order to achieve national reunification. To this end, Hanoi guided and accelerated the build-up of the revolutionary machinery in a concrete form: the NLF (December 1960), the People's Liberation Armed Forces (February 1961), and the People's Revolutionary party (January 1962). And to make the revolution successful, Hanoi let the southern revolutionaries run a relatively independent course. This decision advanced Hanoi's stand from a policy of self-protection to a more ambitious strategy of liberating the South. The third decision of December 1963 was the adoption of an offensive strategy. Meanwhile, Hanoi committed itself to a really determined and active program of aid for the southern revolutionaries. By making this decision, Hanoi promoted itself to an aggressive, specific, and effective position toward the South. As of December 1963, it would have been a miracle if both Hanoi and Washington had reversed their commitments to the war.

Although Hanoi in late 1963 had decided to fight, its strategy was to confine the war to one country—South Vietnam. Ho Chi Minh may have taken into consideration the neutralization of Laos (1962), China's advice, and Khrushchev's cool attitude.[87] But such strategy was adopted mainly because of Ho Chi Minh's fear of America's massive intervention

[87] For a discussion of the cool Soviet attitude toward Hanoi, see King C. Chen, "North Vietnam in the Sino-Soviet Dispute, 1962–64," *Asian Survey* (September 1964), 1023–1936.

and his hope to keep the North out of the war. The Tonkin Gulf Resolution shattered his hope completely.

POSTSCRIPT

On April 30, 1975, the assaults of the Viet Cong and North Vietnamese forced the Saigon government to unconditional surrender. In a period of two months, the North Vietnamese drove Saigon's troops to a total collapse and compelled the hasty and complete evacuation of American personnel. The tragic Vietnam war was over. It was the final victory of Hanoi and the Viet Cong, and a great, humiliating failure of American intervention there.

In retrospect, it is evident that the North Vietnamese and Viet Cong followed closely Hanoi's three decisions of 1959–1963. They accomplished almost all of the objectives as laid down by Hanoi—i.e., the overthrow of the Saigon government (Diem, Thieu, Huong, and Minh), the departure of all American personnel, and the "liberation" of the South. The final goal that remains to be achieved is the national reunification of the South with the North. As Saigon has been renamed "Ho Chi Minh City," the first cornerstone of reunification has been quietly and cleverly placed. They will accomplish this goal in due course probably through a general election. The completion of the Vietnamese revolution is at hand. With the recent takeover of Cambodia by the Khmer Rouge and the shaky coalition government in Laos, a Communist victory throughout Indochina seems to be only a matter of time.*

* The author would like to express his appreciation for financial support for this study to the Research Institute on International Change, Columbia University, and the Faculty Research Council of Rutgers University.

21

Political Polarization in South Vietnam: U.S. Policy in the Post-Diem Period*

George McT. Kahin

IN A PERCEPTIVE BOOK on Kennedy and Johnson written a decade ago, Tom Wicker, then head of the Washington Bureau of *The New York Times* observed that "after the fall of Diem there were visible signs in South Vietnam of a growing 'neutralist' sentiment, and . . . the generals who had come to power were probably in the best position of any government before or since to make a political arrangement with the Viet Cong, and through them, with Hanoi."[1] He concluded that:

It is entirely possible, then, and it may even be likely that the overthrow of Diem and the accession of Big Minh . . . had created one of those rare moments in the troubled history of the Second Indochinese War when a negotiated peace, arising out of some form of reconciliation between the Saigon junta and the National Liberation Front, was genuinely possible.[2]

The accuracy of Mr. Wicker's assessment is substantiated by information I have secured over the past ten years through interviews with most of the key Vietnamese actors[3] and from pertinent declassified U.S. government documents released to me over the last four years under the Freedom of Information Act.[4] Equally important,

*The present article forms the basis for a more extensive treatment that will constitute a chapter in a forthcoming book on the political level of American intervention in South Vietnam. For providing support that has made research for this study possible, I wish to express my gratitude to the Guggenheim and Luce foundations and the Cornell Southeast Asia Program. I am also grateful to Mai Elliott for the translations from the Vietnamese language that I have used.

[1] Tom Wicker, *JFK and LBJ: The Influence of Personality Upon Politics* (Baltimore: Penguin Books, 1969 and 1970), p. 188.

[2] *Ibid.*, p. 190.

[3] Among others, these include Generals Duong Van Minh, Tran Van Don, Ton That Dinh, and Nguyen Khanh, as well as the Minh Government's Prime Minister, Nguyen Ngoc Tho. This research involved visits to Vietnam in 1966-7, 1970, 1971 and 1972.

[4] I wish to express my gratitude to the archivists of the Lyndon Baines Johnson and John F. Kennedy Libraries, especially Martin Elzy and Megan Desnoyers, for their generous assistance. Likewise, I wish to thank the several, usually already heavily burdened, desk officers in the Department of State and elsewhere in the government upon whom fell the task of processing the

these data also describe the efforts made by the Johnson administration to ensure that no such political settlement would take place.

It may seem puzzling that just three months after encouraging a group of Vietnamese generals to remove Ngo Dinh Diem from power, the administration should acquiesce so readily in their ouster by another group. In large measure this was a consequence of Washington's alarm over the political prospects perceived by Mr. Wicker. Less than two months after General Duong Van Minh's junta took power on November 1, 1963, the senior advisors President Johnson inherited from President Kennedy had not only become deeply disappointed at the new Saigon government's unresponsiveness to U.S. prescriptions in the military field, but were becoming acutely concerned that it might negotiate a "neutralist" solution involving an end to the fighting and a compromise agreement with the National Liberation Front (NLF). Such an agreement would, of course, have meant an end both to the fighting and to the United States' military and political role in Vietnam.

The political consequences of Diem's overthrow and the new possibilities this opened up were interpreted very differently in Washington and Saigon. Initially misled by wishful thinking and an apparent inability to sense the depth of the desire for peace among the South Vietnamese, the Johnson administration misread both the character of Minh's new Saigon government and the political context within which it operated. The dominant view among the President's advisers had been that removal of Diem and his brother Ngo Dinh Nhu would insure a more effective and vigorous prosecution of the war against the forces of the National Liberation Front. They now also expected that the new leadership in Saigon would accept greater American direction of the fighting and an escalation of U.S. military participation that would extend to the bombing of North Vietnam.

However, the key members of the new government's Military Revolutionary Committee (MRC)—Generals Minh, Tran Van Don, Ton That Dinh and Le Van Kim[5]—and their civilian Prime Minis-

---

requests for declassification of documents that I made under the Freedom of Information Act. Although permission for release of many of the most important documents bearing on U.S. political intervention in Vietnam has been refused, enough have been released to have made the effort to secure them worthwhile.

[5] Minh, Don and Dinh were respectively Chairman, 1st Deputy Chairman and 2nd Deputy Chairman of the MRC's 12-man Executive Committee, and Kim was its General Secretary and Member for Foreign Affairs. Concurrently Don served as both Minister of Defense and Chief of Staff of the Armed Forces. Dinh served as Minister of Security, and until January 5, 1964, was also Commander of the III Corps. The other eight members were Maj. Gen. Tran Van Minh, Maj. Gen. Pham Xuan Chieu, Maj. Gen. Tran Thien Khiem, Brig. Gen. Do Mau, Maj. Gen.

ter, Nguyen Ngoc Tho, had a set of priorities that differed markedly from those of the administration in Washington and hinged on a political rather than a military solution. They did not believe that they could win a military decision, and they saw the ouster of Diem and Nhu as opening up fresh possibilities for settling the outstanding issues in Vietnam through peaceful means. They looked towards a negotiated agreement among the Vietnamese parties themselves without American intervention. They saw the NLF's rapid growth in the final year of the Diem regime as arising primarily from its having become the symbol of opposition to that widely hated government. With Diem and Nhu removed, however, the NLF was, in their view, deprived of its major focus of opposition and, indeed, insofar as many of its adherents were concerned, much of its *raison d'être*. They saw it as preponderantly non-communist in memberhsip, with its leadership heavily dependent upon the Cao Dai and Hoa Hao religious sects along with other elements that had also rallied to its standard primarily because it was the only effective channel of opposition to Diem.[6] Thus, Minh and his chief lieutenants concluded that with the NLF's backing and political potential substantially diminished they now had scope for building a popular base strong enough for them to negotiate with it on favorable terms.

Along with his closet supporters, Minh tended to regard Huynh Tan Phat, Nguyen Huu Tho and other NLF leaders as "former bourgeois colleagues" whose political views had not greatly changed since their departure from Saigon only a few years before. Saigon's new leaders believed that on basic issues the divergence in viewpoint between the NLF leaders and themselves was not wide enough to prevent a mutually acceptable compromise. Minh himself insisted in private that he and his group were *non*-communist rather than *anti*-communists emphasizing: "you must understand the distinction, because it is an important one." Ten years ago in Saigon his Prime Minister, Nguyen Ngoc Tho, described the new leadership's plans to me in these words.

The strategy of the new government was first to consolidate itself with the Cao Dai, Hoa Hao, Cambodian minority, etc. and then to try to bring over the NLF out of opposition and into support of what would be termed a

---

Mai Huu Xuan, Maj. Gen. Le Van Nghiem, Brig. Gen. Nguyen Van Thieu, and Brig. Gen. Nguyen Huu Co.

[6] Douglas Pike, a U.S. Foreign Service Officer regarded as a specialist on the NLF's organization, acknowledged that the Cao Dai constituted "the bulk of the early NLF support" and that the Hoa Hao was also "an early and major participant in the NLF." Douglas Pike, *Viet Cong* (Cambridge, MA: MIT Press, 1966), pp. 68-9, 369.

649

government of reconciliation. At this time the NLF was overwhelmingly non-communist, with the PRP [People's Revolutionary Party—its avowedly communist component] still having no dominance and indeed only a minor position within the organization. The effort envisaged was to try to bring over first the most detachable elements within the NLF—particularly elements of religious sects.

The second step envisaged was for the launching of a government of reconciliation which would be one wherein all elements of the NLF would be welcome to participate in an electoral process. The NLF was then sufficiently free of Hanoi's control to have made this process quite possible. We would have striven for a neutral government—not a government without an army, but one without foreign troops or bases and one whose neutrality in international affairs would incline towards the West. Unfortunately there were leaks of our plans and it is apparent that the American government got wind of them.[7]

Whether or not they were correct, the top leaders of the Minh government believed there were good prospects for reaching a mutually satisfactory compromise, and with Minh's brother a member of the NLF, contact was not difficult. Indeed, only a week after the successful coup against Diem and Nhu, the NLF in a conciliatory manifesto called upon the new government for negotiations to reach a ceasefire, free general elections and the subsequent formation of a coalition government "composed of representatives of all forces, parties, tendencies and strata of the South Vietnamese people." It made clear, as it had previously, its view that reunification with the North was to occur neither immediately nor automatically, but was something to be realized "step by step on a voluntary basis, with consideration [given] to the characteristics of each zone, with equality, and without annexation of one zone by another." In the meantime, it called for an "independent" South Vietnam that would carry out a policy of neutrality, not adhere to any military bloc, not permit any foreign country to establish troops or bases there, and which would stand "ready to form together with the kingdom of Cambodia and Laos a neutral zone on the Indochinese peninsula."[8] (Note North Vietnam's exclusion.) Throughout the period that the Minh government held office the NLF continued to urge this course.

American officials, of course, were not privy to the Minh govern-

---

[7] The essentials of the views he expressed here were similar to those conveyed to me by General Minh, and consistent with what both of them gave in confidence to a senior political officer of an embassy of a major power friendly to the U.S. and to two senior correspondents, respectively from *The New York Times* and *Le Monde*.

[8] For a fuller text of this appeal, see George McT. Kahin and John W. Lewis, *The United States in Vietnam*, Rev. Ed. (New York: Dell Publishing Co., 1969), pp. 473-6; also pp. 134-7.

650

ment's hopes for negotiated settlement, nor apparently did they suspect it of even considering such a course until well into January 1964. However, considerably before this their high expectations for greater military aggressiveness by Saigon's forces were already being keenly disappointed. Not only was there no recoupment of the considerable areas yielded to the NLF during the last year of Diem's rule, but there were further territorial losses. Although some U.S. officials saw this as an inevitable initial consequence of the extensive shakeup of local administration caused by the sudden replacement of so many Diemist officials, others ascribed it to the new government's reluctance to carry out offensive military actions. General Paul Harkins, head of the U.S. military mission to South Vietnam, had been opposed to the ousting of Diem, as had his mentor Lt. General Maxwell Taylor, Chairman of the U.S. Joint Chiefs of Staff, and John McCone, head of the CIA.[9] From the outset Harkins and his staff were cool towards Minh's government. Its military stance now drove them to outright opposition and gave them ammunition for securing wider administration support for their attitude. Ultimately, Saigon's lack of aggressiveness on the field of battle was one of the factors that contributed to the disaffection of even those U.S. officials who had most opposed Diem and had initially most strongly supported the new government.

For its part, however, the new leadership believed that its immediate plans for attracting uncommitted rural elements and the outer circle of the NLF were quite incompatible even with the level of military activity carried out under the Diem regime, much less with the increased effort now urged by the U.S. Nor, of course, could an emphasis on military offensives provide a suitable context for the negotiations into which they hoped to enter with the NLF.

The time was propitious, the Minh government believed, to launch a major effort to attract a large part of the NLF's non-communist following to its side through a positive rural welfare program involving decentralized governance that encouraged local initiative. It insisted upon embarking on a new approach that would permit peasants to remain in their scattered homes, close to their ancestral graves and free to organize their own local defense units, relying on their own self-interest and in accordance with local circumstances. Minh and his senior colleagues believed that such a program under locally-rooted leaders (rather than the alien northern Catholic ad-

---

[9] See the oral histories of Taylor and McCone held in the Lyndon Baines Johnson Library.

651

ministrators that Diem relied on so widely) was more likely to win peasant allegiance than the U.S.-backed "pacification" effort with its emphasis on aggressive military activity and dragooned population control—the system based on barbed-wire-enclosed strategic hamlets that had been championed by General Harkins and so disastrously administered by Diem's widely hated brother, Ngo Dinh Nhu. In its effort to build support in the rural areas, then, the Minh government was unwilling to reconstitute those many strategic hamlets that had been torn apart by internal pressures or overrun by the forces of the NLF, for it regarded the "pacification" system as so oppressive and unpopular as to be largely ineffective militarily and counter-productive politically. Minh expected that through its new program his government could initially draw away at least 30 per cent of the NLF membership, and more later. And, indeed, before the end of 1963 a significant minority of its Cao Dai adherents had rallied to Saigon.[10]

By early January, the Minh government's rural welfare system had been introduced as a pilot project in Long An province, a vital, strategically-located area abutting on Saigon and heavily influenced by the NLF—a region where most of the strategic hamlets had ceased to function by the end of Diem's regime. Taking advantage of the fact that this was Minh's home area, that he was very popular there, and some of the new local officials were members of his family, the new Saigon government appeared to be making significant progress in establishing its control. This success strengthened its conviction that the new approach should supersede the strategic hamlet system. General Le Van Kim, who was in charge of designing and administering the program—and who regarded it as still being in an exploratory and uncompleted stage—would brook no interference by U.S. officials, military or civilian, and he refused to permit any of them to participate in the planning process. This decreased the possibility of persuading American officials of the program's virtues, and General Kim's attitude understandably aroused suspicions among them, nourishing their belief that the new government was uncooperative.

On several other major issues related to the conduct of the war and the American role therein, the Minh government also refused to go along with Washington's expectations and stood firm against recommendations urged by the Pentagon. Of these, probably the most

---

[10] See Hedrick Smith in *The New York Times*, December 28, 1963. Douglas Pike (*Viet Cong*, p. 369) speaks of the Cao Dai elements defecting "en masse" from the NLF following the end of the Diem regime, but this exaggerates considerably the scale of the movement.

important was the U.S. military's plans for bombing the North.[11] The prescription advocated by the U.S. Joint Chiefs of Staff and their Chairman, General Taylor, called for the "aerial bombarding of key North Vietnam targets, using U.S. resources under Vietnamese cover, and with the Vietnamese openly assuming responsibility for the actions."[12] The fact that General Harkins and Ambassador Lodge were seeking the new leadership's backing for the bombing well before President Johnson had agreed to it suggests that they may have hoped to strengthen the Joint Chiefs' case by assuring him that Saigon stood behind the proposal. However, the new Saigon leadership quickly rebuffed these efforts.[13] Minh and other senior members of the Military Revolutionary Council (MRC) insisted that the NLF was still under southern direction, and that even if Hanoi's influence within it were dominant, bombing the north would not, as the Americans argued, provide leverage on the struggle in the south. They also emphasized to U.S. officials that such an action might well provoke Hanoi into launching a ground force riposte across the 17th parallel that could not be contained by Saigon's forces. Furthermore, the MRC's top leadership believed that such bombing would undermine its own nationalist legitimacy and lose it popular support. A senior South Vietnamese General, Nguyen Van Chuan, has provided an account of a major confrontation that arose over the bombing issue during a meeting between McNamara, Harkins and Lodge with Generals Minh, Don and Le Van Kim:

The Americans said it was necessary to bomb North Vietnam. The Armed Forces Council represented at this meeting by Minh disagreed with this American policy right at this meeting. General Minh mentioned two reasons: (1) bombing North Vietnam would not produce good military results; on the contrary it would do more harm to innocent Vietnamese; (2) by doing so we would lose the just cause because we had [thus far] accepted that we were fighting a defensive war and had ascribed the role of aggressor

---

[11] Generals Minh, Don, and Dinh, and Prime Minister Tho, all regarded their opposition to the U.S. military's bombing plans as the major reason for the coup that was ultimately mounted against them.

[12] See "Memorandum for the Secretary of Defense from the J.C.S. 22 Jan. 1964," in *Pentagon Papers* [henceforth *PP*] Gravel Ed. (Boston: Beacon Press, 1971), Vol. III, pp. 498-9, and also p. 35. (Among other things they also recommended that the U.S. "commit additional U.S. forces as necessary, in support of the combat action in South Vietnam" and "in direct action against North Vietnam." In response to a directive apparently from the JCS, General Harkins and Saigon CIA's Covert Action Branch on December 19, 1963 forwarded a plan, supported by CINCPAC, providing for a "spectrum of capabilities for the RVNAF (South Vietnam Airforce) to execute against North Vietnam." *PP*, Gravel Ed., Vol. III, p. 117.

[13] According to Prime Minister Nguyen Ngoc Tho, Lodge had urged a program of bombing the North as early as "about three weeks after Diem had been overthrown," with the new government from the outset refusing to support any such action.

to the Communists [accusing them] of sending troops to the South, committing crimes in the South, etc. If we bombed the North we would bring war to the North and we would lose our legitimate cause.[14]

At this time opposition to bombing appears to have been fairly widespread among members of the Saigon officer corps, and it is significant that as much as five months later McNamara reported that even General Khanh, regarded as the most cooperative and hawkish instrument of U.S. policy yet to appear, emphasized that he was not yet ready for a move against the north and that such action would require a U.S. promise of protection against any reprisal.[15]

The Minh leadership also opposed any greater American role in directing military operations conducted by the South Vietnamese army and refused to accept persistent American proposals for increasing the number of U.S. military and civilian advisers, especially introducing military advisers down into the district and sub-sector levels. More than that, they called for pulling American advisers out of their existing positions with battalions and permitting them no role below the level of regiment. They believed that any increased American visibility would have serious adverse political consequences, robbing their government of legitimacy in the eyes of the population and undercutting its nationalist credentials at precisely the time it had an opportunity to develop them. Aware of the stigma of foreign dependency attached to the previous government, which had been known as the "My-Diem" (American-Diem) regime, they wished to decrease the visibility of Americans, rather than give them the greater public prominence that these U.S. programs would inevitably entail.

The Minh government's spirited opposition to the continuing U.S. pressures for expanding the role of American advisers is reflected in an account of a top-level meeting held with U.S. officials on January 10, 1964:

General Kim [Le Van Kim, Secretary General of the MRC] stressed the extreme undesirability of Americans going into districts and villages. It would play into the hands of the VC and make the Vietnamese officials look like lackeys. There would be a colonial flavor to the whole pacification effort. Minh added that even in the worst and clumsiest days of the French they

---

[14] Chuan's interview with *Hoa Binh* (a moderate Catholic newspaper), Saigon, July 20, 1971. General Chuan had received his military training in France, and became the first Vietnamese to serve as director of the Dalat Military Academy. In 1960 as commander of the Fifth Division, he helped put down the attempted coup against Diem. However, in November 1963, as head of G-4 on the General Staff, he played an important role in the coup that ousted him.

[15] This is referred to in a cable to Ambassador Lodge from the President, May 14, 1964 (National Security Files [hereafter NSF], Country File, Vietnam, Vol. 9, Cables, LBJ Library).

654

never went into the villages or districts. Others present went on to add that they thought that the USIS [United States Information Service] should carry out its work strictly hand-in-hand with the province chief. When Lodge pointed out that most of the USIS teams were Vietnamese, Minh said, "Yes, but they are considered the same as Vietnamese who worked for the Japanese and the same as the Vietnamese who drive for Americans and break traffic laws."[16]

In response to this stand, the Joint Chiefs of Staff cabled CINCPAC on January 14, 1964, that McNamara was "seriously concerned regarding ... Minh's assertion that no advisers are desired beyond the regimental level. The Secretary considers, and JCS agree, that this would be an unacceptable rearward step." McNamara, the JCS and the State Department then prepared a cable of guidance which was dispatched to Lodge three days later, stating: "We deem it essential to retain advisers down to sector and battalion level as we now have them, and consider establishment of subsector advisors as highly desirable improvement from our viewpoint."[17] However, Minh and his top associates remained adamant on this issue, refusing to yield to the continuing U.S. pressures.

In similar fashion, they strongly resisted channelling U.S. funds directly to local levels of administration, thus by-passing the Saigon government. Speaking for Minh, General Kim insisted that such support could only be on a government-to-government basis. The new government also withstood U.S. attempts to assume an expanded role within Saigon's security apparatus, which it believed was already encumbered by too many American advisers. The consequent tension came to a head when General Mai Huu Xuan, concurrently head of the National Police and Mayor of Saigon, became so infuriated by persistent American pressure and continuing lectures that he ordered the top U.S. adviser out of his office, admonishing: "If you Americans can't protect your own President from assassination, why should we follow your advice with respect to our own internal security?"[18]

Of more fundamental concern to President Johnson and his senior advisers than the differences over these various issues, however,

---

[16] *PP*, Gravel Ed., Vol. II, p. 307.

[17] *Ibid.*, Vol. II, pp. 307-8.

[18] Corroborated by General Ton That Dinh, then Minister of Security in the Minh government, and General Tran Van Don, its Minister of Defense. The CIA's Saigon station criticized Xuan's handling of police affairs, reporting to Washington that he continued "to pack the Directorate-General and police with old cronies, some of whom are of questionable repute and to pursue with perhaps greater than necessary zeal the roundup for questioning of officials connected with the Diem regime." CIA, *Situation Appraisal as of 30 November 1963*, distributed 2 December 1963 (LBJ Library).

655

were the anti-war pressures within South Vietnam, which they feared might impel the new Saigon government towards an accommodation with the NLF. The administration's growing apprehension on this score was fueled by several international developments. Among the most important of these were DeGaulle's well-publicized and continuing offer, first made on August 29, 1963, to cooperate with the people of Vietnam in an effort to unify their country in peace, free of outside influences;[19] Sihanouk's proposals in September and November for the neutralization of Cambodia; and Sihanouk's call for a federation of neutralized Indochinese states, including South Vietnam— a move in line with the NLF's statement of November 8, and which the NLF specifically endorsed on December 13.[20] Nor were these initiatives without wider outside support. Thus, two days after the NLF's November 8 proposal, *The New York Times* editorialized that "a negotiated settlement and 'neutralization' of Vietnam are not to be ruled out" and that the time had come to try to restore the Geneva Agreements by negotiations.

Within this context anti-war pressures inside South Vietnam appeared all the more dangerous to American officials. For the neutralization being discussed by De Gaulle, Sihanouk and the NLF called for an end to all external military ties and any foreign military presence. In the case of Vietnam this, of course, would mean removal of the United States' military and political presence. In such an event no Saigon government could hope to resist popular pressure for an end of the fighting and negotiation of a compromise political settlement with the NLF. In the face of these developments the whole rationale of the U.S. intervention would be undermined. The presidential advisers who had so vigorously championed that course had reason to fear that their own credibility and careers would be damaged, for such an outcome would provide the clearest demonstration of the error and futility of their past recommendations. There could also be serious domestic political repercussions damaging to the administration as a whole.

Even if the question of neutralization were confined to Cambodia, American officials feared that the discussions might also raise hopes in Vietnam. Ambassador Henry Cabot Lodge, then, viewed the pro-

---

[19] *The New York Times,* August 30, 1963.

[20] *NLF Radio,* December 13, 1963. The culminating external event in building up a climate of opinion acceptant of the possibility of a neutralist solution came on January 25 with France's recognition of the People's Republic of China and the attendant speculation that the West's opposition to a China regarded as supportive of Hanoi was diminishing.

656

posed conference on Cambodian neutralization as "disastrous," cabling on December 4: "It is inconceivable to me that a conference like this could do other than foment and encourage neutralism which is always present in varying degrees here in South Vietnam . . . any encouragement of neutralism will impair the war effort."[21]

Protean terms at best, "neutralism" and "neutralization" often took on ambiguous meanings as Americans and Vietnamese applied them to Vietnam. But in the most fundamental sense the Vietnamese used these terms to signify a situation wherein they themselves, without any foreign intervention, could work out their own internal settlement. The most immediate attraction was, naturally, peace, and thus a CIA report on this period concluded that for "many rural inhabitants" neutralism meant simply "an end to the war."[22] But beyond that, much of the population—urban and rural—realized that this goal could be achieved only through a political settlement reflecting compromise by both Saigon and the NLF. Minh and the other top government leaders were intent on trying this route. Thus, although they publicly opposed De Gaulle's and Sihanouk's neutralization proposals, they were at the same time attracted to what U.S. officials regarded as the inevitable internal consequences of a neutralist foreign policy. It was precisely these consequences that were most incompatible with U.S. objectives.

Despite General Minh's public stand against neutralism, there was, as Hedrick Smith reported to the *New York Times*, "widespread speculation in the Saigon press and in intellectual circles that neutralist politicians might be given a role in the Government . . . even rumors of neutralist sentiment within the military junta."[23] Symptomatic of the U.S. Embassy's alarm was its mid-December report to Washington that the Minister of Security in Minh's government, General Ton That Dinh, "is so concerned over Sihanouk's conference proposal that he is considering how to accommodate himself to a neutral solution for Vietnam." In response, Under-Secretary of State George Ball cabled: "As precautionary measure it seems to us useful to make special effort to reassure Dinh and others who may also be concerned. Nothing is further from USG mind than 'neutral solution for Vietnam.' We intend to win."[24]

---

[21] Lodge to Secretary of State, December 4, 1963 (NSF, Vietnam, Vol. 1, LBJ Library).

[22] CIA Weekly Report, *The Situation in South Vietnam 28 February 1964*, p. 4.

[23] *The New York Times*, December 10, 1963.

[24] Ball to American Embassy, Saigon, Immediate, December 16, 1963 (NSF, Vietnam, LBJ Library).

In accounting for the "real reasons" for the overthrow of the Minh government, General Tran Van Don, its Minister of Defense, was on the right track when he wrote: "Our problems apparently started with American Secretary of Defense McNamara during his visit to Saigon...."[25] Following a brief trip to Vietnam, December 18-20, Secretary McNamara and John McCone, Director of the CIA, both reported to President Johnson in highly adverse and alarmist tones.[26] McNamara criticized ineffective direction of military operations, the absence of "realistic pacification plans" and the fact of there being "no clear concept on how to reshape or conduct the strategic hamlet program." He concluded that the Vietcong had made great progress since the coup, with the only exception to the "gloomy southern picture" being "the possible adherence to the government of the Cao Dai and Hoa Hao sects." But it was evident that his primary worry was the prospect of neutralization. To this concern he addressed the entire two-sentence summary of his report: "The situation is very disturbing. Current trends, unless reversed in the next 2-3 months, will lead to neutralization at best and more likely to a Communist-controlled state." Both McNamara's alarm and the possibility of deeper American intervention came through clearly in the final sentence of the main body of his report: "We should watch the situation very carefully, running scared, hoping for the best, but preparing for more forceful moves if the situation does not show early signs of improvement."

McCone reported that the "NLF's appeal to the people of South Vietnam on political grounds has been effective, gained recruits for their armed forces, and neutralized resistance." He concluded that the new government had not yet demonstrated that it could "properly administer the affairs of the country" or successfully prosecute the war, and he seriously doubted its political stability. Indicative of his lack of confidence in the new leadership were his plans for "dispatching to Saigon a number of our 'old Vietnamese hands' for temporary duty to assist in developing the necessary covert resources of native case officers and agents to inform us concerning the effectiveness of the MRC and the public acceptance of the new government."[27]

---

[25] Tran Van Don, *Our Endless War Inside Vietnam* (San Rafael, CA: Presidio Press, 1978), p. 133.

[26] *Memorandum for the President*, 21 December 1963 from the Secretary of Defense (NSF, Vietnam, Vol. 2, LBJ Library).

[27] Letter of Dec. 23, 1963 to the President from John A. McCone, Director of Central Intelligence, with McCone's attached memorandum: *Highlights of Discussion in Saigon 18-20 December 1963*, dated December 21, 1963 (NSF, Vietnam Vol. 2, LBJ Library).

658

With the administration increasingly fearful that the Saigon government might yield to pressures for a neutralist solution, President Johnson's advisers prevailed upon him to throw his own weight against such a move, and, accordingly, in his New Year's message to Minh he strongly attacked neutralism as "another name for a Communist takeover." The neutralist tide did not abate, and American disillusionment with the military policies and performance of Minh's government mounted.[28] During January it became even more evident that the military and political objectives of the Johnson administration and those of General Minh differed more fundamentally than had been the case under Diem. Major opposition to the Minh government spread from the Department of Defense and the CIA to affect even Roger Hilsman, the Assistant Secretary of State for Far Eastern Affairs, and finally Ambassador Lodge himself. Both of these leading proponents of ousting Diem and Nhu eventually withdrew their support of the new government.

To understand the events leading up to the overthrow of the Minh government at the end of January 1964 it needs to be appreciated that removal of Diem and Nhu had not brought about solidarity either among American officials concerned with Vietnam policy or within the South Vietnamese military establishment. There had been a basic difference between the State Department and the Pentagon over whether Diem should be ousted, with Lodge and elements in the State Department championing this course, and the U.S. military leadership and the CIA unsympathetic to it. It was well known to Minh and his supporters that the Department of Defense's representative in Saigon, General Paul Harkins, had strongly opposed Diem's overthrow. Consequently, they mistrusted this head of the U.S. military mission, regarding him as a "symbol of the old order." Lacking effective influence with the new government, Harkins' position was weakened vis-à-vis that of Lodge.[29] The increased distance between the two men was widely known, and if prior to the ouster of Diem they appeared to be estranged team members, thereafter they hardly seemed to be on the same team. Thus, McNamara in his report to President Johnson of December 21, 1962 stated:

The Country Team is the second major weakness [that is, after the Minh government]. It lacks leadership and is not working to a common

---

[28] See, for instance, Hedrick Smith in *The New York Times*, February 2, 1964.

[29] See the reports of David Halberstam and Jack Raymond in *The New York Times* of November 13 and 15, 1963, and January 29, 1964.

659

plan. . . . Above all Lodge has virtually no official contact with Harkins. Lodge sends in reports with major military implications without showing them to Harkins.

Under these circumstances it was understandable that Harkins, resenting his subordinate position, and with his retirement no more than six months away, became interested in political initiatives that by-passed Ambassador Lodge.

The tensions within the American "country team" in Saigon, however, were greatly exceeded by those within the South Vietnamese military establishment. Some officers who had supported the coup against Diem were dissatisfied, because they felt insufficiently rewarded under Minh's new order. Others who had been members of rival military alignments opposed to Diem were worried by the new government's transfers designed to break up their groups.[30] Most worried were those officers who had remained closest to Diem at the time of the coup. Several were cashiered or demoted in the early days of the new government, and thereafter the others were fearful lest they should be the next to go. Although Minh's junta proceeded cautiously in the hopes of avoiding pre-emptive actions by insecure officers, their public program against military corruption further worried those senior Diemist officers who were vulnerable to this charge. In assessing this situation, a CIA appraisal of December 7, 1963 concluded that "however desirable and perhaps even necessary" was the "threatened purge of corrupt elements from the ranks of the military establishment from a long term point of view . . . in the short term" it could be expected to have a "disruptive effect on the solidarity of the military establishment."[31]

This was indeed the case, and at least two important backers of the coup against Minh were officers immediately threatened by the anticorruption drive. Major General Le Van Nghiem, Commander of the Special Forces, according to a U.S. military intelligence report, had been charged with corruption as II Corps Commander under Diem, and was now slated for replacement "as soon as the Executive Committee [of Minh's MRC] had consolidated its position."[32] And General Duong Ngoc Lam, commander of the Civil Guard, was

---

[30] CIA, *Situation Appraisal as of 14 December 1963,* distributed December 16, 1963, p. 6 (LBJ Library).

[31] CIA, *Situation Appraisal as of 7 December 1963,* p. 4 (NSF, Vietnam, Vol. 1, J.F. Kennedy Library).

[32] "Background on Coup in S.V.N., 30 January 1964," a report prepared by U.S. Marine Intelligence shortly after the coup.

660

aware that he was slated for investigation on charges that he had profited heavily from misuse of military funds in his charge.[33]

Disaffection of these elements alone would have been unlikely seriously to undermine the Minh government's capacity to prevent a coup, if the balance of power among the Saigon military factions had not been decisively altered by a number of moves urged by the U.S. military. As one chronicler in the Pentagon Papers notes: "U.S. pressure induced the GVN [Government of Vietnam] to break up the palace guard and to move coup-protection Ranger units out into the countryside...."[34] Of greater importance, on January 5, General Ton That Dinh was transferred from his command of the vital III Corps—embracing Saigon and the provinces around it—following persistent pressure by General Harkins and the U.S. Department of Defense.[35] His U.S.-approved successor, Major General Tran Thien Khiem, played a pivotal role in the events that followed, and General Dinh is undoubtedly correct in later perceiving his replacement by Khiem as "a prelude to the coup" that unseated the Minh regime. As General Don observes, this change in command was essential to the prospects of the plotters, for with it they acquired the major armed units needed to carry out their coup. With these in hand, he states, they were finally able to lay concrete plans for their move. Certainly Khiem and his two Catholic division commanders, Brig. Generals Nguyen Van Thieu and Lam Van Phat, provided the dissidents with their essential power base.

Whether or not Major General Nguyen Khanh, I Corps Commander, was less central than Khiem in the first phases of the coup's planning—as some have concluded[36]—he was deeply involved in later stages, was the principal Vietnamese figure in its direction, and headed the government that displaced Minh's. (Khiem was initially

---

[33] Information from General Tran Van Don. See also Robert Shaplen, *The Lost Revolution* (New York: Harper & Row, 1965), pp. 231-32.

[34] *PP,* Gravel Ed., Vol. II, p. 303. The account notes that "other units stayed near Saigon for this purpose." If that was so, when the crisis arose, they were apparently too far from the center of action to play a role.

[35] As early as November 29, General Harkins had cabled General Taylor, Chairman of the JCS, and Admiral Felt, CINCPAC: "General Dinh is still reluctant to give up command of III Corps. I'm still working on this. . . ." Cable (Naval Message) November 29, 1963 (NSF, Vietnam, Vol. 1, LBJ Library). The major and apparently final U.S. effort to secure Dinh's removal was conveyed by Lodge on behalf of President Johnson as part of the third of eleven points of advice presented orally to Minh at the beginning of January (probably January 1st) 1964. White House Memorandum from McGeorge Bundy to General Clifton at LBJ Ranch in Texas for the President, December 30, 1963 (NSF, Vietnam, Vol. 2, LBJ Library).

[36] Cf. Le Tu Hung, *Bon Tuong Da-lat* [The Four Dalat Generals] (Saigon: Dong Nai, 1971), p. 14.

661

to occupy the number two position in Khanh's government.) Khanh's emergence as the conspirators' top leader may have been partly a consequence of the belief, as one Vietnamese account puts it, that "Khiem did not dare to carry out a *coup d'état* himself out of fear that the Buddhists would react strongly against him and accuse him of trying to reestablish the Ngo Regime."[37] It presumably also resulted from the fact that the American military regarded Khanh as abler than Khiem and just as likely to work in concert with U.S. interests. Khanh was held in high esteem by the U.S. military mission to Vietnam,[38] particularly by General Harkins, with whom he was known to have close relations and who considered him "the strongest of all corps commanders."[39] According to a CIA assessment, he had been "consistently favorable to U.S. programs and advice."[40]

Having risen to the rank of Lt. Colonel under the French, Khanh had subsequently distinguished himself in suppressing the coup against Diem in 1960. Diem had rewarded him with a series of promotions, culminating in his appointment as commander of the II Corps in December 1962. Though Khanh claims to have been a principal organizer in the abortive anti-Diem coup plans of August 1963, available evidence for this is inconclusive, and those who led the November coup against Diem were initially unsure of his backing.[41] Khanh finally made clear his support for those who ousted Diem, but he was aware that the Minh government did not completely trust him.[42] The CIA noted his feeling of insecurity and reported that his motivation in supporting the coup against Minh derived in part from

---

[37] *Ibid.*, pp. 11-12. Although nominally a Buddhist, Khiem was "generally identified with the Catholic group," and was regarded as having been very close to Diem. CIA Report, undated (NSF, Vietnam, Vol. 23, LBJ Library). In so identifying Khiem, this report states that "some Buddhist elements have considered him to be a holdover from the Ngo Dinh Diem period," and that "He commanded the forces which relieved the siege of Diem's Palace in the 1960 coup attempt, but went along with the other generals in the successful 1963 coup."

[38] CIA, *Biographic Register*, January 29, 1965 (Office of Central Reference, Washington, D.C., January 29, 1965) (LBJ Library). See also Hedrick Smith in *The New York Times*, November 30, 1963.

[39] Naval Message, Personal, Harkins to Adm. Felt and General Taylor, 29 November 1963 (LBJ Library).

[40] CIA, *Current Intelligence Memorandum*, March 20, 1964, p. vi.

[41] Thus, a retrospective appraisal in the CIA's Office of Central Reference *Biographic Register* of January 29, 1965 states: "During the suspected coup planning of August and September 1963, Khanh gave no indication of being involved in an antigovernment coup plan. He reportedly regarded Ngo Dinh Nhu as the most intelligent and astute individual in Vietnam and as one who could provide the leadership that Vietnam needed. However, Khanh's name was linked with a coup group reportedly directed by Nhu [designed to pre-empt and compromise the leaders of the actual coup] and with one led by Tran Kim Tuyen. . . . Khanh's participation in the November 1963 coup that deposed Ngo Dinh Diem is not clear."

[42] CIA, *Current Intelligence Memorandum*, Annex, March 20, 1964, p. iv.

662

reports that he was being considered for a post abroad which would have removed him from influence on local developments.[43]

As planning for the anti-Minh coup proceeded, its ultimate objective became obscured by the conspirators' immediate goal of removing Nguyen Ngoc Tho from the prime-ministership—a move backed by a growing number within the government's 12-man MRC, and ultimately not contested by its top leaders, except for Minh himself.[44] The plotters' apparent preoccupation with Tho explains in part why the generals who dominated the MRC—Minh, Don, Dinh and Kim—were taken by surprise when they themselves became the target. But a more important reason for their lack of preparedness was their misreading of the U.S. position. In view of what had happened to Diem, they understood very clearly the absolute necessity of retaining American backing for their government, and repeated assurances from Ambassador Lodge and President Johnson's supportive private and public communications convinced them that this remained firm. Thus, the President in his confidential memorandum to Lodge instructed him to assure Minh when he met with him on January 1, 1964 that he had "the complete support of the United States as *the* leader of Vietnam [emphasis in the original]."[45]

However, Minh's government, and apparently Lodge as well, underestimated General Harkins' opposition, and presumably that of his mentor, General Taylor, Chairman of the Joint Chiefs of Staff. General Taylor, who, it will be recalled, was opposed to the ouster of Ngo Dinh Diem, had, along with McNamara, become highly critical of the attitude and actions of his successors. In noting General Harkins' opposition to the overthrow of Diem and the increasing divergence between Lodge and the U.S. military mission, General Khanh put the matter pointedly when in looking back at this episode he stated: "Maybe in the coup of January 30, 1964, the U.S. Army had come to conclude that it too should have the capacity to bring about a coup."[46] Official U.S. statements, however, have disclaimed any

---

[43] CIA, *Biographic Register*, January 29, 1965.

[44] Although Tho had served as Diem's Vice-President, members of the new government regarded him as having acted as a moderating force against repression of the Buddhists, and Minh, in particular, felt he was indispensable to the effective administration of the successor government because of his knowledge of administrative and economic matters. This assessment of his stand regarding the Buddhists was consistent with that of the CIA in its *Situation Appraisal as of 14 December 1963*, distributed 16 December. (LBJ Library).

[45] "Instruction for Oral Presentation," attached to memorandum "To General Clifton at LBJ Ranch in Texas for the President, from McGeorge Bundy," December 30, 1963 (LBJ Library).

[46] Interview with the writer, Ithaca, New York, June 6, 1973.

663

American responsibility and indicated that the Johnson Administration was taken by surprise.[47] Even five years after the event, one of the chroniclers of the *Pentagon Papers* who dealt with this period still maintained that the coup "came as an almost complete surprise to the [U.S.] Saigon mission and to Washington."[48]

The principal Vietnamese actors on both sides of the confrontation—General Khanh himself, as well as Generals Minh, Don and Dinh, together with their Prime Minister Tho—have testified that the U.S. was decisively involved and that there would have been no coup without its backing. These Vietnamese accounts are basically consistent and corroborative, and are strongly supported by the contemporaneous official U.S. government documents bearing on this period that have recently been released.[49] When such documentation is added to data from interviews, the press, and other sources, a fairly clear picture emerges of events leading up to the January 30 coup.

Generals Khanh and Khiem began lining up support in the first days of January 1964. Encouragement from General Harkins conveyed through the U.S. military advisers appears to have been an early element in the process.[50] Minh's Minister of Defense and Chief of Staff, General Don, states that, even before this time, under orders of General Harkins the U.S. officers attached to the four corps commanders had been hard at work trying to convince them of the vir-

---

[47] See, for instance, James Reston and Jack Raymond in *The New York Times*, January 30 and 31, 1964.

[48] *PP*, Gravel Ed., Vol. III, p. 37. The other somewhat more forthright account provided in the *Papers* states that "There is no record of an official U.S. reply" to Khanh's request of January 28 for U.S. support in staging a coup (*ibid.*, Vol. II, pp. 308-9), but obviously no U.S. reply could be "official," for room had to be left for "plausible denial" in case the coup effort failed to oust a government that Washington formally recognized. There is striking incongruity between the *Pentagon Papers'* accounts of the coup against Diem and that against Minh. In view of the issues involved, the ousting of Minh was in fact as much a watershed in the relations between Washington and Vietnam as was the removal of Diem. Yet though the extent of U.S. involvement in the earlier coup is spelled out clearly, there appears to be a deliberate effort to obscure this element in the later one. The chroniclers in the Pentagon-commissioned study were perhaps willing to have the American role in the removal of Diem rather extensively described because of the Pentagon's opposition to it, while the clear involvment of the U.S. Military's Mission in the overthrow of Minh made them reluctant to have this part of the record disclosed.

[49] The Freedom of Information Act has made it possible to get some important material through the now increasingly tight mesh of constraints, even though the Ford and Carter administrations have refused to declassify many documents relating to Minh's ouster that have been precisely identified in requests made for declassification.

[50] Robert Shaplen, who noted that "A number of meetings beetween Khanh and American officers in the North [where Khanh was area commander] took place in the first two weeks of January," is undoubtedly correct in surmising that "it is very likely that they dealt partly with the new coup." Robert Shaplen, *The Lost Revolution* (New York: Harper & Row, 1965), pp. 232-3.

664

tues of a bombing campaign against the north. He views the role of these American advisers as critical in persuading the officers in command of several key units to back the coup.

The most important supporters Khanh and Khiem recruited were a group of officers who were closely associated with the southern faction of the conservative nationalist Dai Viet Party.[51] Most of them were Catholic and had held important positions under Diem. Prominent among them were some of General Khiem's top subordinates: Brig. Gen. Nguyen Van Thieu, Commander of the 5th Division; General Lam Van Phat, Commander of the 7th Division; General Le Van Nghiem, Commander of Special Forces; General Duong Ngoc Lam, Commander of the Civil Guard; and finally—though joining only at the eleventh hour—Colonel Duong Huu Nghia, acting head of the Armored Command. Among the conspirators the principal liaison roles appear to have been played by General Do Mau, who had served as chief of the military security service under Diem and was now Minister of Information in Minh's government; General Duong Van Duc whom the junta had just permitted to return from France; and General Nghiem.[52]

In justifying their plans against the government, the conspirators first spread the rumor, and finally levelled a formal charge, that Minh, Don, and Kim were "pro-French and pro-neutralist."[53] They built upon the fact that Minh's government had encouraged several anti-Diem officers to return from their exile in France, citing their repatriation as evidence that Minh and his top associates were pro-French and receptive to De Gaulle's neutralization plans. Two events in January gave some plausibility to this accusation. First was a statement made by General Don at a Bangkok press conference during a trip that he and General Dinh had made at the invitation of the Thai army. Responding to a question concerning De Gaulle's plan, Don said that he was not against neutralization but that it should not be confined to the south and should cover the north as well. Second, was

---

[51] Khiem, though not a member of this group, enjoyed cordial relations with them as, in fact, had Minh. So important was the role of Dai Viet officers in the coup that subsequently they tended to refer to it as "their" coup. See cable of June 3, 1964, Saigon Embassy to Department of State (NSF, Country File, Vietnam, Vol. II, Cables, LBJ Library).

[52] A U.S. Marine Corps Intelligence report noted that Nghiem had travelled to Hue on January 13 and obtained General Khanh's backing for moves against two of Minh's principal lieutenants—Generals Tran Van Don and Ton That Dinh—as well as Prime Minister Tho, and then returned to Saigon where he was in contact with Major General Khiem and Brig. General Nguyen Van Thieu, who, it notes, were "both essential to the success of the coup." *Background on the Coup in S.V.N., January 30, 1964* (undated, but apparently February 1964).

[53] See joint CAS [CIA]/MACV message to McGeorge Bundy, January 29, 1964 (NSF, Vietnam, Vol. 3, LBJ Library).

665

a dinner which Don gave for two visiting Gaullist deputies from the French National Assembly to which he invited Generals Dinh, Kim, and Xuan. Don and Dinh both state that De Gaulle's neutralization plan was not discussed there, but the conspirators alleged that it had been.

Presumably, these two episodes provided part of the basis for the report by D'Orlandi, the Italian Ambassador to South Vietnam, forwarded by Lodge to Washington on January 20. It alleged that Generals Don and Dinh were potential leaders of a group that might accept De Gaulle's neutralization formula. At the time Ambassador Lodge commented that the U.S. Embassy had no hard evidence that either of the two was flirting with neutralization, but just after the January 30 coup, he cabled Washington that he had had some second thoughts about the matter. He now referred to D'Orlandi as "one of the shrewdest men here," and observed that General Don and General Kim, the junta's Secretary-General, "had never at any time foresworn the possibility of a neutral solution at what might seem to them the proper time." Although acknowledging that they had been working effectively in the effort against the Vietcong, Lodge observed: "But none of us had ever discussed what the next step would be after the Government of Vietnam had reached a position of strength. Perhaps they did favor the French neutrality solution at that time."[54]

As a final step in his rumor campaign, Khanh—through his U.S. adviser Col. Jaspar Wilson—informed Ambassador Lodge that he had come into possession of certain documents. According to Khanh, these proved that Generals Don, Kim and Xuan were "pro-French, pro-neutralist," and about to stage a coup after which they would announce South Vietnam's neutralization. He asserted that in their planning they were in touch with Minh. If the plot were not immediately crushed, Khanh warned, it stood a fair chance of success because a "neutralist platform might strike [a] responsive chord among junior officers."[55] In addition, he and his supporters spread rumors—actually not altogether unfounded—that leading members of the Minh government were preparing to come to an agreement with the NLF.[56]

---

[54] PP, Gravel Ed., Vol.III, pp. 37-9.

[55] Joint Cable CAS/MACV to White House, McGeorge Bundy, January 29, 1964 (NSF, Vietnam, Vol. 3, LBJ Library).

[56] Cf. Jean LaCouture, *Vietnam Between Two Truces* (New York: Random House, 1966), p. 132.

Khanh and his associates never produced these documents or other evidence to substantiate their allegations. But in view of the existing U.S. alarm over the strength of neutralist sentiment in the south, the charge came at a propitious time. The strategy—whether conceived by dissident Vietnamese officers or certain Americans—was effective in providing a sufficiently plausible rationale for the Johnson administration to accept what Khanh described as his own "pre-emptive coup."

At least some members of the American military were not only privy to the coup's planning but were also involved in its implementation. Col. Jaspar Wilson, the U.S. Military Adviser to General Khanh, was in a position to provide a crucial liaison between the coup's top leader and General Harkins, and according to both Khanh and recently declassified U.S. records, he did perform this role.

General Khanh states that in the early morning of January 28, the other coup leaders in Saigon dispatched General Duong Van Duc to Danang to alert him that plans for the coup were ready and that he was expected in the capital the next day to lead it. To check that Duc's assurances of U.S. backing were correct, he sent Col. Wilson to Saigon that same day. Wilson called him back by a pre-arranged code around 3 o'clock that afternoon and assured him that the embassy as well as MACV had no objections and that the action could get underway.

General Harkins in a cable to General Taylor, Chairman of the JCS, sent just after the coup had been completed, reported that at about 3 p.m. on the 28th Colonel Wilson had come to see him at the request of General Khanh to ascertain whether the United States would back a pre-emptive "counter-coup" against individuals who "planned to seize control and immediately announce a position of neutralization." Harkins states he ordered Wilson to go to Lodge and relate his story, and then, according to this cable, he decided to go on what he refers to as "a field trip."[57] Permission for declassification of his dispatches during this crucial field trip has been refused, but one can imagine that he had urgent matters to attend to.

One problem that could hardly have escaped his attention was the disposition at this time of the armored units in the Saigon area. Support from Colonel Duong Huu Nghia, one of the most powerful of the Dai Viet military leaders and acting head of the Capital Ar-

---

[57] Cable from Harkins to Taylor, January 30, 1964 (LBJ Library).

667

mored Command, was pivotal to the success of the coup. Being a friend and appointee of Minh, Nghia upset plans by balking at General Thieu's order that he move all armored units out of Saigon to Thieu's 5th Infantry Division headquarters at Bien Hoa. As a CIA cable stated, "Nghia suspected that Thieu was plotting against Major General Duong Van Minh and informed Thieu that the armored vehicles could not be moved. . . . Nghia also announced his support for General Minh."[58] This unexpected development appears to have arisen around the time Harkins left on his "fieldtrip," and it is probable that one of his top priorities was to induce Colonel Nghia to go along with the coup plans—at least to back the removal of Minh's most important supporters, Generals Don, Dinh, Kim and Xuan. Whatever the case, this CIA report continues: "By January 29, however, Nghia apparently had switched his support to Thieu," who had secured "operational control of both the armored and the Marine Corps on that date"—a temporary change in command that was presumably central to the coup's timing.[59]

According to Harkins' account, upon returning to Saigon on January 29, he checked in with Lodge and was told of Colonel Wilson's latest meeting with Khanh. Harkins states that at 2:15 a.m. on January 30, Lodge sent an aide to alert him that "H-Hour" would be at 4:00 a.m., that Khanh would pick him up at 3:15, and that coup headquarters would be at the Airborne Brigade's command post.[60]

Colonel Wilson reported the coup's progress at frequent intervals to Lodge who quickly relayed the information to Washington. The following nine cables from Lodge to the Department of State on January 30th are instructive.

5:00 a.m.: Colonel Wilson, MAAG Adviser with Khanh, reports from command post airborne brigade at 0435 operation is on schedule and that JGS compound has been secured.

5:42 a.m.: At 0525 Wilson reports everything still on schedule.

6:00 a.m.: At 0550 Wilson reports General Xuan, Security Chief and Saigon Mayor, being detained at Airborne CP. Khanh plans move CP to JGS compound. Wilson will accompany.

6:20 a.m.: At 0610 Wilson reports that General Khiem now present at Air-

---

[58] Central Intelligence Agency, Intelligence Information Cable, *Background of Coup Staged by General Nguyen Khanh,* Saigon, January 30, 1964 (LBJ Library).

[59] *Ibid.* This report went on to state that on January 30 Nighia supported the coup led by Khanh and that Lt. Col. Ly Tong Ba, commander of the 6th Armored Squadron joined Brig. General Lam Van Phat, commander of the 7th Division—like Thieu's 5th Division part of General Khiem's Third Corps—in doing so.

[60] Cable from Harkins to Taylor, January 30, 1964 (LBJ Library).

668

borne CP with Khanh. General Don has been picked up and is under detention. General Kim's house is surrounded . . . . General Big Minh's home also surrounded.

6:45 a.m.: At 0625 Wilson reports that General Nguyen Huu Co, IV Corps, now present in JGS compound with Khanh and Khiem. . . . Wilson instructed to inform Generals Khanh and Khiem that Ambassador Lodge strongly advises all possible efforts be made to avoid bloodshed. Khanh has expressed desired to see Lodge later today.

7:45 a.m.: At 0735 Wilson reports Big Minh on his way to JGS compound under custody. Khanh reportedly states Minh will be offered "figurehead position" if he agrees to denounce neutralism and aligns himself with Khanh's group and their objectives.

9:00 a.m.: At 0840 Wilson reports that Big Minh has arrived at JGS compound. General Thieu (5th Division) and General do Mau have come in and joined General Khanh. . . atmosphere at JGS is described like an election headquarters after a victory.

9:14 a.m.: At 0855 Wilson reports . . . Khanh states he will turn to American Ambassador and rely upon him heavily for political assistance.

Colonel Nghia with his armored troops supported Khanh's actions against Generals Dinh, Don, Kim and Xuan, but refused to countenance Minh's arrest—his tanks being interposed to protect Minh from General Duong Ngoc Lam's Home Guard units, that carried out the arrests of the four other top generals. Thus, although Minh was briefly taken into "custody" for his own protection from some of Khanh's more belligerent backers, he was never arrested and sent to places of detention outside of Saigon as were the other four. This accorded well with American plans. For though Lodge and the State Department were ready to see Don, Dinh, Kim and Xuan go, they did not believe that Minh himself was a neutralist and wished him to remain on as a symbol of continuity in the government Khanh was about to form.

General Nguyen Van Chuan, a high-ranking officer present at the coup leaders' headquarters, has published an account of his impressions. He states that after having been invited by General Khiem to the Joint General Staff Headquarters early in the morning of January 30, "I saw General Khanh, General Khiem, and a number of officers . . . about 15 to 20 people. . . . Among them were a number of senior officers who had been given a leave of absence without pay after the November 1, 1963 coup. . . .." Chuan states that Khanh, who chaired the meeting, charged that Minh's government was "neutralist, pro-Communist and pro-French" as well as incompetent. "Even at that

669

point," he says, "they didn't know what to call the coup d'état to make it sound all right; it was only a while later that they thought of the term 'rectification'. . . ." He recalled that "the thing that stood out at the meeting was the presence of the American colonel who was General Khanh's advisor; during the meeting he telephoned Harkins regularly every five minutes." Finally, Chuan says, Khanh turned the meeting over to Khiem, saying as he left that he had to go see General Harkins.[61]

In commenting on the American role, General Chuan states that, upon arriving at General Khanh's headquarters on the morning of the coup, "I noticed the heavy involvement of the Harkins group. . . . I had the immediate feeling that this action was not being carried out independently," but "was directed by foreigners." He concludes: "It was precisely because [Minh's] Armed Forces had opposed American wishes" for a "plan requiring a U.S. presence and in particular the establishment of an American base in Vietnam" that "the Americans had reason to push for the 'rectification.' "[62]

Whether or not the U.S. military took the initiative in laying plans for the coup, they were at least privy to them well in advance and encouraged particular Vietnamese officers in their execution. The available data indicate that the major channel of intervention was through MACV, the U.S. military command in Saigon. General Paul Harkins and his subordinate, Colonel Jaspar Wilson, played key roles, presumably with the concurrence of their superiors in the Department of Defense, General Taylor and Secretary McNamara. Although the CIA was clearly *au courant* with the final stages of the planning, insufficient data have been declassified to establish whether or not it played an early role. However, it appears that Ambassador Lodge was not brought into the act until after preparations were well advanced,[63] and that he and the Department of State had either little

---

[61] *Hoa Binh* [a moderate Catholic newspaper published in Saigon], July 14 and 16, 1971.

[62] *Loc. cit.*, July 20, 1971. General Chuan's conclusion regarding the centrality of the American role in these events is consistent with the accounts of Generals Minh, Don, and Dinh and Prime Minister Tho.

[63] That as late as January 25 Lodge either had no inkling of plans for the coup or else was trying to keep Minh from suspecting that U.S. support was being withdrawn is suggested by his cable of that date to President Johnson, wherein he asked that he send Minh "a message of congratulations" on "the progress achieved so far." Department of State cable to Harriman from Lodge, January 25, 1964 (NSF, Vietnam, Vol.2, LBJ Library). A knowledgeable French source states that it is the generally accepted thesis that Lodge was presented with a "fait accompli." Georges Chaffard, *Les Deux Guerres du Vietnam: de Vallery à Westmoreland* (Paris: La Table Ronde, 1969), p. 351 f.n.2. Lodge himself a few days after the coup in a cable to Washington stated: "General Khanh's coup was extremely disconcerting at first blush." *PP*, Gravel Ed. Vol. III, p. 38. Very soon after the event the ambassador of a major U.S.-aligned power found

670

or no advance knowledge of the plans. Otherwise, it is difficult to understand Undersecretary of State Ball's cable to Lodge apparently only a few hours after the ambassador had informed him that a coup had been launched.

We have so little info on motivations and other factors involved in current crisis that we leave to your judgment how to handle. Meantime we trust you will make very clear that we had nothing to do with coup. If you consider it advisable and possible there would seem to us to be merit in preserving Minh as head of Government since he appears to have best potentialities for rallying support of people.[64]

But even Lodge had learned of the plans at least a day before the plotters seized the surprised General Minh and the leading members of his government. Whatever their varying depths of involvement,[65] neither the U.S. military mission nor Ambassador Lodge were willing to warn the South Vietnamese government to which they were accredited, and which they officially supported, of the plot to overthrow it.

It is unclear whether the Department of State was keen about the political change that had been brought about, but it had little choice but to go along. If it had any doubts, they presumably were diminished by a CIA situation report from Saigon dispatched just after it was clear that the coup had succeeded: "It is safe to say that Khanh's group will be essentially pro-American, anti-communist and anti-neutralist in general orientation."[66] And insofar as maintaining leadership in the hands of the senior Vietnamese military was concerned, there appeared to be no other options; for, as General Harkins cabled General Taylor, "One thing is for sure with this coup. We've gone through all the eligible general officers."[67]

The Johnson administration accepted the overthrow of Minh's

---

the usually well-informed Lodge to be surprisingly ignorant about the character and views of General Khanh.

[64] Outgoing telegram Department of State 7.47 p.m. January 29, 1964 (LBJ Library). With Saigon twelve hours ahead of Washington time, this presumably reached the Embassy around 8.00 a.m. on the 30th. According to Harkins, Lodge did not inform Washington that the coup was to be executed until about 45 minutes beforehand. Cable from Harkins to Taylor, January 30, 1964 (LBJ Library).

[65] In the scant coverage of the coup provided by the Department of Defense in the *Pentagon Papers*, there appears to be an effort to shift any suspicions of U.S. involvement from General Harkins to Lodge. The Ambassador is portrayed as the American most privy to the coup plotters' plans and as the person who conveyed news of the coup from Col. Jasper Wilson (Khanh's U.S. adviser) to General Harkins, even though Wilson in fact reported directly to the General, who after all, was his immediate superior.

[66] CIA cable from Saigon prepared at 0725, January 30 (NSF, Vietnam, Vol. 3, LBJ Library).

[67] Cable from Harkins to Taylor, January 30, 1964 (LBJ Library).

671

government and promptly pledged support to its successor, even before General Khanh had actually formed a government. Khanh's co-
operativeness and tractability contrasted with the demeanor of his
predecessor. He made it clear, while the coup was still in progress on
January 30, that he was prepared to turn to Lodge for political advice, and he repeated this at their meeting later that day. The next
day he went even further, requesting the ambassador's judgement as
to what sort of government he should form and who would make a
good premier.[68] The U.S. administration evidently appreciated his attitude. Secretary of State Rusk suggested that Khanh should occupy
the premiership as well as the chairmanship of the MRC,[69] and on
February 2, President Johnson sent him a warm and supportive
handwritten note.[70]

Though Khanh wished to keep Minh under arrest along with his
four colleagues, he yielded to American advice and made him a figurehead Chief of State in order to symbolize a continuity and political unity that in fact did not exist. Khanh described the unhappy
Minh's actual powerlessness with a nice precision: he would be "exactly like the King of England," but on a "provisional basis."[71]

The United States, then, played just as critical a role in the ousting of Minh's government as in the much better known removal of
Diem, the Vietnamese leader it had initially established in power.
Nor was this the last time that intervention by the United States was
a decisive factor in ejecting a Saigon government whose policies were
regarded as departing unacceptably from American objectives.
Within a year U.S. officials no longer regarded Minh's successor as a
sufficiently amenable and reliable agent for advancing their policies,
and in February 1965 General Khanh found himself the object of an
American-supported coup as a successful as the one that had enabled
him to replace Minh.

Only with the installation of Ky and Thieu in office in mid-1965
did the Johnson administration remain satisfied that it had as cooperative an instrument as was available for furthering its military and
political goals. Once this had been achieved, "political stability"
again became the watchword of American policy-makers as it had

---

[68] Cables from Lodge to Secretary of State, January 31 and February 4, 1964 (NSF, Vietnam, Cables, Vol. 3, LBJ Library).
[69] Cable from Rusk to Amembassy Saigon, February 1, 1964 (NSF, Vietnam, Cables, Vol.
3, LBJ Library).
[70] White House Central Files (C0312, LBJ Library).
[71] Cable from Lodge to Secretary of State, February 7, 1964 (LBJ Library).

672

been until almost the end of the regime led by Diem. No more coups were to be permitted, and if one threatened—as when later the Buddhist activists marshalled sufficient power to unseat Ky and Thieu— the U.S. threw its weight on the side of its protégés to ensure their continuing ascendancy.

U.S. aims in Vietnam were incompatible with any assertion of the actual balance of indigenous political forces. Quite apart from its role in the broader campaign against the NLF and Hanoi, American power had to be injected in sufficient measure into the area of South Vietnam controlled by Saigon to ensure that the local levers of control remained in the hands of those who were prepared to represent U.S. interests. There the enormous weight of American intervention registered heavily on the political scales, sufficiently offsetting the pulls of indigenous political gravity to maintain in power a leadership devoid of significant popular support. Thus, a rigid polarization was imposed upon the people of South Vietnam wherein they were denied the option of political compromise and permitted only two active choices—supporting either the NLF or a Saigon regime shaped by and dependent upon the U.S.

The U.S. could not cease its political intervention without being prepared to withdraw its military presence and abandon its goals in Vietnam. Successive American administrations found it essential to maintain the United States' own "reliable" Vietnamese agents in power not only to provide the essential base from which to mount the U.S. military effort, but also to contain the powerful forces of neutralism and ensure Saigon's continuing participation in the war.

The nature of U.S. objectives precluded the acceptance by American officials of any significant movement toward the development of a genuinely representative Saigon government, for by its very nature such a regime could not be expected to back those aims. Any Saigon leadership that sought to broaden its popular base sufficiently to stand on its own feet would have had to adjust its policies to accommodate to the widespread yearning for an end to the fighting and a negotiated settlement based upon compromise with the NLF. This was precisely what the government led by General Duong Van Minh planned, and this was a major reason why U.S. officials were behind the coup that ousted it.

Cornell University, U.S.A., August 1979

673

The Search for the
"Breaking Point" in Vietnam

The Statistics of a Deadly Quarrel

JOHN E. MUELLER

University of Rochester

American strategies for success in the Vietnam War, derived at least partly from historical experience, were based on the assumption that Communist forces would reach a "breaking point" after suffering enough punishment. In conformity with this strategy, extensive damage was inflicted to the point where it appears the military costs accepted by the Communists, in comparison with population, were virtually unprecendented in modern history. The central question about the war then is: Why were the Vietnamese Communists willing to accept virtually unprecedented losses for a military goal that was far from central to the continued existence of their state? Some aspects of an answer to this question are suggested; the strategy of attrition is assessed in historical comparison; and the question of where the "breaking point" might have been is discussed.

I personally underestimated the resistance and the determination of the North Vietnamese. They've taken over 700,000 killed which in relation to population is almost the equivalent of—what? Ten million Americans? And they continue to come. I thought that when we had established a position in Vietnam which would be clearly impossible for them to overrun militarily that then the chances were very high that they would pull back— maybe only for a time--but pull back or take part in some serious negotiation.

—*Dean Rusk, NBC-TV interview, July 2, 1971*

In reflecting on America's involvement in the Vietnam war, commentators have often expressed amazement that bright, talented leaders could embark on a policy that proved so disastrous. How could such a massive mistake have been made? To explain the phenomenon, aspects of the decision makers' personalities are often puzzled over, or inadequacies of the bureaucratic decision-making mechanism are

INTERNATIONAL STUDIES QUARTERLY, Vol. 24 No. 4, December 1980 497-519
© 1980 I.S.A.

497

probed (Thomson, 1968; Ellsberg, 1972; Gallucci, 1971; Halberstam, 1972; Janis, 1972). The content of the decisions is often given little consideration. The decisions are assumed invalid because the policy failed, and so hindsight is used to prejudge them.

This article seeks to examine in context the strategic assumptions behind the decisions that led to U.S. involvement in Vietnam— particularly those decisions that led to the major American escalation of 1965. It examines the strategies for success in Vietnam and concentrates on their underlying assumption: that there was some level of punishment at which the Vietnamese Communists would "break."

The article then attempts to estimate the costs borne by the Communists and compares this with the cost typical of international wars in the last century and a half. It is found that, although they were fighting for a goal that was far from central to their continued existence as a nation, *the military costs accepted by the Communists in Vietnam were virtually unprecedented historically.* This suggests that U.S. decision makers were on sound historical ground when they fashioned their strategies for success—they were mistaken, but the mistake was a reasonable one. I conclude with a discussion of the extraordinary ability of the Communists in Vietnam to accept slaughter and maintain morale without "breaking" and with some considerations about where their "breaking point" might have been.

The Consensus of 1965

In 1965 U.S. decision makers confronted a deteriorating situation in Vietnam, a situation that seemed to be leading to an imminent Communist victory (see Lewy, 1978: 43-48). It seemed that only American intervention could prevent a Communist victory, and there was near-consensus that saw the prevention of Communist success in South Vietnam as vital to U.S. interests. There was an eloquent dissenter to this proposition within the administration—Undersecretary of State George Ball—but generally there was broad agreement with reporter David Halberstam's assessment at the time: "Vietnam is a legitimate part of [America's] global commitment. A strategic country in a key area, it is perhaps one of only five or six nations in the world that is truly vital to U.S interests" (1965: 319).

The origin of this consensus, rooted in the Cold War policy of containment, is not the subject of this article.[1] Rather, the question to be considered concerns the American strategies for success in Vietnam. Given that the prevention of Communist victory in Vietnam was seen to be vital to U.S. interests at the time, did the United States have any reasonable hope of military success in Vietnam? And, if so, why did the United States fail?

The "Breaking Point" Assumption

As former Secretary of State Dean Rusk suggests in the earlier quotation, American strategies for success in Vietnam were based on the central assumption that if the Communists sustained enough military punishment they would finally relent, forsaking (at least temporarily) their war effort. It was hoped there was some "breaking point" for the North Vietnamese—some level of punishment at which their morale and resolve would crumble, at which their "will" would be "broken."

In part, this assumption was based on the observation that U.S. goals in Vietnam were somewhat limited. The enemy the United States was opposing in Vietnam was seeking to unify the country under Communist leadership, and American goals were simply to prevent this unification-by-force. The United States was not seeking to overthrow the regime in the Communist north, but only to prevent the extension of its control to the non-Communist south (see Goodman, 1978: 37). In this view the North Vietnamese regime was not fighting for the survival of its state (as were the Germans and Japanese in 1945, for example). They merely had to give up the fight in the south and they would be permitted to retreat to an independent existence in the north.

Accordingly, from the American perspective, the war did not seem to be any sort of "death struggle," as World War II had been. Rather, it was simply a matter of convincing the north that the war in the south was not worth the cost. Sufficiently punished, the Communists could reasonably be expected to relent, at least temporarily, in their effort to extend their area of control.

The American ability to inflict punishment was clear; what was unclear was how much punishment the Communists would take before they would break. Gelb and Betts characterize the thinking this way:

1. For an extended discussion of the origins and development of this consensus, see Gelb and Betts (1979), especially chapter 6. For a discussion of factors in and outside of Vietnam that caused this consensus to change between 1965 and 1968, see Mueller (forthcoming).

53

"How could a tiny, backward Asian country *not* have a breaking point when opposed by the might of the United States?" (1979: 343).

Strategies for Success

Expectations of U.S. success in Vietnam varied. There were apparently some in the administration who were fairly confident of early victory once American might was properly applied,[2] while others feared a long war with no guarantee of early success (see Janis, 1972: 108-112; Gelb and Betts, 1979: 126, 318-322; Ellsberg, 1972). Some more or less specific predictions in mid-1965 included General William Westmoreland's timetable that seemed to suggest a reasonable hope for the defeat and destruction of enemy forces by the end of 1967 and Assistant Secretary of Defense John McNaughton's calculation of a fifty-fifty chance of success by 1968 (Pentagon Papers, 1971: Vol. 3, 482, 484).[3] Defense Secretary Robert McNamara, writing at the end of 1965, saw a fifty-fifty chance of success by early 1967 (Pentagon Papers, 1971: Vol. 4, 624).

However, as suggested above, success, whatever the degree of confidence, was based on the assumption that a point would be reached where, as Westmoreland wrote in 1965, the enemy would become "convinced that military victory was impossible and then would not be willing to endure further punishment" (Pentagon Papers, 1971: Vol. 3, 482). Or, as he put it in 1967, "We'll just go on bleeding them until Hanoi wakes up to the fact that they have bled their country to the point of national disaster for generations. Then they will have to reassess their position" (Lewy, 1978: 73).

There were at least three ways the war might have been successful for the United States. All had historical precedents.

(1) One of these was the "fade away" thesis. Walt Rostow, then Chairman of the State Department's Policy Planning Council, was one who suggested in 1965 that, if all possible routes to victory were denied, the enemy might finally give up "in discouragement," somewhat in the manner of guerrilla defeats in Greece (1946-1949), the Philippines (1945-

---

2. As Moyers put it, "There was a confidence—it was never bragged about, it was just there—a residue perhaps of the confrontation of missiles over Cuba—that when the chips were really down, the other people would fold" (1969: 262). See also Lewy (1978: 30, 41, 164) and Goodman (1978: 2).

3. Westmoreland argues that this common reading of his 1965 timetable is inaccurate (1976: 142-143).

1954), and Malaya (1948-1960) [Pentagon Papers, 1971: Vol. 3, 381-382].[4] Indeed, one could add other examples to this list. Active Communist or Communist-supported guerrilla movements had been successfully undercut by non-Communist forces in Guatemala, Venezuela, and the Congo in the early and mid-1960s.

The CIA assessment accepted by McNamara in 1965 argued that if the Communists see "no prospect of an early victory and no grounds for hope they can simply outlast the U.S." and if North Vietnam is under "damaging punitive attack," then "Hanoi probably would, at least for a period of time, alter its basic strategy and course of action in South Vietnam" (Pentagon Papers, 1971: Vol. 4, 26).[5]

The war, as Westmoreland saw it, was one of "attrition" against "an enemy with limited manpower." "Although the North Vietnamese might constantly rebuild their units," Westmoreland has argued, "they did so each time with manpower less adequately trained" (1976: 153).[6] Thus depleted, they would fade away; in McNamara's words, they "would choose to reduce their efforts in the South and try to salvage their resources for another day" (Pentagon Papers, 1971: Vol. 4, 624).

(2) Another path to success in Vietnam might be through a combination of military effectiveness and diplomatic prowess. Denied victory, the enemy might seek a negotiated settlement, one which would "save the Communists' face without giving them South Vietnam," as Gelb put it (1971: 152). Although neither Gelb nor Rostow see many precedents for this, the Korean War provides an example of a Communist military effort which was thwarted and which led to a negotiated agreement to return to prewar boundaries.

In addition, the Vietnamese Communists had been willing in 1954 to accept a compromise settlement in Indochina rather than continue the war. There had been two or three negotiatied settlements in Laos in which various sorts of compromise partitions were worked out with the Communists. To be sure, these agreements in Indochina were often arrangements to provide a face-saving way for western powers to

4. Roger Hilsman wrote in 1964: "The alacrity with which the Communists fell into line after we introduced troops into Thailand following the fall of Nam Tha illustrates the effectiveness of such moves" (quoted in Gelb and Betts, 1979: 149n).

5. The existence of this CIA conclusion in 1965 runs counter to the argument that intelligence reports of the time were "invariably pessimistic" (Janis, 1972: 111). See also Epstein (1975: 95-100).

6. See also his comments in Thompson and Frizzell (1977: 66). Some military leaders apparently felt the North Vietnamese supply of fighting-age men could be severely depleted, a calculation Defense Department analysts found to be physically impossible. See Lewy (1978: 82-84), Enthoven and Smith (1971: 295-300), Jenkins (1970), and Thayer (1977: 85-92).

withdraw. However, they give evidence of the willingness of Indochinese Communists to accept partitions and at least temporary cease-fires rather than continuing to pursue a costly war. It seemed possible to many that the North Vietnamese would come to their senses after enough battering by the American military machine and seek a reasoned agreement.

(3) A related hope was that a costly war might lead to discouragement on the part of important North Vietnamese allies—the Soviets in particular (for example, see Pentagon Papers, 1971: Vol. 3, 215). As the war escalated and as North Vietnamese dependence on outside aid increased, the outsiders would have more leverage on Hanoi's policy. It could be hoped the Soviets, wooed by the benefits of the policy of detente and already wary of the costs and escalatory dangers of such "wars of national liberation," might be successful in urging their little client into a more moderate stance. When the Yugoslavs cut off outside aid and sanctuary to the Communists in the Greek civil war, the war collapsed—a comforting, if rather ill-fitting, precendent. It could also be pointed out that the Soviets and Chinese apparently had been a moderating influence on the Vietnamese Communists in the negotiation that concluded the Indochina War in 1954. As Bill Moyers put it, "The President—well, most of us shared this at the White House—we felt that he could reason with the Russians and they would deliver" (1969: 270).

American policy makers, then, did have some hope for success in Vietnam. However, these hopes required that the United States would be able to inflict unrelenting punishment on the North Vietnamese, causing their will to be broken. One pushed on, hoping for signs of cracking morale among Communist troops, of defeatism, of shifts to more moderate leadership in Hanoi (as happened in Moscow following the death of Stalin in 1953 and preceding the end of the Korean War), of signs that the Soviets would become cooperative.[7]

7. For specialist Douglas Pike's quest for signs of weakening of will in North Vietnam, see New York *Times*, January 8, 1971. For William Bundy's hoped-for signs that Hanoi might become "discouraged," see Gelb and Betts (1979: 302). For McNamara's growing pessimism on the issue, see Lewy (1978: 77, 384). For the hope in 1969 that Ho Chi Minh's death would usher in more moderate leaders, see Goodman (1978: 102). For the suggestion that "Soviet pressure" had some moderating impact in Hanoi, see Zagoria (1967: 121). For U.S. hopes of Soviet help, see Gelb and Betts (1979: 188) and Goodman (1978: 119-121). There were continual efforts to detect division within the North Vietnamese leadership (Goodman, 1978: 289), but none was ever found (Gelb and Betts, 1979: 332). In a book written after the war, Palmer argues that Communist field commander Nguyen Chi Thanh saw "the futility of continued confrontation with American firepower" in 1966 and protested "vehemently" (1978: 120). However, Palmer seems to be taking a debate over tactics and making it into one over goals; see McGarvey (1969: 7).

It was a strategy that failed, but it was not one that could realistically be discarded at the time. Halberstam, writing at the end of 1967, was pessimistic about the chances of American success in Vietnam; yet, he had to admit that he and other critics might be proved wrong. Perhaps, he said, a victory was possible: "You simply grind out a terribly punishing war, year after year, using that immense American firepower, crushing the enemy and a good deal of the population, until finally there has been so much death and destruction that the enemy will stumble out of the forest, as stunned and numb as the rest of the Vietnamese people" (1967: 58).

Communist Losses in Vietnam—
The "Body Count"

That American and South Vietnamese forces, in conformity with the strategy, were generally successful in inflicting extensive destruction on Communist forces seems undeniable. Estimating the extent of these Communist losses, however, is somewhat complicated. Official statistics for battle deaths in the war are given in Table 1. The figures cover 1965 to 1974 and thus do not include Communist and South Vietnamese losses in the final Communist offensive of 1975.

The figure for Communist battle deaths is, of course, an estimate based in part on the notorious "body count," one of the statistics introduced in Vietnam to get some measure of progress in the war. It is generally assumed that the body count was exaggerated: There was considerable incentive for U.S. and South Vietnamese officers to err on the high side or even to fabricate wildly to impress superiors. It was doubtless common for bodies to be counted twice or for civilian deaths to be included in the body count (Lewy, 1978: 78-82; Kinnard, 1977: 73-75; King, 1972; Mylander, 1974: 80-82). There were errors in the other direction as well. The enemy commonly made great efforts to hide its dead (Lewy, 1978: 54; Leites, 1969: ix, 155), and many deaths from artillery and air strikes were unknown.[8]

Among the defenders of the body count was Lt. General Julian J. Ewell, who greatly stressed it (Kinnard, 1977: 73-74; Lewy, 1978: 142).

8. Lewy quotes a message from the U.S. embassy: "How do you learn whether anyone was inside structures and sampans destroyed by the hundreds every day by air strikes, artillery fire, and naval gunfire" (1978: 443)? See also Westmoreland (1976: 273).

TABLE 1
Total Military Deaths in Vietnam
1965-1974

	Killed
United States	46,498
South Vietnam	220,357
Communists	950,765

SOURCE: Department of Defense, in Lewy (1978: 450-451).

Westmoreland claimed he directed "several detailed studies which determined as well as anybody could that the count probably erred on the side of caution" (1976: 273). One of these was apparently the study which searched 70 captured enemy documents and confirmed the 1966 body count to within 1.8 percent. However, according to Alain Enthoven and K. Wayne Smith, a review by the Defense Department's Systems Analysis Office of the same documents "suggested that the enemy body count was overstated by at least 30 percent" (1971: 290).

In September 1974, after the American withdrawal but before the final South Vietnamese debacle, a former officer in the war, Douglas Kinnard, sent a questionnaire to the 173 Army General Officers who had held command positions in the war. Two-thirds responded; their answer to a question Kinnard asked about the body count is given in Table 2. There are problems in making use of isolated questions from surveys, but it certainly seems fair to conclude that there would be little agreement with Westmoreland's assertion that the body count was an underestimate. The wording on the other two options is unfortunate: It would seem entirely possible for someone to believe *both* that the body count was "within reason accurate" *and* "often inflated." The vagueness of the word "often" gives little clue as to *how* inflated the respondent felt the body count to be. Indeed, it seems rather impressive that 26% found the body count to be reasonably accurate, given the possible mild interpretation of the other alternative.

Nonetheless, the available evidence suggests that the 1974 figure of 950,765 Communist battle deaths is likely to be a considerable overestimation. How much lower should it be?

To approach an estimate, one might look at the other figures in Table 1. According to these, some 267,000 battle deaths occurred among U.S. and South Vietnamese troops. The American figures can be taken as accurate (the figure would be some 10,000 higher if deaths not directly

TABLE 2
Questionnaire of Army General Officers, 1974
(in percentages)

Was body count	
(1) within reason accurate?	26
(2) underestimated even considering the amount added by MACV to account for later deaths of wounded, etc.?	3
(3) often inflated?	61
(4) other or no answer.	10
	100

SOURCE: Kinnard (1977: 172).

linked to the battlefield in Vietnam are included.) The South Vietnamese, who were often fanciful in estimating enemy losses, seem generally to be reasonably accurate with their own losses—the suspicion, in fact, is that there was underreporting of their own losses so that commanders could draw pay for the "ghosts" (Starner, 1974: 17). Also, the figures in Table 1 do not include South Vietnamese battle deaths for the 1975 period. It seems reasonable to conclude, then, that combined U.S. and South Vietnamese battle deaths in the war came to well over one-quarter million.

While Communist military deaths may never have reached the figure of nearly 1,000,000 estimated by the United States, it seems likely that Communist losses in the war were higher—considerably higher—than the combined U.S.-South Vietnamese losses. The American military machine was specifically designed to maximize enemy losses while minimizing American losses, even if the imbalance could be achieved only at enormous monetary cost. Furthermore, even if one assumes that casualties in most ordinary battles averaged out to near-standoffs, the Communists were willing at several points to launch major offensives in which, by all accounts, they suffered enormously: The Tet offensive of 1968 and the Easter offensive of 1972, for example, clearly cost the Communists tens of thousands of lives.[9]

9. After some initial exaggeration, the Communist battle deaths in the Tet offensive were put at 30,000 (Mildren, 1968: 87). The Communist death toll in the 1972 offensive was estimated at between 50,000 and 75,000 (Kinnard, 1977: 150) or close to 100,000 (Lewy, 1978: 198).

59

To this, one must add Communist losses due to long-range bombing and artillery. According to Westmoreland, often these were not included in the casualty figures (1976: 273). The Communists probably suffered considerable losses due to illness and primitive medical care: On the several-month march to the south alone, from 10% to 20% of the men infiltrating reportedly died, largely from malaria (Van Dyke, 1972: 41).

Communist estimates of their own losses are scarce, but one estimate comes from an interview with General Vo Nguyen Giap conducted by Oriana Fallaci in the spring of 1969:

"General, the Americans say you've lost half a million men."

"That's quite exact."

He let his head drop as casually as if it were quite unimportant, as hurriedly as if, perhaps, the real figure were even larger.[10]

It is possible there is a certain amount of perverse bravura in Giap's admission. He may have wanted to convey a casualness about heavy losses to suggest to the Americans that he was willing to pursue the war indefinitely, without regard to costs. (If so, it was a mistake; American military leaders picked up the statement and used it to try to prove the enemy was "hurting.") But Giap was not inept at statistics. His lengthy speeches contain many quantitative analyses, reminding one at times of Robert McNamara (whom he frequently quotes; see McGarvey, 1969: 168-251). Some of his statistics have to be dealt with carefully—he was quick to claim that thousands of American aircraft had been shot down over the north when the United States put the number in the hundreds, a difference largely due, it seems, to the North Vietnamese inclusion of unmanned drones in their tally as well as the well-known phenomenon of double-counting a downed plane by widely separated observers (Van Dyke, 1972: 248; Salisbury, 1967: 140). In general, it would seem unwise to assume Giap's 1969 estimate of his own losses was either wildly uninformed or purely propagandistic.

Another suggestion of the magnitude of Communist losses comes from a report of a postwar tour of a Communist tunnel system in South Vietnam. The captain leading the tour observed that, of 600 men in his battalion, only four survived the war (New York Times, October 13, 1977).

10. Compare Ho Chi Minh's statement: "In the end, the Americans will have killed ten of us for every American soldier who died, but it is they who will tire first" (quoted in Rosen, 1972: 168).

It seems, then, that, while one can be skeptical or even contemptuous of the accuracy of the body count, one cannot escape the conclusion that Communist losses in the war were enormous. But if the body count is assumed to be too high, what might be a more accurate estimate? A reasonable, possibly conservative, estimate might be 500,000 to 600,000 men. This applies a discount that is larger than the 30% figure suggested by Enthoven and Smith. It is approximately twice the combined U.S.-South Vietnamese battle deaths, and it is similar to the figure Giap admitted to in 1969, six years before the end of the war.[11]

Vietnam in Historical Comparison

To compare Vietnam losses with those other in wars, the battle death figure should be calculated as a percentage of the prewar population. A census in North Vietnam in 1960 tallied a population of 15,903,000. The population of South Vietnam at the time is estimated at about 14,000,000 (Encyclopedia Brittanica, 1973: Vol. 23, p. 8). If one assumes that a sizable percentage of the residents of South Vietnam were essentially North Vietnamese in loyalty and in political orientation, then they should logically be added to the population of the north—it was from among them, of course, that the Viet Cong was formed, and it was they who bore the brunt of the fighting from 1960 to 1965. Thus, a combined North Vietnamese prewar "population" could reasonably be set at 20,000,000.

With 500,000 or 600,000 battle deaths, then, this would suggest the Communists lost some 2.5-3% of their prewar population in the war in battle deaths.[12]

11. It might be added that the Communists did not decide to stop sacrificing in 1975—the war just happened to end then. Had the Communist offensive failed, as it had in 1972, it is to be presumed the Communists would still have continued the war, increasing their losses even more. Also, the debacle on the South Vietnamese side in 1975 seems to have been something of a surprise to the Communists. They probably were expecting to pay far greater costs in 1975 (see Lewy, 1978: 211-212). Lewy's own estimate of Communist deaths is 444,000, somewhat lower than the one given here (1978: 453). He derives this by applying the 30% discount suggested by Enthoven and Smith and then assuming that one-third of the remaining dead are civilians. But the Enthoven and Smith discount already seems to take into consideration inclusion of civilians in the body count (1971: 295). Thus, Lewy is, to a degree, subtracting civilians twice. However, the basic conclusions of the following sections hold even if one accepts Lewy's lower estimate.

12. If one uses Lewy's somewhat lower estimate of Communist military deaths, this percentage would be about 2.2. See note 11.

How does this compare with other wars? It is almost unprecedented. Building on classic works by Wright (1942), Richardson (1960), and Klingberg (1966), Singer and Small published in 1972 *The Wages of War*. For the entire period of world history since 1816, Singer and Small set up careful criteria and identified 100 international wars. The set of wars includes imperial and colonial wars as well as wars among major states, and it includes all familiar wars as well as a great many that have long been forgotten. Any international war to which the United States sent troops is included.

For each war, Singer and Small estimated, with varying degrees of confidence, the battle deaths suffered by each participating country.[13] According to these figures, scarcely any of the hundreds of participants in the 100 international wars in the last 160 years have lost as many as 2% of their prewar population in battle deaths. The few cases where battle deaths attained levels higher than 2% of the prewar population mostly occurred in the two world wars in which industrial nations fought with sophisticated machines of destruction for their very existence. In World War II, according to Singer and Small, Germany and the Soviet Union each lost some 4.4% of their prewar populations in battle deaths. In World War I, Germany lost 2.7%, Austria-Hungary, 2.3%; France 3.3%; Rumania, 4.7%; and England, 2.0% (1972: 351-357).[14] The only other war in which losses were as high was the Chaco War of 1932-1935 in which Paraguay lost 5.6% of its prewar population (in winning) and Bolivia lost 3.2%.[15]

One should not assume that these numbers are accurate. However, even allowing considerable room for error, the extraordinary cost borne by the Vietnamese Communists seems clear. In the last 160 years only a very few of the hundreds of participants in international wars have paid such a high price in military deaths.

More specific comparisons may also be in order: How do the costs borne by the Vietnamese Communists compare with those borne by the

13. Singer and Small define battle deaths ("battle-connected deaths") as "personnel who were killed in combat" plus "those who subsequently died from combat wounds or from diseases contracted in the war theater" (1972: 49). This definition is probably less restrictive than the count used by U.S. forces in Vietnam.

14. By contrast, the United States lost 0.1% of its prewar population in battle deaths in World War I, 0.3% in World War II.

15. There was also a war from 1865 to 1870 in which Paraguay fought Brazil, Argentina, and Uruguay. Paraguay may have lost a majority of its population in the war (Klingberg, 1966: 135). This war is excluded from the Singer and Small list for technical reasons: Paraguay's prewar population was too small for it to be considered a significant international entity in their terms.

enemy in the two other Asian wars in which the United States has been involved—the war against Japan and the Korean war? Singer and Small estimate Japanese battle deaths at 1.4% of prewar population. That is, *Communist battle deaths in Vietnam were, as a percentage of the prewar population, probably twice as high as those suffered by the fanatical, often suicidal Japanese in World War II.* Thus, even the Japanese surrendered, giving the fate of their nation over to the mercy of their bitter enemies, well before Japanese battle death proportions reached levels accepted by the North Vietnamese. The Japanese could have continued to fight to defend the home islands in a last "glorious battle," as urged by some of their generals. But their will to continue the fight had been broken by their losses, and peace feelers had been sent out months before the war was over (and long before the atomic bombs were dropped; see Keeskemeti, 1958).[16] In the Korean war the Communists paid heavily, but in the end battle deaths (Chinese plus North Korean) added to less than two-tenths of one percent of the combined prewar population, according to Singer and Small (1972: 349).[17]

Another pertinent comparison would be with the Communist Viet Minh war against French colonialism in Indochina, which lasted from 1945 to 1954. Both sides paid heavily, but losses do not appear to be of the magnitude suffered in the later war. In 1951 the Viet Minh launched three major offensives, all failures, and apparently suffered around 20,000 *casualties;* their battle deaths in the massed battle at Dien Bien Phu in 1954 have been put at 7900 (Jenkins, 1972: 4; Fall, 1967: 487).

These data suggest, then, that American decision makers were on sound historical ground when they hoped and expected that, at some acceptable cost, they could break the "will" of the North Vietnamese. Only occasionally in the last 160 years has a power absorbed battle deaths in an international war in the proportions accepted by the North Vietnamese, and these have chiefly occurred in the murderous totality of the world wars when states were fighting for their survival.

16. If one adds civilian casualties into the consideration, a difference probably still remains. The Japanese, of course, suffered enormously from conventional and atomic bombing in the last months of the war—several hundred thousand deaths. But even a million bombing deaths would still leave total war deaths at less than 3% of the prewar population. The North Vietnamese also suffered heavily from bombing.

17. A war of attrition against a country like China is hardly a conceivable strategy. Looking specifically at the North Koreans, battle deaths rates get very high—perhaps 6% of the prewar population if estimates are accurate. However, the North Koreans lost their war long before costs got this high, and they were saved only by the Chinese entry, which changed the whole nature of the war (see Rees, 1964: 10, 461).

Attrition as a Strategy

One must be careful with these analogies and comparisons. The war in Vietnam was one of attrition, while many of the others were not. For example, the Japanese war was not particularly one of attrition. Surrender was proffered in the face of increasing evidence that invasion would bring physical occupation and defeat.

It has been argued often that the North Vietnamese could only have been defeated by an invasion of North Vietnam itself or, as in the case of Japan, by the credible threat of an invasion (assuming that the invasions did not bring China into the war.) To this, proponents of the attrition theory could make at least three responses.

First, attrition did play a major role in many past wars. While World War I ended only when a western breakthrough made the final defeat of the Central Powers obvious, this breakthrough came after years of brutal attrition had sapped the German will.[18] There are aspects of World War II which are similar, and, surely, the Russian capitulation in 1917 was largely due to the effects of attrition.

Second, unlike, for example, the Germans and the Soviets in World War II, the North Vietnamese were not fighting for the existence of their state in the same direct and obvious sense. While they seemed to fear a U.S. invasion of the north, at least in the early years of the war (Van Dyke, 1972; McGarvey, 1969), no one was confronting them with direct ultimata of unconditional surrender and postwar domination. The North Vietnamese had viable options to fighting it out: in consonance with U.S. hopes, they could fade out of the war or negotiate their way out and console themselves with the thought that they could always renew it later when conditions were better. The powers in the world wars could end them only by accepting either unconditional surrender or highly punitive peace treaties (as at Versailles and Brest Litovsk). The defeat options before North Vietnam were much milder, and surrender by negotiation or by fading away was a reasonable possibility.

Third, the Korean war shows an instance where the Communists gave up the idea of extending control over a new territory, at losses proportionately lower than those suffered by North Vietnam, even though they possessed the ability to continue the costly war; no invasion of China by U.S. forces was really threatened. The Communists' military goals were frustrated—they were "denied victory"—and they

18. See the comments by Robert Komer and Westmoreland in Thompson and Frizzell (1977: 84, 66).

finally accepted a prewar territorial status quo. Again, one could point out that in 1954 the Communists in Indochina accepted (at least temporarily) something far less than their maximum goals.

Sources of Communist Success in the Vietnam War

The Americans hoped in the war in Vietnam that the Communists, if punished enough and if denied victory, would eventually relent in their war aims. This hope, it has been argued here, was not unreasonable: The lesson from history is that nations almost always end wars long before the losses reach proportions suffered by the Communist side in the war in Vietnam.

The question, then, is not so much how the Americans could have made such a foolish miscalculation, but why the Vietnamese Communists were willing to accept virtually unprecedented losses for the sake of a military goal that was far from central to their survival as a nation. Why didn't morale deteriorate as losses mounted? Why didn't a defeatist faction rise? Why did the population continue to accept the leadership's willingness to send thousands upon thousands of young men to the south to be ground up by the American military machine?

Some would argue that the answer to these questions lies in the peculiar political and military structure of the Vietnam war. It was a war of "will," of "patience," they argue, and the North Vietnamese leadership was constantly encouraged by signs of weakening resolution in the United States. As U.S. costs mounted, as the peace movement grew, and as public support for the war dwindled, it can be argued, the Communists were encouraged to continue their costly struggle.[19] Even military setbacks for them, such as the incredibly costly Tet offensive of 1968, was, in the final analysis, a great political success for the enemy because it increased the unpopularity of the war in the United States and helped enormously to activate the peace movement.

There obviously must be some validity to this argument. One must assume the North Vietnamese found signs of crumbling morale in the United States to be encouraging even as American decision makers found the absence of such signs in North Vietnam to be discouraging.

19. Paul Nitze in Thompson and Frizzell (1977: 6); Goodman (1978: 116). American opinion trends are traced and analyzed in Mueller (1973).

However, it seems that the North Vietnamese would have continued the war even without such encouraging signs. Psychologically they seem to have been committed to endless sacrifice, to a long, protracted war. The North Vietnamese leadership was apparently unswervingly devoted to this approach from the beginning—the war would be long and costly, but they would prevail. This willingness to accept high costs was certainly found in General Giap by Oriana Fallaci in her 1969 interview with him. She was impressed by "his capacity for hate and pitiless cruelty"; she found him, when roused, "a gesticulating fanatic with crimson cheeks and hatefilled eyes, frightening." She quotes his poem:

Hit the enemy and run
Lure him into an ambush and kill him
Kill the imperialists with any means that come to hand
Regardless of the risk you may be running.

And his slogan: "Throughout the world, a hundred people die every minute. Life and death don't matter."

Giap's published speeches are impressive in this respect. There is great emphasis on fighting the war with zeal and determination, and troops are urged to inflict casualties mercilessly on the enemy. Nowhere does Giap write about minimizing his own casualties. It seems to be an unimportant part of his military strategy. As McGarvey noted in 1969, Giap "regards any cost in Communist lives as bearable so long as a sufficient number of casualties are inflicted on the enemy and replacements for his troops continue to be available. His is not an army that sends coffins north; it is by the traffic in homebound American coffins that Giap measures his success" (1969: 43). The difference in perceptions is neatly summarized in General Westmoreland's exasperated remark: "Any American commander who took the same vast losses as General Giap would have been sacked overnight" (1976: 251-252).

The acceptance of a long, costly war is found in numerous statements by North Vietnamese leaders. In 1966 Ho Chi Minh said, "We will fight to find victory. Everything depends on the Americans. If they want to make war for 20 years, then we shall make war for 20 years" (Kellen, 1972: 110; note 12). Pham Van Dong, the North Vietnamese Premier, told New York *Times* reporter Harrison Salisbury in 1966, "we are preparing for a long war. How many years would you say? Ten, twenty—what do you think about twenty" (1967: 196)? In 1969, Fallaci asked Giap, "How long will this war go on, General? How long will this poor people be called upon to suffer sacrifice and die?" Giap replied, "It will last as long as necessary—10, 15, 20, 50 years. Until as our President Ho says we have won total victory. Yes, even 20, even 50 years. We aren't afraid, and we aren't in a hurry."

But one can expect such statements from a country's leaders, especially in a war of attrition. It was Lyndon Johnson, after all, who said in 1965, "We will remain as long as is necessary with the might that is required, whatever the risk and whatever the cost" (Lewy, 1968: 50-51), or "We will not be defeated. We will not grow tired" (Johnson, 1971: 142). The statements can be accepted as reflections of the state of things, or they can be brushed aside as empty bravura intended to intimidate the enemy. One hardly expects a leader to say, "If we don't win in six months, we're going to quit."

In the case of the Communist leaders in the war in Vietnam, however, it seems clear that the leaders meant it. What makes it so unusual, so extraordinary when compared with other wars of the last century and a half, is that the leadership slogans seem to have been substantially accepted by their troops and population.

After this trip to North Vietnam in 1966, Salisbury observed,

> I seldom talked to any North Vietnamese without some reference coming into the conversation of the people's preparedness to fight ten, fifteen, even twenty years in order to achieve victory. At first I thought such expressions might reflect government propaganda . . . but . . . I began to realize that this was a national psychology.

In searching for a "clue to the temperature and morale of North Vietnam," he was constantly reminded of the "do-or-die, no compromise, death-before-dishonor" spirit of the Irish rebellion, or of the nineteenth-century Russian zealots "who casually threw away their lives in one desperate attempt after another to bring down the Russian Empire with a single bomb or a single bullet imprecisely aimed against the Czar or his principal ministers" (1967: 144, 142).[20]

20. Cameron quotes a North Vietnamese lieutenant-colonel in 1966: "We have already had great losses, and I am afraid we shall have greater yet. The price of all this is horrible. But quite honestly I do not see how we can lose. How long it will take I do not know. I may not see the end myself. But I expect my children will" (1966: 79).

514 INTERNATIONAL STUDIES QUARTERLY

Equally amazed is Kellen, a World War I psychological warfare officer who conducted a number of studies of Communist morale in Vietnam for the Rand Corporation. The studies included extensive interviews with North Vietnamese and Viet Cong prisoners. His summaries of his research are liberally studded with words like "incredible," "extraordinary," "surprising," and "astonishing." Morale, he found, was maintained as a level "not equalled by the Nazi soldiers in World War II or the Chinese soldiers in the Korean War." He speaks of the soldiers' "apparently inexhaustible courage and morale" and of the leadership's ability "to mobilize the human and material resources for the kind of total war Hitler spoke of but never attained." Kellen found the soldiers greatly resilient after military setbacks and possessed of an unshakable faith in final victory even though they were repeatedly told the war would probably be long and fierce (1972: 103-108).[21]

In assessing the remarkable fighting ability of the North Vietnamese and Viet Cong, Kellen suggests their success comes from a number of sources. They possessed neither fanaticism nor ideological commitment to Communism. Rather, prominent sources of strength included "an astonishing uniform . . . belief in their cause," "a firm belief that they cannot . . . lose the war," and a "deep personal hatred, a true abhorrence of their enemy, the United States," which Kellen finds more unrelieved than the Nazi soldiers' hatred of the Russians in World War II. He also points to an assiduous and apparently generally successful effort through self-criticism sessions to "eradicate fear of death itself" (1972: 104-105).[22]

Others who have studied the North Vietnamese and Viet Cong are also impressed (Berman, 1974; Knoebl, 1967; Pike, 1966; Leites, 1969). In Vietnam, it seems, the United States was up against an incredibly well-functioning organization, firmly disciplined, tenaciously led, largely free from corruption or self-indulgence. To an extraordinary degree, the organization was able to enforce upon itself an almost religious devotion to duty, sacrifice, loyalty, and fatalistic patience. Although the Communists often experienced massive military setbacks and times of stress and exhaustion, the organization was always able to refit itself to

21. In a 1967 speech Giap quotes Ho: "The closer we come to victory, the greater the hardships we must endure" (McGarvey, 1969: 238).
22. Westmoreland observes: "Many captive soldiers had tattoos on their bodies bearing the slogan, 'Born in the north to die in the south.' They told of funeral ceremonies in their honor before they left their villages" (1976: 252; see also Leites, 1969: 155-160).

rearm, and to come back for more.[23] It may well be, as one of the generals surveyed by Kinnard put it, "They were in fact the best enemy we have faced in our history" (1977: 67).

Kellen stresses, "So well-grounded seems their morale, and so self-resurrecting, that it is not really possible to see how it can be broken" (1972: 106). Instead, it was the American will that broke. Although the war in Vietnam did not come out the way American strategists hoped, in the final analysis it does represent a triumph, though a costly one, for the strategy of attrition.

Could the War Have Been Won?

In Senate testimony in 1969, General Westmoreland was asked if he thought the war could be won. "Absolutely," he said. "If we had continued to bomb, the war would be over at this time—or would be nearly over. The enemy would have fully realized that he had nothing to gain by continuing the struggle" (Race, 1976: 393). Admiral U.S.G. Sharp was equally confident—the massive bombing of Hanoi at the end of 1972, in fact, finally and for the first time "influenced their *will* to continue the aggression—we had convinced them that it was, in fact, becoming too costly. . . . Unfortunately, we failed to press home our advantage of the moment" (1978: 255; see also Goodman, 1978: 161). Sir Robert Thompson was also impressed by the 1972 bombing, arguing that "after eleven days of those B-52 attacks . . . *you had won the war. It was over!* . . . They and their whole rear base at that point were at your mercy. They would have taken any terms" (Thompson and Frizzell, 1977: 105).[24]

Others take a longer-term view and one that is more carefully qualified. Lewy suggests that, had the war been fought differently from the beginning—using "surprise and massed strength" at "decisive points," applying careful programs of population security and Vietnamization—the outcome of the war might have been different (1978:

23. This does not mean that the Communists never had morale problems. Indeed, it was one of their chief concerns (see Lewy 1968: 176). In general, they seem to have been particularly successful in bolstering morale when it sagged. Kellen observes that few North Vietnamese and very few cadre were ever taken prisoner; "there have been rather few defectors"; and "there have been no unit surrenders" (1972: 103).

24. This kind of statement does not appear in Thompson's book, *Peace is Not at Hand* (1974).

439-440). Gelb and Betts, somewhat ironically, suggest that "some combination" of these actions might have produced a Communist defeat: "using nuclear weapons, dispatching a million men to fight, removing all sanctuaries and bombing restrictions, running a nearly perfect pacification program, . . . and demanding and receiving . . . fundamental political reforms" (1979: 330).

What such analysts need is convincing evidence that the North Vietnamese "breaking point" had been, or could have been, reached. It seems reasonable to assume there was some level of punishment and defeat at which the Communists would cave in. Indeed, Rosen, in a study of 40 international wars, found that "the party superior in strength but inferior in cost-tolerance (e.g., the United States in Vietnam) is favored, at least by the odds (60/40), to win" (1972: 183). The evidence of this article suggests, however, that the Communists in Vietnam are virtually unique in the history of the last 160 years in their willingness to tolerate casualties. As Colonel Donaldson Frizzell puts it, "Time after time the U.S. and South Vietnamese forces inflicted heavy casualties upon the [Communist] forces. The Communists suffered casualties that decimated their battalions and brigades, literally knocking them out of combat for months." Yet they were willing to take this "terrible punishment and come back for more" (Thompson and Frizzell, 1977: 75).

At no time is there convincing evidence that this punishment was causing the breaking point to be reached. Thompson based his conclusion that the war was won in 1972 on the observations that the North Vietnamese had used up their antiaircraft missiles in the largely deserted Hanoi area and that the mining of the harbor would make the importation of adequate food supplies difficult. Admiral Sharp cites this evidence as well, and also pointed to the testimony of one American prisoner of war in Hanoi who said the bombing raids caused the prison guards to cower with "ashen" cheeks "in the lee of the walls"; the "enemy's will was broken," the prisoner observed. "You could sense it in every Vietnamese face" (1978: 258).

It is difficult to know how to weigh the importance of the color of a prison guard's cheeks, but even granting that that mining and bombing in 1972 caused severe suffering, disruption, and deprivation in North Vietnam (a conclusion for which there is considerable counterevidence),[25]

25. American military experts were observing in 1972 that "after some adjustments, the Soviet Union and China could get enough war material and food into North Vietnam by rail to make up for seaborne supplies cut off by the mining of North Vietnamese ports" (New York Times, May 13, 1972). As for the effectiveness of the bombing (using the new "smart" bombs), the lesson of the famous Than Hoa bridge is instructive. The destruction

it does not follow that the breaking point had been reached (see also Lewy, 1978: 415). The suffering had been escalated several times before in the course of this long war, and each time the Communists had been able to dig in and to accommodate. Morale did not crack.

It is more difficult to argue with Lewy's conclusion that the war could have been fought much better or with the Gelb-Betts list of ingredients for a Communist defeat. It is interesting that neither includes an invasion of North Vietnam in their prescription. This means they assume that the Americans and South Vietnamese might have been able to reach the Communist breaking point: Some combination of punishment and continual military defeat would eventually cause the Communists to give up.

It is impossible, of course, to know where the breaking point might be. It is doubtless true, as Henry Kissinger often observed in apparent exasperation, that North Vietnam can not "be the only country in the world without a breaking point" (Goodman, 1978: 96). However, the evidence presented here should cause one take the North Vietnamese seriously when they talk about fighting for 10, 20, or 50 years and their willingness to suffer endless casualties. Perhaps the breaking point was only a bit higher—at four or five percent of the prewar population. But their tenacity and resiliency after major setbacks would tend to suggest that the breaking point might have been vastly higher, possibly even near extermination levels. As Kellen puts it, "short of . . . being physically destroyed, collapse, surrender, or disintegration was—to put it bizarrely—simply not within their capabilities. . . . Unless . . . we killed more of them than could be in anybody's interest, they could not be overcome" (1972: 106). Thus, while it is obvious they could not be beaten at a cost the United States was willing to pay, it is also possible they would not give up no matter how far the United States escalated the war, no matter how clear and efficient its strategy.

Even dropping nuclear weapons on North Vietnam and on the infiltration trails might not have done the job, unless they were dropped at near-annihilation levels. Exactly how they could be used effectively against the internal war in the south—which is where, as Lewy points out, the war had to be won—is difficult to imagine (1978: 438).

Finally, it might be observed that even an invasion of North Vietnam might not have worked. An invasion, of course, might have led to a

of this bridge on May 13, 1972 (after years of trying) is hailed by Thompson as a great triumph (Thompson and Frizzell, 1977: 104). However, by July the bridge had been rebuilt and it was back in operation until October 6, when it was successfully bombed again. Furthermore, there was an indestructible bypass route 200 yards away (Aviation Week and Space Technology, November 27, 1972: 15).

71

major escalation by the Chinese or the Soviets, and the war against North Vietnam might have been "won" in the same sense that the invasion of North Korea in 1950 "won" the war against that country. But even without such an escalation by Communist allies, it seems possible the United States would find itself bogged down in a lengthy, costly, agonizing guerrilla war, one which would now have been conducted throughout Indochina—a war rather like the one the French fought, and lost, in 1954.

REFERENCES

BERMAN, P. (1974) Revolutionary Organization. Lexington, MA: D.C. Heath. Lexington Books.

CAMERON, J. (1966) Here Is Your Enemy. New York: Holt, Rinehart & Winston.

ELLSBERG, D. (1972) Papers on the War. New York: Simon and Schuster.

ENTHOVEN, A. C. and K. W. SMITH (1971) How Much Is Enough? New York: Harper & Row.

EPSTEIN, E. J. (1975) Between Fact and Fiction. New York: Vintage.

FALL, B. (1967) Hell in a Very Small Place. Philadelphia: J. B. Lippincott.

FALLACI, O. (1969) "Interview with Gen. Giap." Washington Post (April 6): B1, B4-B6.

GALLUCCI, R. L. (1971) Neither Peace Nor Honor. Baltimore: Johns Hopkins Univ. Press.

GELB, L. H. (1971) "Vietnam: the system worked." Foreign Policy 3: 140-167.

——— and R. K. BETTS (1979) The Irony of Vietnam: The System Worked. Washington: Brookings Institution.

GOODMAN, A. E. (1978) The Lost Peace. Stanford: Hoover Institution Press.

HALBERSTAM, D. (1972) The Best and the Brightest. New York: Random House.

——— (1967) "Return to Vietnam." Harper's (December): 47-58.

——— (1965) The Making of a Quagmire. New York: Random House.

JANIS, I. L. (1972) Victims of Groupthink. Boston: Houghton Mifflin.

JENKINS, B. M. (1972) The Seventh Son Leaves for the Front. Paper P-4851 (September). Santa Monica, CA: Rand Corporation.

——— (1970) Why the North Vietnamese Keep Fighting. Paper P-4395 (August). Santa Monica, CA: Rand Corporation.

JOHNSON, L. B. (1971) The Vantage Point. New York: Holt, Rinehart & Winston.

KECSKEMETI, P. (1958) Strategic Surrender. Stanford: Stanford Univ. Press.

KELLEN, K. (1972) "1971 and beyond: the view from Hanoi," pp. 99-112 in J. J. Zasloff and A. E. Goodman (eds.) Indochina in Conflict. Lexington, MA: D.C. Heath.

KING, E. L. (1972) The Death of the Army. New York: Saturday Review Press.

KINNARD, D. (1977) The War Managers. Hanover, NH: Univ. Press of New England.

KLINGBERG, F. L. (1966) "Predicting the termination of war: battle casualties and population losses." J. of Conflict Resolution 10: 129-171.

KNOEBL, K. (1967) Victor Charlie. New York: Praeger.

LEITES, N. (1969) The Viet Cong Style of Politics. Memorandum RM-5487-1-ISA/ARPA (May). Santa Monica, CA: Rand Corporation.

LEWY, G. (1978) America in Vietnam. New York: Oxford Univ. Press.

McGARVEY, P. J. (1969) Visions of Victory: Selected Communist Military Writing, 1964-1968. Stanford: Hoover Institution Press.

MILDREN, F. T. (1968) "From Mekong to DMZ." Army (November): 82-95.

MOYERS, B. (1969) "Bill Moyers talks about the war and LBJ," pp. 261-271 in R. Manning and M. Janeway (eds.) Who We Are. Boston: Little, Brown.

MUELLER, J. E. (1973) War, Presidents and Public Opinion. New York: John Wiley.

———— (forthcoming) "Vietnam revised." Armed Forces and Society.

MYLANDER, M. (1974) The Generals. New York: Dial Press.

PALMER, D. R. (1978) Summons of the Trumpet. San Rafael, CA: Presidio Press.

Pentagon Papers (1971) Senator Gravel Edition, 4 Vols. Boston: Beacon.

PIKE, D. (1966) Viet Cong. Cambridge: MIT Press.

REES, D. (1964) Korea: The Limited War. New York: St. Martins.

RICHARDSON, L. F. (1960) The Statistics of Deadly Quarrels. Pittsburgh: Boxwood Press.

RACE, J. (1976) "Vietnam intervention: systematic distortion in policy-making." Armed Forces and Society 2 (Spring): 377-396.

ROSEN, S. (1972) "War power and the willingness to suffer," pp. 167-183 in B. M. Russett (ed.) Peace, War, and Numbers. Beverly Hills, CA: Sage.

SALISBURY, H. E. (1967) Behind the Lines—Hanoi. New York: Harper & Row.

SHARP, U.S.G. (1978) Strategy for Defeat. San Rafael, CA: Presidio Press.

SINGER, J. D. and M. SMALL (1972) The Wages of War 1816-1965: A Statistical Handbook. New York: John Wiley.

STARNER, F. (1974) "Juggling with the death toll." Far Eastern Economic Rev. (May 20): 17.

THAYER, T. C. (1977) "We could not win the war of attrition we tried to fight," pp. 85-92 in W. S. Thompson and D. D. Frizzell (eds.) The Lessons of Vietnam. New York: Crane, Russak.

THOMPSON, R.G.K. (1974) Peace is Not at Hand. New York: David McKay.

THOMPSON, W. S. and D. D. FRIZZELL. [eds.] (1977) The Lessons of Vietnam. New York: Crane, Russak.

THOMSON, J. C., Jr. (1968) "How could Vietnam happen?" Atlantic Monthly (April): 47-53.

WESTMORELAND, W. (1976) A Soldier Reports. Garden City, NY: Doubleday.

WRIGHT, Q. (1942) A Study of War (2 Vols.). Chicago: Univ. of Chicago Press.

VAN DYKE, J. M. (1972) North Vietnam's Strategy for Survival. Palo Alto, CA: Pacific Books.

ZAGORIA, D. S. (1967) Vietnam Triangle. New York: Pegasus.

The Development of the American Theory of Limited War, 1945–63

MICHAEL W. CANNON

... as a test of war-fighting theories, an actual armed conflict is likely to be as inconclusive or misleading as the absence of war, since every war is the result of a multiplicity of factors combined in ways that are unique to that conflict and since the strategy that may or may not have worked under one set of circumstances might produce a different outcome under other circumstances.

Robert Osgood[1]

I. Historical Antecedents

Wil   illiam Kaufmann once wrote that "attitudes toward war are ... heavily mortgaged to tradition."[2] This is true of the theory of limited war as well. It did not spring full-grown from the head of Mars (to mix mythological metaphors) but has its roots deeply imbedded in American historical tradition. The saga of those who wrote about the theory of limited war is as much a story of their struggles against those tendencies as it is a recounting of their innovations. My purpose here is to analyze what modern writers offer in light of the writings of some of the classical theorists. In order to do this, it is first necessary to develop a framework of what the American theory of limited war embraced during the period 1946 to 1961, roughly the era of its gestation, birth, and maturation. This will take place generally in a chronological sequence with attention being paid to those events, writers, and actors that illuminate or reinforce the

MAJ. MICHAEL CANNON is a 1975 graduate of the United States Military Academy (USMA), West Point, New York. He has held a variety of command and staff positions in the United States, Germany, Korea, and Saudi Arabia. In addition, he has attended the Army's School for Advanced Military Studies and served as an assistant professor in military history at USMA. He is currently the speechwriter for Gen. Edwin H. Burba, Jr., commander of Forces Command.

ARMED FORCES & SOCIETY, Vol. 19, No. 1, Fall 1992, pp. 71–104.

LIVERPOOL JOHN MOORES UNIVERSITY
LEARNING SERVICES

major elements of the theory. Following this, an analysis of the theory will be conducted *within the context of the time.* It is to the roots of the theory that we now briefly turn.

Robert Osgood, in his book, *Limited War,* discussed several aspects of the American way of war. Perhaps two of the most important tendencies were the view that war and peace were distinct and separate entities and that Americans traditionally gave the military its head in the conduct of wars.[3] Moreover, there was the tendency to allow the "great idealistic goals, once put to the test of force, [to] become the rationalization of purely military objectives, governed only by the blind impulse of destruction."[4]

Another scholar described the American style as "the use of force in a great moral crusade in which there is no room for the deliberate hobbling of American power."[5] This all-or-nothing approach was reinforced by American isolationism, leading to what has been referred to as a confusing "confluence of pacifism and pugnacity."[6] WWII, and our rapid demobilization in its aftermath, confirmed the existence of this particularly American style of conflict.

II. *Our* Bomb and Implacable Foes

In the late 1940s, several problems rapidly rose to challenge our traditional attitudes concerning war. The first came from an attempt to rationalize the nation's defense efforts and bring them under more efficient, centralized, civilian control. Although the National Security Act of 1947 created a Department of Defense to oversee three coequal services (Army, Navy, and Air Force), the Secretary of Defense received only limited authority over them. Thus, when the Congress and administration found it necessary to reduce revenues and expenditures, the stage was set "for a bitter interservice debate about roles, strategy, and finance."[7] This debate was made even more vociferous by America's outlook on war. The consensus was that wars of the future would be total in nature.

The atomic bomb was seen as the "sovereign remedy for all military ailments," allowing the United States to achieve success through "annihilative victories."[8] It was a time when it was still "our bomb" and the Soviets had no means for atomic attack.[9] The Air Force thus "held the master card" as its bombers were the most evident means of delivery of atomic weapons of annihilation.[10]

Reductions in the budget and a *de facto* adoption of a policy of total war caused the services to argue over how to divide limited resources and determine what means were to be developed. So, at a time when the services should have focused on a newly defined responsibility to advise the civilian decision makers on ways and ends, they became involved in an increasingly acrimonious debate over means, one that was to continue throughout the 1950s. Others, therefore, were to develop the concepts that were to become the basis of limited war theory.

While the services attempted to come to grips with the ramifications of the National Security Act, the Truman administration grappled with a growing Communist threat. Ultimately, policy makers decided there would be no more concessions to the Soviet Union and the United States "would, in effect, 'draw the line,' defending all future targets of Soviet expansion. . . . "[11] Thus, our period of isolationism came to a close. The superpower conflict slowly emerged as one between two ways of life—totalitarianism and democracy.[12] This meant an "open-ended commitment to resist Soviet expansionism . . . at a time when the means to do so had entirely disappeared."[13] Moreover, it viewed all interests as being of the same level of importance. Previously we defended only our possessions; now we were guarantors of the Free World's security.

The problem lay in reconciling this end with the means available, for "the country had only limited resources with which to fight it."[14] It became apparent that drastic measures would be necessary to cope with the situation. Since it was unlikely that available means would be expanded, "interests would have to be contracted to fit means."[15]

Gradually, two lines of argument arose concerning a possible solution. One was similar to the geopolitics of Sir Halford Mackinder and found support in one of the first papers drafted by the National Security Council (NSC) in March of 1948. This document stressed that the Eurasian "heartland" contained areas of potential strength that, if added to Soviet holdings, would make them vastly superior to the West in manpower and resources. Eight months later, this philosophy was formally expressed in NSC 20/4.[16] The assumption that Europe was the most critical link in the chain of American defenses was to remain at the heart of American security debates throughout the 1950s and 1960s.

The second line of argument centered around how to protect interests of the free world. One view held that the Communists should be resisted at every step, resulting in a "perimeter defense." The other view stressed that the free world needed to distinguish between vital and peripheral interests, strongpointing those crucial to survival. The latter concept emphasized that non-military elements of power were to play the dominant role, a traditional perception of means available to the United States. The "strongpoint" concept retained a Eurocentric orientation. The controversy over which to adopt was to shape much of the discussion of national security issues over the next two decades.[17]

As the Truman administration was in the process of refining and choosing between these two concepts, several events took place that caused a shift in the debate over national security. The 1949 fall of Nationalist China narrowed the concept of the struggle between totalitarianism and democracy to one of communism with democracy. The *implication* of the fall of China was that adversaries were indivisible and that "when any nation went communist American security was lessened."[18]

The most threatening event, however, was the Soviets' early development of an atomic bomb. This set off a discussion in Washington over whether or not to respond by building the hydrogen bomb, a more powerful implement of destruction.[19] Secretary of State Dean Acheson suggested a reevaluation of the nation's military and foreign policy within the context of this question. The product of this reexamination became known as NSC-68, a landmark document in American security policy.

The basis of American defense policy had been established, however. Containment was the goal, Europe the key. Due to the pressures of the time and of our traditional outlook on war, we began to view the Communist threat as one that was coalescing throughout the world and something that should be resisted everywhere with whatever means available. Means to be employed were perceived to be limited, however, due to economic reasons and the traditional American distaste for a large military. This was reflected further in a desire to use our technological advantage to the fullest, exploiting the edge that the atomic bomb gave us. It became, in fact, the centerpiece of American military strategy.

III. NSC-68 and the Great Catalyst

NSC-68 reflected the administration's attitudes about the world and, in a logical fashion, laid out the assumptions underlying the framers' world view. At the same time, it described a course of action for the government to follow to meet the challenges it faced. Due to the events described above, it became evident that both the postwar military-political doctrine and the efforts made in support of that doctrine were grossly inadequate.[20] More importantly, "there was a [general] feeling that the United States was losing the peace."[21] The detailed reevaluation of basic American defense policy thus took place in an atmosphere of crisis. Since the drafting of NSC-68 was kept free of particulars (in terms of costs and force requirements) "the drafters were ... able to concentrate on general considerations of strategy" instead of being "overwhelmed with details about means, to the complete exclusion of any systematic treatment of ends and their relationship to means."[22]

Crucial to NSC-68's conclusions were the assumptions underlying the administration's analysis of the Communist threat. Although the Kremlin was viewed as the source of the principal challenge and danger,[23] NSC-68 shifted "perceptions of the threat from the Soviet Union to the international communist movement. . . ."[24] The framers of the document foresaw a danger of limited Communist military adventures to expand Communist holdings, ensuring that an American atomic riposte would be disproportionate.[25] The Soviet atomic challenge thus threatened to upset a balance of power that was delicately poised and to create a nuclear stalemate between the United States and the Soviet Union by 1954.[26] What the United States required, therefore, was an expansion of means.[27] In order to accomplish this NSC-68 had to "systematize containment, and . . . find the means to make it work."[28]

Although the most important debate focused on whether to build a hydrogen bomb, the underlying question was: "What should the United States do to avoid complete reliance upon nuclear weapons?"[29] The conclusion was that the United States must,

> by means of a rapid and sustained buildup of the political, economic, and military strength of the free world, and by means of an affirmative program intended to wrest the initiative from the Soviet Union confront it with convincing evidence of the determination and ability of the free world to frustrate the Kremlin design. . . .[30]

One of the major aspects of this buildup was to be an increase in the variety of military means available to decision makers. Yet the "disagreements holding back NSC-68's chances of acceptance were not with its premises but with the conclusion that containment of Communism necessarily entailed a diversified and expensive military program."[31] Given this unresolved major issue, the effects of NSC-68 were predicted to be slight. Fortuitously for the framers of the document, the North Koreans invaded South Korea only a few months after the NSC had completed its work, rescuing NSC-68 from oblivion and making it the foundation of American strategy.[32] This limited conflict appeared to validate NSC-68's most important conclusions: existing U.S. forces were inadequate, atomic weapons alone would not deter limited aggression, and Washington lacked the conventional means necessary to cover all contingencies."[33]

For the first time, statesmen, the military, and the general public found themselves obliged to effect a re-examination of strategy.[34] The war "brought home dramatically the possibility of engaging in military clashes with the Soviet bloc which would not resemble World War II . . . [and] the American people were presented with their first full-scale debate as to the acceptability of limiting warfare."[35]

One of the most fundamental assumptions about the conduct of a war with American involvement was now brought into question. Until 1951, most people had taken it for granted that all wars would be fought without restraint or limitation.[36] Since "the Korean War did not turn out that way . . . it seemed to baffle us completely."[37] However, the energies of the decision-makers involved turned to different activities based on their positions: the divisive debate within the military concerning means to be employed continued, the Administration attempted to devise policies that would avoid our involvement in such conflicts, and the theorists focused on the ways to conduct limited war.

There was a widespread perception among military circles that the effort at unification had failed. Instead of cohesion and efficiency the result was "triplification," not the clear-cut decisions on major interservice differences required to weld the three services into a single establishment working toward defined objectives.[38] The services, therefore, continued unabated the debate on means — and to a limited extent, ways — to the exclusion of ends.

The results of the Korean War also energized the strategy intellectuals. Even so, the true "catalyst" that stimulated thought on limited war was the controversial speech given by Secretary of State John Foster Dulles in January of 1954 in which he announced the strategy of massive retaliation. "In criticizing the doctrine . . . analysts were forced to spell out their objections . . . and to grope for an alternative strategy. . . ."[39] Thus began the questioning of our most cherished assumptions about war.

What were the lessons drawn from Korea that remain a part of our intellectual baggage?[40] Perhaps the most important, and the most difficult to cope with, was the identification of what William Kaufmann referred to as "constraints upon . . . accustomed behavior. . . ." In his view:

> All the emotions traditionally associated with war must be inhibited. We are flung into a strait jacket of rationality which prevents us from lashing out at the enemy. We are asked to make sacrifices and then to cheer lustily for a tie in a game that we did not even ask to play. On the military side, the emotional cost can be minimized somewhat by the practice of

rotating troops. On the civilian side, avoidance of unnecessary dislocation to the domestic society combined with careful and authoritative explanations of the alternatives to limited war are perhaps the only resources available. That they will by no means eliminate dissatisfaction with so unorthodox a war may, however, redound to our benefit. For it will be just as well for the enemy to realize that, despite our best efforts at control, our patience is not inexhaustible.[41]

Another, and more dubious lesson, was that "still thinking in terms of total victories or total defeats . . . the United States thought that stalemate was the only alternative to total war."[42] The Korean War also demonstrated some of the major constraints necessary to keep a war limited. In particular, these included a willingness to settle for goals representing a considerable degree of compromise with the enemy, and thus readiness to keep contact with him and to enter into and maintain negotiations with him.[43]

One issue highlighted by the war was hotly debated until the late 1950s. Russell Weigley wrote that "the Korean experience suggested that it was not capacity for mobilization that counted most, but rather the state of readiness" and, even more important, "for conventional surface strength in readiness."[44] By 1960, however, one lesson learned was reflected by Herman Kahn in a RAND report. His contention was that it "is important to understand that we have this asset: the ability to spend large sums of money rapidly."[45] Our ability to mobilize large forces rapidly thus appeared to be a strength.

Yet the question of how much conventional force strength in being was required remained unanswered. Although there was a great deal of discussion concerning how to correct the deficiencies in our mobilization structure, the government gradually turned away from the strategy of fighting a prolonged war. The "new look" was thought to be the answer strategists were seeking, one that accommodated the "new realities."

Although America had dabbled in the realm of limited war theory, it had not done so to any great depth. Glacial, yet important, changes had occurred in the space of four years, however. Isolationism was consigned to the past as the United States realized it must follow a different path. The Free World, of which the United States was the *de facto* leader, was perceived to be engaged in a life-or-death struggle, albeit a nontraditional one, with a monolithic communism as an antagonist. Yet the question of what means could best be used to contain this beast was still unresolved.

IV. The New Look — A Draconian Solution?

Containment remained the national policy under the incoming Eisenhower Administration. The country's national strategy changed to one referred to as the "New Look."[46] Unfortunately, the military strategy component of the new look received the most attention, not only from historians but from contemporary critics as well. This was the strategy of massive retaliation, a strategy shaped by pressures in the political, domestic, and economic spheres.

Eisenhower came into office with many fixed ideas. Ingrained within him was Clausewitz's argument that the military should be the servant of politics and the idea that means had to be subordinated to ends.[47] Moreover, Eisenhower believed that the means available to secure our national objectives were limited. He firmly believed "that the national economy could not support indefinite military expenditures at levels necessary to contain conventional forces." Based on these predispositions, the possible options open to the United States were limited to "economic and military assistance to local [indigenous] forces, and [reliance] upon the deterrent threat of American air and naval power . . . to achieve objectives. . . ."[48]

More crucial were some of Eisenhower's assumptions concerning the world order. In a traditionally American fashion, Eisenhower adopted the slogan, "there is no alternative to peace."[49] War and peace were things apart — the country was either engaged in a struggle in which all of its resources were to be committed, or it was not. This was "an impractical policy," and, along with massive retaliation, contained "all or none statements inapplicable to the real world. . . ."[50]

Eisenhower also perceived American interests to be of a global nature. Like the authors of NSC-68, Eisenhower "believed the world balance of power to be so delicately poised that no further victories for communism anywhere could be tolerated without upsetting it." In his words, "as there is no weapon too small, no arena too remote, to be ignored, there is no free nation too humble to be forgotten."[51] Any nation, therefore, but particularly those butting against the Communist world, should be protected. The concept of a "perimeter," as opposed to the "strongpoint" method of containment, was thus adopted.

Public attitudes toward the war in Korea also limited the actions Eisenhower could take. Voter discontent with the conduct of the war put the Republicans into office and the new administration intended both to extricate the country from the Korean entanglement and to ensure against similar involvements.[52] The major components of the new look would enable Eisenhower to work around this distaste for ground combat as it was to combine "nuclear deterrence, alliances, psychological warfare, covert actions, and negotiations," all of which promised to be cheaper in dollar and human cost than did the prescriptions of NSC-68.[53]

Within this national strategy, "the central idea was that of asymmetrical response—of reacting to adversary challenges in ways calculated to apply one's own strengths against the other sides' weaknesses."[54] This would, it was hoped, "open up a range of possible responses so wide that the adversary would not be able to count on retaining the initiative; lacking that, it was thought, he would come to see the risks of aggression as outweighing the benefits."[55] Moreover, it "implied a willingness to shift the nature and location of competition from the site of the original provocation. . . ."[56] In order to accomplish this at a tolerable cost (for the economic capability of the nation was *the* over-riding consideration), nuclear weaponry would form the basis of our military strategy.[57] The Air Force, therefore, remained Eisenhower's "big stick."

All of these disparate threads came together to form the military strategy known as massive retaliation. This term came to life in a speech given by Eisenhower's Secretary of State, John Foster Dulles, on January 12, 1954. At this time he stated that "no local defense . . . will alone contain the mighty manpower of the Communist world . . . [it] must be reinforced by . . . massive retaliatory power."[58] What was implied was *not* a rejection of that aspect of the new look that stressed these local defense forces. "Rather the Administration was saying that it was not prepared to support local-war forces large enough to deal with all possible aggressive acts of the Sino-Soviet bloc. Therefore local ground defense had to be reinforced by the threat to use America's strategic nuclear power."[59]

The hue and cry over this pronouncement was immediate and extensive. One commentator wrote that

> It seemed almost inconceivable that at the very moment when the loss of our atomic monopoly . . . was becoming an actuality, Mr. Dulles should announce in blatant and offensive terms what he claimed was a new doctrine, the doctrine of depending "primarily upon a great capacity to retaliate, instantly, by means and at places of our choosing."[60]

To many, this was "placing the cart before the horse. . . . Military strategy and force structure should be designed to support the defense needs of the nation—not vice versa. The development should proceed from theater appraisal to strategy to forces. A reverse progression could end in chaos."[61] The result, as manifested in the form of massive retaliation, appeared to be "a single draconian solution."[62]

The next several years saw the development of a great debate on military doctrine. Massive retaliation came under fire for a variety of reasons, but the most vehemently attacked aspects of it were an underlying (and unstated) assumption that it posed great danger to the nation, and that it lacked flexibility. Perhaps one of the most erudite critics was Bernard Brodie. To him, the "American official attitude . . . [seemed] to be one of ignoring Soviet nuclear capabilities as a reality to be contended with in planning." That part of the New Look "which stresses our retaliatory power is based on an assumption that is questionable . . . and . . . is bound to be ephemeral — the assumption that we have a *unique* capability of destroying an opponent by strategic use of nuclear weapons."[63] In the age of nuclear parity, "an unrestricted general war" meant "a catastrophe to which there are no predictable limits."[64]

Another disadvantage of massive retaliation was its lack of flexibility. As early as 1956, the consensus among intellectuals was that American military policy would "have to deal in some way with the possibility of small-scale wars launched in the manner of the Korean attack of 1950 or developing out of guerrilla operations as in Indo-China."[65] Massive retaliation could not cope with this style of war. Most writers at the time felt that the solution lay in the creation of a capability to fight limited wars.

V. The Birth of the Theory of Limited War

Robert Osgood once suggested that "the western definition of limited war, like the theory, reflected not some universal reality but the interests of the western allies, especially the United States, in a particular period of international conflict."[66] Yet the difficulties faced by the theorists were complex and defied simple solutions. The public and classified literature of the period attacked a dilemma that appeared at the time "to be roughly this: to renounce war altogether as an instrument of policy, or to devise a strategy that employs select means of force (nuclear) yet skirts the contingency of mutual thermonuclear annihilation."[67] The main problem of the theorists in the mid-1950s, given the declared policy that nuclear weapons were to remain the basis of American military strategy, was initially to convince decision-makers and the public of the need to consciously consider *how* to limit war.

The introduction of the thermonuclear device posed perhaps the greatest threat to existing perceptions of the world order. The scale of destruction that could be wrought in a war based on massive retaliation against opponents armed with hydrogen bombs was far beyond that which had occurred using the conventional means of WWII. The significance of the new weapons was, however, not readily apparent to all. The theorists of the time were thus "faced with the necessity of exploring the effects of the new type" when they had "not yet succeeded in comprehending the implications of the old."[68]

As one perceptive commentator described it, the potential for a global catastrophe was real. "Given the will, the ability seems to exist, at least on the part of the Soviet Union and the United States, to pound each other to dust." It was obvious that "any effort to restrict conflict must therefore provide a workable policy for keeping this extraordinary capability within the desired bounds."[69] This point was not debated until nuclear parity had been achieved, however. By then a growing number of intellectuals had joined in the fray, with Bernard Brodie wielding perhaps the weightiest cudgel. To Brodie, the United States military was "tensed and coiled for total nuclear war." What was needed was "to rethink some of the basic principles (which have become hazy since Clausewitz) connecting the waging of war with the political ends, thereof. . . ."[70]

Initially this reexamination was directed at one of the theoretical concepts underlying massive retaliation: that of weapons to be employed. The Korean experience was constantly used as an example of what a limited war might be like. Based on the western experience in this arena, Raymond Aron suggested that one of the first questions that should be asked was "what kind of weapons can be used in a limited conflict without provoking a general nuclear war?"[71] Up until the mid-1950s, the nuclear weapon had not posed an escalatory threat. The numbers of weapons stockpiled were so few that there was "no available alternative to a Douhet-type strategy." The thermonuclear bomb, however, "no sooner appeared than it began to be spewed forth in such numbers and began to wax so great in size" that it threatened "to go far beyond the stage that would redeem him [Douhet] from his errors."[72] The development of truly strategic air power in the form of long-range aircraft, coupled with the destructiveness of atomic weapons, meant that instead of being devoted to an action strategy, air power had to be relegated to a deterrent role. The challenge for the West, therefore, was "to assess how little effort must be put into it to keep global war abolished."[73] Decision makers gradually came to support such a position. This was reflected in 1957 when Secretary of State Dulles wrote an article "in which he seemed to retreat from massive retaliation at least partway . . . [and] argued . . . for more emphasis on tactical nuclear capabilities."[74]

The logical question to follow the slowly developing consensus that an all-out total war would be an unmitigated global disaster was how to conduct a war in a fashion required to keep it limited. The theorists again used the Korean experience as a starting point, and the "new theory of limited war owe[d] much . . . to the miscellaneous collection of lessons abstracted from the history of the Korean conflict."[75] The theory that arose was not one that can be traced by a straight-line progression of concepts, however. It was more a collection of nuggets that were washed from the intellectual stream of ideas that poured forth following Dulles' massive retaliation speech. In conceptual terms, the discussion of limits focused on both ways and ends, with the latter being by far the most difficult to deal with in a manner that would provide a guide to practitioners.

VI. Tentative Elements of the Theory

One of the first issues that needed to be explored was how to fight a limited war given the possibilities offered not only by thermonuclear weapons but also by the rapid increase in the availability of smaller weapons. Two concepts were to emerge that addressed other possible uses for nuclear weapons. The first traced its roots directly to massive retaliation and bore the name "graduated deterrence."

Paul Nitze once offered a conceptual device that is useful here for a study of the nation's policies. He claimed that there is a distinction between the "action policy" of a nation and its "declaratory policy." Although massive retaliation was trumpeted as the latter by American policymakers, in actuality its action policy was something different — graduated deterrence.[76] This concept involved tailoring the projected application of nuclear weapons to the importance of the objective to be achieved. The hope was that by guaranteeing an upper limit along a vertical scale of weapons used, an explosion to total nuclear war would be avoided.[77] The question that needed to be answered, however, was "which areas of the world must be protected by the threat of atomic bombing, and which are the areas that must be defended by conventional weapons?" It was a matter of adjusting "the deterrent to the importance of the stake."[78]

Hand in hand with graduated deterrence came the concept of limited nuclear warfare. Bernard Brodie had been one of the first to see the potential for using nuclear weapons tactically "in order to redress what . . . [was] otherwise a hopelessly inferior position for the defense of Western Europe."[79] If a war in Europe using tactical nuclear weapons was carried out with restraint, theorists felt that retaliation on a broader front could be avoided. Using this as an implicit assumption, the discussion turned to a consideration of the means needed to fight such a war and what would be required to keep such a war limited.

Some of the possibilities were so evident as to require only a minimal amount of elucidation. Geographical limits were perhaps the simplest. Within a European context, this devolved into attempting to limit the types of targets to be attacked. The Douhet style concept of "city-busting" was replaced by a more abstract treatment of strategic targets suggesting that perhaps within Europe there were gradations that could be successfully targeted to limit the escalations of violence.

More recent limited wars yielded other lessons. Areas involved in these wars were limited and definable, the contestants did not commit the total military resources available to them, sovereignty was not an issue, and political factors influenced military decisions.[80] Gradually, however, the assumption that there was no longer a serious danger of total war gained wider currency.[81]

Theorists argued that "only a war between a free or would-be free nation on one side and a member of the Soviet bloc or one of its stooges . . . remains . . . a type of limited war vital to our interests. . . ."[82] The concept of limited war thus grew in importance in the American public debate "as an alternative to massive retaliation for the defense of third [world] areas; and the term . . . [became] associated with the use of limited military force in local areas . . . [and] was coopted to refer to . . . war ostensibly between the forces of the free world and those of Communism in a restricted area for less than total goals."[83] Further debate on limited war initially took place with this as a major assumption.

In 1957, two books were released that supposedly "set the terms of discussion" for the debate during the period 1957 to 1960 on limited war.[84] These were Robert Osgood's *Limited War* and what was perhaps the first strategic study in American history to approach becoming a bestseller, Henry Kissinger's *Nuclear Weapons and Foreign Policy*.

Osgood highlighted in his discussion many of the points about the nation's approach to war brought out by earlier writers: the traditional American distaste for war, our tendency to allow wars to grow in violence due to our dissociation of war and politics, and our acceptance of the policy of containment on a global scale.[85] Osgood asked two key questions: how could the United States keep war limited, and how could the United States fight limited wars successfully?[86] He used the majority of his work to address the first question, stressing that political objectives would determine practical limits. It was up to Henry Kissinger to develop an answer to the second.

Much like other critics of the Eisenhower Administration, Kissinger argued for a different approach to policy and strategy. The major assumption underlying his work was that "for better or for worse, strategy must henceforth he charted against the ominous assumption that any war is likely to be a nuclear war." With this in mind, the conduct of a limited war in the nuclear age had "two prerequisites: a doctrine and a capability."[87] Much of Kissinger's book was concerned with laying out a tentative doctrine for the conduct of a nuclear war based on the development of small yield nuclear weapons.[88] His main concern, however, was that policy and strategy find a place for the use of force in a manner less than absolute, that is, that means *and* ways had to be tailored to political ends. Limited nuclear warfare, particularly in a European context, offered a way out.

Osgood and Kissinger apparently shared a set of assumptions. Both saw the existence of an international and unified Communist threat that was aggressively attempting to expand its influence. Although dangerous enough in a conventional environment, in a nuclear one, the possible consequences of conflict were frightening. The consensus was that the first priority of those analyzing strategic issues should be to develop the concepts needed to preclude a nuclear Armageddon and then to develop the wherewithal to conduct wars on a much lower scale of violence. What is most significant about these two writers is that, to a large degree, they represented the mainstream of the intellectual currents of thought on limited war.

Shortly after the publication of these influential books, Thomas Schelling's *The Strategy of Conflict* was released. Schelling amplified a number of thoughts that were then in vogue, particularly on the limiting process. He was more concerned, however, with the role of bargaining and negotiation in limited conflicts. Although to some his argument was an extremely sophisticated development of concepts striving to expand the frontiers of knowledge, to others it was a somewhat esoteric discussion of isolated aspects of limited war theory open to misinterpretation.

One critic has claimed that Schelling argued that "the study of limited war in no way depended on any actual knowledge of war . . . [and that the] strategy of conflict is about bargaining, about conditioning someone else's behavior to one's own."[89] Much of the problem in interpreting Schelling's work centered around the fact that Schelling was not using the term "strategy" as it was used in military circles. Schelling defined strategy as the search for the optimal behavior that should be adopted by a player based on the interdependence of adversaries and on their expectations about others' behavior.[90] By his time, however, the theoretical consensus held that the theory of limited war was part of a view of "a 'strategy of conflict' in which adversaries would bargain with each other through the mechanism of graduated military responses . . . in order . . . to achieve a negotiated settlement. . . ."[91] Military actions could thus be placed from least to most violent along a spectrum from which civilian policymakers could pick and choose at will.

Schelling argued that it appeared to be generally accepted that "there is a rather continuous gradation in the possible sizes of atomic weapons effects, in the forms they can be used, in the means of conveyance, in the targets they can be used on, and so forth."[92] He was not, however, a supporter of the use of nuclear weapons. Instead, he stressed that "what makes atomic weapons different is a powerful tradition that they *are* different,"[93] and he recognized that there was, "a worldwide revulsion against nuclear weapons as a political fact." Thus the only break along the scale of nuclear options was between use and non-use, not a flexible, sliding point somewhere along the scale as postulated by Kissinger.[94]

The discussions of limited war during this explosion of creative thought focused on the *strategic* uses of power. The major concern was how to arrive at limits and only secondarily on how to achieve war aims. Even so, the treatises on war limitation left "much to be desired in our understanding of limits and the limiting process, especially in relation to the political setting of a local war."[95] Schelling was the only one who even attempted to develop a practical approach to conflict termination in a form that could be used by decision makers.

The sole writer to approach the problems found on the battlefield was William Kaufmann. In *Military Policy and National Security,* Kaufmann argued that there appeared to be three preconditions that were required before the enemy had to be blocked and held on the battlefield; the second, that the cost of the "blocking action" had to weigh more heavily upon him than us; the third, that *whatever* the mode of combat our antagonist chose, he would perceive the results of continued combat to be the same.[96]

Kaufmann also offered "several general principles" for battlefield action. The United States had to aim for efficient resistance as quickly as possible while avoiding expanding either the theater of operations or the types of weapons employed. Furthermore, military actions should "symbolize the intention of the United States to confine both the conflict and the issues" to "the narrowest limits commensurate with the security and tactical initiative of our forces." The military objective appeared, therefore, to be "to inflict heavy and continuing costs upon the enemy's forces" with attrition rather than annihilation being the goal.[97] Thus, "any decision to end the war is likely to result more from a sense of futility than from minor losses of territory. . . ."[98]

This sounds like Korea in a nutshell. Perhaps more important than the above, however, was Kaufmann's contention that the United States must "place our military establishment in symmetry with that of the Communist bloc . . . [to] enhance our bargaining power whether over substantive issues or over problems of disarmament."[99] These suggestions were to fall on receptive ears late in the decade, but prior to that, a new crisis had to be overcome.

VII. Limited War Theory Diverted

From a distance of almost thirty years it is difficult to comprehend how the 1959 launching of the Sputnik jolted the American psyche. From the ebullient tone of Henry Kissinger's theories of possible limited nuclear war, the country was unceremoniously shoved face to face with the specter of nuclear annihilation.[100] By 1959, those dealing with national security issues turned once again to the problems of deterring a global catastrophe.

Two writers came to the fore in presenting the unpalatable to U.S. citizens — Oskar Morgenstern and Albert Wohlstetter. Morgenstern trumpeted the fact that the Soviet nuclear accomplishments were "so formidable" that in 1959 the United States "was approaching a peak of danger the like of which has never been experienced by a great nation." His contention, however, was that with the proper developments in technology and strategy, this danger could be overcome. In particular he favored a further development and broadening of America's strategic nuclear arsenal.[101]

Wohlstetter was more pessimistic. In a RAND report (and its unclassified variant that made its way to the public forum), Wohlstetter attacked the commonly held assumption that the nuclear balance was stable.[102] Due to the capability implied by Sputnik, nuclear deterrence of a general war was no longer considered automatic.[103] Since thermonuclear weapons could give an aggressor an enormous advantage, deterrence would require "urgent and continuing effort," since "this technology itself is changing with fantastic speed."[104] Thus, even though it appeared by mid-1957 that the voices of those arguing for a limited war capability were finally being heard, Sputnik "dramatically [turned] . . . the attention of American policymakers and strategists to the new problems of global war in the missile age."[105]

In a move typical of the Eisenhower administration, a civilian committee was formed to look into a number of problems facing the country. Concerning defense, the Gaither Committee report stressed that "first priority must be given to maintaining the stability of the strategic balance. Thus, just as the government was shifting to the view that the strategic balance was inherently stable and *the* problem was maintaining adequate limited war forces, the administration turned back to the belief that no major shift . . . in defense spending was desirable."[106]

Concurrently with this, "the attention of most analysts turned more and more to problems of general war." As Kissinger's arguments were dissected in this new strategic context, it became apparent that they were severely flawed.[107] Complicating matters even further was the Soviet view that "if nuclear weapons are present, any 'small' war will inevitably grow into a 'big' war . . ."[108] Thus, "by the end of the 1950s . . . the possibilities and perplexities of strategic nuclear warfare seemed endless . . . in the short space of little more than ten years, *the planners and their technical collaborators had invented an essentially new mode of warfare* [emphasis added]."[109]

The outcome of the debate on limited war theory remained inconclusive. Not only were "the dynamics of escalation" hardly better understood than in the early 1950s, it was not at all clear what was meant by the term "limited war," either in a nuclear *or* non-nuclear sense.[110] By 1960, the consensus among strategic thinkers was that wars could no longer be deterred by nuclear means and policies at hand. However, strategy "could not be adapted to nuclear weapons leisurely, or through trial and error."[111] One generally accepted doctrine for nuclear use that offered a possible solution came to be known (at least initially) as "flexible response."

Under Eisenhower, war with the Soviet Union called for a general release of all U.S. nuclear weapons in a single "spasm."[112] The incoming Kennedy administration saw the need to provide for a potential "so designed and controlled" that it could attack a wide range of targets in order to give the United States at least the *ability* to fight a nuclear war while limiting world wide damage.[113]

The need for conventional forces gradually came to the forefront of security debates as well. Under Eisenhower, this arm of the military had been allowed to atrophy. Only eleven of the Army's fourteen divisions were rated as combat-effective (and were organized for nuclear conditions under the Pentomic structure). The strategic reserve, formed from the divisions that were not in Korea or Germany, consisted of one division in Hawaii and three in the continental United States.[114] Numerous smaller crises requiring the possible deployment of conventional forces abounded in the late 1950s, undermining the ideas of massive retaliation and deterrence through nuclear superiority at tactical levels.[115] The 1958 Lebanon crisis was perhaps the most visible evidence of the military's conventional impotence.[116] It was apparent that our capabilities did not match strategic realities.

Later, as the means available to decision makers grew, some began to see the role of conventional forces in a new strategic light. While the debate continued, the concepts of graduated deterrence and the spectrum of conflict were brought together to form the "strategy of escalation," a concept that gave conventional forces an important role.

> The idea bore some similarity to a poker game. Presumably, the non-nuclear chips were the easiest ones to play; NATO therefore should have a sufficient supply of them to make a substantial ante in the event the Soviets started the game. Not only would this be a believable step; it would also commit the United States irrevocably to the play. As such, it might well act as a deterrent to Soviet action. If not, it might suffice to cause a Soviet withdrawal from the game. However, if the Soviets persisted, the United States would then have to resort to nuclear weapons, at first on the tactical level; and if that did not work, on the strategic level. The threat of a graduated use of force, in which non-nuclear capabilities would be the leading elements, thus was the only technique that seemed applicable to the threat in Europe.[117]

Although never *formally* adopted by the Kennedy administration, this concept offered the potential for meeting Communist threats at levels below that of nuclear war. Thus, as the Kennedy administration came into office, backers of three capabilities clamored for funds and the attention of policy makers and strategic thinkers: strategic nuclear warfare, tactical nuclear warfare, and limited non-nuclear warfare.[118] Unfortunately, the arena for the interplay of funds, ideas, and policies remained stable for only a brief period before yet another form of warfare burst upon the world scene.

John F. Kennedy entered office through a campaign that had pledged to restore America's flawed defense policies. He had promised to reduce the "missile gap," restore America's conventional forces, and provide for greater nuclear options. In 1961, however, Nikita Krushchev gave a speech that was to have grave repercussions for the American theory of limited war. Krushchev declared that there were three possible categories of wars:

92

world wars, local wars, and liberation wars or popular uprisings. The USSR, Krushchev trumpeted, had the capability and wherewithal to fight, and thus forestall, conflicts of the first two types. Wars against imperialism (the third type) were likely to break out in every continent, however, and Krushchev announced that the Soviet Union would support such conflicts wherever possible.[119]

This was a bombshell for the new President. Although similar wars had been fought before (in Algeria and Indochina), Russia's support for them had been previously tepid at best. Now, however, there appeared a "new and particularly dangerous form" of warfare. Backed by an aggressive Communist bloc and fueled by revolutionary ardor, this "para-war" or "sub-limited war" presented the United States "with a completely new challenge."[120]

The President addressed this threat immediately and put "a great drive" behind a program to develop concepts and techniques to cope with it.[121] To a large degree, the problems of wars of national liberation supplanted the concerns of limited war theorists. Moreover, Kennedy's attention was firmly fixed to the former as he declared, "How we fight that kind of problem which is going to be with us all through this decade seems to me to be one of the greatest problems now before the United States."[122] As John L. Gaddis wrote, the "struggle had been switched from Europe to Asia, Africa, and Latin America, from nuclear and conventional weaponry to irregular warfare, insurrection, and subversion. . . ."[123] Once again, the theory of limited war was derailed.

VIII. The Theory of Limited War — An Analysis

There are a number of pitfalls threatening anyone who attempts to reconstruct a theory as it evolves over time. The benefits of hindsight allow an analyst to neatly build a model that supports the major tenets of an argument instead of seeing a problem in all its complexity. This often leads to portraying a line of thought as either black or white, omitting the subtle shades of grey that so often are vital qualifications. Keeping this in mind, I have attempted to trace general trends and identify common threads that were gradually woven into the fabric of limited war. The result is the tapestry shown in Figure 1.

A number of assumptions were critical to the development of this theory. Perhaps the most important and widest in its implications was the concept of a monolithic Communist bloc within a bipolar world. This implies several terms of reference from which the theory cannot escape.

Figure 1

Elements of the American Theory of Limited War

* Assumptions

    Monolithic Communist Bloc
        Containment and Perimeter Defense
        Eurocentric
        Balance of Power/"Zero-sum" Conditions
        US Interests Indivisible
    General War Unlikely
    Existence of a Spectrum of Conflict
        Graduated Escalation
        Political Elements Dominant
        Military Only One Tool

* Ends

    Containment
    Avoid "Explosion"/Direct Confrontation
    Give US Flexibility of Options

* Ways

    US Troop Presence at Mid-Intensity Levels
    Attrition-Oriented
    Central Control/Direction Crucial
    Relieve Domestic Burdens

* Means

    Limits
        Geographic
        Non-Nuclear Desirable
        Negotiable and Dynamic
    Mid-Intensity Focus
    Sub-Limited War Not a Primary US
        Responsibility

The need to contain the influence of the Soviet Union in order to promote its disintegration led to the adoption of a concept of perimeter defense. Within this context, any gain by the Communist bloc would be a loss for the Free World, and "salami-slice" tactics, the nibbling away of Western interests, had to be prevented. Since the number of *influential* actors was relatively small, the conflict gradually came to be seen as essentially a form of poker between two players. This, in turn, took place along a spectrum of conflict in which the adversarial players would confront one another and gain or lose chips in the context of a "global game."

Given these assumptions, the ends, ways, and means of the American theory as listed were predictable. Although a general, wide ranging nuclear war between the United States and Soviet Union was considered to be unlikely, it was not viewed as impossible. How to avoid an "explosion" from a "local" conflict into a worldwide one was thus a weighty consideration and an important end, second only to "containment." Yet without the ability to apply all elements of a nation's power flexibly, these considerations would be meaningless.

This theory, like all theories, has its weaknesses. Clausewitz offers a number of illuminating thoughts about theory and its role that are applicable to this situation. The "primarily purpose of any theory is to clarify concepts and ideas that have become, as it were, confused and entangled. Not until terms and concepts have been defined can one hope to make any progress in examining the question. . . ."[124] Moreover, the "task of theory . . . [is] to study the nature of ends and means."[125] Yet there are definite limits to what theory can accomplish. "Theory is not meant to provide . . . positive doctrines and systems to be used as intellectual tools."[126] As Clausewitz's acerbic contemporary, Jomini, points out, "theories cannot teach men with mathematical precision what they should do in every case; but it is certain that they will always point out the errors which should be avoided."[127] The problems, however, arise when theory meets reality, for "*theory conflicts with practice.*"[128]

Clausewitz divides "activities characteristic of war" into two categories, "those *that are merely preparations for war,* and *war proper.*" Theory can be applied to both categories, yet "the theory of war, proper, is concerned with the use of these means, once they have been developed, for the purpose of war."[129] It is easier, however, "to use theory to plan, organize, and conduct an engagement than it is to use it in determining an engagement's purpose."[130] It was in this translation of the means available to achieve the ends desired that the supporters of the theory of limited war ran into difficulty.

It is easier, however, to criticize than to praise, to destroy than to create. With this injunction in mind, it is necessary to dwell on the positive aspects of the theory first, before they are overwhelmed by subsequent criticism. The development of the theory of limited war was a broadly based, interdisciplinary effort that was the subject of much heated debate. The result was an intellectual construct that imposed order upon disorder and set the terms for national security concepts that are still in use today. It addressed wide-ranging numbers and types of threats, thus providing policy makers with the ability to do what Clausewitz claimed to be the first and foremost task of the statesman, "to establish . . . the kind of war on which they are embarking. . . ."[131] Thus the concepts and their subsequent development satisfy the "primary purpose" of a theory.

The theorists were at great pains to address the *strategic* uses of power. Their main concern was how to integrate military force into what had become a more deadly and far less forgiving international environment. The focus therefore was on war as a continuation of politics *with* other means. Moreover, they understood that the term "political war" was not an oxymoron. How to establish limits and use force in a manner that would not eclipse their goals was a crucial consideration and worthy of attention, for if war was "a matter of vital importance to the State . . . it is mandatory that it be thoroughly studied."[132] They understood that wars have a dynamic all their own, and if left uncontrolled, have a tendency to escalate in terms of the amount of violence employed and the goals to be obtained. Limiting means and ways thus became a central focus of this theory, and rightly so, for as Jomini points out, "although originating in religious or political dogmas, these wars [of opinion] are most deplorable; for . . . they enlist the worst passions, and become vindictive, cruel, and terrible."[133]

The recognition of the existence of Clausewitz's "paradoxical trinity" in the form of political control, primordial violence, and chance is also evident in the theory. Domestic issues were not neglected, as some later critics charged, but instead addressed within this context. The traditional American approach to war as something akin to a crusade was understood, and theorists contended that it could be changed with the adoption of appropriate measures.[134] The emphasis merely needed to be placed on the aspect of political control to promote success. Thus, if given a "Clausewitzian litmus test," it would appear that the theory would pass. Unfortunately, with the administering of other tests, it does not.

Perhaps one of the weakest aspects was apparent in an area where the theory received high marks — the political use of force. Although the existence of a unified Communist threat is debatable within the context of the time, the theory was based on the assumption that rational actors operate within the international political system. Greatly contributing to the problems of the practical application of the theory was "the Russians' own inconsistency: at no point during the Cold War did their behavior oscillate more between extremes of belligerence and conciliation than during Kennedy's years in office."[135]

The definition of conflict as bargaining between two blocks was also flawed. Bargaining "implies the ability to control precisely the combination of pressures and inducements to be applied, but that in turn implies central direction, something not easy to come by in a democracy in the best of circumstances, and certainly not during the first year of an inexperienced and badly organized administration."[136] It also implies the ability to identify a single threat or single actor against whom one can direct those pressures. Although the existence of a Sino-Soviet split was in evidence as early as 1960,[137] the concept of a monolithic communism retained some credence well into the politics of the 1980s. Moreover, as the perception of a threat changes over a period of time, how does a government orchestrate the "calibration," the measured and incremental use, of incentives and pressure?[138] American involvement in Vietnam lasted close to twenty years. During this period the war changed in nature from an insurgency to a conventional invasion from the north. How and where are pressures to be applied when the threat does not remain constant? Finally, given the possibility that the threat can change, how can limits be imposed that will restrain the war within acceptable bounds? In Vietnam, were pressures to be applied against the North Vietnamese, Chinese, or Soviets — or against the South Vietnamese government? With an increase in the number of actors, the permutations and combinations of successful and unsuccessful inducements interlock in such a way as to be mind boggling; yet this is characteristic of limited wars.

The role of the military in the theory is unclear, as well. Although Kennedy proclaimed that the strategy of flexible response was "to deter all wars, general or limited, nuclear or conventional, large or small — to convince all potential aggressors that any attack would be futile — to provide backing for the diplomatic settlement of disputes — to insure the adequacy of our bargaining power for an end to the arms race," what military forces were to do *in combat* remained uncertain.[139]

Most of the possible uses for the military were couched in euphemistic terms, such as "successful blocking actions," or "blocking the enemy," and so on. What is missing is an understanding of Sun-Tzu's contention that "what is essential in war is victory, not prolonged operations."[140] It is almost as if, in a peculiarly deadly form of hubris, the theorists felt that the military aspects were self-explanatory. Take, for instance, the comments in a speech made by Secretary of Defense Robert McNamara in November of 1963.

In Greece, in Berlin, and in Cuba, Communists have probed for military and political weakness but when they have en-

countered resistance, they have held back. Not only Communist doctrine has counselled this caution, but respect for the
danger that any sizable, overt conflict would lead to nuclear
war. It would follow that no deterrent would be more effective
against these lesser and intermediate levels of challenge than
the assurance that such moves would certainly meet prompt,
effective military response by the West.[141]

To some extent, this is a confirmation of the contention that "in its
search for a way to keep a nuclear conflict within acceptable limits of
damage the Kennedy administration called upon the skills of the commander, but to restrain rather than to expand battlefield violence."[142] Although this neglect of the roles of the military may appear to be a glaring
oversight, the question that should be asked is who was to bring up
military considerations and the peculiarities of battlefield problems. A
large number of the limited war theorists had some prior military service
on which to base their arguments. Yet only a very few military men
attempted to discuss, address, correct, or analyze the theory in the public
domain. There was a great deal of discussion of defense policy and how
to cope with exigencies on the nuclear battlefield, but the question of
what military end states were required to secure political objectives rarely
saw light in print. The services demonstrated a myopic concern with
means (tools available) over ways (manner of employment) and ends.

A final weakness of the theory was the generally accepted concept of
a spectrum of conflict. This retains force even today, as evidenced by the
following quote from *AFM 1–1; Basic Aerospace Doctrine of the USAF.*

Our military forces must be capable of achieving victory across
a wide spectrum of conflicts of crises. This spectrum is a
continuum defined primarily by the magnitude of the declared
objectives.[143]

Although the spectrum is a useful tool, its greatest value is in the
activity Clausewitz called "preparation for war."[144] This is a neat, orderly
device for illuminating the wide variety of roles that the armed forces are
required to fill and graphically highlights problems that are critical in
developing budgets and force structures. It fails, however, to show the
complexities and chaos of warfare and gives a mistaken impression of
how differing types of warfare are interrelated.

Applying the strategy of escalation to this continuum has led to the
concept of "escalation dominance," the idea that superiority at the highest

level of force in use along the scale is the most important aspect of a conflict. Although this concept recognizes that other types of conflict may be going on, it holds that the crucial battles will take place at the highest levels of violence. Perhaps a better representation of warfare is shown in Figure 2, the idea of "spectrum-less conflict." From this vantage point, wars can be interpreted as being multifaceted, with conflicts moving and changing character with bewildering frequency as the means employed and ends sought change. The implication of escalation dominance is that victory can be achieved through raising the level of violence to an extreme the enemy cannot match. The suggestion of this spectrum-less conflict is that differing categories of conflict can be going on independently from or in conjunction with one another. Although one may not lose by escalating, one certainly may not win if other facets of the conflict are ignored.

Yet another implication of the spectrum of conflict is that the military capabilities of the United States must be placed in what John Gaddis referred to as "symmetry" with the USSR. This implies that "you neglect no capability whatsoever . . . [and] with respect to each capability you're almost driven to outspend the enemy appreciably because, by definition, this doctrine concedes him the strategic initiative."[145] The result is that "perceptions of means have played a larger role than perceptions of threats in shaping U.S. policy toward the Soviet Union."[146]

Given the rather harsh criticism that has been heaped upon the altar of limited war theory, the question remains — what is the bottom line? The theory is a product of its era, shaped by pressures and demands of the time that were often beyond the control of the framers. It has a number of glaring flaws that leap out under analysis (admittedly at the distance of some thirty years). Yet the tendency to reject it out of hand, to throw out the baby with the bathwater, needs to be restrained. There are a number of positive elements that can be used in discussions of security issues today.

The first is the recognition that there is a multiplicity of means available to policy makers at all levels of government that can be used in the formulation of strategies. Too often the military solution is trumpeted as the key, too often as nonapplicable. When viewed as merely one aspect of an integrated approach, the benefits of the use of the military element of power can complement the effects of the others. Used alone, it may create far more problems than it solves. More importantly, the military must remain responsive to civilian control, but also retain the ability to adjust the manner of the application of force to enhance the attainment of political objectives.

The second is that containment as an element of policy has withstood

Figure 2

Spectrum-Less Conflict

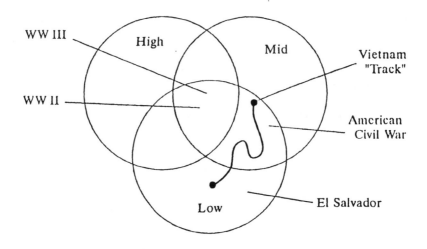

Intensity Levels Defined

High - Nuclear Use
Mid - US Conventional Ground
      Force Commitment
Low - Advisory, Peacekeeping, etc.

the test of time. This is not a new doctrine, however, for as Jomini points out, during the French Revolution of the late 1700s, the *proper* actions for the European monarchies would have been to merely "contain" the revolution within France. Active intervention was not the answer, for "time is the remedy for all bad passions and for all anarchical doctrines. A civilized nation may bear the yoke of a factious and unrestrained multitude for a short interval; but these storms soon pass away, and reason resumes her sway."[147] What has not remained valid is the concept of perimeter defense. More selectivity should be exercised in the selection of U.S. goals and interests, and, just as important, what sacrifices are within reason to secure them. This is especially crucial now that regional conflicts are the focus of defense strategy. Ways and means *must* be subordinated to ends and constantly studied in the light of the dynamics of changing situations.

Finally, the process of limiting wars and their effects should still be regarded as complex processes that at times can defy solution. There are no set methods to go about limiting wars, although some are more readily applicable than others. Geographic scale and scope are perhaps the easiest to maintain and the clearest to demonstrate. Levels of force and types of forces employed are perhaps the most probable limits that will be in use, but these are the ones that are least susceptible to clear and communicable definitions.

It is apparent that the theory of limited war as developed prior to Vietnam had its limitations. Yet it set terms, developed concepts, and established the framework of the debate on security issues that continues even today. Perhaps the greatest compliment that can be paid to it and its intellectual "fathers," however, is that it helped to keep us from a Third World War.

Notes

1. Robert Osgood, *Limited War Revisited* (Boulder, CO: Westview Press, 1979), 8.

2. William Kaufmann, "Limited Warfare," in *Military Policy and National Security,* ed. William Kaufmann (Princeton: Princeton University Press, 1956), 134.

3. Robert Osgood, *Limited War: The Challenge to American Strategy* (Chicago: Chicago University Press, 1957), 29.

4. Ibid., 15.

5. Morton Halperin, *Limited War in the Nuclear Age* (Westport, CT: Greenwood Press, 1963), 19.

6. Gordon Craig, "The Problem of Limited War," *Commentary,* xxv (February 1958), 173.

7. Russell Weigley, *The American Way of War* (New York: Macmillan, 1973), 373. See also Russell Weigley, *History of the United States Army* (Bloomington: Indiana University Press, 1967), 495.

8. Weigley, *Way of War,* 382.

9. Albert Wohlstetter, *The Delicate Balance of Terror* (Santa Monica, CA: RAND Corporation, 1958), 32, RAND P-1472.

10. Weigley, *Way of War,* 372.

11. John L. Gaddis, *Strategies of Containment* (New York: Oxford University Press, 1982), 21.

12. Ibid., 65–66.

13. Ibid., 23.

14. Ibid., 58.

15. Ibid., 21.

16. Ibid., 59. Halford Mackinder was an English geographer who developed, around the turn of the century, the concept of the "heartland." Mackinder felt that the end of exploration was creating a closed political system in the world. Due to the changes in the relative strength of land and sea power, he claimed that the power that controlled the Eurasian land mass could possibly dominate world events, because the heartland was "an ample base for land power, potentially the greatest on earth." Derwent Whittlesey, "Haushofer: The Geopoliticians," in *Makers of Modern Strategy: Military Thought from Machiavelli to Hitler*, ed. Edward Mead Earle (Princeton University Press, 1973), 401 and 405. NSC 20/4 stated that "Soviet domination of the potential power of Eurasia . . . would be strategically and politically unacceptable to the United States."

17. Ibid., 57 and 59.

18. Ibid., 137.

19. Gaddis, *Strategies,* 79.

20. Paul Nitze, "Limited Wars or Massive Retaliation," *The Reporter* (September 5, 1957), 40.

21. John L. Gaddis and Paul Nitze, "NSC 68 and the Soviet Threat Reconsidered," *International Security* 4, 4 (Spring 1980), 170. Paul Nitze was the Director of the Policy Planning Staff on the NSC and the individual who chaired the *ad hoc* committee of State and Defense representatives who drafted NSC-68.

22. Glenn H. Snyder, "The 'New Look' of 1953," in *Strategy, Politics, and Defense Budgets*, ed. Warner Schilling, Paul Hammond, and Glenn H. Snyder (New York: Columbia University Press, 1962), 366.

23. Gaddis and Nitze, "NSC 68," 171.

24. Gaddis, *Strategies,* 239.

25. Weigley, *Way of War,* 382.

26. William Kaufmann, *Planning Conventional Forces, 1950–80* (Washington, D.C.: The Brookings Institution, 1982), 2.

27. Gaddis and Nitze, "NSC 68," 170. George Kennan had argued that "two high-quality Marine divisions . . . would be sufficient to support the military requirement of containment."

28. Gaddis, *Strategies,* 90–91.

29. Nitze, "Limited Wars," 172 and 176.

30. NSC-68, April 14, 1950, 3–69, from "United States Objectives and Programs For National Security" in *National Security Documents* (USACGSC; Ft. Leavenworth, KS 66027).

31. Weigley, *Way of War,* 379. Although some have stated that NSC-68 "put no limit" upon recommended U.S. policies and "paid no attention" to the limitations of budgetary means "this was not the case." The framers of the document "were fully aware . . . of the limitations of means." The conflicts that arose were over the scale of means that were thought to be necessary. Gaddis and Nitze, 174.

32. Weigley, *Way of War,* 398.

33. Gaddis, *Strategies,* 109–110.

34. Raymond Aron, "NATO and the Bomb," *Western World* (June 1957), 11.

35. Halperin, *Limited War,* 22.

36. Arnold Wolfers, "Could a War in Europe be Limited," *The Yale Review* XLV, 2 (December 1955), 214.

37. Bernard Brodie, "Some Notes on the Evolution of Air Doctrine," *World Politics* VII, 3 (April 1955), 368–69.

38. "Memorandum, Subject: Review of the Uncertain Trumpet." A study prepared by the staff and faculty of the Command and General Staff College, 29 March 1960.

39. Halperin, *Limited War,* 2–3.

40. Osgood, *Limited War Revisited,* 6.

41. William Kaufmann, "Limited Warfare," 129.

42. Weigley, *Way of War,* 415.

43. Bernard Brodie, *War and Politics* (New York: Macmillan Publishing Co., Inc., 1973), 114.

44. Weigley, *Way of War,* 396–97.

45. Herman Kahn, *The Nature and Feasibility of Deterrence* (Santa Monica, CA: RAND Corporation, 1960), 35 and 37, RAND P-1888-RC.

46. This term was "first rather narrowly applied to a review of strategic plans and force requirements by the new Joint Chiefs of Staff . . . it later came to denote the substance of the whole grand strategy evolved by the administration in all its aspects. . . . The New Look was both a doctrine . . . and set of actual changes and planned changes in the military establishment." Snyder, 383.

47. Eisenhower. Quoted in Gaddis, *Strategies,* 135.

48. John L. Gaddis, "Commentary," *The Second Indochina War* ed. John Schlight (Washington, D.C.: Office of the Chief of Military History, 1986), 95.

49. P.M.S. Blackett, *Atomic Weapons and East-West Relations* (Oxford: Cambridge University Press, 1956), 19–20.

50. Ibid.

51. Gaddis, *Strategies*, 130.

52. Weigley, *Way of War*, 399.

53. Gaddis, *Strategies*, 161.

54. Ibid., 147–48.

55. Ibid., 151.

56. Ibid., 161. This sounds remarkably similar to the tenets of the now-popular "Competi-
tive Strategies" which many pundits are heralding as a "new" and "innovative" strategy and the older notion of horizontal escalation.

57. Trumpet Review.

58. Dulles, quoted in Halperin, *Limited War*, 22.

59. Ibid., 22. The use of the terms tactical and strategy together indicates a problem that
plagued the national security debates. Although concepts appear to have been important, rigor in developing and holding to definitions to establish the parameters of the
debate does not. This was a major problem with the concept of massive retaliation.
Rather than being perceived as a military strategy that was part of the new look [a
policy that John Lewis Gaddis says "was an integrated and reasonably efficient adaption
of resources to objectives, of means to ends" (Gaddis, *Strategies*, 161)] it took on a life
of its own and was perceived as the *only* option the United States had available.

60. Nitze, "Limited Wars," 40.

61. LTC Gerald Post, *The Strategic Thinking of General Maxwell D. Taylor* (Carlisle Barracks, PA: U.S. Army War College, March 3, 1967), 10–11.

62. Gaddis, *Strategies*, 172.

63. Bernard Brodie, "Unlimited Weapons and Limited War," *The Reporter* Nov. 18, 1954,
17 and 19.

64. Ibid., 16.

65. William Kaufmann, "Force and Foreign Policy," in *Military Policy and National Security*, ed. William Kaufmann (Princeton: Princeton University Press, 1956), 103.

66. Osgood, *Limited War Revisited*, 3.

67. Robert Strausz-Hupe', "The Limits of Limited War," *The Reporter*, Nov. 28, 1957, 31.

68. Bernard Brodie, "Nuclear Weapons: Strategic or Tactical," *Foreign Affairs* 32, 2
(January 1954), 229.

69. Kaufmann, "Limited Warfare," 111.

70. Brodie, "Nuclear Weapons," 229.

71. Raymond Aron, "A Half-Century of Limited War," *Bulletin of the Atomic Scientists*
XII, 4 (April 1956), 102.

72. Brodie, "Some Notes," 367.

73. Blackett, *Atomic Weapons,* 32.

74. Weigley, *Way of War,* 420.

75. Strausz-Hupe, "The Limits of Limited War," 31. Bernard Brodie wrote that Korea "has made it possible for many of us to think and talk about limited war who would otherwise have considered such talk utterly absurd. . . ." Brassey's Annual, 146.

76. Blackett, *Atomic Weapons,* 11.

77. The term "explosion" was normally used to describe an uncontrollable escalation of a small conflict into a central war. The term "central war" was at times used interchangeably with the term "general war." Although the most common use for the latter was in describing a total war between the Soviet Union and United States in which nuclear strikes on each other's homelands were part and parcel of a global conflict, the former was normally restricted to mean a war between the two antagonists that was limited but might not have involved their homelands.

78. Aron, "A Half-Century," 102.

79. Brodie, "Nuclear Weapons," 224–28.

80. (Col.) Thomas L. Fisher, "Limited War — What Is It," *Air University Quarterly Review* IX (Winter 1957–8), 131.

81. Halperin, *Limited War,* 6–7.

82. Fisher, "Limited War," 129.

83. Halperin, *Limited War,* 2.

84. Stanley Peter Rosen, "Vietnam and the American Theory of Limited War," *International Security* 7, 2 (Fall 1982), 83.

85. Weigley, *Way of War,* 412. Osgood, *Limited War,* 28–30.

86. Osgood, *Limited War,* 8.

87. Henry Kissinger, *Nuclear Weapons and Foreign Policy* (New York: Harper, 1957), 123.

88. Halperin, *Limited War,* 5–6. Weigley, *Way of War,* 416.

89. Rosen, "Vietnam," 86.

90. Thomas Schelling, *The Strategy of Conflict* (Cambridge: Harvard University Press, 1960), 3 and footnote.

91. Osgood quoted in Rosen, "Vietnam," 86.

92. Thomas Schelling, *Nuclear Weapons and Limited War* (Santa Monica, CA: RAND Corporation, February 20, 1959), 1, RAND, P-1620.

93. Ibid., 6.

94. Ibid., 1.

95. Halperin, *Limited War,* 11.

96. Kaufmann, "Force," 244.

97. Ibid., 116–17.

98. Ibid., 246.

99. Ibid., 256.

100. Weigley, *Way of War,* 426–27.

101. Morgenstern summarized from Weigley, *Way of War,* 430–32.

102. Wohlstetter, RAND, P-1472, 1.

103. Ibid., 10.

104. Ibid.

105. Halperin, *Limited War,* 7.

106. Ibid., 8.

107. Ibid., 7.

108. Leon Goure', translator, *Soviet Commentary on the Doctrine of Limited Nuclear Wars* (Santa Monica, CA: RAND Corporation, 1958), 8, T-82.

109. William Kaufmann, *The McNamara Strategy* (New York: Harper and Row, 1964), 12.

110. Ibid., 16.

111. Michael Mandelbaum, *The United States and Nuclear Weapons 1946–76* (Cambridge: Cambridge University Press, 1979), viii.

112. Ibid., 108.

113. Kaufmann, *McNamara,* 51–52.

114. Kaufmann, *Planning,* 3.

115. Charles De Vallon Dugas Bolles, "The Search for an American Strategy: The Origins of the Kennedy Doctrine, 1936–61," (Ph.D. diss., University of Wisconsin, Madison, 1985), 535–539.

116. Peter Braestrup, "Limited Wars and the Lessons of Lebanon," *The Reporter* XX, April 30, 1959, 25–27. Braestrup claims the "top-secret" studies were "much less reassuring about our ability to stomp out brushfires." He interviewed 50 top staff and operational officers in the Pentagon and found a number of shocking problems. Eighty percent of the Navy's ships were of WWII vintage or prior and manned at eighty percent strength. Four major ships enroute to Lebanon had breakdowns and one Marine battalion had to transfer to another transport while underway. The Tactical Air Force was as bad off. It received only 6 percent of the total Air Force budget and had less than 58,000 of the service's 850,000 men. Its Transports were so committed to support the Strategic Air Command that only 1200 Army troops were able to be airlifted overseas. The Civilian Reserve Air Fleet was no help either as the "Lebanon crisis came during the height of the summer tourist season."

117. Kaufmann, *McNamara,* 66–67.

118. Ibid., 14–16.

119. Halperin, *Limited War*, 16–17.

120. Maxwell Taylor in a speech given on March 15, 1962 entitled "Our Changing Military Policy: Greater Flexibility," in *Vital Speeches*, 28, 11, 347–49.

121. Robert S. Gallagher, "Memories of Peace and War: An Exclusive Interview With General Maxwell D. Taylor, *American Heritage* 32 (1981), 13. Kaufmann, *McNamara*, 17.

122. Henry Farlie, "We Knew What We Were Doing When We Went Into Vietnam," *Washington Monthly* 5, 3 (May 1973), 11.

123. Gaddis, *Strategies*, 208.

124. Carl von Clausewitz, *On War*, trans. Michael Howard and Peter Paret (Princeton: Princeton University Press, 1984), 132.

125. Ibid., 142.

126. Ibid., 168.

127. Baron Antoine Henri Jomini, *The Art of War*, trans. Capt. G.H. Mendell and Lt. W.P. Craighill (Westport, CT: Greenwood Press Publisher, 1962), 295.

128. Clausewitz, *On War*, 140. Emphasis in the original.

129. Ibid., 131–32.

130. Ibid., 140.

131. Ibid., 88.

132. Sun-Tzu, *The Art of War* trans. Samuel B. Griffith (New York: Oxford University Press, 1982), 63.

133. Jomini, *The Art of War*, 22.

134. Goure', *Commentary*, 3.

135. Gaddis, *Strategies*, 206–7.

136. Ibid., 18.

137. Gaddis, "Commentary," 92.

138. Gaddis, *Strategies*, 243.

139. Ibid., 214–15.

140. Sun-Tzu, *The Air of War*, 76.

141. Kaufmann, *McNamara*, 311.

142. Mandelbaum, *The United States and Nuclear Weapons*, 106.

143. *AFM 1–1: Basic Aerospace Doctrine of the USAF* (Washington, D.C.: U.S. Government Printing Office, 16 March 1984), 1–2 to 1–3.

144. Clausewitz, *On War*, 131.

145. Malcolm Hoag, *On Local War Doctrine* (Santa Monica, CA: RAND Corporation, August 1961), 13, P-2433.

146. John L. Gaddis, "Containment: Its Past and Future," *International Security* 5, 4 (Spring 1981), 83.

147. Jomini, *The Art of War*, 23.

The Social Incidence of Vietnam Casualties

SOCIAL CLASS OR RACE?

GILBERT BADILLO
G. DAVID CURRY
University of Chicago

In the popular protest against involvement in the second Indo-china war, there was widespread belief that black Americans were suffering a disproportionate share of battlefield casualties. In the heat of military and political conflict, there was every reason to believe that the burden was unequally distributed. However, there were a few academic observers who believed that more detailed analysis was required—and that it would have to come at a later date. Such an analysis might well demonstrate that race was not the crucial variable. The research results presented in this article justify the skepticism of this latter group of scholars. This analysis of data on the tracted communities of Cook County, Illinois, indicates that social class—not race—is the factor most responsible for the disproportionate casualty burdens borne by certain American communities and not by others. Neither the ecological nature of this study nor its geographic limitations are sufficient grounds for discounting the relevance of these findings.

Careful analyses of casualty data from American wars are sparse. Albert J. Mayer and Thomas F. Hoult undertook a study of Korean conflict casualties for the city of Detroit using census tracts as the units of analysis.[1] Though certain aspects of their work are questionable, their results show an overrepresentation of blacks among casualties.[2] An analysis of casualty data has been conducted by Maurice Zietlin, Kenneth Lutterman, and James Russell for 380 Wisconsin men killed in Vietnam prior to December 31, 1967.[3] By comparing income and occupational information on the parents of the deceased with similar data for the parents of a one-third sample of male Wisconsin high school seniors from

ARMED FORCES AND SOCIETY, Vol. 2 No. 3, May 1976
©1976 Inter-University Seminar on Armed Forces and Society

[397]

1957, they found that almost twice as many of the total casualties were from poor families relative to the control group (27.2% versus 14.9%). For privates, the results were even more striking, with 32.1% being classified as poor. Workers, regardless of income, tended to be substantially over-represented among the casualty parents in comparison to the control parents. These previous studies show the importance of two variables, race and socioeconomic status, as correlates of casualties. Our purpose is to suggest a model for casualties that more clearly identifies the effects of each of these variables.

SOCIAL STRATIFICATION AND MILITARY ASSIGNMENT

That black Americans are overly represented in combat units and casualty figures has been repeatedly documented. What is at issue is whether race is the determining factor in this overrepresentation or if there is some other factor, specifically socioeconomic status, that can account for this result. In short, do blacks end up in more dangerous military assignments because they are black or because they are poor?

Racial integration in the U.S. military, though marked by turbulent beginnings, has, for the most part, surpassed the same process in civilian life both chronologically and by degree.[4] This development is in good measure the result of the U.S. armed forces' reliance on "meritocratic" criteria as an operational norm in making personnel decisions. The use of such criteria in the assignment process reflects the preoccupation of military elites with rational and bureaucratic efficiency and is indicative of a resultant organizational capacity to conform quickly to political pressures from the policy-making sectors of the society.[5]

In such a rationalistically oriented milieu, an ascribed characteristic such as race becomes irrelevant to the personnel assignment process. However, the same factors that diminish the importance of race as a criterion in assignment decisions may work to increase the significance of attributes derivative of the socialization process, which may be highly correlated with race through the intervention of socioeconomic factors. There exists a large body of literature that emphasizes the relationship of achievement-related variables and degrees of social competency to the occupation, education, and income levels of parents. This is especially noteworthy when we are aware that black Americans are more likely to score low on all three of these latter items.[6]

The second Indochina war produced profound pressures on human behavior in the civilian sector of American life. An as yet unidentified number of young American males avoided military service through emigration or illegal evasion of conscription. Even more individuals sought sanctuary in the universities through student deferments.[7] Occupational movement into deferment-eligible jobs took place but remains unstudied. It would be naive to assume that these same social pressures, away from the battlefield, did not operate among those men, conscripted and volunteers, who did serve in the military during the Vietnam era.[8] Personal preference and a general unbalanced competition between the skilled and unskilled for noncombatant assignments can be assumed to have been made more accentuated by an irony of military reality. Those military occupational specialties (MOS), such as rifleman, which entail the greatest exposure to danger, are the same MOSs which require the lowest level of preservice training and ability. Operating under the combat demands of the Southeast Asian involvement, the U.S. armed forces acted with blind "rationality" when it assigned individuals of lower socioeconomic origins to those positions more susceptible to mortal casualty.

Interestingly enough a reverse phenomenon is operative for assignments in the officer ranks. Two factors are assumed to divide the officers from the enlisted ranks with respect to casualties. First, the negative relationship between socioeconomic status and casualties should be mediated by the gross underrepresentation of blacks and lower-class whites among officers.[9] In the absence of the wide divergence in social background existent among enlisted men, assignment procedures for officers take on a more egalitarian and voluntaristic quality. Hence, the wholesale assignment of lesser qualified individuals from lower socioeconomic origins into positions more susceptible to casualty should not be as characteristic of officer personnel procedures as it is for those of enlisted men. Second, there exists among officers a special sense of military tradition and honor, which could actually create a preference for the more dangerous combat arms assignments.[10] Even from a totally "careerist" perspective, service in a "high risk" combat position can be extremely important in field grade or higher level promotions.

METHOD

Our procedure utilizes the community as the unit of analysis. "Community" for our purposes is defined as one of the U.S. Bureau of the Census-delineated community areas within the city of Chicago and as the separate suburbs within the remainder of Cook County. This provides us with a sample of 101 Cook County communities, for which we derived five major variables.

In our tabular analysis, we have taken the casualty rate of each community as the dependent variable.[11] The Cook County casualty data used in this study included all Army personnel killed in action between

1964 and mid-1968, and all casualties, regardless of branch of service, killed between mid-1968 and 1972. These casualties were allocated to their respective communities by coding their pre-induction home addresses. A casualty rate was computed by dividing the number of casualties under consideration by the total number of males of the same population who were in the age group eligible for military service. In this way, we control for both the age and size characteristics of a given community. For our multiple regression analysis, however, the raw number of casualties per community is used, and the demographic uniqueness of the community is controlled by including the number of males eligible for military service in the community as a separate independent variable.

Two other independent variables, in addition to the size of the age-eligible population, are considered for each community. One is racial composition, which is merely the black percentage of each community according to the 1970 census. The other is an estimate of the socioeconomic level of the community. Our index for the community's socioeconomic status is obtained by summing the Z-scores of each community on three socioeconomic indicators—median family income, percentage of the male labor force in white-collar occupations, and median school years completed. This index is, therefore, a composite measure of income, occupation, and education.

We have also included a measure of military participation as an intervening variable in our multiple regression analysis. The inclusion of such a variable will allow us to consider the possibility that higher casualties among certain segments of the population are simply a function of higher military participation by these segments. Such a finding would considerably undermine our reasons for focusing on personnel assignment practices within the military and require us to shift our attention to the matter of differential recruitment. The level of military participation was obtained by drawing a random sample of Vietnam veterans from the bonus records of the Illinois Veterans Commission.[12] From the addresses included in these files, the number of veterans in the sample from each community was tabulated. It is this number that we use as our measure of military participation for each community.

Since all of the variables can be measured on continuous scales, the mode of analysis chosen for this exposition is multiple regression. The moderate sample size of 101 communities makes procedures such as tabular partialling not as feasible. Multiple regression analysis is especially appropriate for our present purposes since it will represent the degree of relationship between any two variables after controlling for all the other variables in the model. This will enable us to distinguish the direct effect of socioeconomic status on combat deaths separate from the extraneous effects of race and level of military participation. With the use of path analysis, we will then be able to examine the indirect effect of socioeconomic status on casualties as it operates through military participation.

RESULTS

Table 1 provides an overview of the relationship between casualty rates and the racial composition and socioeconomic indicators for the communities in this sample. The more telling standardized regression coefficients are presented in Table 2, while these same figures are used to portray a model of community casualties in the path diagram of Figure 1. All of these statistics make no distinction between officers and enlisted men.

Central attention must be given to the nonsignificant direct relationship (0.06) between racial composition and number of casualties when all other variables are controlled. The source of black citizens among casualties can be found in the significant negative relationship (−0.48) between the percentage of a community's population which is black and the general socioeconomic status of the community. It is the significant negative relationship (−0.32) between the socioeconomic level of the community and its number of casualties, however, which confirms the overrepresentation of all those of lower socioeconomic origins, regardless of race, among casualties of the second Indochina war.

A community's wartime losses are shown by these results to be not significantly related to the level of military participation in the community. As should be expected, degree of military participation is extremely dependent on the number of males who are eligible for military service in the community (0.66) and to a lesser degree on racial composition (0.13) and socioeconomic level (−0.18).[13] It is these results which point to allocative mechanisms within the assignment process of the military as the source of high casualties among certain segments of the population. The policy question of "who shall serve" becomes not nearly so important as "who shall serve how."

That a different casualty calculus is at work for officers and enlisted men is evident in the results contained in Table 3. Here the relationship between socioeconomic level of the community and the number of enlisted casualties is shown to be more significantly negative (−0.35) in the absence of officer casualties. On the other hand, the relationship between the socioeconomic level of the community and the number of officer casualties is shown to be significantly positive (0.25).

These data justify our suggested model for the likelihood of casualty. We argue that among enlisted men, the military assignment process

TABLE 1
Social Stratification of Combat Casualties: Cook County Communities (n = 101)

Indicator		Number of Communities	Casualty Rate per 10,000 Age-Eligible Males
Race (% black)	Less than 10%	63	15.92
	10%–89%	26	12.89
	90% or more	12	19.40
Income (median family)	$ 4,000– 7,000	11	17.19
	7,000– 9,000	7	16.01
	9,000–11,000	22	15.38
	11,000–13,000	33	14.15
	13,000–15,000	17	13.41
	15,000–17,000	6	8.17
	17,000 or more	5	6.27
Education (median for population)	Less than 10	18	19.64
	10.00–10.99	19	17.21
	11.00–11.99	20	13.94
	12.00–12.99	39	12.51
	13.00 or more	5	5.79
Occupation (% of male labor force in white-collar)	Less than 20	11	18.41
	20.00–29.99	23	16.81
	30.00–39.99	26	15.57
	40.00–49.99	15	14.26
	50.00–59.99	7	10.95
	60.00 or more	19	8.72

[402]

114

TABLE 2

Standardized Regression Coefficients for Casualties and Military Participation
as Related to Predictor Variables: Cook County Communities (n = 101)

	Size of Age-Eligible Male Population	Socioeconomic Status	Racial Composition	Military Participation	R^2
Casualties[a]	0.66[b]	−0.32[b]	−0.06	0.03	0.61[b]
Military participation	0.68[b]	−0.18[b]	0.13[c]	−	0.56[b]

a. Based on both all Army casualties from 1964 to mid-1968, and all casualties (regardless of branch of service) from mid-1968 through 1972.
b. Significant at .001 level of statistical significance.
c. Significant at .05 level of statistical significance.

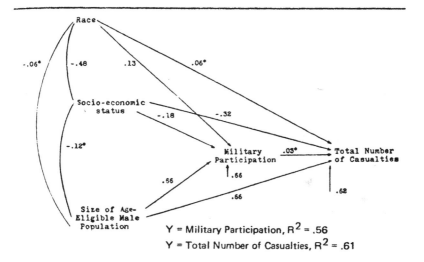

Y = Military Participation, R^2 = .56
Y = Total Number of Casualties, R^2 = .61

* denotes that the partial standardized regression coefficient was not statistically significant

Figure 1: Path Diagram Depicting Relationships Between Race, Socioeconomic Status, Size of Age-Eligible Male Population, Military Participation, and Total Number of Casualties

operated under the norms of bureaucratic efficiency and relied on criteria highly contingent on socioeconomic origins to channel individuals from lower-class backgrounds into positions more susceptible to combat

115

TABLE 3

Standardized Regression Coefficients for Officer and Enlisted Casualties as Related to Predictor Variables: Cook County Communities (n = 101)

	Total Number[a] of Casualties	Size of Age-Eligible Population	Socioeconomic Status	Racial Composition	Military Participation	R^2
Officer	61	0.32[b]	0.25[b]	−0.05	0.06	0.18[b]
Enlisted	762	0.66[b]	−0.35[b]	−0.03	0.04	0.66[b]

a. Based on both all Army casualties from 1964 to mid-1968, and all casualties (regardless of branch of service) from mid-1968 through 1972.
b. Significant at .001 level of statistical significance.

[404]

casualties. Socioeconomic status and not race is the primary sociological determinant of variation in the distribution of casualties.

On the other hand, we suggest that assignment processes operated differently among officers, creating a significantly dissimilar relationship between socioeconomic measures and casualties. Though our data cannot explicitly demonstrate any relationship between normative orientation and casualties, we have speculated that the importance of combat service as an element of career success and the survival of the traditional view of an officer as a heroic leader may have contributed to an overrepresentation of more highly qualified officers from higher socioeconomic backgrounds among casualties.

Casualties must be counted as the greatest cost of a nation's involvement in war. In the Vietnam war, the distribution of casualties became a political issue of great magnitude. The findings of this research obviously do not alter the political and moral issues that have to be confronted due to the unequal distribution of the burdens of war. However, these results call into question the popular view of the incidence of casualties as being oversimplified. At the same time, they reaffirm the observation that casualties do have a social pattern. Though this study by no means supplies a comprehensive overview of this pattern, it is a relevant first step.

NOTES

1. Albert J. Mayer and Thomas F. Hoult, "Social Stratification and Combat Survival," Social Forces 34, 2 (December 1955): 155-159.

2. Specific criticisms of the methodological strategy of Mayer and Hoult are contained in Gilbert Badillo, "Socio-Economic Status, Military Participation, and Casualties," unpublished Master's thesis (Providence, R.I.: Brown University, June, 1975).

3. "Death in Vietnam: Class, Poverty, and the Risks of War," Politics and Society 3 (Spring, 1973): 313-328.

4. An excellent historical narrative of racial integration in the U.S. armed forces can be found in John Hope Franklin, *From Slavery to Freedom* (New York: Knopf, 1974), and Charles C. Moskos, Jr., *The American Enlisted Man* (New York: Russell Sage Foundation, 1970).

5. The importance of the Weberian concepts of rationality and bureaucracy with respect to military institutions is emphasized in H. H. Turney-High, *Primitive War: Its Practice and Concepts* (Columbia, S.C.: University Press, 1949); Stanislaw Andrzejewski, *Military Organization and Society* (London: Routledge and Kegan Paul, 1954); Marion J. Levey, Jr., *Modernization and the Structure of Societies*

(Princeton, N.J.: Princeton University Press, 1966); and Morris Janowitz, *The Professional Soldier* (New York: Free Press, 1971).

6. Here we mention only two of a number of related works: Melvin L. Kohn, *Class and Conformity* (Homewood, Ill.: Dorsey Press, 1969), and James S. Coleman, *Resources for Social Change: Race in the United States* (New York: Wiley-Interscience, 1971).

7. The degree to which this occurred is revealed by a comparison of level of education for Vietnam era veterans and nonveterans in John D. Kasarda and Wayne J. Villemez, "Veteran Status and Socioeconomic Attainment," Armed Forces and Society 2 (Spring 1976)–this issue.

8. We must express our appreciation to James Linger for reminding us that volunteering for noncombat military service was for many Americans an effective means of avoiding being conscripted for combat arms.

9. Discussion of the degree to which blacks are underrepresented in the officer corps can be found in Morris Janowitz, "The Social Demography of the All-Volunteer Armed Force," Annals of the American Academy of Political and Social Science 406 (March, 1973): 86-93; and Morris Janowitz and Charles C. Moskos, Jr., "Racial Composition in the All-Volunteer Force: Policy Alternatives," Armed Forces and Society 1 (Fall, 1974): 109-123.

10. The significance of the heroic ideal for officers even in a modern military establishment is emphasized in Samuel Huntington, *The Soldier and the State* (Cambridge, Mass.: Harvard University Press, 1957); and Morris Janowitz, *The Professional Soldier.*

11. A total of 850 casualty records was used to compute our casualty measures. Roger W. Little, "The Dossier in Military Organization," in Stanton Wheeler, ed., *On Record: Files and Dossiers in American Life* (New York: Basic Books, 1969).

12. Illinois is one of those states which has legislation providing all veterans with active duty experience in Vietnam a financial award of $100 to those individuals returning alive, and $1,000 to the next of kin of casualties. This military participation measure, which is unavailable at the tract level from census records, was created by randomly selecting every seventy-fifth case (944 veterans' records) from the total population of records.

13. Previous and more recent details on the relationship between military participation and race and socioeconomic status are examined in Janowitz and Moskos, "Racial Composition," and Janowitz, "Social Demography."

GILBERT BADILLO, a graduate student in Sociology at the University of Chicago, is currently working on research in military participation.

G. DAVID CURRY is a Ph.D. candidate in Sociology at the University of Chicago and has served in Vietnam. He is currently engaged in a quantitative study of the rank and personnel structure of the U.S. military establishment for the period 1900-1970.

118

Cohesion and Disintegration
in the American Army

AN ALTERNATIVE PERSPECTIVE

PAUL L. SAVAGE
RICHARD A. GABRIEL
St. Anselm's College

Introduction

If societies can be compared in their political systems, they should be comparable in the management of their war making. More importantly, the performance of their military forces can be cross-evaluated respecting cohesion, discipline, and professional leadership. Toward the end of the Viet Nam war, the U.S. Army exhibited clear indicators of disintegration under what appear to be conditions of relatively minimal combat stress.

The purpose of this analysis is to examine indicators of disintegration, together with some historical comparisons, all in the context of socio-military processes which simultaneously appear to affect military cohesion in the U.S. Army. These processes are:

1. *The replacement of a traditional "gladiatorial" officer stereotype with the managerial combat nonparticipant, where efficiency instead of "honor" becomes the performance standard.* The managerial disposition undermines, it seems to us, the sense of military honor. Inasmuch as the latter is involved with "profitless" personal sacrifice, a managerial "commander" may tend to see his troops as a resource base of potential career survival and profitability, not as a moral charge upon his honor and duty rested in reciprocal trust and self-sacrifice.[1]

ARMED FORCES AND SOCIETY, Vol. 2 No. 3, May 1976
© 1976 Inter-University Seminar on Armed Forces and Society

[340]

2. *A radical inflation of officer strengths.* Where the officer percentage of Army strength during World War II and in Korea reached 7% and 9% respectively, by the end of the Viet Nam war officers constituted approximately 15% of total strength. There is further evidence that with the swelling in the officer corps, a corresponding decline in quality occurred.

3. *Destruction of primary military groups.* Military units whose first task is combat resist disintegration principally because of the integrity of the primary military unit—the squad, platoon, or company. The American Army since World War II has experienced a progressive reduction of primary group cohesion until the Viet Nam war, where it may be said it ceased to exist at all. The proximate cause of primary group destruction was the rotation system.

We suggest two interrelated hypotheses:

(1) The United States Army underwent a progressive disintegration and finally an accelerating one over an approximate period, 1961-1971, and that to a significant degree the disintegrative process operated independently of sociopolitical factors in the larger American society.

(2) The disintegration of the Army, together with the dissolution of primary group cohesion, is directly related to the loss of officer professionalism expressed in the pervasive phenomenon of "managerial careerism."

It is, perhaps, useful to define cohesion and disintegration; by defining one, the other follows, since they are reciprocals. Disintegration of a military organization is the emergence of conditions which make effective operations impossible. These conditions are desertion, mutiny, assassination of leaders, and other phenomena at odds with discipline, such as drug usage. Cohesion is assurance that a military unit will attempt to perform its assigned orders or charged mission, irrespective of the situation. Victory or defeat is not a condition of measurement.

It is our contention that a condition of cohesion or disintegration in a military structure is by and large a function of circumstances generated within the military structure. This is to suggest that such factors as the decline in professionalism and the military ethos are more likely to be responsible for disintegration than are factors operant in the society at large. This does not deny, of course, that there are linkages between the larger society and its military structure, for clearly such linkages do exist. With regard to Viet Nam, for example, such linkages were evident in the adoption of a rotation policy designed to avoid a total war footing, the isolation of elites in colleges which acted to reduce the high-quality pool of potential officers, and the obvious restrictions placed upon military operations as a result of domestic political considerations. Yet while we do not imply that military structures are totally independent of wider societal forces, we suggest that other forces internal to the military structure—such as a developed sense of professionalism and an honored military ethic—are far more crucial in determining the degree of cohesion that an army will manifest under stress.

To illustrate the process of military disintegration, historical comparisions are essential. The first comparison is that of the German historical model, an army that maintained its cohesion under enormous pressures even during final defeat in World War II. The German model is appropriate for two reasons. It is a product of western civilization, exhibiting more commonalities with other western armies than differences. In this regard one can point to similarities in organizational and value structures, belief systems rested in patriotism, and conscription based in citizen mass armies.[2] The second reason is that the cohesion of the German Army has been studied in some detail using empirical data.[3]

THE GERMAN OFFICER CORPS
AND THE BURDEN OF SACRIFICE

Despite repeated catastrophes, the Wehrmacht remained so cohesive that it fought effectively until eventually overrun. And indeed, never did it surrender after the fashion of World War I. German speed, discipline, and efficiency in the attack combined with determined, relentless, and methodical resistance over thousands of miles have been attributed to a multitude of generalities including nationalism, National Socialist ideology, and "inherent militarism." Little of the available evidence reveals these factors as important, or indeed that any special *external* sociopolitical factors acted as major influences on military cohesion. Indeed the cohesion of the German Army "was sustained only to a very slight extent by the National Socialist political convictions of German soldiers . . . and that more important in the motivation of the determined resistance of the German soldier was the ready satisfaction of certain primary personality demands afforded by the social organization of the army."[4] German battlefield cohesion related directly to the individual soldier's personal reinforcement due to interactions of esteem and respect with his primary group—squad, platoon, and company—and to his perceptions of his immediate officers and NCOs as men of honor eminently deserving of respect, who in turn cared for their men.[5] German Army officers were very carefully selected and virtually all had education superior to the average German. Moreover, the high selection standards for German officers were maintained throughout the war.[6]

When restrictive standards are combined with very high casualties, the result inevitably is the severe contraction of an officer corps—especially one insisting on rigorous qualification. In 1939, the German Field Army contained 81,314 officers and 2,741,064 enlisted men. Officers constituted 2.96% of total fighting strength; for the German Army as a whole, the figure was 2.86%. The officer/enlisted ratio was 1:34.[7]

German officers clearly suffered losses in much higher proportion than their share of the force strength: that is, 2.86% of officers absorbed 3.5% of the number killed. The German Army lost 1,709,739 men killed in action including 59,965 officers. 30.8% of the German officer corps was killed in action as against 26.1% of the enlisted ranks.[8]

In Germany, military rank and social status overlapped extensively, as did the indicators of sacrifice. Europeans keep track of their nobility by way of such references as the *Almanach de Gotha*. Germans, being the researchers they are, have accounted, in part, for the losses of their noble class in World War II. One source lists 8,284 German noblemen; of these, 4,690 were lost in action, or 56.6% of those listed.[9] Noblemen tended to enter the officer corps, and these high losses are similar to the losses of the officer corps itself, but 25.8% higher. It seems evident that, in some measure, the attitude of deference and respect the German soldier showed his social and military superiors was merited in turn by the willingness of his "betters" to assume the costs of status.

Certainly, a main cohesive factor of the primary group, namely the company, in the German Army was the sense of responsibility and performance of duty demonstrated by German officers. Concern by German officers for their soldiers was, in turn, reciprocated by their men, reinforcing the unit cohesion that remained high in the German Army to the end.[10] To some extent then, military cohesion is a function of the quality of the officer corps, its skill, dedication, and readiness to sacrifice.

The readiness of German officers to lead was apparent to the German soldier; however, this capacity for leadership did not hinge upon a dedication to the "cause"—Nazi ideology or even nationalism.[11] This point is the heart of the Shils and Janowitz study already cited. Such findings, of course, contravene the conventional wisdom which tends to lay military disintegration at the feet of a society badly fragmented. However, in all German field operations, one found a readiness by officers to undertake an inordinate share of risk and to regard any insulation of officers from the risks of battle as dishonorable, regardless of prevailing civil societal disharmony.[12]

The fighting qualities of the German Army in large measure can be attributed to the quality of its leadership. The leadership remained, throughout the war, at a very low percentage of total strength, even declining to half of authorized strength at the end. The Germans, therefore, may have achieved a type of optimum leadership quotient, relying on high quality and low numbers of officers. Officer visibility to the German soldier was apparently maintained at a level sufficient to meet the need on the soldiers' part to be cared for by their officer leaders yet not overwhelmingly through an excessive "visibility of brass." Senior officers, while remote from enlisted ranks and rarely interfering in detail with smaller commands, nonetheless bore a substantial share of sacrifice as the data show and as German soldiers were aware; the front-line soldier knew his officers would remain with him "even unto death." Equal assumption of the burden of sacrifice and death, perceived by German officers as both necesary and right, was not the case with American senior officers in Viet Nam. Indeed, quite the opposite situation occurred.

To be sure, other factors affected military cohesion: the sense of Germany besieged, the traditional deference of a subject-oriented culture, a belief that military service was an honor, some secondary influence in Hitler as a father image, and fear of the security police. But all of these remained far less important than the primary group and its respected leadership. An important additional element adding to cohesion in the German Army was the German policy of rotating divisions out of the line for reconstitution of primary groups.[13] Contrarily, American policy in all recent wars has been to maintain units in combat for protracted periods, keeping them filled by the replacement stream, and, in effect, considerably reducing the maintenance of primary group ties in American units and, hence, unit cohesion.[14]

The German historical model during World War II emerges as one of high military professionalism and cohesion. The cement of the German Army was the sense of the soldier as belonging, of deferring to and admiring immediate leaders who could be counted on to accept sacrifice far beyond what was demanded of the ordinary soldier. Using even these minimal measures of cohesive professionalism the American Army offers an interesting study in contrast.

DISINTEGRATION IN THE UNITED STATES ARMY

In Viet Nam, of course, the American Army underwent no catastrophic reverses and suffered few losses in comparison to the German Army or, indeed, the American Army in World War II. Still, by 1969 the American Army began to disintegrate under comparatively minimal stress.[15] The troubles faced by the U.S. Army ranged from high desertion rates to drug addiction, mutinies, and the "fragging" or assassination of officers and

NCOs. The deserters, "fraggers," and mutineers have often been explained as "understandable" expressions of men engaged in a war both unpopular and without home-front support. Others, especially the military, explained the indiscipline of their troops as an unavoidable product of the permissive society from which the youthful soldier came. Even the draft, it is said, exacerbated the problem of cohesion. Inclined to be invidiously discriminatory, mostly the lower classes were called upon to serve. Privileged upper-status groups, insulated in colleges and universities by the law and the logic of the selective service system, managed, disproportionately, to avoid service. This point may have some virtue in a discussion of cohesion in the American Army. For instance, in World War II, 8.5% of those serving, aged 20-24, had completed four or more years of college. By Korea, this percentage had fallen to 3.9% of all veterans; by Viet Nam, as of 1971, the percentage of those completing four years of college before service fell to 2.6%.[16] Even so, the level of soldiers' education probably has no more than a marginal to overall cohesion, despite the resentment created by the ability to use higher education as a device to avoid ground combat.[17]

Still others have explained the 1969-1971 disintegration of the U.S. Army as an awakening by the ordinary soldier to the immorality of the war and the stirring of "true consciousness." Such ideological perspectives are unconvincing. We know that military cohesion exists quite apart from politics and ideologies in the civilian political systems. Specifically, a sense of active patriotism, nationalism, or other ideologies are not necessarily central to military discipline and cohesion. That is, a continued sense of "cause," at whatever level of saliency, is not vital to military cohesion. In effect, this literature degrades any sense of mission on the part of soldiers, transcendent of the immediate tactical mission.[18]

If home-front support, ideologies, or "system alienation" have little or limited effect on military cohesion, why did the Viet Nam war reveal disintegrative indicators in such clustered profusion toward the end of the war? These indicators include the following: rising desertion rates over a 10-year period with a great acceleration toward the end of the conflict, and in notable excess of World War II and Korean rates; mutinous outbreaks in combat units; and an ever-rising number of attempted and actual murders of officers by their troops.[19] Drug addiction, additionally, became a plague of vast proportions, especially in the last four years of the war. An examination of each of these indicators allows the research to gauge with some accuracy the degree of disintegration within the U.S. Army in Viet Nam and make inferences concerning the major factors associated with decay.

INDICATORS OF DISINTEGRATION

Desertion

One sign of disintegration frequently cited is the desertion rate, a designation assigned a soldier who is absent 30 days without authorization. Table 1 reveals comparative desertion rates for three wars. Desertion rates in Viet Nam far exceed those of World War II and Korea; indeed, the rate reached pronounced proportion between the years 1965-1971, where it increased 468%! In this same period, after 1968, the level and intensity of combat actually dropped off. Thus the data note a paradox: American desertion rates seemed to increase as the level of combat decreased (as measured by deaths in action).

Between 1968 and 1971, the deaths due to hostile action declined steadily each year for an overall four-year decline of 84.6% (see Table 2). In the same period desertion rates each year steadily increased for an overall four-year increase of 60.5%. The data thus suggest that whatever the reasons for increased desertion rates, increased combat loss is certainly not among them. Viet Nam desertion rates exceeded those of World War II by over 10 per thousand at their height, and over 41 per thousand of the Korean War at maximum desertion rates. Indeed, the annual rates of increase in desertions during the Viet Nam war exceeded anything in recent experience, despite the fact that in historical terms it extracted comparatively low sacrifice levels.

"Fragging"

The incidences of fragging during the Viet Nam war were so high as to become one of the outstanding deviant characteristics of the period. Table 3 illustrates the number of fraggings which the Defense Department admits. The assaults by "explosive device" exclude attempts to kill "leadership elements" by other means such as rifle, automatic weapons fire, ambush by claymore mines, and misdirection to hostile ambush. Moreover, the figures released as official conflict with the "official" testimony of Major General Kerwin before a House of Representatives subcommittee on the subject. Since there appear to be no historical analogies for large-scale "fragging," conventional explanations for its occurrence lack credibility. General Kerwin's testimony relied heavily on conventional wisdom referring to the "permissive" society and enlisted men's resentment toward officers and NCOs because of necessary "authoritarian" means "proper in a combat environment."[20] At no time, apparently, has the ethical quality of the officer corps been addressed by

TABLE 1

Desertion Rates, United States Army, World War II, Korea, Viet Nam[a]
in Rate Per Thousand

World War II			Korea			Viet Nam		
Fiscal Year	Rate	% chng. ea. yr.	Fiscal Year	Rate	% chng. ea. yr.	Fiscal Year	Rate	% chng. ea. yr.
1945	45.2	–28.3	1954	15.7	–30.0	1972	53.3	–27.6
1944	63.0		1953	22.3	+ 0.0	1971	73.5	+40.5
1943	Not avail.		1952	22.0	+54.0	1970	52.3	+23.3
1942	Not avail.		1951	14.3		1969	42.4	+45.7
						1968	29.1	+35.9
						1967	21.4	+45.5
						1966	14.7	– 6.7
						1965	15.7	

a. Data source: Department of Defense.

[347]

TABLE 2

Data Relating Overall Army Strength to Overall Viet Nam Forces Level, to Desertion Rates
And Deaths Due to Hostile Action By Year of Engagement

Year	Strength of the Army[a]		Total Ground Forces Strength Viet Nam[b]	Deaths Due to Hostile Action	U.S. Army Desertion Rate per 1,000	U.S. Army Deserters (%)
	Officer	Enlisted				
1965	111,541	1,079,750	184,300	[c]	15.7	1.10 (n=13,177)
1966	117,205	1,296,600	385,300		14.7	3.12 (n=44,244)
1967	142,964	1,401,750	485,600	8,581[d]	21.4	1.73 (n=26,782)
1968	165,569	1,357,000	543,400	9,387	29.1	2.58 (n=39,321)
1969	171,182	1,153,000	475,200	7,043	42.4	4.27 (n=56,608)
1970	160,814	1,161,444	343,600	3,911	52.3	6.07 (n=76,643)
1971	144,595	962,605	139,000	1,449	73.4	7.13 (n=79,027)
1972	120,982	686,692	25,200	195	53.2	5.52 (n=44,643)
1973	117,860	703,031	—	—	37.3	3.95 (n=32,500)
						(Total n=380,445)

a. Strength of the Army figures extracted from fiscal year 1974 *Authorizations for Military Procurement, Research and Development, Construction Authorization for the Safeguard ABM, and Active Duty and Selected Reserve Strengths: Hearings Before the Committee on Armed Services, United States Senate* (see previous fiscal year hearings for additional data). Also, *Department of Defense Appropriations for 1974, Hearings, Before a Subcommittee on Appropriations, House of Representatives* (see previous year hearings for additional data).
b. These figures extracted from the *New York Times* over several years and from the *New York Times Index*.
c. "Killed in Action" as a term was not used in Viet Nam in official reports. Instead the term "Death due to hostile action" was substituted.
d. Cumulative deaths from 1961.

TABLE 3[a]

Assaults with Explosive Devices—Viet Nam (As of 31 December 1972)
Incidents Involving Explosive Devices

	Total Incidents	Category AA[b]	PA[c]	Deaths	Injuries	OFF/NCO	Intended Victim EM	VN	UNK
CY 69	126(239)[d]	96	30	37	191	70	17	7	32
CY 70	271(386)	209	62	34	306	154	40	20	57
CY 71	333	222	111	12	198	158	43	28	104
CY 72	58	27	31	3	19	31	7	4	20
Totals	788(1,016)	554	234	86	714	413	107	59	213

a. Table reproduced verbatim from Department of Defense source.
b. Actual Assaults—Motive determined as intent to kill, do bodily harm, or to intimidate.
c. Possible Assaults—Possible motive determined as intent to kill, do bodily harm, or to intimidate.
d. Figures in parentheses obtained from Congressional Hearings—See Note 20 infra.

the Congress at the time of investigations into military discipline and "fragging."

Mutiny

Concurrent with the surfacing of "fragging" data, more ominous signs of military disintegration became public. Among these signs were "combat refusals." In more rigorous armies they would have been called mutiny—which in fact they were. Inquiries to the Department of Defense extracted the following comment with respect to mutinous outbreaks: "As to so-called combat refusals, data on incidents of this nature are not maintained by the Department of the Army. I do not know the source of the statistics cited by Senator Stennis."[21] We are limited to noting that Senator John Stennis of the Senate Armed Forces Committee observed, during the hearings on the Nomination of Robert R. Froehlke as Secretary of the Army in 1971, that there were 68 refusals to fight in 1968 for the seven combat divisions in Viet Nam, and in 1970 35 "individual" refusals occurred in the First Air Cavalry Division alone.[22] Obviously if this number of mutinies took place in a division with such an extensive (and honored) combat record, the level was probably higher, for example, in the American Division which was involved in My Lai. Even if all other divisions had only the same number of mutinous events as the First Cavalry, then in 1970 there could have been as many as 245 such "refusals" to fight. Without official data we can only infer that if the progressive and symptomatic military disintegration evidenced by desertions and assassinations of leaders is also reflected in mutinous outbreaks, the number of these latter incidents was very probably quite large. Moreover, unlike mutinous outbreaks of the past and in other armies, usually short-lived events, the progressive unwillingness of American soldiers to fight to the point of public disobedience of orders took place over a four-year period between 1968 and 1971, fitting the data on fragging and desertion with a convergent degree of credibility: mutinies occurring in Viet Nam fell into patterned behavior and did not occur as sporadic events.

Drugs

The problem of drug usage among American troops in Viet Nam, particularly hard addictive drugs such as heroin, approaches a situation which is *sui generis*. The acquisition, organized distribution, and use of drugs cannot be dissociated from crime and corruption at high and intermediate command and staff levels. Here we find evidence of an exceptional degree of disintegration not only among the troops of the line but among their leaders as well. Further, when members of the officer corps—some at very high levels indeed—are involved in drug profiteering, it is not unrealistic to expect the stain of guilt to spread to other members of the officer corps and to find that the troops come to hold their officers in contempt. That troops in battle, however minimal the battle, would be subjected to the organized pushing of hard narcotics is without parallel. More extraordinary, drugs were publicly available in places known to all high and low, and little was done to stem the drug trade. Here we find a higher officer corps so committed to policy expediency that the organized distribution of drugs was accepted as necessary to the support of the South Vietnamese government, itself the purveyor of the drugs destroying the army that defended it.[23]

The true extent of hard drug usage by the American troops in the last years of Viet Nam is unknown. The method used for detection in Viet Nam was screening by urinalysis just prior to departure. By this method 5.5% of the troops were shown to have used heroin. Few accept this percentage as realistic since so many ways to avoid detection were devised by the troops being screened. In a 1971 survey conducted by the Human Resources Research Organization (Humrro) of over 40,000 service people worldwide, the extent of drug usage in the services in general and in Viet Nam in particular was found to be over five times as high as "official" figures. Table 4 sets out the Humrro findings.[24]

In Viet Nam, almost a third of the Army had used a hard narcotic while one in five U.S. soldiers used narcotic drugs worldwide. No comparative

TABLE 4

Percentage of United States Army Using Drugs In The Last Twelve Months (1971) By Place of Service

| Service Location | Type of Drug | | | | |
	Marijuana %	Other Psychedelic Drugs %	Stimulants %	Depressants %	Narcotic Drugs %
Continental U.S.	41.3	28.4	28.9	21.5	20.1
Europe	40.2	33.0	23.0	14.0	13.1
Viet Nam	50.9	30.8	31.9	25.1	28.5
Other S.E. Asia	42.0	23.2	24.7	18.1	17.6
Total Army	42.7	29.4	28.0	20.4	20.1

a. *Drug Abuse in the Military: Hearing Before the Subcommittee on Drug Abuse in the Military of the Committee on Armed Services, United States Senate, Ninety-Second Congress,* 1972, p. 127.

modern western population shows rates of hard drug usage remotely resembling those of the U.S. Army in 1971. Further, the introduction, distribution, and sale of heroin in Viet Nam was tied to an organized system operated and run by high-ranking members of the Vietnamese government. More remarkable are judgments about the American "Country Team" headed by Ambassador Ellsworth Bunker. In his work on the production, distribution, and sale of heroin in Southeast Asia, Alfred W. McCoy provides evidence that not only were the American diplomats and military high command aware of Vietnamese official involvement in the heroin racket, but, by burying the facts and blocking investigations, they were also guilty of continued complicity.[25] An even more direct complicity was charged to the CIA, which flew heroin and opium shipments from Laos to Viet Nam by way of Air America, a CIA subsidiary.[26] Both the CIA and the American diplomatic corps frustrated and blocked investigations into the heroin traffic by other elements of the federal government.[27] In any case, heroin usage in the Army is introduced here as another unambiguous sign of military internal decay verging on collapse. No army can function, much less fight, when 28.5% of its troops use heroin, nor can it defer to a leadership that tolerates drug racketeering.

THE AMERICAN OFFICER CORPS

Armies in large measure are products of their leadership: good leadership, dedication, integrity, and competence bring military cohesion. Conversely, bad leadership seems intimately associated with disintegration: a high desertion rate might be explainable, even a mutiny or two, but when desertion, fragging, mutiny, and drug addiction come together in staggering proportions in a short four or five years, oversimplified references to permissive societies and national "fragmentation" because of unpopular wars will not suffice as credible explanations.[28] Knowing well that the heroin racket destroying their forces was operated by their high-ranking Vietnamese allies, in collusion with higher American authorities, not a single senior officer in Viet Nam protested or resigned over the situation. Indeed, there seem to have been no protest resignations by generals for any reason at all while the United States Army was literally coming apart as an effective combat mechanism. Why did all of this occur and in this war alone? To what degree can the officer corps be faulted? How effective were leadership efforts to build primary groups and strengthen morale? How willing was the leadership to share the burden of combat and death by exposing itself to the same hazards as the line soldiers? The answers to these questions certainly would aid in an understanding of the process of disintegration which occurred in the American Army in Viet Nam.

One of the first factors concerning the Army officer corps is its large numbers. Until 1918, the officer corps averaged about 5.3% of the total strength of the Army. In the thirties, officer percentages varied between 7% and 9%. At the end of World War II, officers accounted for 7.7% of the strength, minus Army Air Force strength. Table 5 illustrates the expansion of the officer corps which stabilized at about 11% in the sixties, fell to an average of 9% from 1965 to 1967, and then rose to almost 15% of total strength in 1972, a ratio of one officer for every 5.7 enlisted men. Compared to World War II the number of officers had increased by almost 100%. Even compared to 1965, the beginning of the large Viet Nam build-up, officers increased from 9.4% of total strength to 15.0%—an increase of 59.9%. Taken in association with the data in Tables 2, 3 and 4, expanding signs of disintegration seem to be associated with the extreme expansion of the officer corps to levels unknown in the Army. The German Army, we know, was historically "underofficered." Most armies by American standards are underofficered as, indeed, was the French Army in Indo-China.

Where factors external to the military system cannot clearly be tied to military disintegration, internal factors may have the greatest bearing on disintegration during Viet Nam. Some of the principal internal but generally widespread military conditions linked to disintegration, in association with other influences discussed earlier, appear below:

(1) Relative to their number, the American Army officers did not share the combat burden imposed on their men. Indeed, the total number of enlisted men in the front lines was only a small share of all forces. In 1968, at the height of the build-up, fewer than 80,000 combat troops could be put into battle against a maximum strength of 543,000 in Viet Nam.

(2) The tactical nature of the war and its logistical configuration created a circular rather than linear system; that is, large numbers of officers and men, of mostly noncombat specialties, were in base areas. Accordingly, combat troops were exposed to large numbers of high-ranking officers with conspicuously greater privileges and immunity from harm, this more so than in any previous war.

(3) High-ranking officers were associated with a career system that was manifestly corrupt. Inevitably, troops lost respect for leaders who, acutely aware of drug traffic and profiteering, did little to eliminate these unethical and personally gainful practices.

These conditions focus more on the officer corps than on the Army as a whole, and in particular as the overburden of officers may have affected

TABLE 5
Strength of the Army 1867-1974—Officer/Enlisted Comparison

Year	Officer Strength	Enlisted Strength	Total Strength of The Army	Officer/ Enlisted Ratio	Officer Percent of Total Strength
1867[a]	3,056	54,138	57,194	1:17.7	5.34
1898	10,516	199,198	209,714	1:18.94	5.01
1900	4,227	97,486	101,713	1:23.06	4.15
1918	130,485	2,265,257	2,395,742	1:17.36	5.44
1945	891,663	7,376,295	8,267,958	1:8.27	10.78
	(481,466)[b]	(5,741,729)	(6,223,195)	(1:11.92)	(7.73)
1953	145,683	1,388,182	1,533,815	1:9.53	9.49
1955	121,947	987,349	1,109,296	1:8.1	11.0
1956	118,364	907,414	1,025,778	1:7.7	11.5
1957	111,187	886,807	997,994	1:8.0	11.1
1958	104,716	794,209	898,925	1:7.6	11.6
1959	101,690	760,274	861,964	1:7.5	11.8
1960	101,236	771,842	873,078	1:7.6	11.6
1961	100,335	776,327	876,662	1:7.7	11.4
1962	115,578	950,826	1,066,404	1:8.2	10.83
1963	108,299	867,617	975,916	1:8.01	11.09
1964	110,276	854,950	965,226	1:7.42	11.42

[354]

TABLE 5 (Continued)

1965[c]	111,541	1,079,700	1,191,241	1:9.68	9.36
1966	117,205	1,296,600	1,413,805	1:11.06	8.29
(Buildup)					
1967	142,964	1,401,700	1,544,664	1:9.8	9.25
(Tet)					
1968	165,569	1,357,000	1,522,569	1:8.07	11.01
(fragging begins)					
1969	171,882	1,153,000	1,324,882	1:6.7	13.08
1970	160,814	1,161,444	1,262,258	1:7.2	12.6
1971	148,623	971,871	1,120,494	1:6.5	13.26
(End U.S. ground war)					
1972	120,982	686,692	807,674	1:5.7	14.97
1973	117,860	703,031	820,891	1:5.96	14.35
1974	110,260	689,646	799,906	1:6.25	13.78

a. 1867-1964 Figures from Russell F. Weigley, *History of the United States Army* (New York: Macmillan, 1967) pp. 566-569.
b. Data in parentheses reflect strengths of the Army *minus* Army Air Force. Data from *Strength of the Army 1 June 1945* (Reports Control Number GC—pp. 3-31), Copy No. 40, Dated 5 July 1945.
c. For all officer data after 1965 warrant officers are included. Strength figures gathered from multiple congressional sources but primarily from: *Senate Armed Services Committee and House of Representative Committee on Appropriations*, FY 1966-1975.

[355]

TABLE 6
Officer/Enlisted Ratios World War II, Korea, and Viet Nam[a]

Rank	World War II (1945)[b]		Korea (1953)		Viet Nam (1971)[c]	
	No.	Enlisted Ratio	No.	Enlisted Ratio	No.	Enlisted Ratio
General	1,168	1:4,916	479	1:2,953	498	1:1,952
Colonel	8,547	1:672	5,155	1:274	5,947	1:163
Lieutenant Colonel	22,184	1:258	13,100	1:108	14,577	1:67
Major	48,794	1:118	18,271	1:77	22,266	1:44
Captain	135,348	1:42	33,410	1:42	49,073	1:20
First Lieutenant	166,238	1:35	31,920	1:44	23,907	1:41
Second Lieutenant	75,368	1:76	31,467	1:45	13,666	1:71
Warrant Officer 1-4	23,819	1:242	13,483	1:105	18,689	1:52
Total Officers	481,466 =	1:11.9	147,285 =	1:9.6	148,623 =	1:6.5
Total Enlisted	5,741,729		1,414,711		971,871	

a. Figures for 1945 and 1953 from: *Strength of the Army, 1 June 1945* (Copy No. 40, RCS, GC-P3-31): *Strength of the Army 30 June 1953* (Copy No. 122, RCS, CSGPA-332). Data on Viet Nam peak strength from *Hearings Before The Committee on Armed Services United States Senate. Ninety-Third Congress, on S-1263, Part 8, Manpower,* p. 5443. *Strength of the Army* Reports from 1961 on remain classified according to a Senate source.

b. USAAF strength in World War II subtracted.

c. This date is used since fragging, desertion, and drug indicators were then at their highest.

[356]

the enlisted ranks in terms of military cohesion. Thus the remainder of this study will address each of these conditions as they are seen to be indicators, and perhaps even causes, of disintegration in the American Army in Viet Nam.

OFFICERS IN VIETNAM: A BEHAVIORAL PERSPECTIVE

The numbers of the Army Officer Corps must be understood historically and in terms of officer/enlisted strength ratios. Table 6 shows the comparative growth in the officer corps, by rank, over a period of three wars by officer/enlisted ratios. While increases are clear and interesting to note, it is useful to observe additionally the distribution of casualties by grade in the three wars (see Table 7).[29]

From the data in Table 7, it is clear that there has been a shift in the burden of sacrifice away from colonels and generals despite a huge increase in their relative numbers (see Table 6). But with respect to senior officer losses, 34% more enlisted men died in action in Viet Nam than did generals, compared to World War II loss ratios, and 54% more enlisted men died in action that did colonels in Viet Nam, compared to World War II loss ratios for that rank. There are arguments supporting the growth in senior officer strength: the expansion of technology and its "demand" for officer supervision of complex weapons and communications systems, the number of officers in the pipelines, and those backed up in various schools. These arguments are unconvincing and fail to sufficiently explain the almost endless inflation in the size of the officer corps.

Recapitulating the data on strength ratios and the burden of death, Table 8 summarizes the relation between strength ratios, officers and enlisted men, and the relative deprivation experienced in Viet Nam by each group. Where overall officer deaths in combat may have climbed in Viet Nam in comparison to World War II they have also remained small when the total size of the officer corps is considered. Table 8 reveals that in Vietnam, the costs of war fell increasingly on the lower grades, in particular on lower ranking officers and enlisted men, with high-ranking officer deaths decreasing by at least one-third.

It may be rightly pointed out, of course, that the percentage of *all* officer deaths in Viet Nam (10.7%) when compared to World War II (7.01%) is substantially higher. Yet the Viet Nam officer loss is somewhat misleading since it includes the very high number of warrant officer losses (679 of 3,269 or 21% of total officer losses) which were comparatively low during World War II and Korea. If warrant officer losses are deducted from overall officer losses in Viet Nam then the actual officer loss rate becomes 8.4% of all deaths due to hostile action. It must be pointed out

TABLE 7

Officer/Enlisted Ratios Deaths Among Battle Casualties WAR

Rank	World War II[a] (1941-1945)		Korea[b] (1950-1953)		Viet Nam[c] (1961-1972)	
	No.	Enlisted Ratio	No.	Enlisted Ratio	No.	Enlisted Ratio
General	25	1:6,796	2	1:13,084	3	1:9,074
Colonel	77	1:2,206	5	1:5,234	8	1:3,407
Lieutenant Colonel	338	1:503	21	1:1,246	55	1:495
Major	466	1:365	71	1:369	135	1:201
Captain	2,115	1:80	252	1:104	720	1:38
First Lieutenant	5,168	1:33	716	1:37	1,206	1:23
Second Lieutenant	4,499	1:38	445	1:58	463	1:59
Warrant Officer 1-4	122	1:1,393	23	1:1,138	679	1:40
Total Officer Losses	12,810 =	1:13.26	1,512 =	1:17.31	3,269 =	1:8.33
Total Enlisted Losses	169,891		26,169		27,222	

a. Army Battle Casualties—Final Report, RCS-CSAP (OT) 87, 1953, Adjutant General U.S.A. (U.S. Army Air Force losses excluded).
b. *Battle Casualties of the Army;* RCS–CSGPA–363, 1954, OACSGI, U.S.A.
c. Dept. of Defense *Computer Study of Casualties in Viet Nam.*

that the position of warrant officer in the military status system is anomalous; they are not perceived by enlisted ranks as full officers nor by officers as holding the peer status of the commissioned ranks. Even the Army reporting system often reports warrant officer data as distinct from either enlisted or officer data. Additionally, to the extent that warrant officers saw combat, they rarely did so in field positions, acting almost always as helicopter pilots, an activity which accounted for the great majority of their losses, rather than in combat leadership positions.

Still another aspect of officer losses must be addressed. We know that the assassination of officers occurred and that probably fewer than 10% of the attempted or successful assassinations were reported. Accordingly, some of the officer deaths due to hostile action may be attributed to fragging or other means. Indeed there are some rather curious data in the *Computer Study of Casualties in Vietnam* (see Table 7): the Army lost 89 lives attributed to "intentional homicide"; 534 to "accidental homicide"; and 1,394 to "other accidents," for a total of 2,017. These data were not included in "death due to hostile action" but neither are they explained. Additionally, the losses due solely to helicopter incidents are quite high, with 2,352 attributed to "hostile" action and 1,831 to "nonhostile" causes. Of the total 4,183 deaths due to helicopter incidents, 554 were pilots, and thus officers or warrant officers, lost to hostile action. Since

TABLE 8

Comparative Trends in Relative Strengths By Grade and Losses
World War II, Korea, and Viet Nam

	World War II %	Korea %	Viet Nam (1972) %
Officer strength of the Army	7.29	10.5	14.97[a]
Officers deaths of all deaths due to hostile action	7.01	5.45	10.7 (8.4)[b]
Senior officer strength (Gen.-Maj.) of officer corps	16.74	25.12	29.12[c]
Senior officer deaths of all officer deaths due to hostile action	7.07	4.47	6.1

a. See Table 5. By 1972 officer strength had reached 14.97% of total strength.
b. Percentage in parentheses shows officer losses with Warrant Officer deaths in action removed.
c. See Table 6. General officers alone increased their numbers by 152%. In bureaucratic terms the presence of generals creates the Byzantine effect. The higher the rank the greater pressures for numbers needed to affirm the importance of the personage with the rank—a type of military Parkinsonism.

these deaths were reported as "in action" (and the Army tends to give credit for battle death when it can credibly do so), then as much as 17% of all officer losses might have been associated with helicopter crashes. Further, one recalls that the Army admits to assassination by "explosive devices," and there are few machines easier to sabotage than a helicopter. Regardless of how they die, helicopter pilots and their crews, as with the Air Corps crews of World War II, generally die alone. They do not, as a rule, die at the head of their men and, accordingly, their deaths cannot be seen as having the same impact in terms of reinforcing a perception of a shared burden of sacrifice as would be the death of a platoon leader or company commander.

The available evidence suggests that the higher rate of officer casualties in Viet Nam, compared to that of World War II (found in the officially reported statistics), is highly suspect from a variety of perspectives. While the data are confusing, the fact is that combat enlisted troops did not perceive officers undergoing anywhere near the levels of sacrifice that they felt they themselves were experiencing. The sheer number of officers available made officer status appear as unwarrantedly privileged, and the troops reacted against it.

Assuming a trend in modern American war that the probability of death is increasingly rested on lower ranks, it is obvious that the men sent to die may not only miss the reasons for swollen staffs isolated from the risks of battle but may also come to resent the privileged persons so exempted from death. This hostility can hardly be surprising when the system blatantly shields more and more of even its lower ranking members from hazard due to the organizational structure these officers necessarily support. In other wars, combat troops would never have encountered, and understandably resented, the rear echelon "immunes" in the numbers that were visible in Viet Nam.

The organization of the war in Viet Nam was different and is an obvious cause for combat-participation inequities. No longer a "line" war but a three-dimensional one, Viet Nam was set in base camps and fire bases, where those who fought and those who did not intermingled frequently, often providing the enlisted men with an accurate view as to the exaggerated differences in life style between combat and noncombat troops. The impact of the data in Table 8 and of the foregoing analysis is that the leaders who set the rules of the game—those of duty, honor, and country—did not live up to these rules, the enforcement of which was in their charge. And it seems likely that the troops knew it. If, in addition, the officer corps came to be perceived as careerist "sell outs," liars, and hypocrites, the crumbling of the military organization becomes easily understandable.

THE FRENCH EXPERIENCE AND SOME COMPARISONS

Except for the numbers of men and levels of technology, the military challenge faced by France in Indo-China was not radically different from the one assumed by the United States. At the height of its strength the French Expeditionary Force (FEC) averaged about 151,000. For the French Army as a whole, officer strength approximated 4.9% of total strength, in numbers some 33,000 of a total Army strength of 675,000.[30] French officers lost in action in Indo-China totalled 2,221, or 6.73% of the *entire* French Army officer corps.[31] Accordingly, with a peak strength of 151,000 in the FEC, the probable level of officer strength at a norm of 5% was 7,550. Thus 2,221 officers lost in action constituted some 29% of the French officer corps in Indo-China at peak strength. Of total French Army casualties 11.3% were officers (5,347 officers and total French casualties of 47,048). For all services killed, missing, and dying of battle related causes in Indo-China, officers constituted 11.89%.[32] In comparison, the strength of the U.S. Army officer corps averaged 163,395 for the years 1968 through 1971, and American Army officer deaths due to hostile action amounted to 2% of that strength.

We can find no evidence of a loss of cohesion in the FEC, as measured by the standards of the German Army or those of the U.S. Army. No excessive desertion, drugs, mutiny, or fraggings can be detected. French officers maintained their numbers and quality and accepted a burden of death far exceeding that of the men they led relative to their numbers; that is, no indicators of wholesale disintegration occurred in the French Regular Army or the Foreign Legion, which was exclusively French officered. Further, like the German Army, the French suffered defeats— one of them catastrophic—Dien Bien Phu. None of this appeared to affect French Army cohesion.

In many respects the French Army in Indo-China displayed those "German" qualities of a small but excellent officer corps, i.e., the capacity to retain the respect of the troops and the maintenance of primary groups noted earlier. The French Army was largely volunteer in Viet Nam, but the quality of troops, so far as social origins is considered, was not substantially different from what troops have been historically, i.e., of lower social strata in origin. In any case, by 1970 in Viet Nam, 61% of the U.S. Army was volunteer ("RA"). It is true that comparisons can be driven too far and become incredible, yet French troops fought under conditions far more difficult than those the Americans faced, if only because they lacked widespread helicopter capability and massive air support, as well as useful but marginal devices such as defoliation capabilities. On every count the French ability to maintain cohesion under roughly similar conditions is contrasted with American desertion, officer assassination, drug addiction, and mutiny, indicators which signaled disintegration in the American Army.

THE ENVIRONMENTAL AND OPERATIONAL MILIEU

Over some 11 years (1961-1971) of the Viet Nam war we observed that the officer corps swelled to historically high numbers. At the same time the higher quality pool that might have been available for officer recruitment sought a haven in universities and colleges, which themselves became centers of opposition to the war. ROTC became increasingly unpopular and dried up as a source of leadership. We know from available data that the level of college graduates serving in the Army fell drastically during Viet Nam.[33] The final effect of the quality of officer produced by the need to accept officers of low qualifications remains to be examined. That some connection exists between disintegration and a low-quality officer corps appears evident from the data.

Under ordinary circumstances the lowered quality of the officer corps and their inordinate numbers might only marginally have affected operations and discipline. In Korea and World War II, the direct exposure by enlisted men to officers, and especially senior officers, was strictly limited. Basic training involved, primarily, noncommissioned officers and a few company grade commissioned officers. The same condition existed during combat, however protracted. Indeed, the more protracted the battle and the higher the officer losses, the less were officers encountered on the enlisted man's "perception horizon."

In Viet Nam, conditions were radically different. Aggravating the conspicuous differences in the privileges of rank was the rotation policy employed for officers when combat service became necessary. Officers often served in their (combat) commands for approximately six months of 13. Enlisted men normally had to remain in a combat situation for the entire tour.[34] It cannot have escaped the troops that the central concern of such a policy was career advancement ("ticket punching") and not the pursuit of "duty and honor," much less the stress on the traditional image of a commander dedicated to the care of his men. Together with the general rotation system, even more frequent changes in command only increased turbulence in morale and discipline, and the placement of inexperienced commanders with experienced units—the former always attempting to demonstrate their competence as a means of career advancement often by ill-advised tactics or policy changes—created more turbulence. Troops could hardly build much of a level of respect for their officers in this limited time or under such circumstances. And if troop regard for their officers is important to cohesion, then in a situation which does not permit such regard to develop, given both the shortness of time and the conduct of the officers, primary group cohesion cannot but be affected.

Another probable factor destroying cohesion was the excessive burden of battle placed upon draftees. The data in Table 9 show that both absolutely and proportionately Army draftees in Viet Nam became casualties in greater numbers than did volunteers—"lifers." One of the reasons contributing to this condition was the institutional arrangement created by the Army. Volunteers usually received far more consideration in a choice of schooling—almost inevitably noncombat. Further, it was possible in Viet Nam to get out of the "bush" by reenlisting for a longer term and, perhaps, an extension of tour in Viet Nam. The reward for reenlistment amounted to an assurance of a noncombat assignment. By opting for the professional army one could get out of combat; the hostility of the draftee for the "lifer" is then evident and understandable.

Some of the Army higher leadership, recognizing indicators of disintegration, extend a certain *apologia pro vitis nostris.* One argument heard frequently is that rapid changes in society; the dilution of traditional values; and the rejection of home, family, country, and duty in the nation generally, and among the young specifically, are at fault. This forces the Army to bear the burden of coping with youth poorly socialized by parents or with youth who are self-indulgent, hostile to legitimate authority, and indifferent to the national interest. It is the burden of this analysis that such an argument is open to serious question.

First, sociological and historical research reveal that military systems can persist in disciplined and effective form long after the societies that gave them birth have undergone vast changes. The disciplinary ethos of the Roman legion persisted far past the decay of Roman society and well into the period of "barbarization" of the Roman Army. Additionally, the Prussian tradition persevered through multiple regimes and wars until 1945. Accordingly, there appears no causal relationship between the quality of an army and the quality of its society.

Second, the permissive youth who reject the notions of duty, discipline, and sacrifice tend to be concentrated largely in the middle and upper strata who, for a variety of reasons, have been protected from the draft. Privileged classes are not typical of the enlisted combat soldier. Enlisted combat ranks tend, on the contrary, to be filled by lower-middle and working-class strata, groups lacking the affluence permitting either the luxuries of "dropping out" or finding insulated security from the draft at a university or college. Accordingly, the social population of Army combat

TABLE 9

Distribution of Casualties Between RA Volunteer and
Draftee in Viet Nam[a]

	1968	1969	1970	*Percentage Rate of Increase or Decrease 1968-1970*
Draftee				
% of Army in Viet Nam	42.0	39.0	39.0	−3.0
% of casualties	58.0	62.0	65.0	+7
Volunteer[b]				
% of Army in Viet Nam	58.0	61.0	61.0	+3.0
% of casualties	42.0	38.0	35.0	−7.0

a. *Congressional Record,* August 21, 1970, pp. 29700-29704, (Citing) "National Journal Studies Role of Draftees in Viet Nam."
b. The RA or volunteer in Viet Nam was called a "lifer" by draftee combat troops.

units in Viet Nam was not radically different from the enlisted social types populating armies in western nations for centuries, i.e., rural yeomen and urban working classes. This, therefore, leaves no other implication than that the military subsystem and its leadership had to be at fault when the Viet Nam armies lost coherence and began to disintegrate.

Unit cohesion and traditional discipline were destroyed in Viet Nam because of the military subsystem itself. Past studies on the American Army reveal that, in conflict, the unit of cohesion tends to be the squad. During the Korean War, the primary group contracted to the "buddy" system. By the time of Viet Nam, the buddy system had been destroyed. The results have been that the field army in Viet Nam was substantially made of of military isolates which constituted *noyaus* far more than a "society."[35] Under these circumstances, discipline obviously became increasingly difficult to maintain.

If soldiers committed to Viet Nam combat were forced to function in a progressively unstructured social and military milieu, as this analysis implies, then the lack of effective leadership would only compound the factors leading to disintegration. In the nature of the draft, the burden of battle rested not only upon draftees but also upon enlistees from the lower socioeconomic strata of the country. Men of this social order are often stereotyped as persons subject to impulses of immediate gratification, sudden urges toward violence, and a higher incidence of inability to adapt to military life. If men of these dispositions are placed in a situation where their leaders seem undeserving of respect and where enforcement of traditional and severe discipline is absent, then the incidence of hostile acts by its own troops against the military system and its symbols will increase. Concurrently, if the military system can not, or will not, provide a set of constraining values that serve as guides to behavior, then the tendency to insubordination will be further reenforced.

Senior officers who directed the war in Viet Nam can argue, it is said with some legitimacy, that opportunities for their frequent participation in battle, and thus direct leadership, were relatively limited.[36] Controlling the movement of hundreds or thousands of squad, platoon, and company-sized units; the continuous operation of multiple and complex communications; and problems of supply, transport, and evacuation may have required the presence of senior officers at command centers in base camps rather than in battle, so as to ensure "rational" command control. If this argument be admitted, Viet Nam operations were not consistent with large numbers of generals and colonels intruding their physical presence upon the battle in progress. In this view, the immediate and junior commander on the ground is the best judge of action and therefore requires a high degree of tactical autonomy; a constant presence of senior officers would then tend to inhibit decision-making and to slow tactical reactions unacceptably. In the first place, the war in Viet Nam was one tied intimately to politics, and especially the political culture of the Viet Nam population whose freedom from communist influence was one of the political objectives of the war. Accordingly, by the terms of these conditions of the war, *all* operations should have been subject to intense high command supervision in order to ensure that the violence employed was moderated commensurate with political warfare. By this rubric of political warfare, small unit commanders should not have been permitted to follow the formal doctrines of conventional warfare which dictate tactical autonomy. Instead, all lower level combat commanders ideally should have demonstrated high competence in counterguerilla tactics, while being at the same time closely controlled according to a strict overall counterguerilla policy. However, neither their military training nor their education prepared American troops for this challenge. The lower levels of the army in Viet Nam were indeed amateurs in a "Peoples War," due to the rotation system which limited the vast bulk of forces to 13-month tours, with much the same thing being true of officers at all levels. Clearly, no great expertise could be developed in guerilla warfare by such men.

Given this picture of the war as reasonably accurate, there was a need for the continual presence of highly sophisticated senior officers in action, not merely attempting to lead from helicopters or visiting from time to time the various base camps. The evidence is that the war was not adequately supervised by senior ranks in such a manner as to conduct the war by rules initially laid down by the Army itself. The rules of which we speak are those declaiming, "winning the hearts and minds....," "unconventional warfare," "civic action," and the like. In time, the absence of senior officers from actual battle cannot have escaped the attention of the troops engaged. Insofar as the perceptions of troops toward the war (any war) are conditioned by the military system, visible symbols of the system are necessary to morale. Recall, however, that because of the base system, senior officers were highly visible in noncombat areas. It can be assumed that the idea spread that the generals and colonels not only absented themselves from battle, as their minor losses show, but that they, by their actual behavior, cared little about what the troops did so long as the "forms" were observed (body counts, status reports, reports of "victories"). Why should one then be surprised at a rising incidence of "My Lais"? The eventual breakdown of discipline and respect simply cannot be treated with surprise or amazement.

The clear evidence of a decline of officer quality is illustrated in Table 10. Between 1960 and 1970, Army ROTC recruitment declined over 60%; consequently, the strength of the active officer corps between 1960 and 1972 increased by 57%. Evidently, the Army had difficulty not only replacing its own losses from discharge, but in finding the numbers necessary to fill the expansion pressured by a "felt" need for an ever larger officer corps. However, it is expecting too much to believe that the complexities of the war in Viet Nam could have been coped with by such men. The argument advanced by the Army is that such numbers of officers had to be obtained even if quality were sacrificed (anent the case of Lt. Calley). Yet, historical experience dictates otherwise, as the examples of well-led German and French military forces show. A large army, skillfully led by a small number of dedicated, competent officers, exhibiting a concrete sense of the military ethic, is always more cohesive than a vast mass of poor officers and badly handled troops. All evidence points to the fact that disintegration in the Army relates directly to the character, integrity, and competence of the officer corps. Nothing in the available data shows any connection between disintegration and such external factors as the "permissive society," fragmenting ideologies, or a "nation being torn apart."

THE OFFICER CORPS: ITS SELF-IMAGE

At the end of the Viet Nam experience, a number of books were written about the decayed conditions of the armed services.[37] Among

TABLE 10
Reserve Officers Training Corps Enrollment: 1960 to 1972[a]
(in thousands, for May, end of school year)

Branch of Service	1960	1965	1967	1968	1969	1970	1971	1972
Senior ROTC, total	230	231	216	196	175	123	92	73
Army	133	142	152	141	125	87	63	45
Navy	10	7	9	9	9	8	7	7
Air Force	87	82	56	45	41	28	23	21
Junior ROTC, total[b]	87	88	95	111	122	126	124	121

SOURCE: U.S. Department of Defense, Office of the Secretary, unpublished data.

a. *Statistical Abstract of the United States—1973,* Bureau of the Census, p. 270.

b. Consists of high school, academies, junior colleges, and National Defense Cadet Corps Schools; beginning 1967, includes enrollment in Army, Navy, Marine Corps, and Air Force Junior ROTC, and in National Defense Cadet Corps.

them, Stuart H. Loory's account of a "defeated" American military machine is most interesting.[38] It describes in detail prevailing attitudes and conditions in all of the services, together with a convincing account of an atmosphere of careerism, self-seeking, and exploitation of the enlisted ranks. Loory scarcely sets out to indict the military officer but cannot avoid the indictment. In the end he lets the military off easily since he sees the officer as victimized by a system which "politicized" the military, albeit to the career advantage of the officers. Only by implication does he lay culpability at the feet of an officer corps who betrayed the ethic of the professional soldier, an ethic which is the very creation of those who are supposed to live by and enforce its rigorous standards. This ethic, expressed in three words: Duty-Honor-Country, came to be a function of lip service alone while the actual "sincere" fulfillment of the ideals would destroy a career. More importantly, for our purposes, Loory cites briefly a self-study of the officer corps, its values, standards, and core ethic, the central standards by which any officer was to be judged. Beginning with the core imperative, Duty-Honor-Country, 450 officers were surveyed in 1970 by questionnaire and rudimentary "Q" sort methodology as to their evaluation of the ethical level of the United States Army.[39] The study was directed by then Chief of Staff General Westmoreland and conducted by the Army War College. Some of its more pertinent conclusions are as follows:

The AWC study finds that, "The ideal standards of ethical/moral/ professional behavior as epitomized by 'Duty-Honor-Country' are accepted by the Officer Corps as proper, meaningful, and relevant for the Army of today." However it also notes, "There are widespread and often significant differences between the ideal ethical/moral/professional standards of the Army and the prevailing standards . . . " that are necessary for career advancement. Surprisingly, the study notes that "The variances between the ideal standards and the actual or operative standards are perceived with striking similarity by the cross section of officers queried during the conduct of this study." In point of fact, it would appear that the officer corps itself recognizes the disparity between the ideal and the requirements of career advancement. Indeed, the study suggests that "the junior officers, in particular, were concerned about the unethical practices they observed and were eager to do their part in correcting the situation."

In addressing itself to the causes of this disparity, the study found, "There was no significant evidence that contemporary sociological pressures—which are everpresent—were primary causes of the differences between the ideal and the actual professional climate in the Army; the problems are for the most part internally generated; they will not vanish automatically as the war in Viet Nam winds down and the size of the Army decreases." Following this, it would appear, "The Army rewards system focuses on the accomplishment of short term, measurable, and often trivial tasks, and neglects the development of those ethical standards which are essential to a healthy profession."

Some of the most frequently occurring themes describing disparities between the ideal and the real in the study are, "selfish, promotion-oriented behavior; inadequate communication between junior and senior; distorted or dishonest reporting of status, statistics, or officer efficiency; technical or managerial incompetence; disregard for principles, but total respect for accomplishing even the most trivial mission with zero defects; disloyalty to subordinates; senior officers setting poor standards of ethical/professional behavior." It appears correct to say disparities are encouraged by self-deceptive Army policies "regarding officer evaluation, selection for promotion, career concepts and assignment policies, and information reporting systems." Such circumstances do not aid in the Army's goal of retaining junior officers. The AWC study suggests that while young officers are motivated by principles, these same young officers often find their seniors incompetent, neglectful, and "often out of touch with reality." It is hardly surprising, therefore, that this state of affairs has forced the young officer to choose between the ideals of the service and success.

One cannot but ask whether or not this condition can be changed from within, for one recalls that a basic premise of our analysis is that conditions of disintegration have been brought about internally. In addressing itself to corrective measures the AWC study concluded that,

> The present climate is not self-correcting, and because of the nature and extent of the problem, changes must be credibly instituted and enforced by the Army's top leadership. . . . Correcting the climate will require more than superficial, transitory measures. The climate cannot be corrected by admonitions. Concrete modification of the systems of reward and punishment to support adherence to the time-honored principles of an Army officer is required.[40]

In short the AWC study seems to imply that those who have most benefited by the system can be expected and trusted to change it. We find such an assumption highly spurious.

The AWC study and its findings quoted above makes the statement that the Army's top leadership must institute and enforce changes. Yet in another part of the study we find the following observation which suggests strongly that the Army probably cannot correct its own decayed condition:

the present climate does not appear to be self-correcting. The human drives for success and for recognition by seniors, sustained if not inflamed by the systems of reward and management which cater to immediate personal success at the expense of a long term consolidation of moral and ethical strength would appear to perpetuate if not exacerbate the current environment. Time alone will not cure the disease. The fact also that the leaders of the future are those who survived and excelled within the rules of the present system militates in part against any self-starting incremental return toward the practical application of ideal values.[41]

Reduced to essentials, the Army study leads us to conclude that the military system cannot reform itself because those who enforce the core ethic of Duty-Honor-Country have by the measure of their own success violated the ethic *ab initio*.

CONCLUSION

A stark phrase in the conclusions to the War College study is "disloyalty to subordinates." If disloyalty ranges all the way down, small wonder that the ethical stature of the officer corps came to be communicated to the ranks. We have seen that one of the central elements of cohesion in the German Army was the mutual regard between officers and men. When the time of testing came, the officer corps would not forsake their charge. Has not the reverse occurred in Viet Nam, that in the time of battle and death the officers were not there—especially the senior officers? Moreover, the structure of the war in Viet Nam tended possibly to reenforce the impression upon enlisted personnel that ultimately there was no more purpose to the war than the advancement of officers' careers. If the central concern of the more senior officers was career and promotions, what worse way to destroy career expectancies than first to insist on rigorous standards and then to accept prolonged exposure to the danger of death with combat troops? Under such circumstances cohesive primary groups can scarcely exist, much less overall military cohesion.

Concerning the effects of events external to the Army, the War College study affirms the concept that external sociological pressures are not the primary elements in military performance. We find in the Shils and Janowitz study, that the cohesion of the *Wehrmacht* was a function essentially of internal military factors. The War College study makes basically the same observation. More to the point, the study specifically degrades popular attitudes towards the war as irrelevant.

There is no direct evidence that external fiscal, political, sociological, or managerial influences are the primary causative factors of this less than optimum climate. Neither does the public attitude to the Viet Nam war, or the rapid expansion of the Army, or the current anti-military syndrome stand out as a significant reason for deviations from the level of professional behavior the Army acknowledges as its attainable ideal.[42]

There is no reason to assume that the signs of disintegration emerging from the ranks were essentially derived from external sociopolitical conditions. Accordingly, the connection between an unethical and perhaps incompetent officer corps and an Army of lesser ranks displaying every sign of disintegration is now clearer. The Army exhibited signs of social entropy in the destruction of primary groups, a destruction traceable to rotation systems. However, given, first, the state of the officer corps, its career obsession, and rapid rotation in and out of combat units for the sake of "ticket punching," and second, the sordid condition of American enlisted men, it is a wonder that any cohesion existed at all. Moreover, it is very doubtful that even had they tried the officer corps could have created the necessary primary groups at all, since the growth of mutual regard was precluded by the character and inordinate numbers of the officers themselves, together with the transmission-belt quality of combat replacement.

Reenforcing all other elements affecting the moral state of the Army in Viet Nam was the extraordinary damage done by the drug traffic, which the higher echelons of the Army condoned, if only by inaction. The existence of an organized drug traffic tolerated by civilian policy makers together with the higher officer corps is sufficient evidence of the moral dilemmas of an entire army.

In the end, factors associated with military decay focus on the officer corps, a corps unsure of itself and its standards of conduct, unable to enforce basic discipline, overmanaged with superfluous staff, and held in contempt by their troops. This Army is the reverse of those armies which in history have exhibited high cohesion during periods of retreat or even defeat. Combined with all the other indicators, but essentially the character of the Army officer, the American Army in Viet Nam qualifies as an Army which self-destructed and did so mainly because of internal factors.

NOTES

1. "Because the military establishment is managerially oriented, the gap between the heroic leader and the military manager has also narrowed. . . . The technologist is likely to be most concerned with the means, the manager with the purpose of military policy. . . . Presently the military academies are deeply concerned with whether they can adequately present an image of a 'whole man', who, realistically, is both a modern heroic leader and a military manager." Morris Janowitz, *The Professional Soldier* (New York: Free Press, 1971), p. 425. It may be that the disintegration of the U.S. Army is associated with the rise of the managerials and

their extreme displacement of Janowitz's "heroic" images, i.e., men seeking privilege and displacing men of honor.

2. The general staff organization of the American Army, like that of many other western armies, is a variation of the Prussian system of command and staff. American field regulations governing the conduct of armies in the field are derived also from Prussian influence. For example, see Leon Friedman, ed., *The Law of War*, Vol. 1, (New York: Random House, 1972), pp. xv-xviii.

3. Edward A. Shils and Morris Janowitz, "Cohesion and Disintegration in the German Wehrmacht in World War II," Public Opinion Quarterly 12 (1948): 280-315.

4. Ibid., p. 281.

5. Ibid., pp. 284, 287, 295-297. In addition to the usual esteem held by German soldiers for their immediate leaders, primary group cohesion was further strengthened by a "hard core"which had a "gratifying adolescence under National Socialism" (p. 286). Even this small hard core was oriented toward the military and not toward politics.

6. Ibid., p. 299.

7. Burkhardt Mueller-Hillebrand, *Das Heer 1933-1945, Band III, Der Zweifrontenkrieg* (Frankfurt am Main: Verlag E. S. Mittler & Son, 1969), pp. 248-266.

8. If the average German officer's risk of being killed was far higher than that of his men's, the losses of field grade leadership were even greater. Of 675 general officers on the German Army list, 223 were killed in action (33%). See Josef Folttman and Hans Moeller-Witten, *Opfergand der Generale* (Berlin: Verlag Bernard und Graefe, 1959), p. 85.

9. Dr. Matthias Graf Von Schmettow, *Gedenkbuch des Deutschen Adels* (Limburg a.d. Lahn: C. A. Starke Verlag, 1967), p. x. No similar study exists on American "elites." In any case, the Brahminates of Boston and Virginia do not seem to appear too often in the casualty lists—and clearly not in the Viet Nam war casualty lists.

10. Other data support the sense of duty and cohesion in the German Army. One example was the very low desertion rate. See Shils and Janowitz, "Cohesion and Disintegration . . . " p. 285. Mueller-Hillebrand notes that only 2,600 men were listed as actual deserters in the total Wehrmacht (*Das Heer*, p. 262).

11. See Paul Carell, *Scorched Earth* (New York: Ballantine, 1971), pp. 596-597. In July 1944, the German Central Army Group was virtually destroyed with 28 of 38 German divisions being put out of action. Thirty-one of 47 general officers commanding were lost, approximately 7% of the general officers in the German Army. A sharply illustrative and autobiographical account of small unit warfare and the cohesion of German combat units is Guy Sajer, *The Forgotten Soldier* (New York: Harper and Row, 1971). This account stresses the regard German soldiers had for their officers, especially at the company level. See Shils and Janowitz, "Cohesion and Disintegration . . . " p. 298.

12. The Germans, as with all armies, had their "bombproofs": civilians with assimilated ranks, paper generals whose rank was acquired by politics, SS rear area administrators, Nazi party hacks in ornate uniforms, concentration camp officials. All these were regarded by combat soldiers with contempt. See Sajer, *The Forgotten Soldier* or any standard work on SS *Einsatzgruppen.*

13. Shils and Janowitz, "Cohesion and Disintegration . . . " pp. 287-288.

14. American combat replacement policies have produced combat units composed of men who do not know each other. The phenomenon of units of strangers is,

of course, greater after protracted combat than before. Still, the practice of treating the American soldier as a "component" instead of as a member of a group tends to create a mass army instead of one composed of cohesive units. See Morris Janowitz and Roger Little, eds., *Sociology and the Military Establishment* (New York: Russell Sage Foundation, 1965), pp. 82-83.

15. By minimal stress we mean a situation in which an army, over a protracted time, experiences discontinuous combat, low levels of combat intensity, and low casualties. Historically, many armies have fought under maximum stress and experienced high casualties with no loss of cohesion.

16. Data from unpublished Veterans Administration Reports: *Data on Viet Nam Era Veterans, June 1971* (Washington, D.C.: Reports and Statistics Service, Office of the Controller, Veterans Administration), p. 7. The V.A. data reveal the educational levels for veterans between the ages of 20 to 24 years in three conflicts. More college *dropouts* served in Viet Nam than in World War II, but fewer college graduates served in Viet Nam by some 69.41%.

17. There is some evidence that college-educated middle-class enlisted men decrease cohesion in primary groups. See Charles C. Moskos, Jr., *The American Enlisted Man* (New York: Russell Sage Foundation, 1970), pp. 74-76.

18. Studies of the American soldier in World War II destroyed the conventional image of the ideologically committed soldier. See Samuel Stouffer et al., *The American Soldier*, Vol. 1 (Princeton: Princeton University Press, 1949), pp. 484-489. "The general picture of this volume, of men preoccupied with minimizing their discomforts, acquiring higher rank or pay, securing safe jobs which would offer training useful in civilian life, displaying aggressions against the Army in many different ways, and in getting out of the Army as fast as possible does not suggest a particularly inspired work performance in the American Army." Roger Little found scant sense of commitment and generalized system dedication in the Korean War. See Janowitz and Little, *Sociology*, pp. 77-79. As in the Stouffer study of World War II, the main factor in combat cohesion during Korea was the primary group. But in World War II the American primary group was at the squad or platoon level, whereas by the Korean War the primary group had collapsed to the dyadic buddy system. The smaller primary groups typical of the American Army (compared to the company-sized primary group of the German Army) in World War II, essentially the squad or platoon levels, were largely a condition of a replacement system which kept divisions in protracted combat and thus tended to keep primary groups small. In Korea the same protracted division combat policy was exacerbated by a rotation system which reduced the primary group to a dyad. Cohesion in any military primary group in combat requires some regard for the immediate leader. However, even small-unit combat leadership was weakened in Korea by the unofficial policy of rotating officer platoon leaders from the immediate combat unit to safer positions in the rear as replacement officers became available. Enlisted men served a full combat tour in the line, but officers often did not. In Viet Nam, officers in combat units served approximately six months in combat while their men served 12 months. This will be discussed later as an element in the Army's disintegration. See Roger Little, "Deterioration of Military Work Groups Under Stress," in Morris Janowitz, ed., *The New Military* (New York: W. W. Norton, 1969), pp. 195-223. From a Marxist perspective, John Helmer, in *Bringing the War Home: The American Soldier in Vietnam and After* (New York: Free Press, 1974), argues that the working-class soldier in Viet Nam became "alienated" and did so for "ideological" reasons. Moreover, they actively "resisted" for reasons of class-based ideology. Helmer

surveyed Viet Nam veterans in the Boston area. His sample totaled 90 respondents. See Helmer, *Bringing the War Home*, pp. 43-105.

19. During a Senate hearing (FNU), General Davis stated that there have been "fraggings" (assassinations) of officers in all wars in this country (see Table 3). However, "in World War I, which involved over 4,700,000 American military, fewer than 370 cases of violence directed at superiors were brought to court-martial. This low ratio was fairly constant through World War II and the Korean police action.... Since January 1970 alone, a period during which roughly 700,000 Americans in Viet Nam, there have been 363 cases involving assault with explosive devices ... and another 118 cases termed "possible...." " Officers in the Judge Advocate General Corps have estimated that only about 10% of fraggings end up in court. As will be seen, these figures are low. See Eugene Linden, "Fragging and Other Withdrawal Symptoms," Saturday Review (January 8, 1972): 12. Data on assassination of officers or NCOs is, understandably, difficult to acquire. What data we present above are figures obtained from the Department of Defense and must be treated with suspicion if only because they tend to be overly conservative.

20. Inserted figures in Table 3 are from testimony by Major General Kerwin before a Subcommittee on Appropriations, House of Representatives, Ninety-Second Congress (Department of Defense Appropriations for 1972, Part 3, pp. 473-474). General Kerwin's figures do not agree with those in Table 3. We are inclined to accept the higher figures. Since the Pentagon is understandably sensitive about "fragging," they will not inflate such figures as they did for those such as "body counts." In the same hearing, the general was asked if there were figures on the number brought to trial for such actions. He did not know, but said he would find out. Inserted later in the record was the following: "inquiry to U.S. Army Viet Nam revealed that this information was not available." The probability is that the number of "fraggings" was much higher. Testimony of a General Davis at the same hearing includes, "Fragging is not particularly new in warfare." He cited an incident of threats of violence by men against their officers at the Battle of Cedar Mountain in the Civil War. He denied as well that "fraggings" in Viet Nam were beyond similar violence against officers in other American wars. It may be superfluous to add that General Davis was not in command of military history.

21. Personal letter, Department of the Army, dated 26 July 1972, signed by Clayton N. Gompf, Acting Deputy for Military Personnel Policy and Programs. Such an anomaly in Pentagon data banks seems equivalent to the British Admiralty denying that any record was made of the Bounty Mutiny or, indeed, of the Napoleonic Wars' mutinies, not to mention the French neglecting the mutinies of 1917.

22. Nomination of Robert R. Froehlke: Hearing Before the Committee on Armed Services, United States Senate, June 1971, pp. 9-11.

23. Even though the French army operated in the same area and under similar conditions, no evidence suggests that they experienced a drug problem in the first Indo-China war. Certainly the French command would not have tolerated the fantastic drug network accepted by the American command in Viet Nam.

24. *Humrro Study*, p. 423. Other findings reveal an inverse relation between drugs and the level of education (p. 428); Blacks had a slightly higher use than whites (p. 430); daily usage was higher among technicians than among infantry (p. 432); users reported drugs easily available on base, ship, or in town (p. 439). The data source is a Senate hearing cited in Table 4 which reproduced the Humrro Study quoted.

25. Alfred W. McCoy et al., *The Politics of Heroin in Southeast Asia* (New York: Harper & Row, 1972), pp. 171-172, 218.

26. Ibid., pp. 247, 263-264.

27. Ibid., pp. 350-351.

28. Those so inclined are invited to read in the reports of congressional hearings the weak replies given by generals to questions by senators and representatives about fraggings, mutinies, desertion, and drugs; and they may reflect upon the prolonged unwillingness of the Congress to conduct detailed inquiries as to why such expensive armed systems were allowed to disintegrate. As an example, see Nomination of Robert R. Froehlke: Hearing, p. 220-251.

29. The differences were even greater in Korea than in the other two conflicts (see Table 8). However, our discussion of linear as contrasted to "confined" or "circular" warfare will show why the enlisted personnel in Korea did not perceive the proportionately low number of officer losses as readily as did those in Viet Nam. Troops in both World War II and Korea rarely saw many officers in their transition to the lines, but in Viet Nam they did.

30. *Britannica Book of the Year*, 1954, p. 61. See Orville D. Menard, *The Army and the Fifth Republic* (Lincoln: University of Nebraska Press, 1967), p. 69.

31. Menard, *The Army and the Fifth Republic*, p. 58. Menard observes that during the Indo-China War, one in three graduates of St. Cyr died in Viet Nam. Joseph Buttinger reports that in the entire Indo-China War, 29,605 French and 11,620 Foreign Legionnaires (for a total of 41,225) were lost. The remaining 41,995 were "colonials." See Joseph Buttinger, *A Dragon Embattled*, Vol. 2 (New York: Praeger, 1967), p. 1071, n. 2. One reason the OAS during the Algerian affair was able to persist for so long was that French enlisted men were deeply loyal to their officers, for they saw that French officers never sent their men to die alone.

32. Data from *Secretariat d'etat aux anciens combattants*, personal letter dated September 26, 1974.

33. See notes 16 and 17.

34. The decision to adopt the one-year rotation policy was not purely military, so the Army cannot be held totally responsible. Rather, it was the inevitable result of a politically devised policy of refusing to mobilize the country for war. The Army thus faced the problem of how to command an army without being able to utilize its officers on tours extending "for the duration." They adopted the policy of frequent rotation based on "equity," the expectation that all officers would serve at least one tour. In this sense, the rotation policy was imposed upon the military. Still, the effect of the rotation policy can be exaggerated. The one-year tour was also military policy in Korea during the combat phase, but disintegration indicators were not evident among American units in Korea.

35. See Moskos, *The American Enlisted Man*, pp. 7, 24, 30. See also Little, "Deterioration of Military Work Groups."

36. This argument was made in a personal letter from a senior officer of the United States Army. The same letter justified the discriminatory distribution of losses among RAs and draftees by arguing that enlisted men represent a better long-term investment for the Army and their training should not be wasted.

37. See William L. Hauser, *America's Army in Crisis* (Baltimore: Johns Hopkins University Press, 1973); William R. Corson, *The Betrayal* (New York: Ace, 1968); Edward L. King, *The Death of the Army* (New York: Saturday Review Press, 1972); Ward Just, *Military Men* (New York: Alfred A. Knopf, 1970). King observed that over one-half of the general officers serving in Viet Nam received decorations for

bravery (*Death of the Army*, pp. 103, 210-211). Observing the same curious inflation of awards, Hauser provides further data on decorations given in Viet Nam. In 1968, the total number of Americans killed in all services was 14,592; the total number of awards given was 416,693. In 1970, the number killed was 3,946, and the number receiving awards was 522,905. Some fraudulent awards went to senior officers who received Silver Stars for acts requiring no special bravery or for imaginary acts. See Hauser, *America's Military in Crisis*, p. 175. Moreover, *as casualties lessened and forces were sizably reduced, awards for bravery accelerated*! No student of this subject appears to have noted the anomaly of large numbers of awards for bravery being issued to generals—often accompanied with the purple heart or given posthumously—even though generals were rarely in the field. We have shown that generals in Viet Nam did not die very often. Hauser's book recognizes that the Army is in peril, but he fails to come to grips with the root causes. He tends to attribute blame to forces outside the Army, which we have seen is not justified, and has actually produced a military apologetic. His solution for the regeneration of the Army is to divide the institution into two strata. One level would be an elite, even spartan, fighting force; the other would be a semicivilianized support system. See Hauser, *America's Military in Crisis*, pp. 201-228. Despite general interest in leadership, little attention has been given to the relation between losses and performance in the Israeli Army. In the 1973 War, Israel lost 2,500 KIA, of which 26% were officers. However, of the 2,500 killed, only 85 individuals were "private" soldiers. Thus, more than 95% of the dead were officers and NCOs. See Ward Just, "Israel," Atlantic (June 1975): 11. Just's data, which he attributes to "private" sources, appear credible.

38. Stuart H. Loory, *Defeated* (New York: Random House, 1973).

39. *Study on Military Professionalism* (Carlisle Barracks, Penn.: U.S. Army War College, June 1970). In the survey and in the "Q" sort, the same themes emerged: careerism, self-seeking, and hypocrisy. It should be added that "Q" sorting, properly applied, permits the respondents to evolve as self-selected models. The report gave no details as to the exact "Q Sort Technique," although the method was attributed to Victor H. Vroom, *Work and Motivation* (New York: John Wiley, 1964). See pp. B-30 of *Study on Military Professionalism*. This study, conducted under Army War College control, also surveyed officers at a variety of higher Army schools, including the Staff College and junior officers.

40. *Study on Military Professionalism*, pp. 30-32.

41. Ibid., p. 28-29.

42. Ibid., p. v.

PAUL L. SAVAGE served in combat in Italy in World War II (1943-1945). He was commissioned in 1950 in the U.S. Army and saw duty in a variety of command, staff and military advisory positions. He retired as a Lieutenant-Colonel in 1967 to pursue an academic career. He is now Associate Professor and Chairman, Department of Politics, St. Anselm's College, Manchester, New Hampshire.

RICHARD A. GABRIEL, currently an Associate Professor of Political Science at St. Anselm's College, was commissioned for service in the U.S. Army from ROTC. He served for three years as a military intelligence officer in Europe on the staff of the Supreme Allied Commander, Europe. He retains his commission as Captain on reserve status and has been assigned to military intelligence duties.

West Point at War:
Officer Attitudes and the Vietnam War
1966-72

James Jay Carafano[1]

During the Vietnam War the history faculty at the United States Military Academy at West Point solicited letters from officers on their experiences in Southeast Asia.[2] An analysis of these letters, official records, departmental files, and personal interviews provide a new source for examining the attitudes of professional army officers. This collection suggests that the cognitive values of the military as exemplified by the West Point motto, "Duty, Honor, Country," reflected a far more positive disposition towards duty performance than both contemporary scholarship and popular perceptions recognized.

Why did we lose America's longest war? In part our society created its own "public myth" to help explain the military failure in Vietnam.[3] This myth evolved from the destruction of one fictional, public paradigm and the creation of another. The traditional pre-Vietnam view of the superior moral and military performance of the American Army in war, what Loyd Lewis calls the "John Wayne Wet Dream," turned into a nightmare.[4] It was replaced by a vision which saw American betrayed its institutions. An ineffective military was led by an officers corps which was often incompetent, occasionally corrupt, and always self-serving.

Reinforcing and perhaps influenced by popular perceptions stands a body of scholarship which found the fault of the officers corps in its value system. For example, Edward King wrote in his 1972 book *The Death of the Army* that:

Perhaps the Army became trapped in Vietnam because of pervasive ethical laxness at all levels over the preceding fifteen years. This moral laxness created a new breed of Army officer. The tone of the Army became one of subterfuge, public deception, and promotion of personal self-interest.[5]

This conclusion appeared to be confirmed by an official Army study conducted in 1970 which concluded, there was "a significant difference between the ideal values and the actual or operative values of the Officer Corps."[6] Criticism especially focused on West Point because the

Academy's motto, "duty, honor, country," was recognized by the officer corps as the ideal standard for military ethical, moral, and professional behavior.[7] The West Point motto was the centerpiece of the Army's professed value system and the system failed.[8]

Since West Point represented a touchstone for both the Army and its critics, it is a logical place to begin a revaluation of the issue. This investigation was prompted by a collection of letters written to the Academy by serving officers during the Vietnam War. Although not intended when it was assembled as a tool for historical research, it nevertheless offers one of the largest collections of spontaneous views on the period from a wide range of junior ranking officers.

The letters were collected as part of a project began in 1966 titled the "Adventure Board.' Colonel Thomas Griess, supervisor of military history instruction, selected the title for a specific purpose:

Our effort was aimed at showing the cadets that a military career was challenging and exciting and that it carried great responsibilities for a commander. In other words it was a "great adventure." You must remember that during part of this time we had a bit of a motivational problem with cadets, who were frustrated with growing national attitudes about the war in Vietnam.[9]

The letters were displayed in the rotunda of Thayer Hall, West Point's Main academic building, with displays and maps designed to attract cadet attention and interest.

As to the short comings of this collection, one is obvious. It does not represent all officers. The group who participated in the project can be classified, by virtue of the fact that they did participate, as men who were predisposed towards a positive view of their profession. The former cadets, faculty and their associates that were recruited in this ad hoc program would naturally be considered among those most supportive of the army as an institution. Approximately half the officers responding were West Point graduates. In addition, the fact that an officer even took time to respond to such a query set him apart from others. As one officer reported, "It seems the people in this squadron are good yarn spinners at the bar, but are very reticent to put anything in writing."[10] Only about ten percent of the enquiries resulted in a letter to the department.[11] In short, one would expect that those that did respond would offer a relatively optimistic view of officer life.

Another less obvious problem which makes it difficult to generalize about officer attitudes from any collection of material is the very nature of combat duties in Vietnam. As historian Jeffrey Clarke pointed out in a summary of American strategy:

Throughout the conflict, different levels of enemy activity necessitated different responses from region to region and even from province to province. It is almost impossible to generalize on the nature of the war based on personal experience.[12]

Shelby Stanton illustrates well in his book *Rise and Fall of An American Army* that practices within combat units varied greatly. This was not only the result of the intentions of the enemy and varied terrain, but also the character and tactics employed by different U.S. divisions.[13]

Despite these limitations, however, the West Point letters offer a great deal of utility in accessing attitudes. There was no standard format of reply. Officers wrote about whatever they felt was appropriate. In fact, one of the strengths of the collection is its diversity. In addition, to establish the context in which the letters were written I conducted both oral and written interviews of as many of those involved in the original project as could be located. This material along with relevant departmental records offers a wealth of previously unconsidered historical material.

The question remains, how to analyze this collection? To begin with, their is nothing in the letters about drug abuse, racism, fraggings, war crimes, wide spread ethical conflicts or other problems popularly associated with the moral breakdown of the army officer corps. One possible reason for this is that bulk of the letters are from the period of 1966-69 when it is generally agreed that such problems were less wide spread. It is only in the later letters that signs of an army in crisis are clearly seen. For example, in a 1971 letter to the department an officer wrote:

I am very disturbed by the state of discipline in U.S. troops, even though they do a grand job when bound together by a common threat, the enemy....However, I worry about what will happen when the enemy is not visible or is abstract as in training areas in the U.S. or Europe. I don't think the present state of discipline will hold up.[14]

This kind of letter, however, represented a distinct change from the views given in the bulk of the letters.

A more skeptical approach to the material might be to argue that most respondents simply ignored the negative aspects of the war. This, however, cannot be implied from the character of the letters. Their tone is straight forward and factual. There is little in them that strikes of overt propaganda or false bravado. In fact, in only one letter did an officer described his duties in traditional military heroic imagery. In this letter a captain recalled his first meeting with his men:

I could see that I gathered their attention with my brief remarks as their [sic] was not a sound in the room—a cigarette lit—I brought to life remembrances of Nathan Hale— of Gordon at Khartoum, of Thomas at Chicamagua, of MacArther at Bataan...[15]

This description, however, is absolutely unique. The officers did not view their duties in the larger abstract framework of military tradition or patriotism. On the other hand, the letters are also not on the whole simply cold, dispassionate summaries of tactical lessons learned, although some of them certainly fit into this motif. Rather, many are very sensitive to the realities of war and the stress of combat. One officer, for example, discussed the problems which the increasingly unpopularity of the war posed for him. He wrote:

The men surprised me the other day, sir. After a class I threw the floor open to any questions. And the men started in the PHILOSOPHY of the war in SE [Southeast] Asia. Why is the U.S. involved, what do they hope to gain, how is patriotism and freedom involved.... I was really surprised....[16]

Another wrote about the self doubt of his first experience of leading men in combat:

I had only been a company commander for three weeks and this was a rude way for me to break in. As I sit here and look at the Silver Star I received for that day I wonder if there was something I should have done or could have done to prevent our casualties. I'll probably never really know....[17]

Still another offered a frank assessment of one of his fellow officers:

he leaves in a blaze of glory. He failed to show up for a briefing he was supposed to give Gen. [General] Ploger, 18th Brigade C.O. [Commander] yesterday. His excuse is that he was having a machete chrome plated ir Saigon for the C/S [Chief of Staff]. I'll be glad when we get a new C.O. for B Company.[18]

In analyzing the letters, therefore, I have worked from the premise that they are honest and straightforward appraisals of individual experiences.

The problem still remains of how to synthesize this diverse material into any kind of indicator of officer values. The solution adopted was to examine the letters from the aspect of the West Point motto of "duty, honor, country." This code exemplified the Army's self-established ethical standard. It also represented a focus for criticism. Bruce Galloway and Robert Johnson, for example, in *West Point. America's Power Fraternity* concluded that the Academy motto fostered military elitism. They wrote it:

is identical to the one that appears again and again in the ideology of totalitarianism: "Duty, Honor, Country." This code leaves little room in the life of a West Pointer for a more familiar one, the one that says "Liberty and justice for All."[19]

The importance of the values expressed in the motto for both supporters and critics of the system confirm its utility as a baseline from which to measure officer attitudes.

In particular, analysis focused on evaluating the duty concept as it was expressed in the body of the letters. Duty is defined as consisting of two essential elements. One is the giving of selfless and committed service in the practice of a profession. The second is obedience and loyalty to the authority which delineates duties and responsibilities. It is in this context that the letters, as well as other material from departmental files, were examined.

In considering the first element of the duty concept the overwhelming impression from the letters is that officers were concerned and committed to doing their specific duties as well as possible. For example, in one account a field artillery lieutenant serving as a forward observer with an infantry company wrote:

The Commander was seriously wounded and I took charge of the company. It went through my mind what [a friend] had told me before I left [for Vietnam]. He had an article where an artillery FO [forward observer] had to take charge of an infantry company and I had better study up on infantry tactics. Well, I never thought it would happen to me but it did.[20]

In the middle of a night attack while under fire among the first thoughts of this officer was a concern for his competence to meet the responsibilities placed upon him.

Throughout the letters of their authors express the most satisfaction with themselves when discussing the performance of their profession. A young lieutenant described the sudden responsibilities of the first few moments of battle. He wrote:

I had my radio with me at the TOC [tactical operations center] and proceeded to put it on my back and relay messages to the 105 [mm] howitzer battery. I coordinated with the air observer and instructed him to fire 175 [mm gun], 8" [artillery] and 155 [mm artillery] defensive targets. Then I began to adjust Blue Max [Cobra gunships]. I had to continuously relay messages for both the infantry and artillery, plus coordinate the insertion and aircover for the medevacs [medical evacuations].[21]

Their satisfaction came not from the gratification of a display of personal courage or leadership, but a recognition that they executed their duties in a competent manner.

Nor was a positive attitude towards duty and responsibility limited to combat operations. An engineer lieutenant wrote about a recent bunker building project he had worked on:

You can not imagine the enthusiasm and pride I took in this project.... My one regret is that we rotated out of the DMZ before the finishing touches could be completed.[22]

A positive orientation toward duty performance was a constant throughout the letters of officers in a wide range of assignments.

In further examining attitudes toward job performance the controversial issue of careerism can be accessed. Richard Gabriel and Paul Savage in their 1978 book *Crisis of Command* argued that a careerist mentality among officers was a serious problem during the war. They defined careerism as the product of an attitude in which officers were more concerned with protecting themselves and advancing their careers rather than in doing their jobs. They argue the operative values at work were more suggestive of the managerial attitudes in the business world than those reflected in the West Point motto.[23]

In part the letter do provide evidence of officers seeking specific assignments. For example, some either asked about coming to the Academy or recommended others for teaching assignments.[24] In fact, in the 1960s and early 1970s a popular perception was growing that assignments in certain departments at West Point were helpful in promoting one's career. Of those who taught military history from 1963-70, for example, eight eventually reached the rank of general officer. Interviews with officers who taught at West Point, however, suggest that the success of members of the faculty was not result of a privileged assignment, but a reflection of the specific recruiting policies of individual departments that sought to obtain the best officers available. Colonel Griess, for example, who supervised military history instruction considered one of his primary responsibilities to be the screening and selection of officers. It was during his tenure that the quality of the military history faculty increased and commensurate with it the status of the department.[25]

On reflection, one officer went on to further suggest that concern over assignments among officers was the result of the increasingly inflexible officer management system instituted during the Vietnam era. The revised system limited the time in an officer's career in which he was eligible for certain assignments.[26] As a result, individuals took a more personal and active role seeking positions that would serve as prerequisites to greater rank and increased responsibility. While it is clear that this growing concern among officers over assignment selection existed, there is nothing that indicates it affected their attitudes toward the execution of their duties in specific jobs. Although it was acknowledged that there were individual officers who reflected careerist attitudes, careerism was not endemic to the system.[27] The operative attitude remained that it was important to fulfill all assigned duties and responsibilities as competently as possible.

The duty concept, however, involved more than simply doing a job. the second aspect of duty, the relationship between the officer and his superior must also be evaluated. In this context officers were required not only to give fidelity and loyalty to superiors, but bore a responsibility to ensure that such obedience did not violate the accepted ethical standards of the profession and society. In essence an officer served two masters; his superior and the established standards of his profession.

Several critics of the officer corps writing in the 1970s argued that their dual responsibilities were incongruent. Joseph Ellis and Robert Moore, for example in their critique of West Point titled *School for Soldiers* wrote that the Academy:

never resolved the tensions and contradictions between their obligation to obey orders, their obligation to follow personal ethical principles, and their obligation to serve the national interest.[28]

Josiah Bunting, an Army officer and member of the department of history at West Point recreated this essential moral dilemma in a Vietnam war novel published in 1972 titled *The Lionheads*. Bunting's fictional hero was confronted with an uncompromising choice; obey his commander and pursue a policy which was morally and professionally wrong or oppose the commander and risk damaging his own career.

Some remarks in the Vietnam letters do, in fact, reflect conflict between the individual and the system. One lieutenant wrote, "I don't mind telling you I've mixed opinions about this war—maybe because I'm so far down the chain and some of the rules are hard to play by."[29] Occasions when these officers were at odds with policies or decisions are revealed. The dramatic confrontation between loyalty and morality, however, is not to be found.

More substantial evidence on the tension between loyalty and duty comes from events occurring within the department of history itself. Here there appeared to be two divergent attitudes. One felt that the Army as an institution was incapable of sustaining self-criticism from its officer's without questioning their loyalty and commitment. Principle among this group was a wave of reserve officer who came to teach at the Academy in the late 1960s. As the war in Vietnam demanded an increasing number of officers, some departments at West Point turned to an untraditional method of recruiting faculty. They brought in officers activated only for short service who had already had graduate study or teaching experience at civilian universities. In *School for Soldiers*, Ellis and Moore discuss the "institutional anxiety" caused by the dialectic mix of Army officers and university faculty.[30] Ellis and Moore well understood the problems of the conflicting attitudes of these two groups, since they both came to West Point under the reserve officer program. Reserve officers maintained that their extensive academic training and ability to view the system as an outsider gave them a fresh, objective view of West Point, the army and the conduct of the war.

Not all the officers who experienced conflict over institutional loyalty, however, were among the civilian professors in uniform. Josiah Buntings background, for example, was that of a professional career army officer with a fine combat record in Vietnam. In 1972 he resigned his commission. Among the reasons he stated in his official letter of resignation were:

> I have utterly no faith in the ability of a junior officer like myself—or any junior officer—to effect meaningful and widespread change in the "system."[31]

In that same year he left West Point and published his novel *The Lionheads*.

On the other hand, another persistent attitude was that one could be analytical and critical about America's military policy without betraying a loyalty to the Academy and the army. As one officer recalled:

> You could be critical and that would be the badge of loyalty. Critical because what you saw going on was dysfunctional to the military establishment and its strength. I think criticism emanated from that cause. Just blind slavish support of the war effort was really kind of foolish....[32]

An example of professional self-criticism was the work of Major Dave Palmer. One of the first officers to teach in the department with combat experience in Vietnam, he was assigned the task of writing the instructional material used in the department concerning the war. He did not avoid controversial issues. In his course notes, for example, he criticized the American Army's reliance on technology and firepower.[33] Palmer also wrote a course text which included a chapter on Vietnam. In it he evaluated the overall military strategy of the war and concluded:

> One thing should be made absolutely clear: attrition is not a strategy. It is irrefutable proof of an absence of any strategy. A commander who resorts to attrition admits his failure to conceive an alternative. He turns from warfare as an art and accepts it on the most non-professional terms imaginable. He uses blood in lieu of brains. Saying that political considerations forced the employment of attrition warfare does not alter the hard truth that the U.S. was strategically bankrupt in Vietnam.[34]

He repeated these conclusions in an even more public forum in 1978 in his book *Summons of the Trumpet, A History of the Vietnam War from a Military Man's Viewpoint*.[35] Palmer's self-generated commitment to analyze and critique the army's performance in Vietnam reflected the view of professional Army officers who felt that their experience and familiarity with the Academy and the army gave them insights into the system which their contemporary critics could not appreciate. Palmer remained within the system. In 1986 he was promoted to the rank of a three star general and appointed the Superintendent of United States Military Academy at West Point.

Presiding over divergent views of the war and West Point was Colonel Griess. The evidence suggests Griess worked hard to accommodate contrasting views within the department and allowed officers great latitude in expressing their personal opinions. Therefore, despite signs of friction, it was not official policies of the department or the Academy which forced officers to decide to continue to dissent within the system or get out. The decision to stay or leave was a reflection of individual character and choice and not institutionally driven. Within the department of history, the Army did not force officers to make unsolvable moral choices based on conflicting loyalties.

In summary, the conclusion that there was a moral breakdown of the Army which resulted from divergent operative and stated values is not supported by the evidence in the West Point collection. This is not to suggest that the army, West Point or the officer value system were not affected by the turmoil of Vietnam. The evidence does argue, however, that the origins of the army's failures were not inherent in the character of its institutions. The public myth of the war may have provided a cohesive vision to the Vietnam generation, but it is flawed explanation of the American military experience.

Notes

[1]A version of this paper was presented at the 1987 meeting of the Popular Culture Association in Montreal, Canada. I would like to thank Colonel W.S. Dillard and Edward Krasnoborski who introduced me to the West Point collection of Vietnam letters. This collection is now contained at the United States Military Academy Library under the title *James E. Torrence Collection* (hereafter cited as *T.C.*). I am indebted to Mrs. Marie Capps of the USMA Library for her advice and counsel on cataloguing the collection.

[2]From 1966-69 the Department of Military Art and Engineering taught military history at West Point. In 1969 the department was reorganized and the military history faculty formed the nucleus of the newly created history department. To avoid confusion this paper will use the term history faculty to refer to both. This faculty consisted of active duty Army officers.

[3]Recent works which trace the evolution of America's new "public myth" are John Hellmann, *American Myth and the Legacy of Vietnam* (New York, 1986); Loyd B. Lewis, *The Tainted War, Culture and Identity in Vietnam War Narratives* (Westport, Conn., 1985); Mary L. Bellhouse and Lawrence Litchfield, "Vietnam and Loss of Innocence: An Analysis of the Political Implications of the Popular Literature of the Vietnam War," *Journal of Popular Culture* 16 (Winter, 1982): 157-745.

[4]Lewis, *Tainted War* pp. 25-37 finds the origins of the "John Wayne" image of the American military in the experiences of World War Two. John Shy argues, however, that the popular "can do" perception of the American way of war were

actually commonly held assumptions before the end of the nineteenth century. See John Shy, "The American Military Experience: History and Learning," *Journal of Interdisciplinary History* 1 (Winter, 1971): 220.

[5]Edward L. King, *The Death of the Army, Pre-Mortem* (New York, 1972), p. 75. Other critiques include Ward Just, *Military Men* (New York, 1970); Haynes Johnson et al., *Army in Anguish* (New York, 1972); Richard Gabriel and Paul L. Savage, *Crisis in Command: Mismanagement in the Army* (New York, 1978), and Stuart Loory, *Defeated, Inside America's Military Machine* (New York, 1973).

[6]*Study on Military Professionalism* (Carlisle Barracks, Pa., 1970), p. iii. Gabriel, *Crisis,* pp. 89-94 accepted the War College study as definitive and relied heavily on its conclusions. The study was also cited in Loory, *Defeated,* pp. 334-6. Recent works continue in this vein. See Loren Baritz, *Backfire, A History of how American Culture Led Us to Vietnam and Made Us Fight the Way We Did* (New York, 1985), p. 303-5, and Cincinnatus, *Self-Destruction, The Disintegration and Decay of the United States Army During the Vietnam Era* (New York, 1981), pp. 130-6.

[7]*Study on Military Professionalism,*p. 30.

[8]Variations of this argument can be found in K. Bruce Galloway and Robert Bowie Johnson Jr., *West Point; America's Power Fraternity* (New York, 1973); Richard U'Ren, *Ivory Fortress, A Psychiatrist Looks at West Point* (Indianapolis, 1974); Joseph Ellis and Robert Moore, *School for Soldiers* (New York, 1974); Gabriel, *Crisis,* pp. 91-3; John P. Lovell, "Professionalism and the Service Academies," *American Behavioral Scientist* 19 (May/June 1976): 605-26, and Ward Just, *Military Men,* pp. 15-52.

[9]T.C., Griess, ltr. dtd. October 29, 1986; see also T.C., Palmer, memorandum, subject "Draft Plans for Establishing a Vietnam Information Board," dtd. July 6, 1966; T.C., Schilling, ltr. dtd. September 19, 1966. Findings concerning the decline of interest for a military career among cadets are discussed in Office of Research Study 1b5.8-66-001, *Military Commitment and Entering Class of 1970 and Graduating Class of 1966* (West Point, N.Y., 1966) and *Annual Report for the Superintendent 1966-7,* (West Point, N.Y., 1967), pp. 15-18. The findings of the Academy paralleled those of David Segal and John Blair, "Public Confidence in the U.S. Military," *Armed Forces and Society* 3 (Fall, 1976): 8-9. Segal and Blair note that while on the whole popular trust of the military remained high during the war (1965-75), there was a marked decline in the favorable image of the military among ages 18-24.

[10]T.C., Lyman, ltr. dtd. January 29, 1969.

[11]T.C., Torrence, 5x8 cards titled "Adventure Board, New Instructor Orientation, 1969."

[12]Jeffrey Clarke, "On Strategy and the Vietnam War," *Parameters* 4 (Winter, 1986): 44.

[13]Shelby L. Stanton, *The Rise and Fall of an American Army, U.S. Ground Forces in Vietnam 1965-1973* (Naveto, CA., 1985).

[14]T.C., May, ltr. dtd. April 8, 1971.

[15]T.C., Esposito, ltr. dtd. July 11, 1986.

[16]T.C., Rybicki, ltr. postmarked January 25, 1967.

[17]T.C., Lambart, ltr. dtd. March 3, 1968.

[18]T.C., Smith, diary dtd. August 16, 1966.

[19]Galloway, *West Point,* p. 22.

[20]T.C., Campanella, ltr. undated. This letter was not written directly to the "Adventure Board," but addressed to the author's wife. Campanella's description of the battle is subject to independent verification. The battle he discussed was the subject

of a book by S.L.A. Marshall. Marshall, a combat historian, conducted an in-depth interview of all participants involved immediately after the incident. See Marshall, *Bird* (Garden City, N.Y., 1969), pp. 223-7, 232, 233-4, 243, 276, 281, 286.

[21] *T.C.*, Shulte, ltr. dtd. September 7, 1969.

[22] *T.C.*, Townsend Clarke, ltr. dtd. December 1968.

[23] Gabriel, *Crisis*, pp. xi, 17-8.

[24] For a typical example see *T.C.*, May, ltr. dtd. April 8, 1971.

[25] *T.C.*, Palmer, interview, pp. 3-6; *T.C.*, Flint, interview, pp. 5-6; *T.C.*, Nye, interview, pp. 4-5; *T.C.*, Woodmansee, interview, pp. 7-10; *T.C.*, Griess, ltrs. dtd. April 29, 1970, August 1, 1970.

[26] *T.C.* Flint, interview, p. 4. See also the treatment of this issue in William L. Hauser, *America's Army in Crisis, A Study in Civil-Military Relations* (Baltimore, 1973), pp. 173-86.

[27] *T.C.*, Palmer, interview, p. 5.

[28] Ellis, *School*, p. 207.

[29] *T.C.*, Rybicki, ltr. dtd. March 21, 1967.

[30] Ellis, *School*, pp. 129-34. See also *T.C.*, Nye, interview, pp. 11-15; *T.C.*, Palmer, interview, pp. 22-3; *T.C.*, Flint, interview, pp. 6-7.

[31] *T.C.*, Bunting, ltr. dtd. January 19, 1972.

[32] *T.C.* Flint, interview, p. 8.

[33] *T.C.*, Palmer "Notes for Instructors *Vietnam: The Phalanx of Fire*", see pp. 20-2, 27-8.

[34] Palmer, Dave Richard, *Readings in Current Military History* (West Point, 1969), pp. 94.

[35] Dave Richard Palmer, *Summons of the Trumpet, A History of the Vietnam War from a Military Man's Viewpoint* (New York, 1978), pp. 147-67.

James Jay Carafano is an assistant professor at the United States Military Academy at West Point. He received an MA "with distinction" from Georgetown University.

Patrolling Hill 55: Hard Lessons in Retrospect

A company grade officer's memoir of duty in Vietnam and his reflections on how the Corps adjusted and responded to battlefield challenges quite different from those for which it was specifically organized and trained.

by LtCol Howard A. Christy, USMC(Ret)

We are taught by the book. That is, we are taught the basics of individual and unit discipline and movement under combat conditions. But some have said that we do this so that when the balloon goes up and the lead begins to fly we can throw out the book and play it by ear—but in a disciplined sense, a sense shaped and tempered by all that book learning and training. In Vietnam perhaps we ran across all too many occasions to throw out the book and play it by ear. We were, at least in the beginning, in a new kind of war for us, one for which the book had not been definitively written. But I wonder if we were wise to have thrown the book out with such regularity. On the other hand, I wonder if we had the flexibility—the professional sharpness—to reassess our course against what turned out to be an extremely resourceful enemy.

This article deals with some of the foolishness and perhaps the lack of flexibility that occurred in I Corps during the early part of the Vietnam War, and suggests lessons learned that may still have some application today. I was a first-hand participant in the events described, as the combat intelligence officer/briefer in the 3d Marine Division intelligence staff, and later as the commander of Company A, 1st Battalion, 9th Marines. However, in order to reduce personal references as much as possible, I use third-person (e.g., "the company commander" and "the company") throughout. The perspective and conclusions presented are the result of considerable reflection over time; by no means was the apparent interrelatedness of events clear at the time. That might be a lesson in itself.

By the spring of 1966, combat elements of the 3d Marine Division seemed to be carrying out two strategies at the same time: the strategy of counterinsurgency that had been developed re-

cently by American forces in collaboration with the guerrilla-savvy British and French, and a hybrid offensive strategy featuring scattered deployment and saturation patrolling coordinated with elaborately plotted "H & I" (harassing and interdiction) artillery fires. This more offensive strategy received the most emphasis, understandably so since it was more familiar than the land-control, pacification-oriented strategy of counterinsurgency, which in a three-pronged approach employed population control and assistance simultaneously and equally with the more combative counterguerrilla effort. Perhaps saturation patrolling and H & I fires were emphasized also because the first major Marine effort of the war—Operation STARLIGHT in the Chu Lai tactical area of responsibility (TAOR) during the summer of 1965—had been a conventional offensive operation against Viet Cong (VC) forces that stayed to fight instead of employing the more elusive strategy they emphasized later, particularly in the Da Nang TAOR. That is, perhaps the patrolling and H & I strategy was employed in the anticipation that we would regularly meet or "catch out" larger, more-fixed enemy units like those encountered in STARLIGHT. Did our approach work? That is, did it allow us to accomplish our objective?

Whatever may have been the merits of either strategy, it was obvious that the VC were not fools; in fact, they seemed to be quite capable of keeping us at bay while they seemingly moved at will. We knew that the VC were intently and shrewdly watching us. Stories of sand-table mockups of Marine positions painstakingly fashioned by the VC began to be reported by intelligence sources and were also reflected in captured documents, which included precise sketches of our positions. To us, this indicated an impressive knowl-

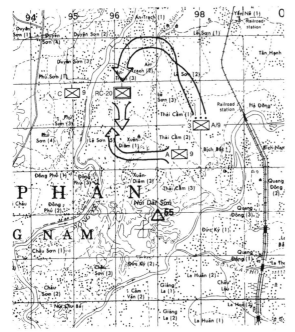

dent the division intelligence staff began a careful study of the incidence of mines and booby traps, and information on that aspect of the war became a priority feature in future intelligence briefings.

About a week later, a VC force of estimated battalion size snuck up on and assaulted the Marine company occupying a remote outpost on Hill 22, on the division's defensive salient northwest of Hill 55. The VC penetrated the perimeter and got all the way to the command bunker before the Marines were able to beat back the attack in desperate hand-to-hand fighting. Later, it was reported that the VC had made an elaborately detailed sand-table mockup of the outpost, then had shrewdly attacked at about 0245 when they knew the Marines were least likely to be fully alert. Though repulsed, they came precariously close to overrunning the outpost. The episode sent a shock through the division.

A few days later, the VC ingeniously employed a mine ambush; that is, they wired together several mines in an elongated "L" shape, sat in wait, then simultaneously exploded all the mines—probably with a hand-operated electric detonator—when a Marine patrol walked into their trap. The ambush was quickly investigated and briefed, and once again a shock went through the division staff.

If nothing else, these incidents pointed to the fact that we were up against a smart, as well as vicious enemy. But had we been alert enough to see it, they also clearly indicated that the VC had developed a strategy of their own, one designed precisely to counter our scattered deployment and aggressive tendencies. "Strategy" is the "science and art of military command exercised to meet the enemy in combat under advantageous conditions." Could these seemingly unprofessional VC commanders have developed such a "science and art"? Could they have assembled a "book" on our tendency to dash aggressively about the countryside in small units aching for a fight? It seems in retrospect that they had. Sad to say, however, the matter never came up for discussion at division intelligence, and over the next several months, Marines kept to their strategy even though they seldom if ever had a significant meeting engagement with a sizable VC force. While at the same time, fully 90 percent of our casualties were being caused by mines, booby traps, and ambushes.

Early in the spring of 1966, a platoon on patrol north of Hill 55 walked into a massive ambush and was annihilated with the exception of two wounded Marines who survived the slaughter by feigning death as the VC poked about among the bodies collecting weapons and ammunition. Investigation revealed that the platoon, by repeatedly patrolling over the same ground, had established a pattern that the watchful VC had been able to spot and for which they prepared a devastating response. By now it should have been painfully obvious that the enemy was employing effective countermeasures and that the aggressive patrolling strategy needed to be reassessed in that light.

edge of our overall order of battle. It was soon obvious that the VC had both the means and the moxie to make mines and booby traps out of just about anything that could be induced to explode.

These and other capabilities were determinable very early in the war. Three stark events in the summer and fall of 1965 if examined together could have given a clue not only of particular tactical capabilities but perhaps something more ominous. In September, one of the battalions of the 9th Marines set up a command post on Hill 55, southwest of Da Nang, and began patrolling in the sector surrounding the hill. One morning—just before the daily 8 a.m. briefing of the division commander was to take place up in Da Nang—the battalion commander, during a short reconnaissance near the north slope of the hill, tripped a booby-trapped 155mm artillery shell that exploded with a roar and blew the colonel to pieces. The tragedy was immediately reported to division, and the intelligence desk officer ran the grim information over to the conference room just as the G–1 portion of the briefing commenced. The G–2 briefer hastily noted the information and silently slipped it to the commanding general immediately before taking his turn on the platform. The general was visibly shaken by the report. He read the note silently, then handed it to the officer beside him and bowed his head. There was utter silence in the room as the note moved up and down the table, then the general grimly nodded for the briefing to continue. Following that inci-

In particular, the aggressive part needed to be rethought. Far too many officers were inclined to aggressively maneuver against every known enemy sighting. Even the commanding general had demanded that his intelligence briefings include reports of every contact with the VC, including, in his exact words, "one-shot misses." Demanding exacting information about the enemy is one thing; blindly chasing after shadows is another. An aggressive strategy is one thing; an overly aggressive strategy under the conditions we experienced is another. In the case of I Corps in 1966, a one-shot miss, or even a fusillade from a tree line, should not have necessarily demanded an immediate frontal assault, especially in light of the knowledge that the enemy was taking advantage of such a proclivity. In conversations between officers, aggressiveness was often the topic of discussion. Not unlike Custer, some seemed to think that it was up to them to end the war then and there, and with dash and flair. In one conversation with a battalion commander the question was put: If a unit was to draw fire from the far side of a wet rice paddy, would he order an assault across the paddy? Without hesitation he said that he would. Not often discussed was individual and unit security, particularly individual dispersion and unit point and flank security. Although such basic concerns may have been taken for granted, failure of senior commanders to continually warn of the crucial nature of unit security in a strategy emphasizing constant aggressive movement was extremely shortsighted. These aspects of the early war—the strategy of saturation patrolling; the counterstrategy of mines, booby traps, and ambushes; the tendency to be overly aggressive; and underemphasis on individual and unit security— were sure to lead to trouble, and the Marines in I Corps continually walked into that trouble.

On 21 May 1966 several weeks after the above-mentioned ambush, another company was assigned to carry out a County Fair counterinsurgency operation at the little village of Thai Cam (2) also in the area north of Hill 55. The counterguerrilla aspect of the operation went off without incident, and by noon the troops had little or nothing to do as the attached medical and other relief and assistance people did their work. But gunfire began to crackle off to the west, and the company saddled up for possible action in that direction. Minutes later the battalion commander, who was located at his command post on Hill 55, radioed for a platoon to be detached and flown by helicopter to join the adjacent company, which had become engaged by fire with an enemy force across the river that marked the boundary between the two companies.

Now at least some of the company were perhaps going to have a taste of real war, the old-fashioned kind with which we were the most familiar. Two large cargo helicopters flew in and picked up the 3d Platoon (with a section of machineguns attached), and within the hour the entire company was ordered to move directly to the

scene of the battle and engage the enemy in support of the other company. The troops climbed onto the two battle tanks and two amphibious tractors at hand (attached for use in the County Fair) and moved due west to the river, jumped off, formed a skirmish line with two platoons abreast, and proceeded to move north.

The company was no sooner organized and moving than it met headlong a large group of VC almost nonchalantly streaming south, obviously out of ammunition and unaware of what they were blundering into. A slaughter commenced during which every VC soldier was killed, most by the withering enfilade poured into them and some by hand-to-hand fighting. It was thrilling. For once it was hard-nosed Marines in a classic skirmish assaulting straight into and vanquishing the enemy—like at Saipan or Inchon. Somewhat ironically, the company, in its assault up the river, recovered from the vanquished foe the very M1917A4 machineguns lost in the ambush (described above) that had earlier annihilated the Marine platoon that had patrolled the same route once too often. (It was later determined that the VC unit involved in both incidents was the RC-20th Company.) But the story is not yet complete, nor is the irony.

As the company thus proceeded up the river bank doing its dirty work, a pathetic voice came over the battalion tactical net. "Help," he pleaded weakly. "I'm dying, and I'm the only one left," or words to that effect. The battalion commander broke in, told the company commander to concentrate on the battle at hand, and addressed himself to the caller. What followed was a wrenchingly sad but at the same time eloquent conversation between the two. The colonel, like a father talking to his injured child, soothingly began, "Now, son, we hear you, and we're going to help you." Thence proceeded the necessary communications between the commander and the badly wounded young Marine (his shoulder had been shattered by machinegun fire) to effect a rescue. The Marine had no idea where he was, but the colonel was able to ascertain that he had an unspent white-star cluster

These aspects of the early war—the strategy of saturation patrolling; the counterstrategy of mines, booby traps, and ambushes; the tendency to be overly aggressive; and underemphasis on individual and unit security— were sure to lead to trouble, and the Marines in I Corps continually walked into that trouble.

with which he could signal his location. With the colonel gently and patiently telling him what to do step by step, on the count of three the flare popped only a few hundred yards from the assaulting force's position. The company commander, having heard the entire communication, entered the net and told the colonel that he had the position in sight, and since the battle was well in hand, he could move there immediately by am-

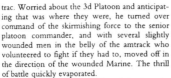

trac. Worried about the 3d Platoon and anticipating that was where they were, he turned over command of the skirmishing force to the senior platoon commander, and with several slightly wounded men in the belly of the amtrack who volunteered to fight if they had to, moved off in the direction of the wounded Marine. The thrill of battle quickly evaporated.

Below, Marines from Company B, 1st Bn, 9th Mar recover the bodies of their comrades from the 3d Platoon who lost their lives during the action on 21 May 1966.

The scene was sickening. There indeed was the 3d Platoon, or what was left of it. The two helicopters had landed in a large, dry rice paddy—right in the middle of the RC-20th. The battalion commander, the one who had shown such kindness to a single wounded Marine, had little more than an hour before ordered that Marine and many others straight into the fray by helicopter without any effort to secure a landing site. He put them, not behind or alongside the company to which they were to be attached, where security for the landing and at least some semblance of mission orientation could have been established, but across the river from that company where they were to operate as a separate maneuver element. Essentially, in his zeal to aggressively close with the enemy, the battalion commander chanced everything on a blind guess. Unfortunately, he could not have guessed more wrongly.

The RC-20th immediately turned its attention from the Marines across the river and poured fire point-blank into the 3d Platoon as the Marines desperately scrambled out of the helicopters. In the frantically confusing situation, the helicopter crews had only one option—to abandon the already scattering troops and escape as best they could. With the troops running in every direction to get away from the helicopters and many men falling from the hail of fire, regathering everybody proved impossible. Six Marines were killed outright—most as they attempted to exit the helicopters. An additional 25 Marines and corpsmen were wounded, among them the platoon commander. The irony was made complete by the fact that the VC had at least two "old" Browning M1917A4 light machineguns that fired well, and both of the 3d Platoon's brand-new M60s had immediately jammed. (Marine infantry units had begun replacing their M1917A4s with M60s in the early spring of 1966).

When the company commander and his party arrived, only two pockets of men remained unhurt. Eleven were cowering in one bomb crater, and five more were grimly awaiting the end in another nearby crater. Then there was the wounded Marine on the top of the ground by himself. No person in any group knew if anybody else remained alive. The platoon sergeant, who was with the group of 11, later explained that they had attempted to maneuver, but with their machineguns jammed, there was little chance of gaining a balance of fire. Further, every time someone lifted his head above the edge of the crater the VC raked him with fire. Neither the group of 11 nor the group of 5 had a radio, and with the platoon commander and his radioman being shot down, all command and control were lost. From the moment the platoon landed to the moment the wounded Marine finally made his feeble appeal, the platoon was entirely cut off. They never had a chance.

There were, fortunately, some magnificent displays of professionalism, courage, and compassion by individual Marines and Navy corpsmen—displays by young enlisted men that in a way saved the bacon for us supposed "professionals" who had precipitated this shameful affair. Splendid leadership and heroism were displayed in the group of five, for example. Upon interview, four of the Marines, all Caucasians, reported how, as they crouched there, a young black machinegunner calmly said he would take charge. Assuming that they would be assaulted and killed or captured, he ordered each man to inventory his ammunition and trade around so that each had an equal share; each man would save one round to kill himself if necessary, and all would stand at the ready, back to back, and await the expected assault on their hole. Then they would go down fighting, taking as many VC with them as they could. Melodramatic stuff, but the Marines who told the story were deadly serious.

Earlier, and at the height of the bedlam, one of the corpsmen ran to one wounded Marine and gave him lifesaving first aid, then ran to the next fallen Marine, then to the next, and on to the next. Surviving Marines told that the corpsman, while attending the fifth wounded Marine, was shot down, a bullet through his head. He had knowingly sacrificed himself to do his duty. (He was still alive when evacuated but probably died on the way to the hospital.)

Somehow, probably from information reported by the helicopter crews that had taken the 3d Platoon into the fray, a helicopter medevac team arrived on the scene while the situation was still in chaos. The crew flew into the bloody field seven times—several times directly into enemy fire. During the first sorties they took so many rounds into and through their helicopter that they had to replace it in order to continue. Just after the detachment with the company commander arrived, the medevac crew returned for the sixth time and picked up the remaining wounded, including the lone Marine who had called for help, and then came back once more to pick up the dead. Wanting every able-bodied man to concentrate on the possibility of another attack, the company commander ordered them to stick to their weapons and proceeded alone to help the corpsman/crew chief load the dead on the helicopter. It was a gruesomely difficult task: the dead Marines, their bodies drained of blood, handled much like what might have been large sacks of potatoes that had been smashed by a sledgehammer; like so much mush they flopped about heavily and awkwardly in the effort to half heave, half yank them up into the helicopter. The bodies filled the belly of the helicopter and the crew chief had to sit atop the mound of corpses for the return flight. As the helicopter lifted off, the two men's eyes met. On the crew chief's face was an unforgettable look of shock and anguish. He seemed to be expressing, though without words, how terribly sorry he was that he could not have saved them all.

More melodrama, perhaps, but these descriptions, at the risk of pushing too hard to make the point, are inserted here to convey a sense of the human tragedy that more likely than not occurs when officers throw out the book, play it by ear, and cavalierly hasten to order other men into terrible situations.

What foolishness! Under the conditions, there was no clear reason to have been so hasty and to have risked so much. Had the 3d Platoon been dropped into that horrible trap sooner it would likely have suffered far worse, since the VC company that engaged them would have had more ammunition with which to finish the platoon off. Those who survived were extremely lucky; the VC did run out of ammunition and withdrew— south down the river bank and to their destruction at the hands of the skirmish line moving north.

Chance destruction of the RC-20th aside, should we have been dashing about looking for a fight so recklessly? Should any unit be dropped into an unsecured landing site unless the situation is desperate? In the case of the company to which the 3d Platoon was to be attached, their situation was not desperate. They were merely exchanging fire with the enemy across a river and had plenty of room to maneuver. The words "was to be" are intentional. The 3d Platoon never saw, nor was it ever seen by, the company to which it was supposed to have been attached; nor is it apparent that anybody in that company attempted to establish contact beyond perhaps trying to contact them by radio. One has to wonder why, when that medevac crew kept coming in across the river in plain sight and hearing, somebody in the company did not at least warn battalion that the to-be-attached unit might be in trouble. On the other hand, why should they have? Technically, the 3d Platoon was not yet an attachment under the company's responsibility; it was still a separate command under battalion responsibility. Did the other company commander even know they were there? Owing to the sensitivity of the episode, such things were not discussed later. Whatever the whole story might have been, obviously the 3d Platoon was sacrificed for no other reason than a chance that through aggressive maneuvering in the blind they might keep a VC unit in place. That is insufficient justification for blindly jeopardizing the lives of a reinforced rifle platoon and several helicopter crews. The entire incident simply should not have happened, and it would not have happened had we better balanced our stewardship to our men with our disposition to aggressiveness. But then Marines are always aggressive, and commanders had little time to learn their trade and make their mark.

Returning to the saturation patrolling strategy, the troops derisively called the incessant patrols "activities." Although in a few instances a single "activity" probably flushed out an enemy unit, and a few others may have deterred an enemy attack, the continuous employment of patrols around the clock kept the troops in a constant state of exhaustion while at the same time offering easy targets for an enemy that, as already indicated above, had the capability and cunning to take advantage of the opportunities that the strategy presented them. Didn't this strategy violate or misapply any number of the principles of war, those principles that are considered the "enduring bedrock of doctrine"? Arguably, such a strategy can be justified under the principles of objective, maneuver, and offensive. But what about mass, economy of force, unity of command, security, simplicity, and surprise? The enemy always knew right where we were, and they knew that we would constantly present ourselves in vulnerable little pieces and that those little pieces would wander about seemingly willy-nilly over the same terrain day after day and night after night. And complicating the issue, all patrolling had to be orchestrated, lock step, around those elaborately plotted and timed H & I fires. All the VC had to do was observe, plant mines and booby traps, and use the hit and run tactics that they often employed in coordination with deadly ambushes. That is, the Marines seemed to be employing a strategy that in violating most of the principles of war all-too-easily accommodated the strategy consistently being employed against them by enemy commanders who took advantage of every element as if they had conceived those bedrock principles themselves. Add to that a tendency on the part of Marine commanders to be overly aggressive and the conditions for disaster were ripe.

Moreover, still another factor mitigated against us— our general disdain of the enemy. Were the VC equal to the challenge? By all means they were. They probably were as adept at employing mine warfare as any military force in history. We saturated the battlefield with little patrols and chased after every burst of fire; they saturated the battlefield with traps, baited us with scattered fire, and waited for us in ambush. The VC were not merely a bunch of stupid little people in black silk pajamas, conical straw hats, and shower shoes made from old tires. They were intelligent, cunning, able, well trained, largely professional, and relent-

> . . . the continuous employment of patrols around the clock kept the troops in a constant state of exhaustion while at the same time offering easy targets for [the] enemy. . . .

Above, in an engagement shortly before the action described in this article, Marines from 3d Bn, 9th Mar engage VC forces during Operation GEORGIA, south of Da Nang in April–May 1966.

about eight men under the command of a lance corporal or corporal. That is, those maneuver elements that were supposed to be able to fix and destroy a fanatic enemy were little more than glorified fire teams often led by newly arrived junior NCOs barely older and better trained than the youngest and least trained men under them. It seemed little short of suicidal to send these weak little units out on the extended "activities" expected under division policy. In early June the battalion commander at Hill 55 was urged by subordinates to beef up offensive patrols to platoon size for several reasons, among them leadership and experience, firepower, maneuver capability, and sheer size sufficient to resist an ambush. The battalion commander naturally hesitated making a decision that might be considered contrary to division policy, but on the other hand, he could not dismiss the rationale presented. On the merits, and possibly somewhat influenced by the tragic results of his decision of 21 May, he approved increasing the size of offensive patrols from squad to platoon.

What about troop strengths? In 1966 the 3d Marine Division was chronically short of personnel. The above-described company is a good case in point; it averaged about 150 men on any given day. Casualties totaled 100 between March and July, and 4 of them were lieutenants. These painful losses were in addition to the normal attrition that arised as a result of the single-year rotation policy that prevailed throughout the Vietnam War. This policy resulted in a steady drain of experienced men, often at times when units could ill afford to lose them. These endemic shortages in both numbers and experience, in combination with the requirement to saturate the operations area with patrols around the clock and the Marine Corps' "can do" spirit, created an extremely dangerous, sometimes almost debilitating situation. It appears that the Corps' personnel administration structure was not geared to keep up in 1966. Is it now? If not now, or if always fighting shorthanded is taken for granted, are field commanders prepared, either by training or philosophy, to make the necessary operational adjustments to keep the fighting machine healthy enough to carry out the mission?

Combining enemy mines, booby traps, caves, tunnels, wire, dikes, ditches, ambushes and selected attacks with our willy-nilly "activities" carried out by exhausted and understrength units and the VC's uncanny ability to orchestrate the mix to their advantage, the early part of the war was hell. It was nasty, humorless, exhausting, and terribly discouraging. In another kind of bitter irony, an awful incident occurred in late June 1966 that seemed to neatly but searingly bind up the whole ugly mess.

Near the river that flows past Hill 55 on the south, the rice paddies did double duty by yielding rice during the northeast monsoon and corn during the dry season. By June the corn stood about 7 feet high, just the perfect addition to the

less. And they were fanatically determined killers. They hated us passionately and would never rest until we were gone from their homeland forever, dead or alive. Having no mass, no fighter planes, no artillery or tanks or naval guns or B-52s with which to pulverize the landscape with arc lights, they dug ditches, tunnels, and caves, and planted barbed wire, booby traps, and mines—all brilliantly and perfectly adapted to counter the strategy of aggressive saturation patrolling. The so-called ambushes we claim to have employed in tandem with patrols were nothing more than patrols that stopped longer at one of their checkpoints. In fact they were a joke; it is likely that Marines never closed a successful ambush against the VC, since the VC always knew where the ambushes were. Perhaps one of the lessons we seemingly never learned is that we were fighting a smart and dedicated—and sophisticated—enemy.

The RC-20th VC company made only one mistake on 21 May: It abandoned an extremely effective strategy and fought for too long in one place. Nevertheless, up to the moment of destruction it had been enormously successful; it annihilated one platoon and almost annihilated another in addition to killing several more with mines and booby traps (including a battalion commander) before succumbing to their own annihilation. Regardless of their relative success, the other VC in the region probably learned well from the RC-20th's one big mistake. We, however, seemingly never learned. Rather than learning, our revenge on the RC-20th and recovering our weapons may even have been seen as a vindication of our strategy, not a lucky stroke owing to a VC mistake that was not likely to be repeated.

After the incident of 21 May, the company took up defensive duty for the southern part of the battalion command post perimeter at Hill 55—with the usual additional responsibility of saturation patrolling. The company was so short of personnel that squad patrols (the commonly employed patrol was squad size) consisted mostly of dikes, ditches, wire, and mines to present patrolling Marines with bad situations. Late one afternoon the 1st Platoon while on patrol entered one of those rice paddy/cornfields. At the far side of the field the point squad came abruptly upon a high dike behind a ditch and topped by barbed wire. The squad leader halted his unit and radioed the situation to the platoon commander, who decided to come up to see for himself. He unwisely brought with him the platoon sergeant, platoon guide, and the platoon's complement of radiomen and corpsmen. They approached, then intermingled with the squad, which had already become badly bunched up—first because of the dense growth and then from piling up on the fenced dike. The platoon commander looked the situation over and ordered the squad to move around the obstacle and continue on the previously assigned heading. And to his credit he ordered everybody to spread back out since they were so dangerously bunched up.

It was too late. The first man to move tripped a large mine planted at the base of the dike. Two Marines, including the platoon sergeant, were killed instantly. The platoon commander was saturated with shrapnel, the man who tripped the mine had both feet blown off, and 14 others were also wounded, most of them seriously. It was probably the worst mine tragedy in the war up to that point.

The physical evidence of the tragedy was starkly clear upon inspection the next morning. Shrapnel had cut a swath through the corn, and the broken stalks lay in an arc away from the point of the blast. Thick puddles of coagulated blood marked the place where every Marine had fallen, and the puddles were close together. When the report of the tragedy reached division, a formal investigation was immediately launched with both the company and battalion commander being named as parties. The investigating officer was a lieutenant colonel who had just arrived in country and was being assigned to the 9th Marines. Fortunately, before he came down to Hill 55 he took the opportunity to interview the wounded before they were airlifted out of country. Most or all who were able to speak reported that before the incident strong measures—to include a 10-pace minimum interval—had been consistently carried out to avoid just such a tragedy, and the investigation concluded without culpability being assigned. Not that this in any way ameliorated the tragedy that had occurred.

With the exception of the events of 21 May, every casualty suffered by the company between March and July 1966 was due to mines, booby traps, and VC ambushes while the men were carrying out "activities" during which they never saw the enemy.

Did our approach work? Did it allow us to accomplish the objective? Two years after returning home I bumped into a classmate from The Basic School at the Camp Pendleton post exchange. He had just returned from Vietnam. He had been a rifle company commander in the vicinity of Hill 55. He recalled that it was nasty, humorless, exhausting, and terribly discouraging. And his company suffered many casualties on mines and booby traps while hardly ever setting eyes on the enemy. His was at least the 12th rifle company to have patrolled Hill 55 (at least four battalions had been assigned in that vicinity between 1965 and 1967). How many more companies bled there and to what end? Was it all in vain?

Suffice it to say, in conclusion, that battle commanders should stick by the book (the basics) as much as they can—at least as regards individual and unit security—and play it by ear only when the conditions absolutely dictate. But at the same time we must be flexible enough to reassess and respond, intelligently and quickly, boldly even, to whatever strategy the enemy may employ to counter us. Battle commanders must be ever vigilant regarding the condition of their men, and allow that condition to influence their approach to the mission. It is true, whether we like it or not and "can do" spirit notwithstanding, Marines can easily be pushed to exhaustion and can absorb bullets and shrapnel just as easily as any other foot soldier. If they are killed or maimed because of constant exhaustion, or while on details that foolishly play into the hands of the enemy, it is not their fault; it is their commander's fault. And surely, one of the deadliest ways to play into the hands of the enemy is to blindly drop troops into unsecured landing zones.

Lastly, the commander's responsibility as the guardian of the welfare of his men must take precedence over any personal motive. How often are decisions on the battlefield entirely consistent with the real mission, and how often are they influenced by the urge, for example, to be dashing, aloof, and cavalier? In the final analysis, the best battle commanders, in addition to being highly competent, are—consistent with the mission—also highly dedicated to the welfare of their men. That any Marine's vanity be the cause of another Marine's death is more than tragic; it is criminal.

US MC

>LtCol Christy, who was awarded a Silver Star for his actions on 21 May 1966, retired from the Marine Corps in 1975 after 20 years of service in infantry and intelligence. He currently directs the Office of Scholarly Publications at Brigham Young University where he received a master's degrees in American history and library science. He has written numerous published works on Utah history and geography.

Paradox of Power: Infiltration, Coastal Surveillance, and the United States Navy in Vietnam, 1965-68

☆

Clarence E. Wunderlin, Jr.

COASTAL surveillance patrols, operations in keeping with one of the historic missions of navies everywhere, have often been ill-conceived and poorly conducted and have seldom received scholarly attention. From the American Revolution to the Vietnam War, the United States Navy has rarely been properly prepared or even inclined to undertake these basic naval operations. The Continental Navy's inability to inform General Washington about enemy movements before the capture of Philadelphia affords just one example drawn from those dark days of 1777. In the "undeclared and limited" Quasi-War with France, the United States Navy groped haphazardly at surveillance of the nation's coastline before Secretary of the Navy Benjamin Stoddert shifted that service's efforts to combat a Caribbean *guerre de course*. But secretaries and admirals from Ben Stoddert to the present have eschewed such modes of unconventional warfare in a Mahanian quest for great fleets and decisive battles. In its haste to confront the Japanese Combined Fleet in the Pacific during World War II, the navy often failed to interdict the infiltration of supplies to enemy-held island fortresses.[1]

1. William James Morgan, ed., *Naval Documents of the American Revolution*, vol. 9, *1777* (Washington: GPO, 1986), especially 90-91, 107, 110, 347; Michael A. Palmer, *Stoddert's War: Naval Operations During the Quasi-War with France, 1798-1801* (Columbia: University of South Carolina Press, 1987); for a more

The Journal of Military History 53 (July 1989): 275-89 © American Military Institute

★ **275**

Given the unique circumstances of the Vietnam War, it is not surprising to find strategic and operational flaws hindering those coastal surveillance efforts. Forced by the constraints of limited war largely to disregard important Cambodian sanctuaries, the navy then failed to interdict infiltration along numerous waterways along the Vietnamese border. It is this failure at the strategic level that needs closer scrutiny.

Not surprisingly, in a war that has generated a vast amount of literature, naval strategy and operations in Vietnam—particularly surveillance and interdiction patrols, decisive only when the cumulative effect of their operations is tallied—have received little notice. Only a small number of scholars have focused on the achievements of that brown water navy in Vietnam.[2]

It was after March 1965 that the navy began an extensive effort to interdict the infiltration of men and materiel along the twelve-hundred-mile South Vietnamese coastline. As they evolved their "denial of victory" strategy, Johnson administration policymakers perceived that this interdiction effort was crucial to the conduct of the war. By early 1965 the administration was determined not to lose a war in which the

---

recent example of the problem of coastal surveillance and interdiction in the midst of offensive operations, see Samuel E. Morison's account of the battle for Leyte in 1944. *History of United States Naval Operations in World War II*, vol. 12, *Leyte, June 1944–January 1945* (Boston: Little, Brown and Company, 1958), especially 380, 387–88.

2. The best general survey of the war remains George C. Herring, *America's Longest War: The United States and Vietnam, 1950–1975* (New York: John Wiley and Sons, 1979). On the origins and escalation of United States involvement, the most significant works are Ronald H. Spector, *Advice and Support: The Early Years, 1941–1960*, United States Army in Vietnam (Washington: GPO, 1983); Leslie H. Gelb and Richard K. Betts, *The Irony of Vietnam: The System Worked* (Washington: Brookings Institution, 1979); Larry Berman, *Planning a Tragedy: The Americanization of the War in Vietnam* (New York: W. W. Norton and Company, 1982); Alexander S. Cochran, Jr., "Eight Decisions for War: January 1965–February 1966," in John Schlight, ed., *The Second Indochina War: Proceedings of Symposium Held at Airlie, Virginia, 7–9 November 1984* (Washington: GPO, 1986). An official treatment of early naval operations is in Edward J. Marolda and Oscar P. Fitzgerald, *From Military Assistance to Combat, 1959–1965*, The United States Navy and the Vietnam Conflict (Washington: GPO, 1986). Recent additions to the literature on in-country naval operations are Edward J. Marolda, "The War in Vietnam's Shallows," *Naval History* 1 (April 1987): 12–19, and Thomas J. Cutler, *Brown Water, Black Berets: Coastal and Riverine Warfare in Vietnam* (Annapolis: Naval Institute Press, 1988). Earlier works on the in-country naval war include R. L. Schreadley, "The Naval War in Vietnam, 1950–1970," *U.S. Naval Institute Proceedings* 97 (May 1971): 181–209; and James H. Hodgman, "Market Time in the Gulf of Thailand," U.S. Naval Institute *Naval Review, 1968*, 36–67.

enemy was achieving stunning military and political successes almost daily. In a series of decisions made between December 1964 and the Honolulu Conference in February 1966, Johnson and his war managers opted to intensify gradually the war effort in Indochina, while postponing the politically and strategically painful decisions for withdrawal or unlimited war against the Democratic Republic of Vietnam (DRV). Over the course of these thirteen months, the president and his advisors hoped to maintain flexibility by escalating America's military presence in the South within the parameters of limited war. During this crucial year, the United States government determined to force Hanoi to the bargaining table by demonstrating to the Communists their inability to liberate the South from the government of the Republic of Vietnam (GVN). Although American civilian and military policymakers could not conceive of losing, the United States quickly became trapped in a no-win war of attrition, conducted to meet a set of quantifiable strategic goals, without ever determining a clear path to victory.[3]

In the desperate days of early 1965, as Communist main force units chewed up one Army of the Republic of Vietnam (ARVN) battalion after another, naval strategists tasked Pacific Fleet units with a coastal surveillance and interdiction mission. As early as December 1963, admin-

---

3. The dissolution of the Republic of Vietnam's state apparatus and political hegemony in the early days of 1965 was a culmination of a decade of political, economic, and ethno-cultural instability that dated back to the early days of the Diem Regime. The government of South Vietnam (GVN) displaced traditional and imperial governance with a political system widely perceived as illegitimate. In response to Diem's effective—although ruthless and indiscriminate—counterinsurgency effort, the Communist National Liberation Front assumed the revolutionary initiative in 1959-60. The Communists quickly separated the GVN from the nation's populace through a reign of terror, while building their movement through a variety of constructive civic action programs. On the revolutionary movement, see William J. Duiker, *The Communist Road to Power in Vietnam* (Boulder, Colo.: Westview Press, 1981), and Jeffrey Race, *War Comes to Long An: Revolutionary Conflict in a Vietnamese Province* (Berkeley: University of California Press, 1972), 3-140; see also Spector, *Advice And Support,* 329-48.

On the early decisions to escalate and follow a war of attrition, see especially McGeorge Bundy Memorandum for the President, February 7, 1965; John McNaughton Memorandum, "Action for South Vietnam," March 10, 1965; and Maxwell Taylor for the Undersecretary of State, June 3, 1965, Cable No. 4035, National Security File, National Security Council History, "Deployment of Major U.S. Forces to Vietnam, July 1965," Lyndon Baines Johnson Papers, Lyndon Baines Johnson Library, Austin, Texas. Secondary works that have treated the decision-making process and the absence of strategic thinking are Cochran, "Eight Decisions for War," 65-80; Herring, *America's Longest War,* 145-55; Berman, *Planning a Tragedy,* especially 31-78. Berman's study draws heavily on the above cited NSC history.

---

istration officials began pondering the extent of seaborne infiltration into the South. Secretary of Defense Robert S. McNamara and Vice Chief of Naval Operations Admiral Claude V. Ricketts both expressed concern that supplies were coming by sea, especially through Cambodia, and being shipped along Mekong Delta waterways to main force Communist battalions. At McNamara's request, Admiral Harry D. Felt, commander in chief, Pacific, sent a team headed by Captain Philip H. Bucklew to Saigon to find some answers.[4]

From Bucklew's report and from later Center for Naval Analyses (CNA) research, we can draw a clear picture of the infiltration problem between 1964 and 1968. Bucklew described a three-pronged infiltration system, consisting of landborne transport along the Ho Chi Minh Trail through Laos, seaborne infiltration along the RVN coast, limited to "deliveries of high priority items and key cadre personnel," and shipments through the ports of Sihanoukville and Kep to secure Cambodian sanctuaries. Bucklew warned that existing South Vietnamese coastal patrols were insufficient to guard the coast, recommended that United States Navy units should augment their efforts, and—most significantly—argued that a coastal quarantine would fail without accompanying operations to seal off inland infiltration routes, especially along the Cambodian border.[5]

These Cambodian sanctuaries loomed as the most significant source of materiel for enemy troops in the southern half of the RVN between 1965 and 1968. Bucklew clearly believed that the infiltration of munitions from Cambodian sanctuaries, not from coastal junk and trawler traffic, was the major threat to the southern provinces (III and IV Corps Tactical Zone).[6] CNA research further clarifies the picture of infiltra-

---

4. Marolda and Fitzgerald, *From Military Assistance to Combat*, 302.

5. Bucklew's conclusions can be found in "Report of recommendations pertaining to infiltration into South Vietnam of Viet Cong personnel, supporting materials, weapons and ammunition" (hereafter cited as Bucklew Report), 15 February 1964, Vietnam Command File, Box 63, Operational Archives, Naval Historical Center (hereafter cited as OA, NHC).

6. To support operations in South Vietnam's III and IV Corps Tactical Zones, the Viet Cong developed a vast border sanctuary complex. Especially in the "Parrot's Beak"—that portion of Cambodia that juts into the natural geographical approaches to Saigon—the Communists constructed facilities that "serve as reservoir and pumping stations for the provision of war materials." Under the direction of COSVN (Central Office for South Vietnam), Rear Service headquarters coordinated the off-loading of cargoes at the ports, the transportation of munitions to border depots by either cover organizations or secure chartered trucking companies, and distributed the materiel to border sanctuaries in the Parrot's Beak, Angel's

tion during these years. Although the Military Assistance Command, Vietnam (MACV), had evidence as early as 1964—when it was upgraded to a truck route—that the Ho Chi Minh Trail through Laos supplied Viet Cong troops as far south as lower II Corps in the Central Highlands, the trail did not assume primacy until 1968. Even as late as December 1968, the trail could not handle the requirements of III and IV Corps, when coupled with the requirements of the fierce battle for the northern provinces.

Furthermore, CNA research reveals that Cambodia was the major supply point for IV Corps Tactical Zone as early as the 1950s, although the port of Sihanoukville was not handling munitions on a large scale until 1966. "All-source reporting for 1964–1965 indicates massive equipping of enemy forces in III and IV Corps coinciding with shipments from Cambodian military warehouses. There were implications of high-level Cambodian military or government complicity," according to CNA analysts.[7] By April 1968, a Naval Forces, Vietnam (NAVFORV) intelligence study estimated that approximately 175 to 200 tons of munitions, exclusive of foodstuffs, arrived in Cambodian ports monthly—an estimate that later turned out as extremely conservative. This logistical support alone exceeded estimated requirements for Viet Cong troops in IV Corps Tactical Zone, requirements that approximated twenty-eight tons per month. The excess amounted to enough provisions to supply the majority of Viet Cong operations in II and III Corps as well. Naval leaders assumed that Viet Cong troops were storing the enormous excess (which outstripped even the needs of Cambodian armed forces) in caches for future operations—caches which allied ground forces often uncovered in search-and-destroy operations inside Republic of Vietnam borders.[8]

Wing, and Fishhook regions. See Operation Order, COMNAVFORV No. 201-70, 180142Z SEP 69, Annex C, Intelligence, in supplemental materials to Judith Erdheim, *Market Time,* deposited in OA, NHC; on the establishment of the border sanctuaries in Cambodia, see Race, *War Comes to Long An,* 84–85.

7. Victory Daniels and Judith C. Erdheim, *Game Warden,* Center for Naval Analyses Study CRC 284 (unclassified) (January 1976), Appendix A, quote on p. A-4. Vietnam Command File, Box 254, OA, NHC. Marolda incorrectly concludes that the navy's successful Market Time operations forced Communists to begin using Cambodian ports after 1966 as a substitute, thus setting the stage for the 1968 offensive in the southern provinces. "The War in Vietnam's Shallows," 15.

8. Daniels and Erdheim, *Game Warden,* ibid., Appendix A, 2–6. Although it was conceivable that trawlers could have furnished a large portion of this logistical support, intelligence reports as early as 1966 detailed a complex support system, beginning with Cambodian port facilities, and noted five major crossing points into Vietnam from Cambodia. *Game Warden,* Appendix A, 4.

Despite the primacy of Cambodian sources of war materiel as early as 1964, many civilian and naval leaders were obsessed with nagging doubts about the infiltration of personnel and supplies along the South Vietnam coastline—doubts fueled by numerous unsubstantiated reports. But the capture of an ammunition-laden North Vietnamese trawler at Vung Ro Bay in February 1965 substantiated in the mind of Vice Admiral Paul P. Blackburn, Jr., newly assigned commander of Seventh Fleet, that the "numerous unconfirmed reports of sea infiltration in the past" possessed a frightening validity.[9]

This threat of seaborne infiltration was not negligible and had existed for some time. Both steel-hulled fishing trawlers from the North and shallow-draft coastal junks and sampans sought to weave their way through the crowded shipping lanes and heavy coastal commercial traffic to deliver munitions to numerous shallow and densely covered inlets along the South Vietnam littoral.[10] Senior naval commanders did not know in February 1965 that infiltration into South Vietnam by ocean-going fishing trawlers had begun as early as the late 1950s. To support regulars engaged in major campaigns, steel-hulled trawlers usually carrying one hundred tons or more of materiel shouldered the major burden of this infiltration.[11] The North Vietnamese eventually built or received from the People's Republic of China twenty-five trawlers.

9. The Bucklew Report in Vietnam Command File, Box 63, OA, NHC. Quoted material is from p. 2. On the use of Cambodian ports to supply the Viet Cong *in 1964,* see Appendix 1, 3. On seaborne infiltration, see also Schreadley, "The Naval War in Vietnam, 1950-1970," 186, and Marolda and Fitzgerald, *From Military Assistance to Combat, 1959-1965,* 299, 301-51. Bucklew's views can be found in Oscar P. Fitzgerald Interview with Captain Philip H. Bucklew, 10 July 1978, OA, NHC. In the interview, Bucklew claimed that "we were never convinced that many of things claimed or suspect really occurred. There was never any indication of infiltration of troops over the coastal channels. As I recall, there were three boats that were shot out of the water and there was no real indication that it was military supplies." Bucklew interview, 4. On the Vung Ro Incident, see Marolda and Fitzgerald, *From Military Assistance to Combat,* 513-15.

10. For the navy's analysis of the physical geography of the South Vietnamese littoral and problems facing surveillance operations, see Operation Order, COMNAVFORV No. 201-70, 180142Z SEP 69, Annex C, Intelligence, (declassified), and Memorandum from Chief, Naval Advisory Group, Military Assistance Command, Vietnam, 23 September 1965, "Study on Waterborne Infiltration into South Vietnam," (declassified) both in supplemental materials to Erdheim, *Market Time,* OA, NHC.

11. Most of these fishermen were 275-300 gross tonnage, diesel-powered ships of about one hundred feet in length with a draft of six and a half to eight feet. Most had 12.7-mm machine-guns as armament. See Appendix II, "Resume of Major Infiltration Attempts By Sea Since February 1965," in Naval Forces, Vietnam

Although few trawlers sailed south during the first three years, infiltration increased markedly once Viet Cong operations intensified in 1962, with twenty trawlers sailing in 1963, possibly fifteen the following year, and seven in early 1965.[12]

Even after the Vung Ro incident, civilian and military leaders remained uncertain of the magnitude of the coastal infiltration prob-

(hereafter cited as NAVFORV), *Monthly Historical Supplement*, March 1987, OA, NHC. Often seaborne infiltration followed an elaborate pattern. Most trawlers charted an intricate five- to ten-day course embarking from Haiphong Harbor, sailing through the Hainan Straits, southward into the South China Sea, then approaching directly perpendicular to the coastline. Favorable landing sites were the mouth of the Sa Ky River, Lo Dieu Beach, and Hon Heo Peninsula along the Annamite coast, and the Bo De River mouth and U Minh Forest in the Delta. Ships dashed to shore under the cover of darkness before moonrise or after moonset. Tidal conditions figured significantly in a trawler captain's considerations, especially if he charted a course for the Mekong Delta which necessitated an approach at high tide. Operation Order, COMNAVFORV No. 201-70, 180142Z SEP 69, Annex C, Intelligence, and CICV Special Report SR 67-002, "VC/NVA GUNRUNNERS," 9 August 1966, deposited with supplemental materials to Erdheim, *Market Time*, OA, NHC.

On the receiving end, the Vietnamese Communists in the South established a sophisticated support network. In the northern provinces, several units such as the Fiftieth Viet Cong Main Force Battalion distributed munitions inland. In the Delta, the support system encompassed units of an even higher echelon than battalion. By early 1966, intelligence sources suspected that a four-battalion support group, based in Kien Hoa Province, received, stored, and secured materiel received from the seaborne infiltration system. In the Delta, the A101 Group consisted of four battalions and a Group Headquarters: the headquarters and its 518th Security Battalion based in Kien Hoa; two unidentified battalions probably located in Vinh Binh and Ba Xuyen; and the 330th Battalion probably located in An Xyyen. CICV Special Report SR 67-002, "VC/NVA GUNRUNNERS," 9 August 1966, ibid.

12. By 1960 the DRV had organized what would eventually become the 125th Naval Transportation Group, directly subordinate to Military High Command in Hanoi, to plan and operate the naval support function. Operation Order, COMNAVFORV No. 201-70, 180142Z SEP 69, Annex C, Intelligence, ibid. Infiltration by sea was sporadic from 1960 to 1963, with a Viet Cong junk captured off Ly Son Island, Quang Ngai Province, on 31 January 1960, and cache of over two hundred tons of ammunition found in An Xuyen Province in August 1962. Especially after the Diem assassination in 1963, the Viet Cong intensified activities against the South Vietnamese government and army. The Central Committee resolved to support units in the South in campaigns against ARVN units and government-created Strategic Hamlets. Initially the North Vietnamese supplied units in the South through the Ho Chi Minh Trail complex in Laos. This logistical system soon bogged down under the weight of tons of heavy equipment destined to outfit regular battalions in the South, reinforced by some twelve thousand North Vietnamese personnel. Combined Intelligence Center, Vietnam, CICV Special Report SR 67-002, "VC/NVA GUNRUNNERS," 9 August 1966, (declassified), ibid. See also Marolda and Fitzgerald, *From Military Assistance to Combat*, 299, 301.

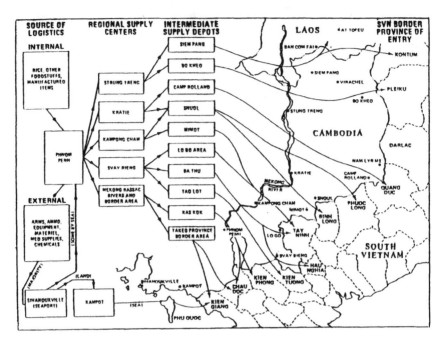

Logistical flow of Vietcong supplies from Cambodia to South Vietnam, 1966. (Source: Victory Daniels and Judith C. Erdheim, *Game Warden* [Washington: Center for Naval Analyses, 1976], A-3.)

lem. This ignorance stemmed directly from a failure of intelligence gathering and analysis. Naval intelligence admitted that "the rate and effectiveness of the sea infiltration program is largely unknown." This "major intelligence gap" resulted from ineffective surveillance of North Vietnam and the lack of an intelligence operative network throughout Indochina as a whole. At the time, the navy had little information upon which to base its estimates of coastal infiltration.[13]

13. C. H. Miller Memorandum for the Director of Naval Intelligence, 4 February 1965, Office of the Chief of Naval Operations files (hereafter cited as 00 files), 1965, Box 15, OA, NHC. On the inadequacy of intelligence, see also Oscar Fitzgerald Interview with Vice Admiral Paul P. Blackburn, 26 November 1973, 34–35, OA, NHC. A consensus about the overall pattern of maritime infiltration between 1960 and 1967 emerged afterwards, but operational commanders possessed little intelligence to guide them during the period. Daniels and Erdheim, *Game Warden*, Appendix A, p. A-1.

But naval leaders acted anyway. They inaugurated an extensive surveillance effort along the South Vietnam coastline without precise knowledge of enemy infiltration and, to a large degree, disregarded Bucklew's conclusions about the relative importance of coastal infiltration. After a week of planning with MACV in March 1965,[14] Admiral Blackburn inaugurated combined surveillance operations with the United States and Vietnamese navies to counter this perceived threat to the coastline. Initially two destroyers comprised the patrol force for an operation eventually code-named Market Time. On 15 March, the Johnson administration approved Blackburn's activation of Task Force 71—the Vietnam Patrol Force. Within two weeks, ten Seventh Fleet ships were patrolling the coastline, supported by shore-based SP-2H Neptune and carrier-based A-1H Skyraider patrol planes.[15]

In the March planning session, naval officers developed a basic concept for a combined United States–Vietnamese operation.[16] The Vietnamese Navy's Junk Force would conduct most patrols at the coastline, while the United States Navy would handle the more conventional sea patrol effort with ships and aircraft employing radar and visual search. Planners divided the South Vietnamese coast into eight (later nine) continuous-patrol areas stretching out to an average depth of thirty-five to forty nautical miles. Within these patrol areas, the navy created three barriers to infiltration. The outermost barrier consisted of aerial surveillance increasingly done by sophisticated antisubmarine warfare planes. Within the forty-mile limit, Seventh Fleet deployed first destroyers (DDs), then destroyer escorts (DEs) and radar picket escort ships (DERs), as well as minesweepers (MSOs and MSCs).[17]

14. Between 3 and 10 March, representatives from Naval Advisory Group and the MACV operations staff met with a liaison officer from Seventh Fleet and the Deputy Chief of Staff for the Commander-in-Chief, Pacific Fleet (CINCPACFLT). See Naval Advisory Group, MACV, *Historical Review* (hereafter cited as NAG, *Historical Review*), March 1965, Box 69, Vietnam Command File, OA, NHC.

15. NAG, *Historical Review*, March 1965, ibid.; Marolda and Fitzgerald, *From Military Assistance to Combat*, 517–19; Schreadley, "The Naval War in Vietnam," 188.

16. When interviewed, Blackburn described the cynical manner in which he and his planning officer established Market Time patrol patterns to please the technocrats of the Defense Department, knowing full well at the time that the patrols bore no relation to any enemy threat. Blackburn interview, 45–46.

17. In July DEs and DERs, with smaller yet still effective 3-inch guns, replaced all the heavier gunned DDs, which in turn formed the core of the navy's gunfire support Cruiser-Destroyer Group (Task Group 70.8) offshore. NAG, *Historical Review*, July 1965, Vietnam Command File, Box 69, OA, NHC. An MSO is an ocean-going minesweeper; an MSC, a coastal vessel.

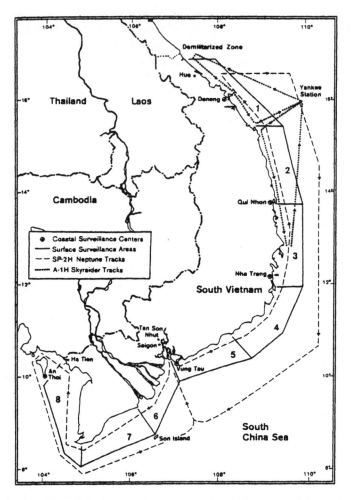

Market Time patrol areas. (Source: Edward J. Marolda and Oscar P. Fitzgerald, From Military Assistance to Combat, 1959-1965, The United States Navy and the Vietnam Conflict *[Washington: GPO, 1986], 518.)*

In conjunction with this American effort, Vietnamese Navy (VNN) patrol craft and junks initially handled most of the inner barrier or coastline patrols. But by April 1965, MACV believed that the VNN could not carry out effective surveillance of the voluminous junk and sampan

A "Swift": the PCF-4. This craft was the first United States loss during operation Market Time. On 14 February 1966 it struck a mine off Rach Gia. (Photo courtesy U.S. Naval Institute.)

traffic, especially along the coast south of Vung Tau and in the Gulf of Thailand. United States Navy advisors fleetingly considered supplementing the VNN with Patrol Craft, Fast (PCF), commonly called Swifts. But "the unwillingness of the VNN to patrol effectively with junks now," American naval advisors argued, "and the known reluctance of the VNN to accept new ideas and operational concepts in any timely manner, indicates that they will not use the SWIFT as envisioned. Therefore it is imperative that SWIFTs be manned by USN personnel until the VNN shows adequate ability to perform."

Even if they had possessed the will, the Vietnamese had few trained personnel in the technical ratings needed to man sophisticated patrol vessels. Based on their assessment of patrol requirements and utilization rates, but with no hard evidence on the magnitude of enemy coastal junk traffic, Naval Advisory Group (NAG) then suggested that the navy send fifty-four Swifts to Vietnam—a decision ratified by Secretary of Defense Robert S. McNamara in July. In addition to the Swifts, the navy deployed United States Coast Guard patrol craft (WPBs) to patrol inshore waters and block infiltration at the Demilitarized Zone and in the Gulf of Thailand at the Cambodia-RVN border. Surveillance centers were established at Danang, Qui Nhon, Nha Trang, and Vung

Tau on the South China Sea, and at An Thoi on Phu Quoc Island in the Gulf of Thailand.[18]

Although its effectiveness against largely unmeasurable enemy junk traffic along the coastline is debatable, the elaborate patrol network effectively curtailed trawler infiltration by late 1967. But as Admiral Elmo Zumwalt quickly grasped after assuming command of Naval Forces, Vietnam, in 1968, the navy had not used precious boats and men in the most productive way to block the major sources of infiltration. Postwar evaluations reveal the flaws of a naval strategy that permitted the enemy to wage a tactically disastrous, but strategically decisive offensive in early 1968.

Admiral Blackburn, possibly the most bitter critic of coastal surveillance, described Market Time as an "over-reaction." In explaining the commitment of vast resources of men and materiel to coastal patrols, he blamed the army "who were selling an excuse for their poor performance." Critical of the Office of the Secretary of Defense for promoting extensive coastal patrolling at the expense of other missions, Blackburn charged that "McNamara and his boys put intense heat on many. Like so many of their strongly held ideas, this one wasn't very bright." Other participants in the naval war questioned the extent of the coastal infiltration threat; some even pondering what the results would have been with a reduced commitment to Market Time.[19]

With the inauguration of Operation Market Time, and its systematic patrols and aerial reconnaissance flights, came a relative disregard for the infiltration of war materiel through Cambodian ports and sanctuaries. It was not an outright dismissal, but rather a failure to appreciate

---

18. VNN patrol boats did not have radar in sufficient numbers, rarely conducted alert patrols, and, as of early 1965, had a poor overall effectiveness rating. The United States Joint Chiefs of Staff wanted to improve the VNN, not just have Americans supersede it. In Saigon, the Naval Advisory Group wanted the VNN to maintain at least sixteen sea force patrols and two hundred junk patrols along the coastline at all times. R. L. Kalen Memorandum for the Secretary of the Navy, 17 April 65, 00 files, 1965, box 13, Operational Archives; on the Swifts and the VNN, see NAO Memorandum, Subject: "Use of SWIFT-type boats in the Vietnam coastal patrol," 1 April 1965, and NAG, *Historical Review*, March 1965 and July 1965, Vietnam Command File, Box 69, Operational Archives; Hodgman, "Market Time in the Gulf of Thailand," 38–41; Schreadley, "The Naval War in Vietnam, 1950-1970," 188–91; Marolda and Fitzgerald, *From Military Assistance to Combat*, 517.

19. Blackburn reply to Questionnaire, n.d., in supplemental materials for Erdheim, *Market Time*, deposited in OA, NHC. Lieutenant Commander Ian M. Bailey "was never really sure just how big the coastal infiltration threat was." Bailey Memorandum to Mrs. Judy Erdheim, 12 February 1974, ibid. Commander Robert K. Leopold replied to Erdheim's questionnaire by stating that he did not "believe that

Bucklew's warning in 1964. Without the interdiction of the munitions disembarked at the ports of Sihanoukville, Kep, and Kampot, then stockpiled in Cambodian sanctuaries, and eventually distributed along the vast waterways of the Delta region to support enemy offensives, the security of III and IV Corps Tactical Zone would remain in doubt.

What effort did the navy make to prop up its strategic weak link? Naval commanders tasked the "Game Warden" River Patrol Force (Task Force 116) with this interdiction mission. Task Force 116 combined numerous small river patrol craft, Seawolf helicopter units, and elite SEAL commando teams in an effort to curtail enemy movement along the waterways of the Delta and its adjacent Rung Sat Special Zone—the forest of assassins, a dark and bloody ground straddling the water approaches to Saigon. Regardless of the force's numerous achievements, intelligence analysis revealed that "from 1966 to 1968, Game Warden failed to capture a single important shipment of war material. This did not imply the enemy was not making large shipments, however, since he had accumulated enough to mount the Tet offensive." Task Force 116's meager, although always aggressive, defense of the Delta's major rivers and other primary canals and waterways proved woefully inadequate to accomplish their primary mission.

"Evidence showed that enemy was infiltrating supplies with impunity over the Cambodian border," according to the CNA. "In March 1968, NAVFORV analysts felt that massive infiltration over the Cambodian border was taking place, especially between Ha Tien on the Gulf of Thailand and Chau Phu on the Bassac River." Intelligence estimates from 1967, well in advance of the Tet Offensive, revealed that Communists were infiltrating along routes not covered by these wardens of the waterways. Indeed, Task Force 116 had only succeeded in chasing the enemy onto the secondary waterways of the Delta, especially the

---

a reduced Market Time effort would have resulted in significantly increased infiltration." Leopold Response To Market Time Questionnaire, 12 April 1974, ibid. Lieutenant Commander John D. Broglio declared that "the initial scope was adequate but that it ultimately grew completely out of proportion to the threat and in many cases was so large as to be completely self-defeating." Broglio to Chief of Naval Operations, 2 April 1974, ibid. See also R. J. Johnson to Judy Erdheim, 25 April 1974, and A. J. Krekich to Erdheim, 10 May 1974, ibid. Some naval officers even criticized the employment of assets against the trawlers. "The forces employed in Market Time were extravagant in relation to the threat and the value of the cargo delivered by the trawlers," wrote Rear Admiral H. S. Ainsworth, Commander Patrol Wing South Pacific, Ainsworth Response, ibid. For a contrasting view to this analysis, which emphasizes the adequacy of the operation, see Vice Admiral J. H. King, Jr., Memorandum for the Operations Evaluation Group of the Center for Naval Analyses, 23 February 1974, ibid.

extensive canal systems, rather than stopping the flow of materiel altogether. The ARVN, responsible for the defense of IV Corps Tactical Zone, possessed insufficient forces of questionable effectiveness that even collaborated at times with the enemy smugglers.[20] After a failure by Allied forces to halt waterborne infiltration in-country, Communist main force maneuver battalions mounted a determined, albeit unsuccessful, offensive in the southern provinces.

With the Tet Offensive came a high-water mark in coastal surveillance operations. To sustain their main force battalions locked in a desperate battle for over twenty key South Vietnamese cities and towns, the DRV sent five fishing trawlers southward. Their mission of mercy turned quickly into a disaster as the effective Market Time units easily intercepted their less than surreptitious entry into RVN waters. After interception, one vessel turned back; Market Time units forced a second ship aground near Danang; a third vessel took fire from Task Force 115 off the coast of Ca Mau; navy units riddled a fourth while it was aground northeast of Nha Trang; a fifth ship reversed course and headed home after it was spotted. The enemy had finally sent infiltrators in numbers commensurate to the surveillance effort; the trawlers paid the price. Market Time units operated with unquestionable effectiveness under the most stressful of combat conditions.[21]

Although the navy had performed well in the preceding three years and during the 1968 crisis, Tet brought American naval commanders to the stark realization that their strategy was flawed. The full import of Bucklew's 1964 warnings was now painfully obvious. With the change of naval command in the autumn of 1968 came a massive overhauling of naval strategy and operations. Cognizant of the strategic threat posed

20. Daniels and Erdheim, *Game Warden,* 37, Vietnam Command File, Box 254, OA, NHC. This CNA study concluded that Market Time and Game Warden were both highly effective within the limits of their operations. A task group commander in the Gulf of Thailand observed that the shipment of materiel by coastal junks and sampans had halted, "partly because of Market Time and partly because the VC could use the inland waterways without fear of disruption." A most telling remark. But in fairness to Task Force 116, the study declared that "by October 1968, Game Warden forces had secured many sections of the major Delta and RSSZ [Rung Sat Special Zone, near Saigon] rivers for commercial use. Routine VC tax collections had been interrupted along these major rivers. SVN government curfews were being enforced, and became effective weapons against the VC." *Game Warden,* 37. For an engrossing but less critical account of river patrolling, see Cutler, *Brown Water, Black Berets,* 137–209.

21. Marolda and Pryce, *Short History of the United States Navy and the Southeast Asian Conflict,* 48–49.

by the sanctuaries to the defense of III and IV Corps Tactical Zones, Vice Admiral Elmo Zumwalt, the new commander, Naval Forces, Vietnam, focused his Sea Lords campaign on the interdiction of infiltration across the Cambodian border. With Sea Lords, the navy attempted to seal off the waterways into South Vietnam with extensive patrols on the inland waterways connecting Cambodia to Vietnam.[22] So it took the traumatic jolt delivered during the Tet Offensive to awaken naval planners to their strategic flaws, then it took a change of command before that service would act.

Despite a preponderance of force, an obviously flawed plan negated the effectiveness of American naval power between 1965 and 1968. With one arm already bound by the constraints of limited war, the United States lowered its guard by refusing to seal off the Cambodian border waterways. It waited four years after the Bucklew report to institute an integrated campaign of interdiction along coastline and internal waterways. It is doubtful that an integrated effort early in the war would have staved off eventual defeat, but it would have changed the face of the Delta war.

Given its record during three years preceding the Tet Offensive, Operation Market Time might just represent the entire American war effort in microcosm. Elaborately planned and painstakenly conducted at the operational level, the naval effort in Vietnam was nonetheless strategically ill-conceived. Often successful, although questionable from a cost-effectiveness standpoint, Operation Market Time could not in itself decisively end Communist infiltration. Better suited and more inclined to patrol the seas, the United States Navy then failed to interdict infiltrating materiel at the strategic point. The navy fought its war for the southern provinces, regardless of whether it was the right one.

---

22. Sea Lords "was a Delta-wide operation coordinating the combined assets of TF 115 (Market Time), TF 116, TF 117 (Mobile Riverine Force), and U.S. and Vietnamese ground forces." It was initiated to "continually harass VC strongholds" as well as interdict infiltrating supplies. Daniels and Erdheim, *Game Warden*, 38. According to Cutler, naval intelligence officers finally realized that Bucklew was correct in his 1964 predictions, after analyzing Communist logistics systems in early 1968, after the offensive. Cutler, *Brown Water, Black Berets*, 285–86.

THE SIGNIFICANCE OF LOCAL COMMUNIST FORCES IN POST-TET VIETNAM

By Peter Brush*

The February 1997 issue of *Vietnam* contained my article "The War's 'Constructive Component,'" an examination of counterinsurgency operations during the Vietnam War. In his editorial comments in that issue, editor Colonel Harry Summers took exception to my conclusion, saying it ignored "the last seven years of the war during which guerrillas played an insignificant part."

Summers' conclusion is one of the themes of his important work *On Strategy: A Critical Analysis of the Vietnam War.* In that book Summers quotes former U.S. Army Chief of Staff Fred C. Weyland who claims that the Viet Cong (VC) were destroyed during Tet 1968; "eliminated" at the direction of the North Vietnamese Communists. Also noted is that the VC comprised no more than 20 percent of the Communist fighting forces after 1968. This article examines the Viet Cong in the post-Tet 1968 period in order evaluate the significance of their role in the fighting during the years between the 1968 Tet offensive and the fall of Saigon in 1975.

Army General Earle Wheeler, Chairman of the Joint Chiefs of Staff from 1964 to 1970, did not think the Viet Cong had been eliminated. In a cable dated March 1 1968 to General William Westmoreland, commander of US forces in Vietnam, Wheeler admitted that counterinsurgency programs had been brought to a halt. To a large extent, the VC now controlled the countryside. The VC were rebuilding their infrastructure via recruiting and infiltration and over-all recovery was "likely to be rapid."[1] John Paul Vann, a former Army lieutenant colonel before becoming advisor for counterinsurgency operations in II Corps, felt Westmoreland had been duped by army briefers who over-stressed enemy body counts as a measure of success. Vann wrote in March 1968 that the VC were "being given more freedom to intimidate the rural population than ever

---

*Peter Brush is a contributing editor to *Viet Nam Generation*, a journal of recent history and contemporary issues. He has taught history and political science at Clinton Community College and Empire State College in Plattsburgh, New York. He has authored many articles on the history of the Vietnam War. He spent Tet 1968 in the Marine Corps with a heavy mortar battery in Vietnam, and today is a librarian at Vanderbilt University in Nashville, Tennessee.

Journal of Third World Studies, Vol. XV, No. 2
© 1998 by Association of Third World Studies, Inc.

before in the past two-and-a-half years."[2] Further, as will be shown, there are simply too many references to Viet Cong military actions after Tet to support the conclusion they had been eliminated.

Does the claim that the VC comprised no more than twenty percent of Communist military forces mean they were insignificant? In 1968, the Marine Corps force in South Vietnam numbered 86,000 men ashore. That year the total number of US troops in Vietnam was 549,000.[3] Although the Marines supplied less than 16 percent of total US forces, no one claims that the Marine force in Vietnam was insignificant. It takes more than percentages to demonstrate significance.

Historian Ngo Ving Long claims that the VC achieved dramatic gains while receiving relatively light casualties during the first phase of Tet 1968. Long notes that officials and academics in both the United States and Vietnam claim only the North Vietnamese played the decisive role in the liberation of the South in the period after Tet. Officials in North Vietnam have gone so far as to restrict debate on the conduct of the war in order that the official party line go unchallenged. Long claims this view is incorrect, that it cannot be supported by current research, and in reality southern revolutionaries rebuilt their connections between villagers and soldiers in 1971 and 1972 to a level which allowed a respite from their Tet losses.[4]

According to Long, all of the VC forces were not killed in the Tet fighting because many of them did not participate in the attacks. For example, Saigon, the main target of Phase 1 of the Tet Offensive, was assigned the largest number of VC attack forces by the Communist National Liberation Front. These forces were divided into two commands, Northern and Southern. Long An Province supplied most of the forces that attacked Saigon from the Southern Command. Eight Southern Command VC battalions were sent to Saigon. None of them were able to break through Saigon's defenses to link up with VC sapper units. Consequently, all of these forces were withdrawn from the city to the surrounding countryside and their losses were low. In the heaviest fighting the Southern Command participated in, the equivalent of only one platoon became casualties.[5]

As allied commanders withdrew their troops from the countryside to defend Saigon and other urban areas, VC guerrillas were able to defeat government regional and local militias. This allowed the NLF to expand its control in rural areas. It was this expansion of NLF control that encouraged the Communists to launch Phase 2 and 3 of the Tet Offensive.

According to a classified NLF study, Long An was the province where its forces sustained the highest level of casualties of all provinces in the South during all phases of Tet. Nevertheless, in late 1968, U.S. officials still regarded

Long An as being largely under NLF control.

After Tet the allies attempted various counterinsurgency measures to regain control of the countryside. One manifestation of the acknowledgement by the allies that the Viet Cong were filling the void caused by the withdrawal of US/ARVN forces from rural areas of South Vietnam was the Phoenix Program. Implemented from 1968 until 1972, Phoenix had as its objective identification of the Viet Cong, building support among the local South Vietnamese in combatting the Viet Cong infrastructure (VCI), and eventually reducing and eliminating the Viet Cong as a military and political force.

Robert Komer managed the pacification program in 1967 and 1968. Komer set quotas for all of South Vietnam: He wanted 3,000 Viet Cong neutralized each month. William Colby, who replaced Komer as head of pacification, stated in 1971 that 28,000 VCI had been captured in South Vietnam under the Phoenix Program, 20,000 had been killed, and another 17,000 had been detected.[6] Had the Viet Cong been eliminated or reduced to insignificance during Tet 1968, there would have been no need for the Phoenix Program.

Further evidence of increased VC influence is provided by events in Ben Tre Province (also known as Kien Hoa). Most of the province was under NLF control at the beginning of Tet. Long a VC stronghold, Ben Tre had the distinction of being the most heavily bombed province in the Mekong Delta during Phase 1. Its capital, with a population of 140,000, was the place an American officer claimed, "We had to destroy the town to save it." Ben Tre became the scene of massive allied counterattacks beginning in July 1968. During that year the NLF expanded its influence in Ben Tre, adding an additional ten percent of the total provincial population to areas under its control.[7]

In July 1969 the allied Hamlet Evaluation System (HES) indicated that 74 percent of the population of South Vietnam was subjected to covert Communist activity and another five percent was under their convert control. Only 38 percent of the population was considered free of Communist influence. Later US data suggest that as late as June 1971 Viet Cong were conducting activities among two-thirds of the population of South Vietnam.[8]

According to Long's view, the Viet Cong could have minimized their casualties by breaking off combat after their Phase 1 gains. Instead, the Communists were ordered to mount the second and third phases, which left revolutionary forces in forward positions until the fall of 1968. Here they suffered severe losses when subjected to allied firepower. Hanoi compounded its errors by finally ordering VC units to withdraw to border sanctuaries in Laos and Cambodia, effectively surrendering populated areas to the Army of the Republic of Vietnam (ARVN) and US forces without a fight.

Later, NLF forces paid a high price when they returned to the villages to rebuild their infrastructure. Additionally, North Vietnamese Army (NVA) troops sent south in the 1969-1970 period operated ineffectively and suffered increased casualties due to this lack of infrastructure. According to southern revolutionary leaders, 1969 and 1970 were the most difficult years of the war. The difficulties of this period were caused by decisions the Communists made themselves, and not directly by actions of the US or South Vietnam. Local revolutionary forces were able to reclaim the initiative in 1971 and 1972, aided in part by the redeployment of allied forces for the invasions of Laos and Cambodia. Simultaneous with these invasions was an increase in NLF urban operations.[9]

Were Viet Cong activities militarily significant during the period between the withdrawal of US forces and the fall of Saigon? This significance can be gauged by references to them in military histories of the period. One account is provided by General Van Tien Dung, Chief of Staff of the (North) Vietnam People's Army.

According to Dung, Hanoi's Party Central Committee recognized the significance of the southern revolutionary forces. Its 1974 Twenty-First Conference Resolution stated as one of its goals the need to raise the will to struggle and step up organizational discipline in order to guarantee victory for all three kinds of troops: main-force units, regional-force troops, and local guerrilla militia.[10]

After building up its forces during the 1973-1974 period, Hanoi decided to test its strength against Saigon forces. Remote Phuoc Long province was chosen as its first target. In 20 days of fighting, a combination of main-force (i.e., NVA) and regional forces (i.e., VC) liberated both Phuoc Long town and province from ARVN control. This was the first province lost to the Communists by the South Vietnamese government.[11]

Saigon's next loss was Ban Me Thuot. Dung notes that people from the local revolutionary apparatus gave advice to NVA forces as they prepared their attack plans. Further south, in Tay Ninh province in 1974, local forces from Phu Yen were ordered to block Route 7 to prevent the escape of ARVN troops toward Tuy Hoa.[12]

In the northern provinces, Dung notes that seven regional force battalions, along with 100 armed special assignment squads and local armed forces, mounted a series of attacks in Mai Linh district. The district town was knocked out, eleven other installations were destroyed, and the Communists were able to propagandize a large area which included 53 villages with a population of over 20,000. On March 24 and 25, the NVA 2d Division, in coordination with local forces, destroyed the ARVN 4th and 5th regiments while liberating Tam Ky and Tuan Duong. In Quang Ngai it was regional forces who liberated the northern part of the province. When Danang fell, it was "members of our revolutionary infrastructure" who raised the Communist flag over city hall.[13]

In March and April 1974, Communist forces launched a series of attacks in the central coastal plain. Dung credits regional armed forces, along with the people, for the liberation of Qui Nhon town as well as Phuoc Ly and Phuoc Hai peninsulas.[14]

In early April the Communists began preparations for the final attack against Saigon. An official from Communist Zones 8 and 9 noted that while previously this area only had two regional force battalions, by April it had increased its forces to five battalions. In one day Rach Gia had mobilized 200 recruits to form an additional provisional battalion, and "every village had a company of guerrillas." Weapons and munitions for these forces were sent down from the regional level as well as taken from the enemy, providing equipment for these new units. Their continuous activities tied down a number of ARVN main-force units in IV Corps, and diverted some activities of Saigon's air and naval forces.

The revolutionary infrastructure inside Saigon was kept busy when the fighting began. The party committee spread propaganda leaflets by the hundred of thousands. Members of the Saigon municipal party committee, members of special ward committees, hundreds of party members, thousands of members of various mass organizations, and tens of thousands of people could be mobilized to support the attack forces. A political infrastructure existed in every section of town. Hundreds of loudspeaker cars were readied and thousands of meters of cloth were delivered to tailor shops to be sewn into flags.[15]

Far from being eliminated or insignificant, according to Dung, regional forces were bigger and stronger than ever before. The revolutionary forces in the final attack included sappers, special action units, armed security forces, self-defense units, and mass political forces. Their role was to capture bridges, guide mainforce units into the city, neutralize traitors, and mobilize the masses for an urban uprising. Plans for participation were passed all the way down to the neighborhood level.[16]

It was a combination of main force, regional force, and militia of Ba Ria that liberated a large section of that province. Regional and guerrilla forces liberated Cu Lao Cham Island on March 30. Party members liberated Cung Son Island and turned it over to regular soldiers for administration. Local forces also assisted in the liberation of Cu Lao Xanh and Hon Tre Islands.[17] Regional forces and guerrilla militia, in coordination with main force units, surrounded My Tho and Can Tho in the Mekong Delta and interdicted movement of ARVN forces along Route 4.[18]

Dung's book was written for a Vietnamese audience. As Long notes, the Communists have sought to minimize the role of local forces in the conquest of South Vietnam. Nevertheless, however much minimized, Dung's version of the final offensive indicates the Communists assigned a significant role to local revolutionary forces.

Truong Nhu Tang, the Viet Cong Minister of Justice during the war, notes it was the NLF's 9th Division that provided security for the founding congress of the Provisional Revolutionary Government in 1969. The following year saw large-scale combat as the VC 5th, 7th, and 9th Divisions fought ARVN and Cambodian army units during the withdrawal of NLF headquarters elements into Cambodia. By 1972, according to Tang, the Viet Cong were better placed than ever before to exploit the weaknesses of the South Vietnamese government and their American supporters.[19]

On May 21 1972, Communist forces occupied Loc Ninh. It was the NLF flag that was raised over the captured city after it had fallen to regiments of the VC 5th Division. As survivors of the Loc Ninh attacks fled, the VC 9th Division was probing An Loc and the VC 7th Division blocked Route 13, resulting in a siege of five ARVN regiments that would last until June 18.[20] On December 2, men of the 10th VC Sapper Regiment blew up the Nha Be tank farm, the largest oil storage facility in South Vietnam. Tang notes the participation of the VC 3d, 7th, and 9th Divisions in the capture of Phuoc Long province in January 1973.[21]

Not only Communist writers ascribe a role to the Viet Cong in post-Tet events in Vietnam. Colonel William E. Le Gro, author of *Vietnam from Cease-Fire to Capitulation* (published by the U.S. Army Center for Military History), notes that intelligence sources revealed the Communists force deployments in early 1973: NVA main forces would contain the ARVN in its bases while NLF forces would invest the hamlets and villages. That month saw NLF flags raised in hamlets of western Hieu Duc district, southern and western Dai Loc, Dien Ban, northeastern Duc Duc, western Duy Xugen, and parts of the Que Son District of Quang Nam Province. On January 28, local forces attacked along Route 1 between Danang and the Bong Son pass to the south, cutting the highway in several places. In MR2, local forces interdicted Route 20 in Lam Dong Province in late January. Le Gro notes that VC units up to regimental size were still considered to be predominantly Viet Cong and not North Vietnamese.[22]

Viet Cong units during this period were not confined to propagandizing the hamlets and villages. In October 1973 an inferior VC unit drove elements of the 11th ARVN Ranger group from their dug-in positions on Hill 252 near Quang Ngai City. Two months later the VC 95th Sapper Company infiltrated the command post of the 68th Ranger Battalion and inflicted over 50 casualties, including the battalion commander and his deputy. On occasion, VC units filled in for NVA units, maximizing the flexibility of Communist forces on the battle-field. In the Northern Provinces, at the time of the second anniversary of the cease-fire, local units relieved the NVA 325th Division on the My Chanh line, allowing the 325th to move toward Hue.[23]

Le Gro places significant VC units in MR3 during this period. During February 1974 the NVA 6th Regiment of its 5th Division was given the assignment of cutting roads around Tay Ninh. This force was assisted by a VC regiment and at least three local battalions. VC forces launched rocket attacks in the Central Highlands in early 1975 as Saigon forces began their final crumble. And so it went throughout the country during March 1975: Local forces assisted the NVA in overrunning the 102nd PF Battalion in Hau Duc, local forces participated in the NVA onslaught against the ARVN at the An Khe Pass, and local forces inflicted heavy casualties on Saigon territorials in Long An Province near the capital.[24]

A Rand Corporation report prepared for the Secretary of Defense in 1978 provides additional evidence of Viet Cong military activity after Tet 1968. A battle near Hue in March 1974 between Saigon and Communist forces reportedly cost the NVA and VC over 1,000 killed. Later, as ARVN troops evacuated Hue and withdrew southward, the city of Danang moved toward chaos. The ARVN 3rd Division commander reported that VC sapper units in the city contributed to the confusion.[25]

The South Vietnamese government (Government of Vietnam, or GVN) sought to consolidate its forces in Military Regions 3 and 4 after the loss of the northern regions. Units withdrawn from MR1 (formerly I Corps) were added to the six ARVN divisions, two armored brigades, various Ranger groups, and Regional/Popular Forces organic to MR3 and MR4 in order to provide for the continued defense of South Vietnam. The Rand study notes that most of the GVN indigenous units were themselves already hard pressed and tied down by local Communist forces and could not be disengaged to form reserves to meet fresh enemy units moving into South Vietnam from the north. Examples include the ARVN 25th Division near Tay Ninh, and the ARVN 7th, 9th, and 21st Divisions in the Mekong Delta: all tied down by local Communist forces. According to the Commander of the Capital Military District, this was a lesson the Communists learned from the failed 1972 Easter offensive. Additionally, local units seized captured ARVN vehicles for transportation to Long An Province where they threatened to cut a major communications link between Saigon and the Delta. The South Vietnamese Joint General Staff deployed its 22nd Division from Binh Dinh Province to counter this threat.[26]

Historian John M. Gates indicates the importance of Viet Cong forces at the time of the 1973 cease-fire, particularly outside of MR1. Although throughout South Vietnam local units provided only 16.9 percent of total Communist strength, they provided over 50 percent of the administrative and service personnel. In MR3, the area around Saigon, local forces provided 20 percent of the combat troops and almost 70 percent of support troops. In MR4 (the Mekong Delta), the percentages were over 40 percent of the combat troops and over 90 percent of the service and administrative personnel. The ARVN Chief of Staff for MR2 estimated that in 1975, Communist regular units made up less than fifty percent of the forces in this area.[27]

At the time of the 1973 cease-fire, Communist forces in South Vietnam consisted of about 148,000 combat troops, 16,000 men assigned to antiaircraft regiments and 71,000 support troops. Opposing them was an ARVN force with an assigned strength of 450,000, a Navy of 42,000, an Air force of 54,000, Popular and Regional Forces totaling 525,000, and a Women's Armed Forces Corps with 4,000 members. As Army historian Le Gro notes, these gross figures of 235,000 Communists verses 1,075,000 South Vietnamese troops tell little about relative combat power.[28] Communist strength in the South was devoted almost exclusively to offensive operations, while GVN forces were assigned to fixed defensive missions.

It is difficult to accurately determine the Viet Cong contribution to total Communist strength. North Vietnamese who infiltrated south in 1964 and 1965 were often assigned as replacements to Viet Cong units. Many of these people were originally from the South and had moved North at the time of the Geneva partition in 1954. In later years, many VC were added to the ranks of existing regular NVA units. Compounding the problem is that some VC units had their Tet 1968 casualties replaced by North Vietnamese while maintaining their Viet Cong unit designations. One study claimed that by mid-1968, one-third of the men in VC units were North Vietnamese.[29]

Besides providing manpower for direct combat operations, the Viet Cong functioned as an interface that facilitated the operation of North Vietnamese main-force units in the South. The intimate NLF knowledge of conditions in the South allowed North Vietnamese forces to operate with a minimum ratio of combat to support units. An example of this is provided by the rice war in the Mekong Delta. Nearly 90 percent of Communist rice requirements were filled from South Vietnam sources. The Viet Cong, often recruited locally, were able to exert control over rice-producing hamlets, protect the activities of rice-requisitioning parties, secure the lines of communication for movement of food supplies, and prevent the intrusion of Saigon forces into the rice-producing areas (primarily in the Mekong Delta).[30] It was this "fifth column" function that enabled the Communists to deploy a greater number of units for offensive operations than the ARVN despite the Communists' 4.5:1 overall disparity in total force levels.

Truong Nhu Tang, then the NLF Minister of Justice, describes the victory parade in Saigon after the final Communist offensive. Representatives of various mass organizations filed by the reviewing stand. These were followed by military units of the NVA, "troops from every North Vietnamese Army unit, all of them wearing distinctive new olive-colored pith helmets." Tank squadrons, antiaircraft batteries, artillery units, and Soviet missiles lumbered past under the protective cover of air force overflights. Finally several unkempt and ragtag looking Viet Cong units appeared. In alarm, Tang turned to General Dung who was standing next to him. Tang asked quietly, "Where are our divisions one, three, five, seven, and nine?"

After staring for a moment, Dung replied that the army had been unified. It was then, in 1975 and not 1968, that it became clear even to the leaders of the NLF that their forces had been rendered insignificant, and that the Front had no further role to play in the revolution. It had become only a minor obstacle to North Vietnam's consolidation of power in the South.[31]

VIET CONG STRENGTH AND ORDER OF BATTLE
Late January 1973

	MR1	MR2	MR3	MR4
Viet Cong Combat Troops:	3,000	6,000	5,000	11,000
Viet Cong Administrative and Service Troops:	6,000	8,000	11,000	12,000

NOTE: VC units usually contained NVA fillers. VC units ranged in composition from predominantly VC to predominantly NVA. Communist strength included 15,300 VC/NVA in separate combat platoons not included in the following units.

South Vietnam Military Region 1

120th VC Montagnard Inf (150)
42d VC Rcn (150)
70th VC Sapper (150)
145th VC Inf (150)

South Vietnam Military Region 2

45th VC Inf (150)
67th VC Inf (200)
408th VC Sapper (200)
Khanh Hoa VC Sapper (200)
481st VC Inf (200)
482d VC Inf (150)
251st VC Inf Bn (150)

South Vietnam Military Region 3

10th VC Sapper Bn (100)
12th VC Sapper Bn (150)
8th VC Arty Bn (150)
168th VC Inf Bn (150)
368th VC Inf Bn (150)
1st VC Inf Bn (150)
6th VC Inf Bn (150)
20th VC Inf Bn (150)
445th VC Inf Bn (150)
9th VC Inf Bn (150)
269th VC Inf Bn (150)
508th VC Inf Bn (150)

South Vietnam Military Region 4

DT1-1 Regt (600)
207th VC Sapper Bn (100)
309th VC Arty (150)
209th VC Inf Bn (100)
268C VC Inf Bn (150)
271St VC Inf Bn (150)
278th VC Inf Bn (150)
279th VC Inf Bn (200)
295th VC Inf Bn (300)
310th VC Inf Bn (200)
512th VC Inf Bn (300)
516A VC Inf Bn (200)
516B VC Inf Bn (150)
590th VC Inf Bn (150)
502D VC Inf Bn (200)
514C VC Inf Bn (200)
D-1 Regt (600)
D-3 Regt (1000)
2012d VC Sapper Bn (150)
2014th VC Sapper Bn (150)
2311th VC Arty Bn (100)
2315th VC Arty Bn (100)
Tay Do Inf Bn (100)
U Minh 10th Inf Bn (250)
U Minh 2d Inf Bn (100)
764th Inf Bn (150)
857th Inf Bn (100)

Source: Colonel William E. Le Gro, *Vietnam from Cease-Fire to Capitulation*, (Washington, D.C.: U S. Army Center for Military History), 1981, pp. 28-30.

NOTES

1.   Robert Buzzanco, "The Myth of Tet," in Marc Jason Gilbert and William Head (eds.), *The Tet Offensive*, Westport, CT: Praeger, 1996.

p. 239.

2. *Ibid.*, p. 244.

3. George R. Dunham and David R. Quinlan, *U.S. Marines in Vietnam: The Bitter End, 1973-1975*, Washington, DC: Headquarters, U.S. Marine Corp), 1990, p. 266; William C. Westmoreland, *A Soldier Reports* (Garden City, NY: Doubleday), 1976, p. 359.

4. Ngo Vinh Long, "The Tet Offensive and Its Aftermath," in Gilbert and Head, *The Tet Offensive*, pp. 90-91.

5. Long, "The Tet Offensive and Its Aftermath," pp. 106-107.

6. Neil Sheehan, *A Bright Shining Lie*, (NY: Random House), 1988, pp. 732-733.

7. Long, "The Tet Offensive and Its Aftermath," p. 108.

8. Thomas C. Thayer, *War Without Fronts* (Boulder, CO: Westview Press, 1985, p. 206.

9. Long, "The Tet Offensive and Its Aftermath," pp. 89-90.

10. Van Tien Dung, *Our Great Spring Victory: An Account of the Liberation of South Vietnam* (NY: Monthly Review Press), 1977, p. 11.

11. *Ibid.*, p. 22.

12. *Ibid.*, pp. 46, 95.

13. *Ibid.*, pp. 101, 105, 109.

14. *Ibid.*, p. 113.

15. *Ibid.*, pp. 151, 164, 172-173.

16. *Ibid.*, pp. 182, 187, 188.

17. *Ibid.*, pp. 218, 221.

18. *Ibid.*, p. 249.

19. Truong Nhu Tang, *A Vietcong Memoir*, (NY: Vintage Books), 1985, p. 147, 179-181, 204.

20. *Ibid.*, 205 William S. Turley, *The Second Indochina War*, (NY: Westview Press, 1986), p. 145.

21. Tang, *A Vietcong Memoir*, pp. 232, 250.

22. William E. Le Gro, *Vietnam from Cease-Fire to Capitulation*, (Washington, DC: U.S. Army Center for Military History), 1981, pp. 23, 24, 25, 15.

23. *Ibid.*, pp. 63, 139.

24. *Ibid.*, p. 143, 153, 156, 161, 167.

25. Stephen T. Hosmer, Konrad Kellen, and Brian M. Jenkins, *The Fall of South Vietnam: Statements by Vietnamese Military and Civilian Leaders*, (Santa Monica, CA: Rand), 1978, p. 1-3, 110 n33.

26. *Ibid.*, p. 116.

27. John M. Gates, "Revisionism and the Vietnam War" in William Head

and Lawrence E. Grinter, *Looking Back on the Vietnam War*, Westport, CT: Praeger, 1993, p. 180; see also the Appendix.

28.   Le Gro, *Vietnam from Cease-Fire to Capitulation*, p. 30.
29.   Michael Lee Lanning and Dan Cragg, *Inside the VC and the NVA*, (NY: Ivy Books), 1992, p. 52.
30.   Le Gro, *Vietnam from Cease-Fire to Capitulation*, p. 65.
31.   Tang, *A Vietcong Memoir*, pp. 264-265.

The Attack on Cap Mui Lay,
Vietnam, July 1968[*]

☆

Faris R. Kirkland

T O minimize the uncertainties inherent in large military operations, especially those involving more than one service, armed forces rely on doctrine and procedure. The efficiency in joint operations displayed by the U.S. forces since 1989 is to a large extent a consequence of a decade of effort by the J-7 section of the Joint Staff.[1] But prior to the 1980s, joint operations were ad hoc affairs dependent on face-to-face coordination among the participants to build mutual respect, understanding, and trust. During the war in Vietnam elements of the Army, Navy, Air Force, and Marine Corps collaborated routinely at low echelons of command. The only extensive operation involving substantial forces of all four services took place during the first week of July 1968. It was an attack by fire on North Vietnamese Army (NVA) installations

---

* An abridged version of this article, "Thor: A Case Study in Multi-Service Coordination," appeared in the February 1993 issue of *Field Artillery,* the professional bulletin of the U.S. Army Field Artillery Center. The author wishes to thank John P. Butler and Richard L. Boylan of the National Archives; Jack Shulimson and J. Michael Miller of the Marine Corps History Center; Glenn E. Helm, John Reilly, and Mike Walker of the Navy History Center; Jeffrey J. Clarke, George L. MacGarrigle, and Jim Knight of the Center of Military History, and Sheldon Goldberg of the Air Force Historical Center, for their professionalism, guidance, and support.

1. The concept of joint operations is described in the Capstone Manual, Joint Publication (JP) 1-0. JP 3-0 lays out doctrine. Matters relevant to each of the primary staff fields are in five Keystone Publications. There are manuals on specific types of operations. For each type of operation there are guides on tactics, techniques, and procedures to facilitate detailed coordinations. For a study of joint service coordination in specific operations, see Robert B. Killibrew, "Force Projection in Short Wars," *Military Review* 69 (March 1989): 2–9; Ned B. Ennis, "Exercise Golden Pheasant: A Show of Force." *Military Review* 69 (March 1989): 25–26.

on Cap Mui Lay. Code-named Thor, it illustrates the difficulties of planning and executing large-scale joint operations prior to the J-7 era.

Though Thor has escaped the notice of historians thus far, it is worthy of attention in the context of the Vietnam War as well as being a milestone in U.S. joint operations. Ronald Spector, in *After Tet: The Bloodiest Year in Vietnam,* described 1968 as the critical year, a year in which both sides "believed themselves to be on the offensive against a seriously weakened enemy."[2] The NVA since 1966 had been seeking to "place the two [northern] provinces [of the Republic of Vietnam—Quang Tri and Thua Thien] within North Vietnam's boundary as a bargaining point in any peace negotiations."[3] Both sides knew that "The fate of the peace talks [that began in May 1968] turn[ed] on the military situation in Vietnam."[4] Operation Thor, by crippling the ability of the NVA to conduct offensive operations at the eastern end of the Demilitarized Zone (DMZ), influenced that situation.

Historical Background

In January 1966, the North Vietnamese Army laid the foundations of their plan to seize Quang Tri and Thua Thien provinces by transferring responsibility for military operations from Military Region 4, which operated in South Vietnam, to Military Region 5, which comprised the southern part of North Vietnam. In April and May 1967, the NVA attacked Khe Sanh at the western end of the DMZ and conducted a ground assault on Con Thien toward the eastern end. In August and September, they mounted an intense artillery attack on Con Thien. Between December 1967 and January 1968, the NVA concentrated eight divisions against the northern provinces. They laid siege to Khe Sanh on 21 January, and launched the Tet offensive on the night of 30–31 January. The NVA main effort during the Tet offensive was in the north, and their most significant achievement was the seizure of Hué.[5]

In addition to maneuver forces, the NVA concentrated artillery along the DMZ. By March 1968 3rd Marine Division intelligence (G-2) had identified six artillery regiments and two separate battalions facing the division—a total of about 160 guns (see Table 1). NVA heavy artillery units used 152-mm gun-howitzers and long-range, flat trajectory 122-mm and 130-mm Russian guns emplaced in caves that provided superb

2. Ronald H. Spector, *After Tet: The Bloodiest Year in Vietnam* (New York: Free Press, 1993), 24.

3. Willard Pearson, *The War in the Northern Provinces* (Washington: GPO, 1975), 10.

4. Nicholas Katzenbach, quoted in Spector, *After Tet*, 144.

5. Pearson, *War in the Northern Provinces*, 9–13, 17, 29–47.

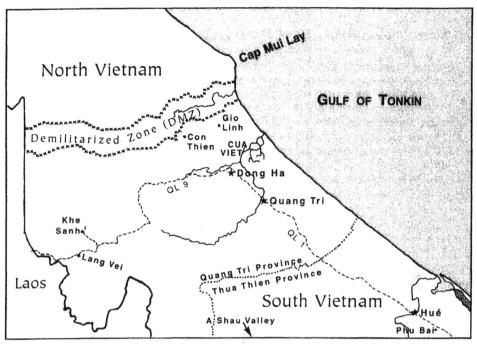

Map 1. *Cap Mui Lay and northern Republic of Vietnam.*

protection against both artillery and air attack. The NVA prepared many more positions than they had guns, and moved the available weapons around frequently.[6] Superior numbers, long range, forward positioning, and protected emplacements gave the NVA artillery fire superiority over the Marines holding the DMZ.[7]

U.S. action to counter the NVA along the DMZ was complicated by inter-service issues. Lieutenant General Robert E. Cushman, command-

6. Commanding General, 3rd Marine Division, to Commanding General, Provisional Corps Vietnam, 24 March 1968, letter, Subject: Enemy Artillery Concentration in the Cap Mui Lay Area, Marine Corps History Center Archives, Washington Navy Yard, Washington, D.C. (Hereafter cited as MCHC.)

7. Ibid., Inclosure 1, "The Cap Mui Lay Sector (CMLS): Its Influence on Friendly Operations and a Proposal for Reducing Deployment Thereon," 2–3; Melvin F. Porter and A. W. Thompson, *Operation Thor* [and supporting documents] (Headquarters Pacific Air Forces: Contemporary Historical Evaluation of Combat Operations [CHECO], 29 January 1969), p. 2, Simpson Historical Research Center, Air University Library, Maxwell Air Force Base, Alabama. (Hereafter cited as CHECO Report with page number or supporting document number.)

Table 1
North Vietnamese Artillery in the DMZ, May–July 1968[8]

Unit	Location	Comments
38th Regt.	vic. Khe Sanh	308th Divisional Artillery
54th Regt.	central DMZ	320th Divisional Artillery
68th Regt.	vic. Khe Sanh	304th Divisional Artillery
78th Regt.	DMZ	325th Divisional Artillery
84th Regt.	eastern DMZ	Rocket artillery
164th Regt.	DMZ	130-mm gun
204th Bn.	YD 194 646	130-mm gun
13th Bn.	DMZ	120-mm mortar
unknown units	DMZ	122-mm gun, 152-mm gun-how.

ing III Marine Amphibious Force (III MAF), was responsible for operations in the five northern provinces, including Quang Tri and Thua Thien. General William C. Westmoreland, Commander in Chief of U.S. forces in Vietnam (U.S. Military Assistance Command, Vietnam—MACV), saw the NVA concentration in the north as posing a grave threat, and he did not have confidence in the Marines.[9] On 22 January 1968 he wrote, "[T]he military professionalism of the Marines falls far short of the standards that should be demanded of our armed forces."[10]

He had, a year earlier, initiated planning for a division-sized force to reinforce III MAF. In April 1967, he assigned Task Force Oregon, with three brigades under the command of Major General William B. Rosson, to III MAF. It operated in the southern portion of the III MAF zone, and it released the 3rd Marine Division to garrison the DMZ from Khe Sanh to the sea. At the same time, work began on the McNamara Line, a series of remote sensors to detect NVA infiltration along a line from Con Thien to Gio Linh.[11]

When the siege of Khe Sanh began, Generals Westmoreland and Cushman agreed that it should be held. The defense was based on con-

---

8. XXIV Corps Artillery, Assistant Chief of Staff for Intelligence (S-2), Intelligence Summaries (April–December 1968), 6-68, 7-68, 8-68, 9-68, Box 1 (6-17-8-1), Record Group 472 (U.S. Army, Vietnam), National Archives and Records Administration, Washington, D.C. (hereafter cited as RG 472, NA); HQ XXIV Corps, AVII-ATC, to COMUSMACV, 16 August 1968, letter, Subject: Combat After Action Report (RCS: MACJ 3-37) (K-1), p. 4, MCHC.

9. Lewis Sorley, *Thunderbolt—From the Battle of the Bulge to Vietnam and Beyond: General Creighton Abrams and the Army of His Times* (New York: Simon and Schuster, 1992), 390–91; Spector, *After Tet*, 118.

10. Westmoreland to [General Earle G.] Wheeler [Chairman, Joint Chiefs of Staff], MAC 01011, 220052Z January 1968, quoted in Sorley, *Thunderbolt*, 391.

11. Spector, *After Tet*, 13–14, 224.

centrated aerial bombing of NVA maneuver forces around Khe Sanh or assembling north of the DMZ. Westmoreland assigned General William W. Momyer, the commander of Seventh Air Force, responsibility for all air operations—including those by III MAF's 1st Marine Air Wing—in the southern portion of North Vietnam. Control of their own close air support was an integral part of Marine Corps doctrine, and the Marines were infuriated. General Cushman complained to his superiors in the Marine-Navy chain of command, but in vain.[12]

On 25 January General Westmoreland established a MACV Forward command post under his deputy, General Creighton Abrams, in the III MAF zone. In Abrams's opinion, Major General Rathvon McC. Tompkins, commander of the 3rd Marine Division, was not in control of the situation at Khe Sanh, and General Cushman's actions to recapture Hué were unlikely to be decisive, so he took over the battle in the northern provinces.[13] By the time Hué was recaptured on 25 February, senior Marines resented the Army and Air Force for usurping their prerogatives, and senior Army commanders doubted the Marine commanders' ability to conduct major operations.

To reinforce III MAF and alleviate the Marines' resentment, Westmoreland dissolved MACV Forward on 10 March and replaced it with Provisional Corps Vietnam (PCV).[14] PCV was a tactical headquarters under the command of William Rosson, now a lieutenant general, and subordinate to III MAF.[15] It controlled the Army 1st Air Cavalry and 101st Airborne Divisions, and the 3rd Marine Division. The corps opened the road to Khe Sanh in April (Operation Pegasus), conducted the first raid on the NVA logistics system in the A Shau Valley in April and May (Operation Delaware), and destroyed North Vietnamese units remaining in Quang Tri and Thua Thien provinces during June.[16]

12. Tab E, MACV Directive No. 95-1, Subject: Aviation Procedures for Fire Support Coordination and Control in the TALLY HO Area, 21 January 1968; Pearson, *War in the Northern Provinces,* 13–14, 17, 31–34, 71–72.

13. Sorley, *Thunderbolt,* 213–16.

14. Major General Willard Pearson was chief of staff of MACV Forward and of Provisional Corps Vietnam until June 1968. His book, *The War in the Northern Provinces,* provides a detailed description of the events leading up to Operation Thor.

15. Provisional Corps Vietnam was the only U.S. corps in Vietnam. On 15 August 1968, it was redesignated XXIV Corps. Sorley, *Thunderbolt,* 219; Pearson, *War in the Northern Provinces,* 66–68; Steve E. Dietrich, "Corps-Level Command-&-Control in an Unconventional Conflict: U.S. Army Field Forces in Vietnam," working paper, U.S. Army Center of Military History, July 1989, 32.

16. HQ XXIV Corps, letter, Subject: Operational Report of Headquarters, Provisional Corps Vietnam for Period Ending 31 July 1968, RCS CSFOR-65 (R1), 20 August 1968, p. 3, Box 1 (6-17-8-2), RG 472, NA; letters of 23 March, 1 April, 22 April, 28 April, 2 May, 12 May, and 13 May 1968 from the S-3 of Provisional Corps Vietnam Artillery to his wife (March–July 1968), in the possession of the author (hereafter cited as PCVA S-3, with date); Spector, *After Tet,* 134–35, 207.

The Paris peace talks began on 13 May, and were immediately dead-locked.[17] The North Vietnamese, though they had suffered heavily in the battles of Khe Sanh and Hué, still had several divisions facing the 3rd Marine Division, and their artillery still had fire superiority along the DMZ. They continued offensive operations in an effort to influence the peace negotiations.

The Cap Mui Lay Fortified Zone

Cap (cape) Mui Lay is a perturbation in the coastline just north of the 17th parallel. The coast of South Vietnam tends northwesterly for 130 kilometers, then at the 17th parallel turns abruptly straight north for 14 kilometers to form Cap Mui Lay before resuming the northwesterly tendency. The centerline of the DMZ begins at the 17th parallel also. The configuration of the coastline offered the NVA a zone twenty-four kilometers wide and fourteen kilometers deep in which to concentrate ground forces directly north of Dong Ha and the Cua Viet River. They fortified Cap Mui Lay with underground barracks, munitions dumps, and air defense, field, and coastal artillery positions, while maintaining the facade of existing farm villages and trails.[18]

The NVA artillery inflicted casualties on maintenance and logistics personnel at the main Marine base at Dong Ha, 17 kilometers south of Cap Mui Lay, and harassed lighters unloading cargo ships on the Cua Viet River, the supply route to Dong Ha.[19] Coastal artillery on Cap Mui Lay "caused [U. S.] naval gunfire ships to stand 12 to 18 kilometers off-shore generally."[20] Destroyer guns with ranges of 13.7 (5"/38 guns) to 18 kilometers (5"/54 guns) were unable to attack the installations on Cap Mui Lay effectively. Only the 8-inch main batteries of cruisers could hit targets protected by the coastal batteries.[21]

The Air Force found that Cap Mui Lay had "a formidable air defense system comprising multiple automatic weapons, radar-directed guns, and surface to air missiles . . . [which had] succeeded in denying the area to effective aerial observation, and had limited the accuracy of air support. This high-threat counter-surveillance screen of AA [antiaircraft]

17. Spector, *After Tet,* 142.
18. CHECO Report, 17.
19. Major Leonard Blasiol, "Operation Thor" (undated typescript, MCHC), 1; U.S. Seventh Fleet Monthly Historical Summary, July 1968, 31, folder: 7th Flt. Prov. NGFS, July 1968, 1 of 2, Navy History Center Archives, Washington Navy Yard, Washington, D.C. (hereafter cited as NHC).
20. Enemy Artillery Concentration in the Cap Mui Lay Sector(S); Commanding General Prov Corps V, PHB, to Commanding General III MAF, DNG, 120750Z July 1968, Subject: Preliminary Report: Operation Thor, MCHC.
21. "The Cap Mui Lay Sector (CMLS)," 1, 3.

installations, coupled with the enemy's expert use of camouflage and constant, covert movement of his artillery, had to a great extent limited friendly knowledge of enemy artillery deployment in the CMLS [Cap Mui Lay sector]."[22]

The NVA camouflage and antiaircraft weapons made it impossible for aviators to bomb accurately and for air observers to spot the fall of shot for the artillery.[23] Colonel David L. Jones's 108th Field Artillery group had conducted a counterbattery program using the sound, flash, and radar detection capabilities of Battery F (Target Acquisition), 26th Artillery. But the only American artillery permanently positioned near the DMZ capable of matching the 27.2-kilometer range of the NVA 130-mm guns were two batteries of 175-mm guns of Army Lieutenant Colonel James C. Barnes's 8th Battalion, 4th artillery, and Marine Major E. B. Beall's 155-mm 5th Gun Battery. From time to time Lieutenant Colonel Robert H. Kamstra's 2d Battalion, 94th Artillery, reinforced the 108th Group with three more 175-mm batteries. To enable them to support action in any direction, U.S. guns were in open positions vulnerable to NVA fire. Because of this vulnerability, American heavy artillery was positioned an average of eighteen kilometers south of the five kilometer-wide DMZ, and had only a marginal capability to attack targets north of it.

Their counterbattery efforts frustrated, the Marines tried three times to organize joint operations to destroy the NVA field, coastal, and air defense artillery. General Tompkins described these initiatives in a letter to General Rosson when the latter took command of PCV: "Operation Neutralize by the Air Force with no concurrent planning with Marine Corps or Navy commands [was ineffective]. Operation Rope Yarn was to have been a joint Navy, Air Force, Marine Corps operation that was dissipated due to the lack of resolve at the command level and no aggressive action against the threat was made. The last effort was an operation called 'Head Shed.' A joint planning conference was proposed by CG, 3rd Marine Division, that resulted in the three services, Air Force, Navy, and Marines, executing an operation that . . . because of weather had marginal effect."[24]

The most dangerous aspect of Cap Mui Lay was its capability of "[concealing], staging and infiltrati[ng] . . . men and equipment into [South Vietnam]."[25] Between 27 April and 6 May, the 320 NVA Division

---

22. CHECO Report, 1.

23. Blasiol, "Operation Thor," 2; Commanding General Prov Corps V, PHB, to Commanding General III MAF, DNG, 120750 2 July 1968, Subject: Preliminary Report—Operation "Thor," Par. 1a(1) and 1a(2), MCHC.

24. Enemy Artillery Concentration in the Cap Mui Lay Sector(S), par. 1.

25. U.S. Seventh Fleet Monthly Historical Summary, July 1968, 31, NHC.

attacked toward the Marine combat base at Dong Ha with forces from Cap Mui Lay. The NVA renewed the attack on 29–31 May.[26] The attacks, which came close to succeeding, were in one-division strength. If the NVA overran Dong Ha and nearby South Vietnamese cities it would have rendered the DMZ meaningless, substantially changed the military situation, and weakened the allies' position at the peace negotiations.[27] By late June the PCV G-2 estimated that the NVA had one and one-half or two divisions in Cap Mui Lay.[28]

Planning for Operation Thor

On 29 February 1968 General Cushman had directed 3rd Marine Division "to concentrate AO [air observer] effort toward locating and subsequently destroying enemy artillery/rocket positions which are capable of delivering fire on the Cua Viet River and port."[29] On 11 March, its second day in business, PCV advised III MAF that General Westmoreland had visited PCV and told General Rosson to "increase reconnaissance and strikes against enemy artillery in the DMZ; degradation of 50 percent is hoped for."[30] General Tompkins, in a letter to PCV on 24 March pointed out that "[Cap Mui Lay] is not accessible to Marine AOs because of flight restrictions [by MACV Directive 95-1] as well as the effective enemy deployment of AAA [antiaircraft artillery] therein."[31] In an inclosure to his letter he recommended an attack by fire on the Cap Mui Lay fortified zone by a joint task force of aircraft, warships, and field artillery. Recognizing that the operation would pose problems of coordination and control similar to those in an amphibious assault, he proposed that it be organized around a naval task force with the Navy in

26. Major Miles D. Waldron and Spec. 5 Richard W. Beavers, "The Critical Year, 1968. The XXIV Corps Team" (undated typescript official history in U.S. Army Center of Military History library), 37–64; Keith William Nolan, *The Magnificent Bastards: The Joint Army-Marine Defense of Dong Ha, 1968* (Novato, Calif.: Presidio Press, 1994); Headquarters, 1st Battalion, 40th Artillery, 10 August 1968, letter, Subject: Operational Report of 1st Battalion, 40th Artillery (105mm SP) for period ending 31 July 1968, Box 1 (6-17-8-2), RG 472, NA.

27. Philip B. Davidson, *Vietnam at War: The History, 1946–1975* (Novato, Calif.: Presidio Press, 1988), 478–79.

28. Headquarters, XXIV Corps, AVII-ATC, letter, Subject: Combat After Action Report, 16 August 1968 (RCS MACJ-3-37) (K-1) (4), Box 1 (6-17-8-2), RG 472, NA.

29. Commanding General III MAF to Commanding General 3rd Marine Division, 291022Z February 1968, MCHC.

30. Commanding General PCV to Commanding General III MAF, 110514Z March 1968, Subject: Visit of COMUSMACV to Headquarters, Provisional Corps Vietnam (TS), MCHC.

31. Enemy Artillery Concentration in the Cap Mui Lay Sector (S), par. 3.

control and using amphibious warfare doctrine.[32]

On 25 April members of the staffs of 108th Group and 12th Marines (the 3rd Marine Division's artillery regiment) briefed the PCV Artillery staff on the threat from Cap Mui Lay and the Marines' plan for an attack by fire. Most of the PCV Artillery staff thought the difficulties of coordinating a complex operation through the chiefs of four service components would be insurmountable, but the commander of PCV Artillery, Brigadier General Lawrence H. Caruthers, Jr., directed his staff to develop a plan.[33] Two days later the 320 NVA Division launched the first of its attacks on Dong Ha and precipitated the battle of Dai Do.

On 28 April a delegation from PCV and 3rd Marine Division went to MACV headquarters to explain the problem and propose an attack by fire which PCV Artillery, as the organic fire support coordination agency for the corps, would coordinate. MACV tentatively approved the concept. PCV Artillery prepared an outline plan and code-named it Thor. General Rosson approved the plan and sent it to III MAF on 15 May. On 20 May an NVA coastal battery on Cap Mui Lay hit an American destroyer,[34] and the same day General Cushman sent a message to MACV describing the threat posed by Cap Mui Lay.[35] On 24 May, Major General Raymond G. Davis took command of 3rd Marine Division and urged the implementation of Thor. On the twenty-sixth General Cushman sent the Thor plan to General Westmoreland.[36] On 29 May the NVA launched its second division-sized assault on Dong Ha out of Cap Mui Lay. The next day Rosson told PCV Artillery to develop an operation plan.

On 7 June 3rd Marine Division learned that "the MACV Planning conference had disapproved Operation Thor, and that the matter would probably be referred back to III MAF and PCV to be handled as an operation using organic capabilities."[37] An informal report reached PCV Artillery headquarters that Seventh Air Force had refused to participate unless it controlled the operation.[38] Most of the members of the PCV Artillery staff expressed relief.[39] They would have been responsible for failure, which was likely, or for disaster, which was possible. To attack the NVA artillery with massed fires, the short-range U.S. howitzers (8-inch with sixteen kilometer and 155-mm with fourteen kilometer range) would have to occupy positions close to the southern edge of the DMZ.

32. "The Cap Mui Lay Sector (CMLS)," 6–7.

33. PCVA S-3, 25 April 1968.

34. Enemy Artillery Concentration in the Cap Mui Lay Sector (S).

35. Commanding General III MAF to COMUSMACV, 2000282 May 1968, cited in CHECO Report, 4.

36. Headquarters, XXIV Corps, Combat After Action Report, 16 August 1968, 5.

37. 3rd Marine Division Fact Sheet, 9 June 1968, MCHC.

38. 7th Air Force's objections are laid out in detail in CHECO Report, 5–7.

39. PCVA S-3, 7 June 1968.

213

Positioning medium and heavy artillery batteries in forward positions would expose them to infantry as well as artillery attack. Reconnaissance and strike aircraft and gunfire support ships would also be at risk. Exceptionally refined coordination and highly competent performance by elements of four services beset by stronger than usual antagonisms would be necessary to achieve success and avoid heavy losses.

On 11 June, General Cushman sent a message to Westmoreland reviewing his previously expressed concerns about the dangers posed by the NVA stronghold in the Cap Mui Lay area and stating his "conviction that a major operation is required in order to do this job and do it right."[40] He included the operation plan the PCV Artillery staff had prepared. It called on MACV to commit all of its naval gunfire ships and the bulk of its Air Force and Navy aerial strike assets to augment the 1st Marine Air Wing and the Army and Marine medium and heavy artillery with PCV. Command and coordination relationships were labyrinthine. (See Table 2 below.)

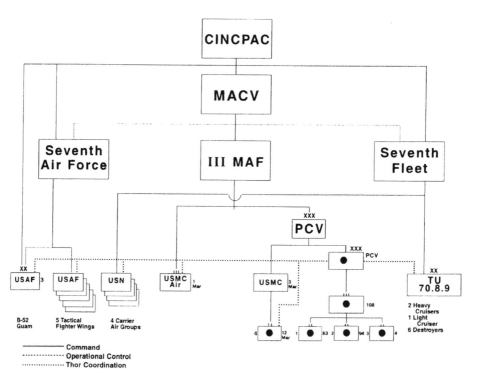

40. Commanding General III MAF to COMUSMACV, 110112Z June 1968, MCHC. Quoted extensively in CHECO Report, 4–5.

Operation Thor was to have three phases. Phase I was two days of air attacks by B-52s and fighter bombers on positions previously used by NVA field, air defense, and coastal batteries. Its purpose was to limit enemy capabilities to respond by fire, and to uncover additional targets. During the aerial attack Army 8-inch howitzer batteries and Marine 155-mm howitzer batteries would move close enough to the DMZ to enable them to mass fire on most targets in the Cap Mui Lay sector. Phase I was to be under the control of Seventh Air Force.

In Phase II artillery, warships, and aircraft would conduct two days of "integrated attacks concentrated in the [Cap Mui Lay Sector] to secure a permissive environment for [air observers and forward air control] aircraft and close-in [naval gunfire] support."[41] Coastal and air defense weapons were the focus of Phase II. III MAF, using the Thor command post operated by PCV Artillery, was to control fighter bombers, artillery, and naval gunfire. This contravened the MACV Single Manager Concept that assigned Seventh Air Force responsibility for control of flying and firing in the southern part of North Vietnam.

Phase III was the payoff. For three days artillery air observers and forward air controllers would fly along and then into Cap Mui Lay. They would use observed air strikes and artillery and naval gunfire to destroy any NVA installations and weapons. The operation was to be controlled by III MAF. This phase would complete the elimination of immunity from surveillance that had enabled the NVA artillery to gain fire superiority, and that had provided concealment for their maneuver forces.

Phase IV, a continuing program of close aerial observation and photo reconnaissance with immediate fire on any artillery or air defense positions that revealed themselves, was to follow the seven days of concentrated attacks. Seventh Air Force would be responsible for coordination and control.

The fundamental concept of the operation was to protect friendly forces by using the capabilities of each fire-delivery system to cover the vulnerabilities of the others.[42] During Phase I, the B-52s would be protected from all but surface-to-air missiles by altitude, and electronic warfare aircraft would neutralize NVA missile systems. The fighter-bombers in Phase I would be protected by surprise, the effects of the B-52 strikes, and radar-seeking missiles. The intense aerial attacks would distract the NVA from the artillery units moving up to the DMZ.

In Phases II and III strike aircraft were to be protected in the target areas by artillery and warships firing on NVA air defense guns and mis-

41. Ibid.

42. Commanding General PCV to III MAF, 7th Air Force, 7th Fleet, 3rd Marine Division, and others, 240418Z June 1968, Subject: OPORD 15-68 (THOR), MCHC; Briefing Outline: Operation THOR Box 1 (6-17-8-2), RG 472, NA.

sile systems. The trajectories of the shells and the flight paths of the air-craft were to be coordinated so that the planes were not endangered, and the last shells would explode only seconds before the aircraft arrived over their targets so the enemy gunners could not engage them. Heavy and medium howitzer batteries, positioned within one to three kilome-ters of the DMZ, would be vulnerable to infantry that could reach them in a few minutes from the DMZ, and to mortar and machine gun fire from within the DMZ. Two or three infantry battalions were to safeguard the batteries, but their most substantial protection would be from the massed artillery, warships, and fighter bombers assembled for the oper-ation. Naval gunfire support ships, if fired on by coastal batteries, could call on field artillery and fighter bombers for protection.

In Phase III observation aircraft approaching and overflying the for-tified zone would have all fire-delivery systems at their disposal. Any antiaircraft weapons that fired at them would be the target of massed fires.

Targeting for Phases I and II would not be precise. NVA weapons were mobile, and intelligence about their locations deteriorated rapidly.[43] The NVA used telephonic communication rather than radio, so tracking units by their electronic emissions was not possible. The attacks in Phases I and II would be on positions that had been used, but might not be occupied. On the other hand, the attacks in Phase III would be on targets under observation at the time of the attack.

On 19 June, General Rosson advanced the start date of Operation Thor from mid-July to the first week of July. His decision, which was the first indication that the operation would actually take place, shocked the PCV Artillery staff. One of the senior officers got drunk in despair.[44] The next day, 20 June, NVA artillery hit the ammunition dump at Dong Ha and destroyed most of the ammunition available for Thor.[45]

On 21 June MACV approved Operation Thor for planning[46] and an initial coordination meeting was held for Army, Navy, Marine, and Air Force representatives at PCV Artillery headquarters. It was a stormy meeting; every participant had a keen awareness of the complexity, dif-ficulty, and danger inherent in a four-service attack in a confined space against a powerfully armed adversary. Several expressed the opinion that Thor was an infeasible plan dreamt up by staff officers who were unaware of the realities of air and ground operations. Some staff officers were evidently acting under instructions from their commanders to bring forth objections to either force the abandonment of the operation

43. CHECO Report, 2.
44. PCVA S-3, 19 June 1968.
45. Blasiol, "Operation Thor," 5.
46. COMUSMACV to Commanding General III MAF, 200705Z June 1968, MCHC.

or release their units from participation. The expected misunderstandings arising from service-specific terminology, procedures, and equipment[47] were exacerbated by the climate of mistrust that existed at senior levels of command. The briefing officers from PCV Artillery encouraged participants to discuss technical issues with each other and to share their specialized expertise to find solutions. To a remarkable degree this nondirective approach succeeded both psychologically and technically.[48]

The most serious problem was airspace coordination. The Air Force used an airborne command post and the Marines used ground-based control stations. Radio and radar frequencies were incompatible, identification systems differed, and procedures differed. Warrant officer technicians from different services, brought to the meeting to provide technical justification for canceling the operation, got together and found they talked the same language. They worked out systems whereby the Air Force, Marines, and Navy could fly in the same air space under common control. From there they arranged check-in procedures, holding points, entry and egress corridors, and altitude limits to avoid shellfire from artillery and warships.

Army, Navy, and Marine officers developed deception measures to cover the easily observable movements of heavy artillery from the southern part of the PCV zone to the DMZ. These included the use of Navy landing craft that would go out of sight of land after picking up artillery pieces, Army personnel wearing 9th Division patches at the quayside to give the impression that the guns were going south rather than north, and Army and Marine engineers who would prepare firing positions while appearing to be doing routine work on the McNamara Line of sensors.

Army, Air Force, Marine, and Navy officers coordinated procedures for communicating target information from their own sensors and reconnaissance systems to command posts and thence to ships, squadrons, or batteries. They calculated the capacity of available networks and compared them with the expected volume and speed, and service-specific requirements. In some cases existing communications could be temporarily dedicated to Thor; in others new networks had to be set up. Communications had to include a dedicated teletype circuit between Seventh Air Force headquarters and the Air Force 1st Mobile Communications Group at Phu Bai airfield, and a retransmission link from the airfield to PCV Forward (the Thor CP) at Dong Ha. All Thor traffic was to have Flash precedence. It would include requests for B-52

---

47. Terry J. McKearney, "Rethinking the Joint Task Force," *United States Naval Institute Proceedings* 120 (November 1994): 56.

48. CHECO Report, 10; PCVA S-3, 12 June 1968; Briefing Outline: Operation THOR.

strikes (Arc Light missions) and 7th Air Force Daily Frag Orders assigning targets to tactical fighter wings.[49]

On 22 June PCV sent the final preparatory instructions for the construction of forward firing positions, and for the use of psychological operations assets to exploit the shock of Thor.[50] On 25 June MACV issued the initiating directive for Operation Thor. It confirmed Seventh Air Force control and coordination responsibility for Phases I and IV; III MAF control for phases II and III.[51] On 26 June the staff of PCV Artillery moved to Dong Ha to organize the PCV Forward/Thor command post in the 108th Field Artillery Group combat operations center. On 27 June Major General Richard G. Stillwell assumed command of PCV.

On that same day the PCV ammunition officer began a massive effort to assemble 155-mm, 175-mm, and 8-inch artillery ammunition from throughout Vietnam. No logistician believed that the ammunition requirements for Thor could be met, and when the ammunition dump at Dong Ha was blown up on the 20th, many saw that as the *coup de grace* for the operation. In what is probably the most extraordinary achievement of Operation Thor, the ammunition officer arranged a network of heavy Air Force transports to bring ammunition to Dong Ha, then for shuttles of trucks to carry it to battery positions near the DMZ. The gunners took the shells from the tailgates of the trucks to the gun breeches. They never ran short.

Also on the twenty-seventh, a second coordination meeting was held by Seventh Air Force at Udorn, Thailand. Air Force, Navy, and Marine aviators coordinated remaining control issues such as a minimum radar-directed bombing altitude to permit concurrent bombing and artillery fire during periods of low visibility. [52]

Meanwhile, three aircraft carrier battle groups and a nine-ship naval gunfire support group were moving into position. Tension was high. One artillery officer received his briefing from the PCV Artillery staff and was appalled by the prospect of taking a heavy artillery battalion to within two kilometers of the DMZ. As he went out the door, he shouted at the

49. Commanding General Prov. Corps V to CO 63d Signal Battalion, 281221Z June 1968, Subject: Teletype Message Support for Operation THOR, MCHC.

50. Commanding General PCV to Commanding General III MAF, 220649Z June 1968, MCHC; Commanding General PCV to Commanding General III MAF, 220950Z June 1968, Subject: Psyop in Operation Thor, ibid.; COMUSMACV to Commanding General III MAF, Commander 7 AF, 300817Z June 1968, Subject: Operation THOR, ibid.

51. COMUSMACV to Commanding General III MAF, Commander 7AF, 251124Z June 1968, Subject: Initiating Directive, Operation THOR, MCHC.

52. CHECO Report, 7–10; XXIV Corps, Combat After Action Report, 8–9.

operations officer, "You murderer!"[53] On 30 June, MACV issued the execute order for Operation Thor.[54]

The Battle

Air assets arrayed for Thor included the entire B-52 force and nearly fifty fighter and attack squadrons (see Table 3, next page). B-52 raids, called Arc Lights, usually comprised six aircraft attacking a one by two kilometer target area. Each B-52 carried about twenty-five tons of 500 or 750 pound bombs—as many as one hundred bombs per aircraft. B-52s flew at 40,000 feet; NVA soldiers on the ground neither saw nor heard the planes; only the sudden simultaneous explosion of three bombs, each with a lethal radius in excess of 100 meters, on every football-field sized bit of ground.[55]

The fighters and attack aircraft carried smaller loads but dropped them with greater precision guided by radar, forward air controllers in low-flying aircraft, or the pilots' own views of the target. Marine ground-based air traffic controllers and the Air Force Airborne Command and Control Centers coordinated one low-flying strike sortie every three minutes into Cap Mui Lay. On 1 and 2 July the 3rd Air Division flew 114 B-52 sorties, the 1st Marine Air Wing sent in 240 sorties and the aircraft carriers *Bon Homme Richard, Ticonderoga,* and *Constellation* sent 192 strikes.[56] The powerful NVA air defenses fought back with guns and missiles. They shot down an Air Force F-105 on 1 July. A helicopter attempting to rescue the pilot was damaged, and the mission was called off. A second mission on 2 July succeeded. An A-1H supporting the rescue crashed, killing the pilot.[57]

During Phase I, 8-inch and 155-mm artillery batteries moved to firebases A-2, A-3, and A-4 within eighteen hundred to three thousand meters of the DMZ (see Table 4). These bases had been used before by direct support artillery battalions, but not by heavy units. The anxiety felt by many members of the artillery units moving to forward positions was justified. The NVA controlled the DMZ by patrolling and fire. By the

---

53. PCVA S-3, 26 June 1968.

54. COMUSMACV to Commander 7 AF, Commanding General III MAF, 300817Z June 1968, Subject: Operation THOR, MCHC.

55. CHECO Report, 16; COMUSMACV to AIG 7860, 141440Z July 1968, Subject: ARC LIGHT Strike Results 30 June–6 July 1968 (CHECO document 19).

56. Seventh Fleet Monthly Historical Summary, 4; First Marine Aircraft Wing to III MAF, letter, Subject, Commander's Daily Summary, 010901H–020900 July 1968, 020901H–030900H July 1968, MCHC.

57. Report to 7th Air Force HILLSBORO and ALLEY CAT ABCCC REPORTS, 1–7 July, p. 1 (CHECO document 16); Extract, Weekly Air Intelligence Summary (7th Air Force), 20 July 1968 (CHECO document 17).

Table 3
Aviation Assets Committed to Thor

Unit	Base	Equipment

AIR FORCE[58]
Seventh Air Force—General W. W. Momyer

Unit	Base	Equipment
3rd Air Division	Guam	B-52H
8th Tactical Fighter Wing	Ubon, Thailand	F-4D
433, 435, 555 Tac Ftr. Sqdns.		
12th Tactical Fighter Wing	Cam Ranh Bay, RVN	F-4C
355th Tactical Fighter Wing	Takhli, Thailand	F-105D/F
333, 354, 357 Tac Ftr. Sqdns.		
366th Tactical Fighter Wing	DaNang, RVN	F-4C
4, 389, 390, 480 Tac Ftr. Sqdns.		
388th Tactical Fighter Wing	Koret, Thailand	F-105D/F,
34, 35, 44, 469 Tac Ftr. Sqdns		F-4D
432nd Tactical Recon. Wing	Udorn, Thailand	RF-4C
13 Tac Ftr. Sqdn.		
37th Tactical Recon. Wing	Phu Cat, RVN	F-100F
20th Tactical Air Support Sqdn.	Da Nang, RVN	0-1, 0-2

MARINES[59]
1st Marine Air Wing—Maj. Gen. C. J. Quilter

Marine Air Group 11—Col. Robert D. Slay

Unit	Base	Equipment
Reconnaissance Sqdn. VMCJ-1	Chu Lai, RVN	10 RF-4B,
		7 EF-10B
		4 EA-6A
Attack Fighter Sqdn. VMFA 122	Da Nang, RVN	13 F-4B
Attack Fighter Sqdn. VMFA 542	Da Nang, RVN	13 F-4B
Attack Sqdn. VMA (AW) 242	Chu Lai, RVN	9 A-6A

Marine Air Group 12—Col. C. B. Armstrong, Jr.

Unit	Base	Equipment
Attack Sqdn. VMA 121	Chu Lai, RVN	19 A-4E
Attack Sqdn. VMA 211	Chu Lai, RVN	20 A-4E
Attack Sqdn. VMA 233	Chu Lai, RVN	17 A-4C
Attack Sqdn. VMA 311	Chu Lai, RVN	20 A-4E

Marine Air Group 13—Col. J. H. Berge, Jr.

Unit	Base	Equipment
Attack Fighter Sqdn. VMFA 115	Chu Lai, RVN	14 F-4B
Attack Fighter Sqdn. VMFA 314	Chu Lai, RVN	12 F-4B
Attack Fighter Sqdn. VMFA 323	Chu Lai, RVN	12 F-4B

NAVY[60]
Attack Carrier Air Wing 14—Cdr. Kenneth E. Enney

Unit	Base	Equipment
Fighter Sqdns. VF-142, 143	USS Constellation	24 F-4B
Attack Sqdns. VA-27, 97	USS Constellation	25 A-7A
Attack Sqdn. VA-196	USS Constellation	11 A-6A

Attack Carrier Air Wing 19—Capt. Phillip R. Craven

Unit	Base	Equipment
Fighter Sqdns. VF-191, 194	USS Ticonderoga	21 F-8E
Attack Sqdns. VA-23, 192	USS Ticonderoga	28 A-4E
Attack Sqdn. VA-195	USS Ticonderoga	15 A-4C

Attack Carrier Air Wing 5—Cdr. D. B. Miller

Unit	Base	Equipment
Fighter Sqdn. VF-51	USS Bon Homme Richard	13 F-8E
Fighter Sqdn. VF-53	USS Bon Homme Richard	13 F-8H
Attack Sqdns. VA-93, 212	USS Bon Homme Richard	28 A-4F
Attack Sqdn. VA-94	USS Bon Homme Richard	15 A-4E

Attack Carrier Air Wing 6—Cdr. L. Wayne Smith (July 7 only)

Unit	Base	Equipment
Fighter Sqdns. VF-33, 102	USS America	25 F-4J
Attack Sqdns. VA-82, 86	USS America	23 A-7A
Attack Sqdn. VA-85	USS America	11 A-6A, 3 A-6B

Table 4
Artillery Committed to Thor[61]

Provisional Corps Vietnam Artillery, Brig. Gen. Lawrence H. Caruthers, Jr.
108th Field Artillery Group—Col. David L. Jones

Units	Service	Weapons	Battery Positions
8th Bn., 4th Arty.	Army	8-175-mm guns	Btry. A YD 210674 (C-1)
			Btry. C YD 222590 (Dong Ha)
2nd Bn., 94th Arty.	Army	12-175-mm guns	Btries. A&C YD221589 (Dong Ha)
			Btry. B YD144618 (C-3)
1st Bn., 83rd Arty.	Army	11-8-inch howitzers	Btry. A YD 117695 (A-4)(Con Thien)
			Btry. B YD 214739 (A-2)
			Btry. C YD 211733 (A- 2)
1st 8" Howitzer Btry.	Marines	4-8 inch howitzers	YD 176721 (A-3)
4th Bn., 12th Marines	Marines	24-155-mm howitsers	2 Btries. YD 117695 (A-4)(Con Thien)
Btry. K, 4th Bn.	Marines		1 Btry. YD 214739 (A-2)
13th Marines			1 Btry. YD 176721 (A-3)
5th 155-mm Gun Btry.	Marines	6-155-mm guns	YD 122592 (Cam Lo)

58. DCS Combat Operations to DO, letter, 25 July 1968, Subject: After Action Report Input—Operation THOR(U) with Tab A, CHECO Report, Document 7; 7th AF to aviation units participating in Thor, 210045Z July 1968, Subject: Congratulatory Message on Operation Thor.

59. Chief of Naval Operations, OPNAV Notice 03110 31 July 1968—Allowances and locations of Navy Aircraft. 1st Marine Air Wing Command Chronology, July 1968, NHC. Marine Air Group 11 Command Chronology, July 1968; Marine Air Group 12 Command Chronology, July 1968; and Marine Air Group 13 Command Chronology, July 1968, MCHC. Unit histories of VMA 223, VMA 311, VMFA 115, VMFA 323, and VMFA 542, MCHC library. Peter B. Marsky, *U.S. Marine Corps Aviation 1912 to the Present* (Baltimore: Nautical and Aviation Publishing Co., 1987), 229–30, 236–37.

60. United States Seventh Fleet Monthly Historical Summary, July 1968, pp. 23, 32, NHC; Chief of Naval Operations, OPNAV Notice 03110 31 July 1968—Allowances and locations of Navy Aircraft; CO USS *America* (CVA-66) to COMAIRNAVLANT, letter, Subject: USS *America* CVA-66/Commander Attack Carrier Air Wing Six WESTPAC Deployment Cruise Report (1968); command histories for USS *Bon Homme Richard,* CVW-6, 14, and 19, Squadrons VA-23 and 196, VF-33, 53, and 142; dictionary histories of VA-82, 85, 86, 93, 94,97, 192, 195, 196, 212 and VF-27, 51, 102, 191. (All documents in NHC.) See also René J. Francillon, *Tonkin Gulf Yacht Club* (Annapolis, Md.: U.S. Naval Institute Press, 1988).

61. Letters, Subject: After Action Report, Operation Thor: Headquarters 1st 8-inch Howitzer Battery, FMF, 12 July 1968; Headquarters 8th Bn., 4th Artillery (175-mm) (SP), 11 July 1968; Headquarters 4th Bn, 12th Marines, 16 July 1968; Headquarters 1st Bn., 83rd Artillery (8") (SP), 10 July 1968; Operational Reports for Period Ending 31 July 1968 RCS CSFOR-65 (R1) for 8th Bn, 4th Artillery (revised) (8 September 1968), 1st Bn, 83rd Artillery 1 August 1968, and 2nd Bn, 94th Artillery (8 August 1968), XXIV Corps Artillery S-3, Box 1 (6-17-8-2), RG 472, NA; CO 5th 155-mm Gun Battery (SP) (Reinf) to CO 1st Bn 13th Marines, letter, Subject: Command Chronology for Period 1 July to 31 July 1968, 4 August 1968, MCHC. The 5th 155-mm Gun Battery is not mentioned in the Thor Operations order or in the after-action reports by PCV Artillery, PCV, or III MAF. However, the battery command chronology and ammunition expenditure reports by XXIV corps make it clear that it took part.

LIVERPOOL JOHN MOORES UNIVERSITY
LEARNING SERVICES

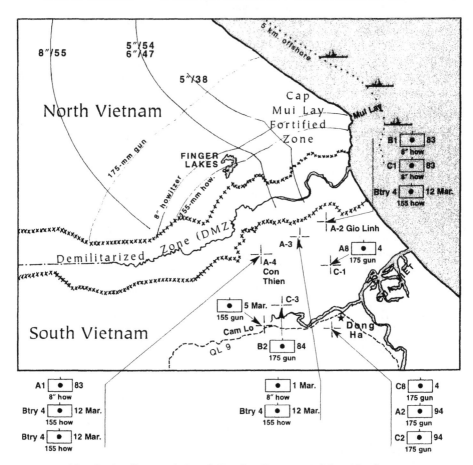

Map 2. *Artillery and Naval Gunfire Coverage of Cap Mui Lay,
1–7 July 1968.*

afternoon of 2 July ten heavy and four medium batteries were laid and
ready to fire. The 8-inch and 155-mm howitzers could reach one-half to
two-thirds of the targets in the Cap Mui Lay fortified zone; the 175-mm
and the 155-mm guns could cover the entire zone (see Map 2).

While B-52s and fighter-bombers hit suspected NVA artillery, air
defense, and coastal batteries, the ships of Task Unit 70.8.9 closed to
within ten kilometers of Cap Mui Lay (see Table 5). They were not fired
on. From ten kilometers offshore the cruisers *St. Paul* and *Boston* could
hit three-fourths of the Cap Mui Lay sector with their 8-inch guns. The

Table 5
Naval Gunfire Support Assets Committed to Thor[62]
Task Unit 70.8.9 - Rear Admiral S. H. Moore

Ship	Armament
USS *Boston* CAG-1	6-8″/55, 10-5″/38
USS *St. Paul* CA-73	9-8″/55, 12-5″/38
USS *Providence* CLG-6	3-6″/47, 2-5″/38
USS *Henry B. Wilson* DDG-7	2-5″/54
USS *Cochran* DDG-21	2-5″/54
USS *Turner Joy* DD-951	3-5″/54
USS *O'Brien* DD-725	4-5″/38
USS *Boyd* DD-544	4-5″/38
USS *Benner* DD-807	6-5″/38

light cruiser *Providence* (6-inch guns) and the destroyers could hit coastal targets.

To make productive use of the large force assigned to Operation Thor, the PCV Artillery staff, integrated with the staff of 108th Artillery Group and functioning as PCV Forward, worked around the clock in two shifts. It evaluated information on potential targets, decided which were worth attacking, selected delivery systems, and scheduled attacks. Targets of opportunity were the most important. In most cases they were NVA weapons or maneuver forces firing on a friendly aircraft, ship, or battery. Attack had to be rapid and effective because of the vulnerability of friendly forces.[63]

Target information came from four sources. The richest but least timely was aerial photo reconnaissance by the Air Force 432nd Tactical Reconnaissance Wing or the 1st Marine Air Wing's tactical reconnaissance squadron, VMCJ-1. Aerial photos were taken, developed, analyzed, and evaluated within eight to twelve hours. Real-time targets came from side-looking airborne radar, aerial observers, and ground based sensors. The latter included Battery F, 26th Artillery's sound and flash bases, the

62. CTU 70.8.9 to USS *Boston, Providence, St. Paul, Benner, O'Brien, Boyd, Turner Joy, Cochran, Henry B. Wilson*, R 071622Z July 1968, NHC; Raymond V. B. Blackman, *Jane's Fighting Ships, 1962–63* (London: Sampson Low, Marston, 1962), 217–18, 321, 328, 330, 332, 334, 337; CTU 70.8.9 to AIG 460, 0 030753 Z July 1968, Subject: NGFS Assignments 4 to 25 July inclusive, NHC. The cruiser *Providence* is not listed in the Thor operations order or in after-action reports by PCV Artillery, PCV, or III MAF, but these messages and XXIV Corps ammunition expenditure report showing expenditure of 6″/47 ammunition makes it clear that she took part.

63. XXIV Corps Artillery, 25 August 1968, letter, Subject: Operational Report of Corps Artillery (Provisional) Vietnam for Period Ending 31 July 1968, RCS CSFOR-65 (R1) 4, S-3 Operations Reports, Box 1 (6-17-8-2), RG 472, NA.

235th, 239th, 240th, 245th, and 250th Field Artillery Radar Detachments, five radars belonging to 12th Marines, and an experimental MITHRAS integrated artillery detection system (flash, laser, and acoustic means) the 12th Marines had set up at firebase A-4. MITHRAS detected forty-one targets, including two surface-to-air missile batteries, and was used to register artillery.[64]

PCV Forward preempted all cable paths between 108th Field Artillery Group and 3rd Marine division, and 63rd Signal Battalion installed special communications systems solely for Thor. Communications with fire support ships went through naval gunfire liaison officers using 3rd Marine Division's one secure voice circuit. Air liaison officers at PCV Forward had communications with the Air Force Airborne Command and Control Center. A representative of 3rd Marine Division communicated by FM radio with maneuver units, and by telephone with 1st Marine Air Wing and Marine air control teams. The 108th Field Artillery Group had phone and radio communications with field artillery units and ground-based sensors. Eight sole-user voice circuits were installed by 63rd Signal Battalion to link MACV, PCV, PCV Forward, and 3rd Marine Division.

These communications were only marginally adequate. There was no secure voice circuit between PCV Forward and Seventh Air Force or with the admiral commanding TU 70.8.9. The Air Force radar bombing control team (ASRT) at Camp Carroll was only ten miles west of Dong Ha but it never received written target lists from PCV Forward in time to program strikes on the targets. Air Force and Army personnel worked out a system during the operation to telephone the coordinates of targets in the clear using a low-level "KAC" code. Decrypting target data delayed the receipt of targeting orders at the squadrons until midnight.[65] A further deficiency was lack of a daily air courier to carry target lists to TU 70.8.9 and Seventh Air Force.[66] Some communications, particularly the naval gunfire liaison officer's secure circuit to TU 70.8.9 and the 7th Air Force teletype to Phu Bai and thence to PCV Forward, were always saturated. That the communications networks did not collapse was remarkable given the complexity of the linkages and the heavy traffic. Because the commander of the 63rd Signal Battalion had been in on the planning from the beginning, he was able to install the communications quickly

64. Ibid., 2, 4; Headquarters XXIV Corps, AVII-ATC, 16 August 1968, Subject: Combat After Action Report (RCS: MACJ 3-37) (K-1), pp. 6–8, 11; Blasiol,"Operation Thor," 6.

65. Extract, Taped Record, "Thor Critique, ABCCC at UDORN, 13 Jul 68," pp. 2–4 (CHECO document 14).

66. Headquarters 7th AF to Commanding General PCV, date unknown, Subject: PCV Targeting, Op THOR (CHECO document 21).

when MACV decided on 25 June to implement Thor six days later.[67]

The air strikes and naval gunfire of Phase I were sufficiently effective that warships were able to close to within five kilometers of the coast on 3 July and fire forty missions. The NVA did not fire back. From these positions the 8-inch guns of the _Boston_ and _St. Paul_ could reach 90 percent of the Cap Mui Lay zone; 5-inch guns of the _Henry B. Wilson, Cochrane,_ and _Turner Joy_ and 6-inch guns of the _Providence_ could reach 45 percent of the zone; and the 5-inch cruiser secondary guns and main batteries of _O'Brien, Boyd,_ and _Benner_ could reach highway 1A along most of its length (see Map 2).[68] The bombardment during Phase I also weakened NVA air defenses enough for Army and Marine light observation planes to begin flying along the DMZ on 3 July.[69]

One of the most critical tasks facing PCV Forward, the Air Force Airborne Command and Control Center and ground-based Direct Air Support Center, and the Marine ground-based control teams was airspace coordination. It had been the primary focus of the preliminary conferences, but the agreements fell apart in the face of interservice mistrust as Phase II began on 3 July.

The plan for protecting strike aircraft from NVA antiaircraft fire was to have artillery or naval gunfire neutralize the NVA weapons until just before the aircraft released their bombs. But on 3 July the controller in the Air Force Airborne Command and Control Center called PCV Forward and asked to have the artillery and ships cease fire thirty minutes before strike aircraft were due in. His position was that fliers do not like to share airspace with artillery shells, and the Air Force had always been responsible for airspace coordination. The PCV operations duty officer argued that shutting down flak suppression fire would expose the planes to the full effects of NVA antiaircraft fire. He conferred with the Air Force controller for several impassioned minutes on the radio. Neither would abandon what he considered to be correct procedure. Thor was unusual in using artillery and naval gunfire for flak suppression. Most air strikes in North Vietnam had no friendly artillery in range to support the aircraft so there had been no need for coordination. Aerial attacks on NVA forces in South Vietnam usually did not face formidable antiaircraft defenses, so flak suppression was not often necessary. To the great credit of the officer in charge of the Airborne Command and Control Center, he real-

---

67. XXIV Corps Combat After Action Report, 16 August 1968, 9; XXIV Corps Artillery, 25 August 1968, letter, Subject: Operational Report of Corps Artillery (Provisional) Vietnam for Period Ending 31 July 1968 RCS CSFOR-65 (R1), 14.

68. USS _Turner Joy_ to AIG 7678, 021730 July 1968; USS _Benner_ to AIG 7678, 031456Z July 1968; and USS _Boyd_ to AIG 7678, 031605Z July 1968, NHC.

69. XXIV Corps Combat After Action Report, 16 August 1968, 6.

ized that Thor was different, and he withdrew his demand for a cease fire.[70]

On 3 July the target list grew as air observers examined Cap Mui Lay from low altitude. An unexpected problem emerged because the Air Force used a computerized target list and PCV Forward used a manual system. The Air Force could not deal with a target that was not in their computer, but the new targets were often fleeting and there was not time to program them into the computer. A system was cobbled together whereby PCV Forward would assign a new target the number of another target that was already in the Air Force computer and that was in the same grid square as the new one. Then oral instructions were given to the pilot flying the mission to look for the new target by reference to the old one. It was cumbersome but it worked.[71]

On 4 July a Marine F-4B from VMFA 115 was hit by automatic weapons fire. The crewmen ejected and were rescued. The next day an A-4 and an F-8 from USS *Ticonderoga* collided near their carrier. Both pilots ejected and were rescued. The same day the Air Force lost an F-100F to possible battle damage. Both crew members bailed out over the sea and were rescued.[72]

Phase III was the decisive part of Thor. On 5 July 0-1 observation aircraft flew north of the DMZ for the first time, and the next day Army and Marine 0-1s examined the Cap Mui Lay sector from the coast to the Finger Lakes Area calling in artillery. Air Force forward air controllers in 0-2s and F-100Fs called in air strikes. The air observers and forward air controllers found that no farming or other domestic activity was taking place in the Cap Mui Lay sector. What once had been villages were now fortified billets, storage facilities, and gun positions. One air strike on a "village" led to eighteen secondary explosions over a ninety-minute period. Naval gunfire support ships fired eighty-seven missions.[73] Airspace coordination reached a high level of efficiency. There were no incidents of aircraft being hit by artillery or naval gunfire. Tactical coordination also was effective. On one occasion an Army air observer found an NVA artillery piece, Marine artillery bracketed it, and an Air Force fighter-bomber destroyed it.

70. PCVA S-3, personal communication.

71. Ibid.; CHECO Report, 22–23.

72. Commanding General III MAF to COMUSMACV, 141538Z July 1968, Subject: Preliminary Report, Operation THOR (CHECO document 12); Report to 7AF, Hillsboro and Alleycat ABCCC Reports, 1–7 July 1968, 2 (CHECO document 16).

73. XXIV Corps Combat After Action Report, 16 August 1968, 6; Blasiol, "Operation Thor," 9–10; CHECO Report, 17.

Analysis

Operation Thor was terminated at 2400 hours on 7 July.[74] Army, Navy, Marine, and Air Force personnel had worked together around the clock for a week to hit Cap Mui Lay with 8,363 tons of bombs and 42,209 shells. Friendly losses were one Air Force pilot killed and one Army soldier slightly wounded, and four aircraft shot down and two lost in an accident. PCV, or XXIV Corps as it was renamed in August, claimed the destruction of 789 antiaircraft guns or positions, 179 artillery pieces or positions, 143 bunkers, five rocket or mortar positions, nine surface-to-air missile installations, and 359 structures. In addition, Thor caused 290 secondary fires and 334 secondary explosions.[75]

Though no U.S. personnel could go into Cap Mui Lay to inspect the damage, III MAF accepted the claims and described Thor as a striking success in reports to MACV. The Marines commissioned a monograph about it that may be a part of the Marine Corps history of operations in Vietnam.[76]

Rear Admiral S. H. Moore commanding Task Unit 70.8.9, the naval gunfire support force, was lyrical in his praise of his nine ships for their work off Cap Mui Lay: "The devastating firepower and precise accuracy of your long deadly naval rifles have weeded out a high threat area at the enemy's front door. The destruction wrought, the enemy forces put to flight, the heartfelt thanks from our forces ashore when you destroyed before their eyes the enemy fire closing in on them, are high tributes indeed to your professional, hard working and sleepless crews. The performance of TU 70.8.9 destroyers and cruisers in Operation Thor against the enemy was in keeping with the highest traditions of the U.S. Navy. Well done to all hands."[77]

Admiral Moore also complimented the commander of Task Group 73.5, the logistical support force afloat: "Truly outstanding. The flexibility and endurance of your support units in response to our many and constantly changing requirements enabled us to meet our commitments

74. Frag Order 1 to PCV OPORD 15-68 (Thor), 060915Z July 1968, cited in letter from Headquarters 108th Field Artillery Group, 31 July 1968, Subject: Operational Report of 108th Field Artillery Group for Period Ending 31 July 1968, RCS-CSFOR-65 (R1), 3, XXIV Corps Artillery, S-3 Operations Reports, Box 1 (6-17-8-2), RG 472, NA.

75. Appendix I, Thor Ammo Expenditures, Bomb Damage Assessment/Gun Damage Assessment to CHECO Report, 29; CTG 70.8 to CTE 70.2.1.1, P 081445Z July 1968, NHC; Inclosure 4, Ammunition Expenditures, Bomb Damage/Gun Damage Assessment) to "Thor" After Action Report, XXIV Corps Combat After Action Report, 16 August 1968, S-3 After Action Reports, Box 1 (6-17-8-2), RG 472, NA.

76. Blasiol, "Operation Thor."

77. CTU 70.8.9 to USS *Boston, Providence, St. Paul, Turner Joy, Cochrane, Boyd, Benner, O'Brien, Henry B. Wilson,* R 071622Z July 1968, NHC.

continually and effectively. The damage our guns inflicted upon the enemy emenwted [emanated] from the holds and tanks of your ships. Hearty thanks and well done."[78] Praising subordinates in electrical messages that one's superiors will read is a common way to call one's own outstanding leadership to the attention of those superiors. Still, Admiral Moore's messages suggest that Operation Thor was unusual, difficult, and an achievement in which the Navy took pride.

The vice commander of Seventh Air Force, Major General Robert F. Worley, sent a congratulatory message to participating Air Force units,[79] but his headquarters took issue with both the claims of damage inflicted and the massive resources committed. Seventh Air Force said there was clear photographic evidence of only two artillery and eleven antiaircraft weapons being destroyed.[80] Headquarters, Pacific Air Forces prepared a report on Thor in which it concurred in Seventh Air Force's skepticism.[81] This critique must be set against the reports of Army and Marine air observers, flying low and slow over Cap Mui Lay, who had a clear view of NVA weapons and structures while they were under fire.

The only joint headquarters in the theater, MACV, adopted the views of the Army, Navy, and Marine commanders.[82] Although it is inevitable that most of the American ordnance blew up North Vietnamese dirt and trees, there is indirect evidence with which to evaluate both the outcome of the attack and the appropriateness of dedicating massive resources to it. First, after Operation Thor, it was possible for light aircraft to fly over the Cap Mui Lay area—until 1 November when President Johnson forbade further flights over North Vietnam.[83] Second, after Thor the intensity of NVA artillery fire from the Cap Mui Lay sector fell by 80 percent.[84]

78. CTU 70.8.9 to CTG 73.5, R 071620Z July 1968, Subject: Operation Thor Logistical Support, NHC. The logistics ships included tankers *Caliente* (A0-53) and *Kennebec* (A0-36); ammunition ships *Haleakala* (AE-25) and *Paricutin* (AE-18); stores ship *Pictor* (AF-54); fast combat support ship *Camden* (ACE-2), and combat store ship *Niagara Falls* (AFS-3).

79. 7 AF to 3rd AIR DIV (and other units), 210045 July 1968, Subject: Congratulatory Message on Operation THOR (CHECO document 18).

80. Headquarters 7AF to DASC Victor, Hué Phu Bai, 1002307Z July 1968, Subject: Operation THOR (CHECO document 15); Headquarters 7th Air Force, letter, Subject: BDA Operation THOR to DIT (Col. Jones), 30 July 1968.

81. CHECO Report.

82. Headquarters United States Military Assistance Command, Vietnam, Command History 1968, 1: 408–9.

83. Headquarters XXIV Corps Artillery, 25 August 1968, letter, Subject: Operational Report of Corps Artillery (Provisional) Vietnam for Period Ending 31 July 1968, RCS CSFOR-65 (R1), 3; Blasiol, "Operation Thor," 11–12.

84. Headquarters Provisional Corps Vietnam, Daily Intsum (intelligence summary), 1 June–31 July 1968. Between 7 and 30 June there were eighty-seven NVA artillery attacks; between 8 and 31 July there were only seventeen. Box 1 (6-17-8-1), RG 472, NA.

Third, there were no more ground attacks launched from Cap Mui Lay during the Paris peace talks.

The defeat of the Tet offensive, the elimination of Cap Mui Lay as a secure base for excursions across the DMZ, and the defeat of the NVA second stage offensive in August and third stage offensive in October spelled the defeat of the NVA plan to change the military situation by conquering Quang Tri and Thua Thien provinces. These victories gave American commanders sufficient confidence to recommend a bombing halt to help get the peace talks started. On 15 October the bombing stopped, and two weeks later the North Vietnamese dropped their other eight conditions and began to negotiate matters of substance.[85]

As an example of a joint operation, Thor ranks somewhere between the landing at Vera Cruz in 1847,[86] and Desert Storm in 1991. It was an improvised, seat-of-the-pants operation run at a very low level and largely dependent on the development of trust developed through face-to-face encounters for its success. There was no joint task force commander designated, and responsibility for control and coordination shifted with the phases of the operation between III MAF and Seventh Air Force. General Westmoreland and his staff assigned missions to service components and left the tasks of coordination and direction to III MAF, which delegated them to PCV, which delegated them to PCV Artillery—a brigade-level headquarters.

Decentralization of responsibility for execution to a low-level headquarters could be interpreted as an effort by senior commanders to distance themselves from a potential catastrophe. PCV Artillery lacked the personnel necessary to conduct direct coordination with key personnel on warships and in aviation squadrons; it lacked the technical expertise to anticipate the concerns of personnel from other services; and it lacked the authority to compel compliance. These apparent weaknesses actually enhanced the effectiveness of coordination because they allowed the good will and professionalism of participants from all four services free rein. Many became intrigued with the complexity and importance of a task they saw as worth doing. Members of the different services cross-pollinated each other with ideas, came up with creative solutions, and came to trust each other in the process.

Air Force and Marine aerial photo reconnaissance crews, Army and Marine air observers in their light observation planes, sailors on Navy warships, members of Army and Marine artillery batteries, and crews of Navy, Air Force, and Marine attack fighters all knew the great risks they ran in approaching Cap Mui Lay more closely than had been possible for

85. Spector, *After Tet*, 295–99, 304.
86. Paul C. Clark, Jr., and Edward H. Moseley, "D-Day Veracruz, 1847—A Grand Design," *Joint Force Quarterly*, Winter 1995–96, 102–15.

two years. They were all dependent for their survival on the competence and dedication of members of other services. Thor was particularly significant as a psychological victory, a triumph of trust at the working level over doubt and resentment generated by interservice rivalry and hostility.

Thor left two legacies for the Army after the war. General Caruthers became Assistant Commandant of the Field Artillery School (1968–72) and introduced Thor into the combined arms curriculum at the School. It is likely that officers who have worked on J-7 doctrine or who planned Desert Storm knew about the problems Thor encountered. Lieutenant General William E. DePuy, assistant Vice Chief of Staff in 1969, asked General Caruthers to prepare a briefing to support DePuy's efforts to convince Deputy Secretary of Defense David Packard to fund Tacfire, a second-generation field artillery fire control data system. Caruthers used Thor to illustrate the need for Tacfire's capabilities to coordinate fire in future joint operations. Packard was convinced, the Army bought Tacfire, and it guided fire support during Operation Desert Storm.[87]

87. Brigadier General L. H. Caruthers. Jr., to F. R. Kirkland, 18 March 1992, letter.

760 ★

Tonnage and Technology

Air Power on the Ho Chi Minh Trail

Darrel D. Whitcomb

(Overleaf) Trucks roll down
the Mu Gia Pass in 1967.

(Right) The OV-10 Bronco
performed well for its forward air controllers.(Photo
courtesy of the author.)

(Below) The forward air
controller searches for targets.(Photo courtesy of the
author.)

D uring our nation's long involvement in the wars in Southeast Asia from 1961 to 1973, United States air forces engaged in combat in almost all parts of the theater and performed all of the classic missions, from air superiority to routine daily resupply. But one of the most focused and intense efforts was the series of campaigns to interdict or cut the Ho Chi Minh Trail—the main supply route—which ran from North Vietnam through southern Laos and eastern Cambodia and branched off into South Vietnam at several places. That effort, which spanned several years and peaked between 1969 and 1972, was a failure. The constant aerial bombardment exacted a heavy price from the North Vietnamese truck drivers and support troops below. But the Trail stayed open throughout the conflict. It was the North Vietnamese "Road to Victory," for it led to their defeat of the South in 1975. The lessons of that failure are worth noting. And though unformed and unstructured, they occurred to one young U.S. Air Force pilot in the waning days of that conflict.

It was April 1972. The Vietnam War, America's longest, refused to end. In fact, events had taken a dramatic turn for the worse because North Vietnam had brazenly unleashed massive formations of tanks, artillery, and infantry which, in three separate attacks, were slicing into South Vietnam. It would come to be called the "Easter Offensive." Across the border in Laos, a young Forward Air Controller (FAC) was patrolling his assigned sector over the Ho Chi Minh Trail, just north of the critical road junction at Tchepone. New to the 23rd Tactical Air Support Squadron (TASS) at Nakhon Phanom Air Base in Thailand, the eager OV-10 pilot was earnestly searching the road network for signs of enemy movement.

THE EAGER OV–10 PILOT WAS EARNESTLY SEARCHING THE ROAD NETWORK FOR SIGNS OF ENEMY MOVEMENT

All of the roads showed indications of heavy activity from the fully laden trucks hauling supplies south for the blossoming offensive. But where were they hiding?

He was interrupted by a call from Hillsboro, the orbiting command and control C–130 aircraft. The controller told the FAC that he had a flight of two F–4s in the area that was low on fuel, and needed a target so that they could drop their bombs and return to base. Did he have a target for the flight?

The FAC was caught slightly off guard. He had just arrived on station in his assigned area and had not yet had a chance to find anything in the morning haze. Usually, the first FACs up each day would find residue from the work of the AC–130 gunships the night before. But it took time to reconnoiter all of the roads in the sector. Searching quickly, he spotted two trucks which apparently were stalled in a small river. He told the controller on Hillsboro to send the fighters to his assigned strike frequency.

Dutifully, the fighters checked in with him. They were two F–4s from Udorn Air Base, Thailand, and their call sign was "Merco." Each was carrying twelve Mk-82, 500-pound bombs. The FAC gave them his position so that they could rendezvous. The fighters headed to the FAC's location and found him orbiting above the target.

He quickly passed them a target brief, including such basics as target elevation, winds, known enemy defenses in the area, and the nearest friendly airfield, should they need to divert from the strike. He also told them where to bail out in the immediate area if they were hit by enemy fire. The fighters acknowledged all of the information. The FAC then said that he would like them to make four passes each on the trucks, dropping three bombs on each pass. The flight leader hesitated—why so many passes? The FAC responded that the area was quiet, that he had so far that morning seen no enemy anti-aircraft

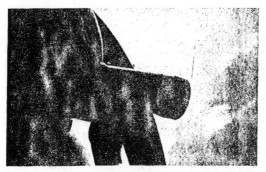

Colonel Darrel Whitcomb is an Air Force officer currently assigned as the individual mobilization augmentee to the commandant of the Air Command and Staff College at Maxwell AFB, Alabama. He was graduated from the U.S. Air Force Academy and served as a forward air controller, flying the OV-10 and O-1 from 1972 to 1974. He flew combat missions over Laos, North and South Vietnam, and Cambodia. Col. Whitcomb is a graduate of the Army Command and General Staff College and the National War College. He has published several articles on the Vietnam War and is completing a manuscript on the rescue of Bat 21.

6

(Right) The spiderweb of trails with a myriad of bomb craters shows the difficulty of cutting the trail in two. (Photo courtesy of the author.)

Below) Southeast Asia and its important geographical features. (Map courtesy of the author.)

THE AIR FORCE HAD BEEN INVOLVED IN EFFORTS TO "ISOLATE" THE BATTLEFIELD IN SOUTH VIETNAM BY INTERDICTING THE FLOW OF SUPPLIES FROM THE NORTH

guns. He wanted to kill those trucks and knew that the odds of destruction increased if the fighters made multiple passes. The fighters acknowledged his request.

Briefing complete, the FAC rolled his aircraft in towards the target and fired a smoke rocket, which exploded near the river. The FAC saw the plume of white smoke blossom on the ground. The FAC then talked them from the smoke to the actual trucks. They were ready.

The flight leader attacked with his first three bombs. They fell to the north of the target. The FAC cleared the second fighter to make his first bomb run. But as the second aircraft dived at the ground, two anti-aircraft guns opened up and "hosed off" numerous rounds at it. The pilot jinked left and right as he pulled off of the target, but his bombs hit one of the trucks. Curiously, it did not burn.

Spooked by the ground fire, the flight leader told the FAC that they would make only one more pass on the target. He acknowledged and cleared them to attack. The guns continued to fire from their unknown locations. The lead plane's bombs were once again wide of the mark. But as before, his wingman dropped his remaining bombs on the second truck. It was a good strike.

Elated, the young FAC reported his success back to Hillsboro and continued his mission

throughout the rest of his sector for his assigned time on station. When his time was up and his fuel was low, he returned his OV–10 to Nakhon Phanom. There, he reported to the intelligence shop to pass along his sightings for the day and the results of the air strike. The "old head" sergeant was curious about the air strike and asked the FAC to point out to him on the map where it had taken place. Dutifully, the FAC did so. The sergeant laughed knowingly. Those trucks had been there for years. This was the third time that they had been personally debriefed to him as having been "destroyed." They were a perfect decoy.

Chagrined, the young FAC felt foolish at his naivete. The whole endeavor had been a waste. More importantly, he had asked the fighter crews to risk their lives for nothing. It was beginning to occur to him that perhaps the whole war effort was following the same pattern.[1]

As it had been at the onset, the American war in Southeast Asia was by 1972 once again an air war. Most ground forces had been withdrawn. Other than the advisors, those ground units that remained were performing base security duty while the Army of the Republic of Vietnam (ARVN) fought the battles. The few remaining Americans still engaged in combat were fighting from the air.

American air power was still considerable in the theater and was performing a rear guard role as the U.S. disengaged. But although the basic decision to withdraw had been made in 1968, the actual period of withdrawal from 1969 to 1972 saw some of the greatest bloodletting of the war. This was due in part to the extensive use of air power. By 1972, the question was how to withdraw the remaining forces while securing the return of American prisoners and leaving South Vietnam reasonably secure.[2] The order of these deeds suggest their priority.

Since the halt of all bombing of North Vietnam in 1968, the Air Force, with some exceptions, had been involved in efforts to "isolate" the battlefield in South Vietnam by interdicting the flow of supplies from the North. The intent was to create a shield behind which South Vietnam could strengthen its military and build a stable society.

235

BY CONTROLLING SOUTHERN LAOS, NORTH VIETNAM COULD USE IT AS A HUGE LOGISTICAL BASE AND ... MOVE UNITS INTO ALMOST ANY PART OF SOUTHEAST ASIA

We called it "Vietnamization." This shield was necessary because of the strategic realities of the war. North Vietnam still held to its objective of uniting the two countries under Hanoi's control. South Vietnam continued to resist.

Increasingly, North Vietnam was using its main force Army (NVA) to prosecute the war, and it had to be supplied from the north. The primary conduit for moving soldiers and supplies south was the Ho Chi Minh Trail. Earlier in the conflict, North Vietnam also infiltrated men and materiel into the South by boat along the coast and over-land from ports in southern Cambodia along the "Sihanouk" Trail. But these paths were of secondary importance and had been cut off by decisive ground and naval actions. That left only the overland route. It would not be easy.

The Ho Chi Minh Trail had its genesis in 1959. At a Politburo meeting in May of that year, the North Vietnamese Communist Party leaders decided to unleash an armed revolt against the Saigon government and support armed struggle in the South. In making such a momentous decision, they realized that their comrades in South Vietnam would need manpower and materiel support from the North. The question then became how to get it there. To solve that problem, the Central Military Committee established an organization called Group 559 (based on its beginning in the fifth month of 1959), with the mission of creating and operating an overland supply system. Ho Chi Minh turned to one of his subordinates, Vo Bam, and said:

Comrade Vo, build me a supply road by hand from Hanoi to Saigon with five main North-South

routes and twenty-one East-West branches. Even though it will be an elephant-sized project, keep it secret and hidden. And when it is complete, report back to me.[3]

A "riser" in the NVA, Vo Bam sprang to the task. Using cadres of engineers and support troops, he began the long and laborious process of creating what would become the most critical logistical and communications link of the entire war.[4]

These developments did not go unnoticed by the U.S. At one point in 1961, plans were drafted to insert an American combat force of soldiers and marines to seize several towns in central Laos, including Tchepone, and create a barrier from the Thai border along Route 9 to South Vietnam. The operation never took place. Instead, American political leaders put their faith in the "neutrality" of Laos as established by the agreement which emanated from the Geneva Conference of 1961-1962. At that conference, fourteen nations, including the U.S., agreed to declare Laos a neutral nation, controlled by a regime comprised of three factions: royal forces, neutralist forces, and Communist forces. At the request of the Communist forces, NVA troops drove neutralist forces from their position along Route 9 in Laos prior to the implementation of the agreement. They then took *de facto* control of a corridor in Laos ultimately up to eighty kilometers wide, from north of Tchepone to south of Moung Phine. The Laotian Communists agreed to this arrangement, but directed the North Vietnamese to keep it secret. Vo Bam began moving his people into Laos. His engineers and construction crews went to work on the mountain trails through the Trung Son Mountain Range which split the area from north to south. They would turn those trails into truck capable roads. Within a year, the trucks were running south.[5]

Some have argued that that was a serious—perhaps the most serious—American error of the war, because southern Laos was the key terrain of the entire theater. By controlling southern Laos, North Vietnam could use it as a huge logistical base and, with well built roads, move units into almost any part of Southeast Asia. It was a premier strategic advantage.[6]

From the signing of the agreement, North Vietnam never observed Laotian neutrality. They realized the advantage they had gained. Still in the embryonic stage, the Ho Chi Minh Trail was beginning to evolve into the strategic corridor which would give the North access to all areas of South Vietnam, Cambodia, and most of Laos. Ultimately it would connect the roads coming south from the Chinese border and docks of Haiphong and the battle areas as far south as the Mekong Delta. It would consist of literally hundreds of roads and bypasses, over 10,000 miles in total length. Like a spider web, it would link all of the strategic areas of Southeast Asia. By 1975, it would give the North Vietnamese Army unsurpassed mobility.[7]

These trucks were wending their way through the Mu Gia Pass in early 1967.

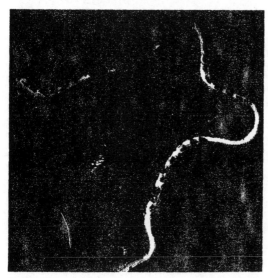

8

236

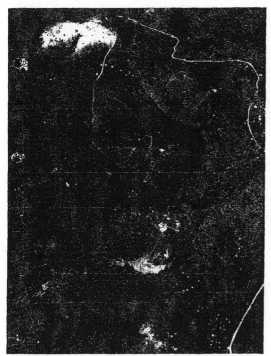

The Ho Chi Minh trail was a
network of passages
through the mountains.
(Photo courtesy of the
author.)

**THE MISSION
DESCRIBED
UNDER
COMMANDO
HUNT WAS
DEFENSIVE
IN NATURE,
AND
CLEARLY
REACTIVE
TO THE
ENEMY'S
INITIATIVES**

The North Vietnamese efforts did not go
unchallenged. As the war progressed, American
and ARVN special operations teams were constantly introduced into the Trail complex to
observe traffic and harass the engineer units. At
least twice, in 1965 and 1967, American and
South Vietnamese military leaders again advocated using regular forces to cut the Trail and
build a fortified barrier against the North
Vietnamese. In both instances, President Lyndon
Johnson rejected the proposals.[8]

Instead, others suggested technological solutions. In 1966, Secretary of Defense Robert
McNamara convened what came to be known as
the "Jason" group to study air operations against
North Vietnam. Among other things, the group
recommended that an anti-infiltration barrier be
built across Laos. Part of the effort would be the
use of electronic sensors to detect enemy movement. The physical barrier was never built, but
the sensors were developed and placed along the
Trail. The program was called IGLOO WHITE.[9]

Starting in 1961, air power was also used
against the Trail. Under Operations STEEL TIGER
and TIGER HOUND, special units out of the air
bases in Thailand used refitted A–26s, AT–28s,
AC–47s, and A–1s left over from the Korean War

to attack what targets they could find.[10] FACs
assigned to the 23rd TASS flying O–1s would spot
for them. The larger F–105s and F–4s were also
used. The priority for them was the ROLLING
THUNDER missions being flown against North
Vietnam. But when these missions were prevented by bad weather, these aircraft were also
available. Indeed, during the northeast monsoon
season, from November to April, most "fast-
movers" were used against the Trail. And B–52s
flew many strikes against the early Trail, but
their priority was ground support for troops in
South Vietnam. All of that would change in 1968.

That year was the watershed year for the U.S.
in the war. The debacle of Tet led to the demise of
President Johnson's administration, the end of
the bombing of North Vietnam, and the strategy
of withdrawal and Vietnamization under
President Richard Nixon.

Upon taking office, President Nixon ruled
against resuming air strikes against North
Vietnam. Instead, the planes sitting in abun-
dance on airfields and aircraft carriers in
Southeast Asia would be used to cover America's
withdrawal from the war. They would be used as
the shield necessary to buy time for
Vietnamization and withdrawal. President Nixon
said at a press conference, "As far as air power is
concerned, let me also say this: As we reduce the
number of our forces, it is particularly important
for us to continue our air strikes on the infiltration routes."[11] The plan was to attack the Ho Chi
Minh Trail wholesale with air power. It would
expand the use of the two "Ts" of American military power—tonnage and technology.

The effort would be a series of campaigns from
November 1968 to March 1972 called COMMANDO
HUNT I through VII. The COMMANDO HUNT objectives were twofold: first, to reduce the logistical
flow by substantially increasing the time needed
to move supplies from the north to the south; second, to destroy trucks and supply caches along
the roads and streams and in the truck parks and
storage areas along the Ho Chi Minh Trail in
Laos and its tributaries into Cambodia and South
Vietnam.[12]

Air power is primarily—although not exclusively—an offensive weapon, best used in hitting
clearly defined enemy vital centers, or, in other
words, in taking the war to the enemy. Yet the
mission described under COMMANDO HUNT was
defensive in nature, and clearly reactive to the
enemy's initiatives. Given such a nebulous mission, the Air Force was groping for direction.
Emphasis shifted to tactics, techniques, and high
technology employed under a pervasive managerial concept evolving as a substitute for strategy.[13]

The tonnage necessary for the endeavor was
certainly available. Freed from missions against
North Vietnam, several hundred fighter aircraft
were readied to strike Trail targets. In October
1968, 4,700 sorties were flown against STEEL
TIGER—as that part of Laos was now designated.

(Above) The southern end of the Mu Gia Pass.

(Below) This AP–2H of U.S. Navy Squadron VAH-21 was used to drop sensors along the trail. (Photos courtesy of the author.)

bottlenecks and constantly attacked. Bombs were used to cut the roads or cause landslides. Area denial weapons like CDU-14 "Gravel," CBU-4? WAAPM (wide area anti-personnel mines), or bombs with delay seismic fuzes were then dropped over the site to keep work crews from rapidly repairing the damage.[16] Some sites were bombed so heavily that they resembled craters on the moon. So many bypasses were created to get around all of the bomb craters and destruction that the Trail looked less like a throughway than a plate of spaghetti.[17]

Once again, planners turned to technology for solutions. They noted the earlier use of sensors along the Trail under IGLOO WHITE which had been recommended by the Jason group. They were also encouraged by the use of sensors in locating and destroying North Vietnamese units besieging Khe Sanh in 1968.

They contacted the Defense Communications Planning Group (DCPG) in Washington which had developed IGLOO WHITE. It was under the command of Air Force Lt. Gen. John Lavelle. That organization was working on a concept called the "automated battlefield." General William Westmoreland, the commander of American forces in Vietnam, explained this concept in a speech to the Association of the U.S. Army in October 1969. He told them, "I see battlefields or combat areas that are under 24-hour real or near real-time surveillance of all types. I see battlefields on which we can destroy anything we can locate through instant communications and the almost instantaneous application of highly lethal firepower."[18]

Under this concept, high technology sensors communications, and weapons would replace soldiers on the ground. DCPG had already developed a whole series of electronic sensors. One was basically a microphone which would transmit whatever sounds it heard. Another sensor would

The next month, that number increased sharply to 12,800.[14]

Air planners recognized that there were actually four types of targets to be struck. First, there were the supply trucks. Second, there was the Trail itself, the road beds and, in some cases, waterways over which the trucks traveled. Also included in this category were the equipment and facilities of the work battalions which labored to keep them open. Third, there was the terrain. The Trail snaked through mountain passes and under jungle canopy. Passes could be blocked and foliage could be destroyed with bombs or defoliants. Lastly, there were the anti-aircraft guns and, later, SAMs which were being brought south in increasing numbers to protect the Trail.[15]

Operationally, the Ho Chi Minh Trail complex was divided into a series of sectors searched by FACs during the day and FACs and gunships at night. "Target Boxes" were selected at key road

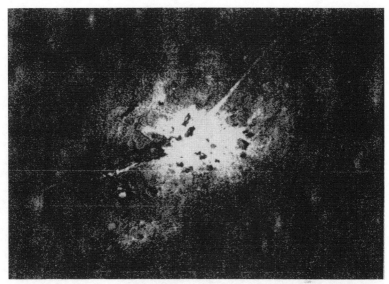

A dust cloud marks the location of what once was a truck on the trail. *(Photo courtesy of the author.)*

ONE AIR FORCE OFFICER CROWED, WE GOT THE HO CHI MINH TRAIL WIRED LIKE A PIN BALL MACHINE

THE GUNSHIPS WERE EQUIPPED WITH SOPHISTICATED SENSORS WHICH COULD SEE THROUGH SOME FOLIAGE AND THEN AIM THE HEAVY CALIBER WEAPONS

pick up the vibrations of people or vehicles moving nearby. Building on IGLOO WHITE, Seventh Air Force implanted thousands more along the Trail. The sensors were then tied by relay aircraft to two huge IBM 360 computers at Nakhon Phanom. There, the data could be analyzed and transformed into targeting information. Controllers would contact the orbiting command and control aircraft and have them respond to activations with air strikes.[19] When fully operational, it was an extensive system. Controllers bragged that the enemy now had nowhere to hide. One Air Force officer crowed, "We got the Ho Chi Minh Trail wired like a pin ball machine."[20]

To provide for around-the-clock and all weather operations, the Air Force introduced several modifications to aircraft. F–4s and RF–4s were refitted with LORAN navigational gear so that the crews could easily use the targeting data passed by the controllers. Seventh Air Force also upgraded several SKYSPOT radar sites to allow the radar controllers to guide fighters on blind strikes. Additionally, they also introduced a vastly upgraded force of eleven B–57Gs with forward-looking radar infrared and low-light-level television and laser ranging devices.

They also improved the fixed-wing gunship force. Since the beginning of interdiction along the Trail, orbiting gunships had been used. Initially, they were old AC–47s firing 7.62mm Gatling guns. These were replaced by AC–119s and eventually by AC–130 Spectre gunships firing two 20mm Gatling guns, two 40mm Bofors cannons, and a 105mm Howitzer. Additionally, the gunships were equipped with sophisticated

sensors which could see through some foliage and then aim the heavy caliber weapons. One device could sense truck engines when they were running. Given their ability to spend hours orbiting over the Trail, they rapidly became some of the most effective weapons against trucks and supplies.[21]

Improvements were also made to the FAC force. The 23rd TASS at Nakhon Phanom was given sophisticated low-light scopes for night use. Additionally, fifteen of the assigned OV–10s were modified to carry LORAN navigational devices and laser guidance emitters boresighted to low-light scopes mounted on the belly of the aircraft and operated by a second crew member in the back seat. The laser and scope combination, called PAVE SPOT, could be used for both target detection and guiding illumination for laser guided bombs.

The 23rd TASS squadron commander, Lt. Col. Lachlan Macleay, first commanded the squadron detachment at Ubon and field tested the system in Cambodia. He built up a team of young, enthusiastic, and creative pilots and navigators to make the system work. They faithfully followed the procedures suggested by the various experts sent over from the States to explain its use. But they soon discovered that the suggested techniques were impractical for combat use. Lt. Col. Macleay gave them free reign to develop any tactics which they felt would make the system most useful. They rapidly discovered that the system had great flexibility and could be used day or night. Its only limitations were the lack of laser guided bombs, bad weather, or the lack of creativ-

(Top) An F-4D loaded with Mk-82 500-lb. bombs at Da Nang.

(Above) The close-up of the same F-4D shows the fuse extenders on the bombs, making them "Daisy Cutters." (Photos courtesy of the author.)

ity by the users. In short order, they had destroyed most targets in northern Cambodia worthy of a laser guided bomb. Thereafter, the PAVE NAILS began flying over the Ho Chi Minh Trail.

During their creative exploration of the system's capabilities, they discovered that the combination of the laser and the LORAN allowed them to plot locations on the ground accurately. The backseater could find a target using the magnification of the scope. He could then "designate" it with a laser beam and the LORAN would provide the coordinates. It was accurate to ten feet. In fact, they discovered that in many cases the system proved that published maps were wrong.[22]

All of this technology was matched to the tonnage and applied to the Trail war. But given the unclear nature of this mission, it was difficult to measure success. Since the target was logistical, the measurement decided upon was the number

of trucks killed. Figures and statistics became "the name of the game." Dry statistical measures of success were institutionalized. As the campaigns evolved, the truck counts rose steadily and were daily reported to the leaders in Saigon and Washington. By COMMANDO HUNT V, in 1971, almost 21,000 trucks were reported as destroyed or damaged.

However, the leaders were deluding themselves. CIA analysts estimated that only 6,000 trucks entered Laos during that period. The discrepancy was based on several factors. First, there was no good way to assess the effectiveness of air strikes. Most bomb damage assessment was done by the aircrews based on strictly visual results. Since large counts were sometimes the basis for awards, reports became unduly optimistic. Second, some vehicles were obviously bombed and reported destroyed numerous times. Third, aircrews considered their weapons to be more effective than they really were. In 1971, Seventh Air Force ran tests to determine the effectiveness of the gunships. Results indicated that kill reports were overstated and that accounting systems and campaign results had to be reevaluated.[23]

There was another factor which should have caused a reevaluation of the results had it been understood at the time. As America stepped up the Trail war with tonnage and technology, the enemy reacted with countermeasures. Most obvious, of course, were the air defenses. The number of guns steadily increased along the Trail. By 1972, they were joined by SA-2 radar guided missiles and, on occasion, even MiGs from North Vietnam.

Second, the North Vietnamese discovered that Americans liked to run on schedules. Therefore, they plotted the time of the day when aircraft were least active over the Trail and began to run their trucks during those times. In effect, the North Vietnamese got inside the American "managerial loop."[24]

Third, they fell back on a timeless expedient—deception. Firepower can be converted into wanton waste if the individual delivering that firepower can be convinced to strike targets which do not exist and bypass legitimate ones. The North Vietnamese discovered how their adversaries determined their targets. They knew that the crews spotted targets visually, while intelligence personnel found them though electronic devices. The North Vietnamese became masters at both forms of deception. Their motto was, "Walk without tracks, cook without smoke, speak without sound."[25]

Visually, they employed numerous stratagems to deceive the FACs and reconnaissance pilots. The troops were advised to act like chameleons and change their skin to match the surrounding environment in which they were operating so that "even if an 'old woman' or a 'blockhead' leans over and looks all day, they will not see a thing."[26]

All villages and truck storage areas were heav-

12

240

ily camouflaged, and were practically invisible from the air. Even cooking smoke was vented—in some cases for miles—so that it would either dissipate or appear far from the real campsite. Conversely, on occasion, the North Vietnamese would start small caches of supplies on fire, and wait for the Americans to see it and respond with air strikes.[27]

They would abandon worn out trucks in the open for the same reason or tow them to river fording sites to draw attention there. The sites would always be obvious. Chances were, though, that the real site was not too far away, but under heavy cover, and protected by AAA.

The North Vietnamese also discovered how the electronic sensors worked, and became adept at finding and destroying them. They learned that the acoustical sensors could be easily muffled. A favorite tactic was to cover known sensors and play tape recordings of moving trucks near other sensors several miles away. When planes responded to the transmitting sites, convoys would slowly move by the muffled sites.

The road teams also figured out the seismic sensors. They discovered that they could be deceived by trucks rolling by slowly at fixed intervals or individuals moving in small groups. They also learned that the sensors became highly unreliable during periods of high wind or rain. That was when they would move.[28]

Perhaps the most effective countermeasure was psychological. The North Vietnamese turned the Ho Chi Minh Trail into a national cause. It was celebrated in poem and song, and its very existence in the face of such heavy and sustained American efforts to cut it was a rallying point for the nation. At its height an estimated 50,000 troops of Group 559 and support personnel worked the Trail. They were told, "Let the road wait for vehicles; never the vehicles for the road."[29]

In fact, the personnel assigned to the Trail, perhaps to better handle the psychological impact of the unremitting aerial attacks, bonded together into a closely knit society. Survivors talked about the terror of the bombing attacks, especially the B–52s. When the bombs would start to fall, they would huddle together in the shelters and sing patriotic songs or tell stories to try to divert attention from the havoc. Some would hurl invectives at the nameless, faceless pilots above.[30]

But even without the air strikes, life was hard along the Trail. Most of the North Vietnamese were not used to jungle living. Many succumbed to diseases, especially malaria, which were endemic to the steamy climate and lush vegetation. Where possible, the troops would plant vegetable gardens. It broke the tedium of the hard work, and gave the troops and travelers a valuable and much needed source of vitamins.

There were very few amenities. Some of the more enterprising would collect the discarded tubes from the bomblets or flare parachutes dropped by the aircraft and turn them into decorations or souvenirs. To support the road builders, drivers, and fighters, all types of artisans and specialists were drafted and sent to join them. Their task was to create an atmosphere of "normal" life for those who were working so hard. They would travel through the camps and way stations, putting on shows or announcing the latest news.

Sharing the common threat, and pursuing the common goal, the personnel of the Trail became the community of Trung Son. Their heroes were the truck drivers, whom they admired for their daring and courage. The drivers were called the "pilots of the earth." Unknown thousands died in their trucks. In many cases, the trucks were blown up or pushed off cliffs to prevent road blocks. In these instances, the bodies could not be recovered, and those vehicles became their coffins. In every unit, one individual was assigned the task of reporting the names, birth dates, and villages of those killed. If the body was recovered, the officer would then write the information on a piece of paper and insert it in a small bottle. The bottle would then be put in the mouth of the victim, and the body would be placed in a plastic bag and left along the road for a later pick-up. To honor the dead, the officer would write the name and data neatly with a "very good quality Chinese pen" which he would carry in his pocket.[31]

THE NORTH VIETNAMESE TURNED THE HO CHI MINH TRAIL INTO A NATIONAL CAUSE

When the seismic sensors operated correctly, air strikes left results like these. (Photo courtesy of the author.)

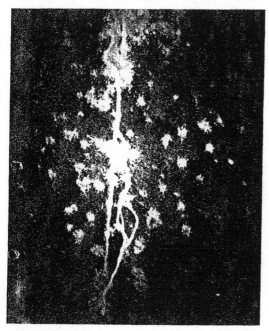

241

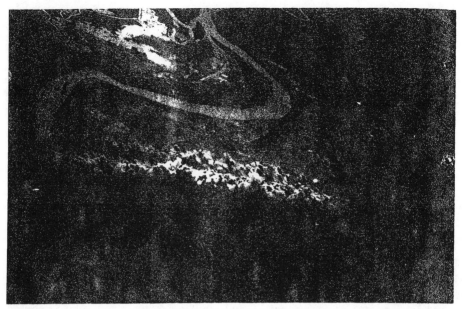

Air strikes like this made the Ho Chi Minh Trail a dangerous place to travel. (Photo courtesy of the author.)

One North Vietnamese writer explained this community and the power of it all.

... there were people from the North to the South, people of the plains and mountains, young and graying men, people of all occupations, the most academic ones included: it was the image of the struggling nation in its entirety.[32]

THE AC–130S NEEDED THE SHADOW OF NIGHT FOR PROTECTION. PERHAPS IT MADE MORE SENSE TO MOVE DURING THE DAY

One incident highlights this entire phenomenon. As COMMANDO HUNT continued, the AC–130s were taking an increasing toll against Trail traffic. They had become the most effective weapon against the trucks and had to be countered. The air defense units would engage them. But they were always escorted by strike aircraft armed to attack and destroy the guns and their crews. Other measures were needed and Colonel Le Xi of Group 559 was sent to investigate.[33]

He met with various sector leaders, who told him of the damage the AC–130s were doing. Then he met with numerous drivers and asked for their thoughts. One stated that he hated the lumbering gunships and their massive guns, which he called the "thug." Another driver observed:

When we stayed quiet, it [the gunship] merely circled overhead. But as soon as we started the engine, it began firing. If we turned off the engine, it would fire a few more rounds and leave. But if we restarted the motor, it would come back at once. The dangerous thing is that it needs neither flares nor guidance by a recon plane.[34]

Comparing this information with technical documents they had on the AC–130, Le Xi concurred that the gunship was a formidable adversary. He asked the drivers if they thought that the "thug" had any weakness. One driver responded that he did not think that the gunship was as good in the daytime. He related a story of how he was driving during the day and observed an AC–130 pass overhead. It did not attack him. Several others joined in with similar vignettes. The colonel pondered, "Move during the day?" It was accepted that trucks had to move primarily at night to avoid the FACs, reconnaissance, and strike aircraft during the day. That threat remained. But the AC–130s with their sophisticated sensors needed the shadow of night for protection. Perhaps it made more sense to move during the day.

Still, the trucks could not move in the open because observation planes, with their fighter-bombers, would spot them. Could more heavily camouflaged roads be cut through the jungle to cover them? Le Xi addressed that question to the engineers. They answered affirmatively and the work teams began. They did not use explosives, so as to avoid detection. Instead, all work was done manually. It was also less disruptive to the jungle foliage. Where the foliage was thin, they would string ropes and hang fast growing vines or leafy creepers.

River fording points were a problem. The real crossings were also heavily camouflaged. Nearby decoys were prepared and were seeded with derelict trucks, which were easily seen. At the

14

actual crossing, observers watched constantly for aircraft. All traffic stopped when they were overhead. When crossing, they moved in groups of three trucks at a time.

The covered roads were eventually extended all the way from the Mu Gia Pass, in central Laos, down to the central highlands of South Vietnam. In some areas, there was not enough vegetation to cover the Trail. There, the drivers coordinated their driving so that they were moving during the periods of lowest aircraft activity. It was an amazing, creative process, harnessing the talents of thousands of ordinary people dedicated to a cause.[35] One nation, struggling in its entirety. That was their view of the war and their objective. Most of the young American airmen were not aware of any of this activity and commitment and did not take the time to think it through. They had no idea of what a continuous, deadly struggle life was down there on the Trail. To the fliers it was war by the numbers and the numbers were good—deceptively so. But something larger than numbers did not tally. Earl Tilford, in his book, *Setup: What the Air Force Did in Vietnam and Why*, explained it:

Undoubtedly, gunships destroyed a large number of trucks while B-52s and fighter-bombers wreaked havoc on the roads and jungles. Whatever tactical advantages were gained, however, paled beside the impact resulting from the enforcement of the managerial ethos that took over during Commando Hunt. In what came to resemble "production line warfare," success was assessed primarily on dubious statistics, the compilation of which became an end unto itself. Statistics, however, proved no substitute for strategy, and for all the perceived success in that numbers game, the Air Force succeeded only in fooling itself into believing Commando Hunt was working.[36]

The aircrews were not fooled. Even though they could not understand what life was like below, they could sense that trucks were getting through. One Air Force pilot, a veteran of many Trail missions later wrote:

... the areas where the targets were relatively hardest to find, with adjustment for the nature of the terrain,... and where the defensive reaction was least predictable and most effective, tended to be precisely those areas most important to the flow of materiel... whoever was in charge had his shit together.[37]

In fact, anyone who spent any time at all on the COMMANDO HUNT campaigns came away with a solid respect for the troops below.

In contrast, comparing our own efforts with those of the enemy, one FAC said, "The effectiveness of our interdiction efforts along the Trail was 'piss poor."[38] And U.S. intelligence knew that there were whole Trail segments about which we knew nothing.[39]

Air power was not the proper weapon with which to cut the Trail—not alone at least. Historically, interdiction was most effective when the enemy was forced to move and increase his logistical needs. We never coordinated our ground and air offensives. The enemy could adjust their operational tempo accordingly, to live on what they could get through the rain of bombs.[40] Moreover, time was on their side.

Used singly, American air power was being wasted; the aircrews could feel it. One young pilot defined the dilemma of the Ho Chi Minh Trail perfectly. Talking about the bombing of the Trail, he said, "A 500 pound bomb makes a hole five feet deep and ten feet across. With fifty coolies filling the hole and packing it with a battering ram, the road can be open again the next day."[41] That was it—the American statistical view matched by the raw human power of the Trung Son community. Those words were spoken in 1964. Eight years later, we were still trying to do the same thing.

General Creighton Abrams, Westmoreland's successor in Vietnam, watched these events with dismay. He also knew the importance of the Trail. In 1970, he had moved decisively to cut off NVA infiltration all along the coast. Additionally, he had sent U.S. and South Vietnamese ground forces into Cambodia to clean out their materiel stockpiles and cut their infiltration routes through that country. He realized that the Trail was the enemy's last conduit, but had come to the conclusion that air power alone would not stop the flow down the Trail. He proposed—and American and Vietnamese political leaders accepted—a bold plan to launch a strong conventional ground force of South Vietnamese armor and infantry to block the Trail and destroy NVA supplies. It would attack west into Laos along the old Route 9 from Khe Sanh to cut the Trail as far as Tchepone. At the same time, it would destroy vast stockpiles which the NVA had been building next to the South Vietnamese border.[42] The operation would be called Lam Son 719.

A force of 15,000 troops entered Laos in early February 1971. Initially, they were met by soldiers from the engineer and anti-aircraft battalions who did not put up much of a fight. ARVN and Marine task forces fanned out and swept through several base areas and destroyed large quantities of trucks and supplies. Then the South Vietnamese forces were counterattacked by five regular divisions of NVA troops with heavy tanks and artillery. The fighting was some of the heaviest of the war.

U.S. and VNAF (South Vietnamese Air Force) air power responded to the needs of the troops on the ground. But the NVA covered their forces with anti-aircraft guns and, in effect, achieved a level of air deniability against the attacking aircraft. The ARVN began to retreat. The retreat nearly became a rout, as the South Vietnamese forces pulled back into their homeland.

Lam Son 719 was at best a partial success. Great quantities of supplies had been destroyed

AIR POWER WAS NOT THE PROPER WEAPON WITH WHICH TO CUT THE TRAIL—NOT ALONE AT LEAST. AMERICAN AIR POWER WAS BEING WASTED

243

and some NVA units had been mauled. But the Trail was not cut for any length of time. Most importantly though, the North Vietnamese had shown that they would fight to hold southern Laos—the key ground of Laos and location of the Ho Chi Minh Trail.

After the battle everyone claimed victory. President Thieu of South Vietnam claimed that Lam Son 719 was "the biggest victory ever." President Nixon told the nation, "Tonight I can report Vietnamization has succeeded." At the same time, Hanoi said that the battle was "the heaviest defeat ever for Nixon and Company."[43]

Each side saw what it wanted to see. President Nixon announced that because of the ARVN's battle success, American withdrawals would be accelerated. Curiously, the battle helped both sides: North Vietnam to consolidate its hold on the Ho Chi Minh Trail and the United States to withdraw. And it bought the South Vietnamese some time because those NVA units which had attacked the ARVN forces in Laos did not follow them back into South Vietnam. They needed time to reconstitute their decimated battalions and replenish their supplies. But having uncontested control of the Trail would make it possible for them to regroup, resupply, and prepare for the battles in 1972—battles which their leaders were planning at that moment, in part because they saw that Vietnamization might just work.

The additional anti-aircraft guns brought in to cover the NVA counterattack stayed in place and supplemented the already frightening inventory of guns. The aircrews noticed it immediately. Throughout the dry season, the situation worsened consistently. By January 1972, the Trail was the hottest that it had ever been; there were guns everywhere. Worse, SA-2 SAM sites had been introduced into Laos and had downed an AC-130 south of Tchepone on March 28.[44]

Additionally, the SAM sites protected the key passes at Mu Gia and Ban Karai. Because of this, the B-52s could not be used to keep them closed. The task fell to the tactical aircraft. But the latter could not continuously devastate the roads like the bombers, and the supplies continued to flow.

The massed guns along the Trail vastly decreased the effectiveness of the FACs and gunships. By the spring of 1972, the gunships were no longer sent into the high threat areas and the FACs were not even allowed to perform visual reconnaissance along some main routes. The NVA had successfully challenged us for air superiority over major and critical sections of the Trail.[45]

The air defenses and deception were protecting the large troop and armor formations heading south. They were the wherewithal for the upcoming invasion. COMMANDO HUNT had failed and the air effort, while looking good statistically, had been wasted. The aircrews sensed it, the generals at Seventh Air Force knew it. We had lost the battle of the Ho Chi Minh Trail.[46] It was a loss of huge proportions because, given the strategic

realities of the theater, the Ho Chi Minh Trail was North Vietnam's operational "center of gravity." That was why they had fought so tenaciously to protect it. It was key to their strategy for defeating the South with modern, conventional forces, and they made it impervious to American and South Vietnamese air power.[47] South Vietnamese soldiers and marines from Quang Tri to An Loc would pay for that failure under the merciless pounding of the North Vietnamese artillery, rockets, and tanks. Indeed, the failure of the campaign was immediately obvious when enemy tanks appeared on all three fronts and within sixty miles of Saigon. These "prime" targets had not been conclusively detected or effectively interdicted as they moved south through the Trail complex.[48]

Perhaps in mute testimony, by the end of 1972, the IGLOO WHITE system was all but shut down. It had not been "cost effective." Over $3 billion had been spent on the program and the trucks were still rolling.[49]

Throughout 1972, as American air forces returned to the skies of North Vietnam, NVA engineers and battalions along the Trail continued to improve it and develop it into an all-weather road. Indeed, after the cease-fire and American withdrawal in 1973, they moved massive amounts of vehicles and supplies south to begin replacing their losses from the battles past. And they expanded the road network throughout Southeast Asia.

All critical areas of the Trail were heavily camouflaged and protected by massed guns and SAMs. The South Vietnamese Air Force could not effectively penetrate the air defenses to attack their supply and troop columns. Of the 2,000 plus aircraft the VNAF was left with, almost half were helicopters. Only 391 were jet-propelled fighter or attack aircraft. These were all older A-37s or F-5s. They had no aircraft with electronic warfare capability, which could neutralize the enemy's air defenses. U.S. leaders knew that South Vietnam would need some form of interdiction aircraft. They were left with only a small number of AC-119s—the same planes which had been driven away from the Trail by the crack gunners in 1972.[50]

Additionally, the NVA were being heavily supplied with the heat-seeking SA-7s. Yet the U.S did not supply the VNAF with equipment which would counter these deadly missiles. Consequently, South Vietnam could not effectively block, threaten, or even observe major portions the Ho Chi Minh Trail.[51]

This enabled North Vietnam to move large combat formations rapidly over large distances with relative impunity. Fifteen years of effort and battle to build and protect the Trail had paid off It was the key link in the North's war effort. I gave the NVA critical, unhindered mobility throughout Southeast Asia, and most important tantly, it was unassailable by the South Vietnamese.

BY JANUARY 1972, THE TRAIL WAS THE HOTTEST THAT IT HAD EVER BEEN; THERE WERE GUNS EVERYWHERE

THE AIRCREWS SENSED IT, THE GENERALS AT SEVENTH AIR FORCE KNEW IT. WE HAD LOST THE BATTLE OF THE HO CHI MINH TRAIL

16

244

THE HO CHI MINH TRAIL PROVIDED US WITH A STRATEGIC VANTAGE GROUND FROM WHICH TO FIGHT AND DEFEAT THE ENEMY

As 1974 ended, North Vietnam would move the majority of its reequipped army through this road net to destroy the southern army and conquer South Vietnam. In 1976, to celebrate the first anniversary of their great victory, the leaders of North Vietnam rewarded Group 559 by presenting it with the title of "Hero of the People," for brilliantly fulfilling its mission. The citation stated:

This network of strategic roads extended from the starting base in the North to all southern battle-fronts.... Combined with local roads, this network of strategic roads ensured steady communications and liaison with all fronts.... This is one of our Party's outstanding political and military successes.... During the war, the Trung Son Road [Ho Chi Minh Trail] provided us with a strategic vantage ground from which to fight and defeat the enemy.... The Trung Son Road joins North and South and unites the country.[52]

And unification of the two nations under the control of North Vietnam was the objective!

Used alone, air power was unable to cut the Ho Chi Minh Trail. First the U.S. and then the South Vietnamese air forces could not overcome the air defenses and deception efforts of the enemy to effectively staunch the flow of men and materiel to the South. That strategic network of roads, so long in building, and paid for in blood, paved the way for the North's defeat of South Vietnam. It was Ho Chi Minh's "Road to Victory." ∎

NOTES

1. Author's personal flight log and recollections.
2. Earl H. Tilford, *Setup: What the Air Force Did in Vietnam and Why* (Maxwell Air Force Base, Ala.: Air University Press, 1991), p. 215.
3. Larry Rottmann, *Voices from the Ho Chi Minh Trail* (Desert Hot Springs, Calif.: Event Horizon Press, 1993), p. 125.
4. "Opening the Trail," *Vietnam Courier*, Number 5, 1984, p. 9.
5. *Ibid.*, p. 14. Also, Douglas Pike "Road to Victory: The Ho Chi Minh Trail," *War in Peace*, Vol. 5, No. 60 (1983-84), p. 1196.
6. Norman B. Hannah, *The Key to Failure, Laos and the Vietnam War* (New York: Madison Books, 1987), p. xiii.
7. Pike, p. 1197.
8. Col. Harry G. Summers, Jr., *On Strategy: The Vietnam War in Context* (Carlisle Barracks, Pa.: Strategic Studies Institute, U.S. Army War College, 1981), p. 73.
9. Tilford, p. 133.
10. John F. Guilmartin, "Bombing the Ho Chi Minh Trail: A Preliminary Analysis of the Effects of Air Interdiction," *Air Power History*, Vol. 38, No. 4 (Winter 1991), p. 4.
11. *New York Times*, November 13, 1971, p. 1.
12. Tilford, p. 173.
13. *Ibid.*, p. 167.
14. *Ibid.*, p. 173.
15. *Ibid.*, p. 174.
16. *Ibid.*, p. 181.
17. Pike, p. 1197.
18. Paul Dickson and John Rothchild, "The Electronic Battlefield: Wiring Down the War," *The Washington Monthly*, May 1971.
19. *Ibid.*, p. 177.
20. "The Air Force's Secret Electronic War," *Indochina Chronicle*, October 15, 1971, pp. 2-6.
21. Tilford, p. 179.
22. Interview, author with Col. Lachlan Macleay, USAF (Ret.), February 1, 1993.
23. Tilford, p. 184.
24. *Ibid.*, p. 219.
25. "Recalling Rain of Death on the Ho Chi Minh Trail," *International Herald Tribune*, April 28-29, 1990.
26. "Value of Camouflage," *Quan Doi Nhan Dan*, Hanoi, August 21, 1971, p. 3.
27. Interview, author with Lt. Col. Jack Butcher, USAF (Ret.), March 21, 1993. In 1971, 1st Lt. Butcher

was shot down in an OV-10 over the Ho Chi Minh Trail. He was captured, but escaped for several days and evaded along the Trail before being recaptured and taken to Hanoi.
28. "The Tropical Tree," *Quan Doi Nhan Dan*, Hanoi, August 18, 1972.
29. Rottmann, p. 139.
30. "Recalling Rain of Death on the Ho Chi Minh Trail," *International Herald Tribune*, April 28-29, 1990.
31. *Ibid.*
32. *The Ho Chi Minh Trail* (Hanoi: Foreign Languages Publishing House, 1985), p. 19.
33. "Supply Trucks Moving Down the Trail in Daylight," *Vietnam Courier*, No. 5, 1984, pp. 15-18. Indochina Archive.
34. *Ibid.*
35. *Ibid.*
36. Tilford, p. 185.
37. Guilmartin, p. 12.
38. Interview, author with Mr. Gary Ferentchak, April 24, 1993. In 1972, Capt Ferentchak was a FAC assigned to the 23rd TASS.
39. Eduard Mark, *Aerial Interdiction: Air Power and the Land Battle in Three American Wars* (Washington, D.C.: Center for Air Force History, 1994), p. 332.
40. Guilmartin. pp. 6, 14.
41. "Laotians to Let U.S. Planes Bomb Ho Chi Minh Trail," *New York Times*, December 21, 1964, p. 1.
42. Keith W. Nolan, *Into Laos, The Story of Dewey Canyon/Lam Son 719 Vietnam 1971* (New York: Dell Publishing, 1986), p. 30.
43. Tilford, p. 204.
44. David K. Mann, "The 1972 invasion of Military Region I: Fall of Quang Tri and Defense of Hue," Project CHECO Report, March 15, 1973, p. 11.
45. Mark, pp. 336, 346.
46. Tilford, p. 220.
47. *Ibid.*, pp. 218, 220. Also, *The Ho Chi Minh Trail*.
48. Mark, p. 368.
49. "Resounding Success or Costly Failure?" *Philadelphia Inquirer*, December 14, 1972.
50. Jack S. Ballard, *Development and Employment of Fixed-Wing Gunships 1962-1972*, (Washington, D.C.: Office of Air Force History, 1982), pp. 253, 258.
51. Maj. George R. Dunham and Col. David A. Quinlan, *U.S. Marines in Vietnam: The Bitter End 1973-1975* (Washington, D.C.: History and Museums Division, HQ USMC, 1990), pp. 13, 14.
52. *The Ho Chi Minh Trail*.

The CIA and the "Secret War" in Laos: The Battle for Skyline Ridge, 1971–1972

☆

William M. Leary

BETWEEN December 1971 and May 1972, one of the great battles of the Vietnam War took place in northern Laos when over twenty battalions of the North Vietnamese army assaulted positions held by some 10,000 Lao, Thai, and Hmong defenders. Yet few people have heard of the battle for Skyline Ridge. Press coverage of the engagement was slight, and public interest—at least in the United States—was minimal. Historians of the Vietnam War also have ignored this major battle, perhaps because it had limited impact on the outcome of the war. Still, the battle for Skyline Ridge deserves to be remembered. The culmination of efforts by the U.S. Central Intelligence Agency to direct a major and lengthy war in Asia, it was an impressive—if temporary—victory for the anti-Communist forces in Laos.

I

By 1971 the no-longer-secret war in Laos had been going on for more than a decade.[1] Prior to the Geneva Agreements of July 1962 on the neutrality of Laos, United States military personnel had taken the leading role in training and advising indigenous forces. Indeed, under the terms of the Geneva Agreements, which called for the removal of all foreign military personnel from Laos, the United States withdrew 666 individuals.[2] The Central Intelligence Agency, by contrast, had assigned only

---

1. The best general accounts of the war are Charles A. Stevenson, *The End of Nowhere: American Policy toward Laos since 1954* (Boston, 1972), and Arthur J. Dommen, *Conflict in Laos: The Politics of Neutralization*, rev. ed. (New York, 1971).

2. North Vietnam, in contrast, formally withdrew only forty of its estimated six thousand troops in Laos at the time of the cease-fire. Statement of Ambassador G. McMurtrie Godley, 22 July 1971, in U.S. Senate, Committee on Armed Services,

The Journal of Military History 59 (July 1995): 505–18 © Society for Military History

★ **505**

nine paramilitary specialists, assisted by 99 Thai Special Forces–type members of the Police Aerial Reinforcement Unit (PARU), to train and support Hmong tribal forces in the northern part of Laos, which constituted the Agency's main program in the country.[3]

When fighting broke out again in Laos in 1963 and 1964, officials in Washington considered reintroducing a sizable number of U.S. military personnel into the country to train and advise the Royal Lao Army. Leonard Unger, the American ambassador in Vientiane, opposed the idea. "As will be recalled," he cabled the State Department in June 1964, "experience in '61–62 with MAAG [Military Assistance and Advisory Group] was not a happy one. MAAG and White Star [Special Forces] teams did a highly commendable job under difficult circumstances, but their experience demonstrated that it is almost impossible to put any real spine into FAR [Forces Armée Royale or Royal Lao Army]."[4]

Acting upon Unger's recommendation, Washington decided to maintain the thin fiction of the Geneva Agreements—which the Communist Pathet Lao and their North Vietnamese backers had ignored but never formally repudiated. The ineffective Royal Lao Army would be given a minimum of support. At the same time, the Central Intelligence Agency was assigned responsibility to train, advise, and support Hmong forces in northern Laos, and to recruit, train, advise, and support volunteer Lao troops in the southern part of the country. The CIA presence in Laos was to remain small. As Unger's successor, William L. Sullivan, explained, Unger was a "most reluctant militarist and took care in establishing the paramilitary operation to be sure it was designed to be reversible. Consequently, only a small portion of it was actually present in Laos, and all its supporting elements were housed in Thailand, under a secret agreement with the Thai."[5]

Although critics of U.S. policy later would portray the CIA as responsible for the "secret" war in Laos, they failed to take into account the circumstances surrounding the employment of the intelligence agency. Given the nature of the Geneva Agreements, Under Secretary of State for Political Affairs U. Alexis Johnson once explained to a congressional

Hearings on Fiscal Year 1972 Authorization for Military Procurement, 92d Congress, 1st Session (Washington, 1971), 4270. See also Norman B. Hannah, The Key to Failure: Laos and the Vietnam War (Lanham, Md., 1987), 59.

3. Edward G. Lansdale to Maxwell D. Taylor, "Resources for Unconventional Warfare, S.E. Asia," n.d. [July 1961], The Pentagon Papers (New York Times ed., New York, 1971), 130–38.

4. Unger to the Secretary of State, 15 June 1964, Declassified Documents Reference System (DDRS), 1989: 2100. The U.S. military assistance program is detailed in Timothy N. Castle, At War in the Shadow of Vietnam: U.S. Military Aid to the Royal Lao Government, 1955–1975 (New York, 1993).

5. William L. Sullivan, Obbligato (New York, 1984), 210.

committee, the CIA "is really the only other instrumentality that we have."[6] G. McMurtrie Godley, U.S. ambassador to Laos, 1969–73, agreed. "These operations that the CIA are conducting in Laos," he testified in 1971, "were not initiated by them." The task, he emphasized, had been assigned by the President.[7]

Between 1964 and 1967, the CIA-supported Hmong army in northern Laos, the main area of conflict, fought a highly successful guerrilla war against a mixed force of Pathet Lao and North Vietnamese troops. The high point of this phase of the war came in the summer of 1967. Royal Lao Army and Hmong units had blunted the enemy's dry season offensive of winter-spring 1966–67, causing local CIA officials to issue an optimistic appraisal of the situation in Laos. Hmong forces, a CIA Intelligence Information Cable argued, had gained the upper hand in the war: "They now have the option of attempting a permanent change in the tactical balance of power in North Laos."[8]

Unfortunately, the North Vietnamese recognized the danger. Beginning in January 1968, Hanoi introduced major new forces into Laos and relegated the Pathet Lao to a support role for the remainder of the war. By March, the CIA estimated that there were 35,000 North Vietnamese regular troops in Laos—and the number would continue to grow.[9]

The fighting in Laos took on a more conventional nature, characterized by engagements between large units. The North Vietnamese, tied to unpaved road networks for their supplies, took the offensive during the dry season, which usually lasted from early winter to early spring. The U.S.-backed forces in Laos responded during the summer months of the rainy season, exploiting the mobility provided by the transports and helicopters of Air America, the CIA-owned airline.

The main strategic prize in northern Laos was the Plaine des Jarres (PDJ), a circular plateau measuring five hundred square miles in area and with an average elevation of thirty-five hundred feet. The PDJ's attractive rolling grasslands and tree-studded hills saw some of the most intense fighting of the war, with control of the area passing from one side to other, depending upon the season.

6. Johnson testimony on 22 July 1971, U.S. Senate, Committee on Armed Services, *Hearings on S. 939 (H.R. 8687)*, 92d Congress, 1st session (Washington, 1971), 4293.

7. Godley testimony, 22 July 1971, ibid., 4278.

8. Central Intelligence Agency, Intelligence Information Cable IN 19395, 29 July 1967, DDRS, 1992: 3089. For a passionate discussion of the Hmong role in the war, see Jane Hamilton-Merritt, *Tragic Mountains: The Hmong, the Americans, and the Secret Wars for Laos, 1942–1992* (Bloomington, 1993).

9. Central Intelligence Agency, Special National Intelligence Estimate 58-68, 21 March 1968, DDRS, 1989: 1865.

Beyond the PDJ to the south lay a series of high mountain ridges that eventually gave way to the lowlands of the Mekong River valley and the administrative capital of Vientiane. The Hmong controlled these mountains. Their charismatic leader, Vang Pao, made his headquarters in the valley of Long Tieng (also known as Lima Site 20-Alternate), some twenty miles southwest of the southern edge of the PDJ. Skyline Ridge, just to the north of Long Tieng, commanded the mountain valley and led to the major refugee center of Sam Thong, five miles of narrow, twisting road to the northwest.

In January 1970, the North Vietnamese army launched a strong attack across to the PDJ, aimed at Hmong defenders who had been weakened by losses suffered during the past two years of heavy fighting. Ambassador Godley acted upon pessimistic appraisals of the Hmong ability to withstand the enemy assault and on 23 January asked Washington to authorize the use of B-52s against North Vietnamese army troop concentrations. His request caused considerable soul-searching in the highest echelons of the Nixon administration. No one wanted to disturb the fragile equilibrium in Laos. "It would not make any sense to expand the conflict in Laos," national security adviser Henry Kissinger observed, "except for the minimum required for our own protection, while we were busy withdrawing troops from South Vietnam." Nonetheless, the situation was deemed so grave that President Richard M. Nixon approved Godley's request. On 17 February shortly after receiving a formal request from the Royal Lao government, Operation Good Look began with the first B-52 strikes on the PDJ. Over the next three years, 2,518 B-52 sorties would drop 58,374 tons of bombs in support of U.S-backed forces in northern Laos.[10]

The B-52s may have slowed the enemy offensive, but they failed to stop it. By 21 February the North Vietnamese army had overrun the entire PDJ and threatened Hmong positions at Sam Thong and Long Tieng. Edgar M. "Pop" Buell, senior official of the U.S. Agency for International Development in northern Laos, told the press that the Hmong might be making their last stand. Vang Pao's forces had lost more men in the last six months than during any comparable period during the past ten years. "It's all been running and dying," he said, "just running and dying."[11]

The CIA agreed with Buell. The Hmong have fought well, an intelligence estimate observed, but "they are battle weary and their losses over

10. Henry Kissinger, *White House Years* (Boston, 1979), 448–57; Department of Defense, "Report on Selected Air and Ground Operations in Cambodia and Laos," 10 September 1973.

11. Hugh D. S. Greenway, "The Pendulum of War Swings Wider in Laos," *Life* 68 (April 1970): 32–36.

the past year or so have exceeded their capability to replace them." Obviously, air power was not enough. If nothing was done to replenish the dwindling manpower resources, the situation in Laos would continue to deteriorate.[12]

The prospect for fresh troops grew brighter when Thailand offered to send volunteers to fight in Laos during the current crisis if requested by the Royal Lao government. The State Department, Kissinger reported, "strenuously resisted" the proposal, while other government agencies were unenthusiastic. President Nixon, however, gave his approval. On 17 March as the North Vietnamese army occupied Sam Thong, 300 Thai troops arrived at Long Tieng.[13]

The first battle for Skyline Ridge began on 20 March 1970, when enemy troops occupied positions on the high ground overlooking Long Tieng. Thanks to the timely reinforcements, plus the employment of tactical air power, the enemy assault fell short of its objective. On 26 March the North Vietnamese relinquished their forward positions and began to retreat toward the PDJ.[14]

During the wet season of 1970, the Hmong went over to the offensive, as usual, but this time their gains were limited and their losses were heavy. Lao authorities, recognizing the declining strength of the Hmong and the poor quality of their own forces, in June asked the Thai government to supply regular troops on a more permanent basis to fend off the North Vietnamese. While the Thais were anxious to stop the North Vietnamese short of the Mekong River, they were reluctant to send large numbers of regular army units into Laos and thereby take a more prominent role in the war. Instead, officials in Bangkok agreed to recruit "volunteer" battalions which would be led by regular army officers and NCOs. The cost of the units would be underwritten by the U.S. government.[15]

The enemy again took the initiative with the appearance of drier weather. The North Vietnamese army offensive during the winter of 1970–71 was even stronger than the previous year's attack. Supported by new roads through Sam Neua and Xieng Khouang provinces, the North Vietnamese committed some 8,500 troops against Hmong defenses at

12. Central Intelligence Agency, Office of National Estimates, "Stocktaking in Indochina," 17 April 1970, DDRS, 1977: 270C. The Hmong continued to suffer severe casualties. In 1971 losses totaled 2,259 killed and 5,775 wounded. See Arnold R. Isaacs, *Without Honor: Defeat in Vietnam and Cambodia* (Baltimore, 1983), 169.

13. Kissinger, *White House Years,* 448–57; *Washington Evening Star,* 18 March 1970.

14. Harry D. Blout, "Air Operations in Northern Laos, 1 April–1 November 1970," U.S. Air Force CHECO Report, 15 January 1971, U.S. Air Force Historical Research Center (USAFHRC), Maxwell AFB, Ala.

15. Theodore Shackley, *The Third Option* (New York, 1981), 122–24.

Long Tieng. The situation became critical in mid-February 1971 as 122-mm rockets and mortar rounds began to fall into the Long Tieng valley.[16]

The U.S. Air Force, as it had in the past, made a maximum effort to stop the North Vietnamese. Due to declining resources in Southeast Asia, however, sorties averaged only sixty per day, less than half the number of the previous year. On 14 February one of these sorties produced unfortunate results when an F-4D dropped two CBU-24 cluster bombs eight hundred meters short of its target. The "friendly fire" killed one Hmong, wounded seven others, and destroyed most of the CIA compound at Long Tieng.[17]

The enemy siege continued for another two months. In mid-April, as the monsoon rains began to fall, the tide of battle changed. Reinforced by several Thai battalions and CIA-supported irregular troops from other sections of the country, Vang Pao's forces launched a counterattack that cleared Skyline Ridge by the end of the month. It had been a close call for the defenders of Long Tieng. And they knew that the future likely would bring even worse.[18]

II

On the eve of the last and greatest battle for Skyline Ridge, 1971–72, the CIA's presence had grown far beyond Ambassador Unger's minimalist objectives due to the expanding nature of the war, but it still remained small, especially inside Laos. According to one knowledgeable CIA official, the total number of people at Udorn in Thailand and inside Laos—"including all support personnel, the contract wives, and some military detailee technicians"—never exceeded 225. This included some 50 case officers.[19]

At the top of the command structure for the conduct of the war stood Ambassador Godley. By presidential directive, the ambassador was responsible for "overall direction, coordination and supervision" of all

16. Harry D. Blout and Melvin F. Porter, "Air Operations in Northern Laos, 1 November 70–1 April 71," U.S. Air Force CHECO Report, 3 May 1971, USAFHRC.

17. Frank J. Adamcik, "Short Rounds," U.S. Air Force CHECO Report, 15 July 1972, USAFHRC.

18. William W. Lofgren and Richard R. Sexton, "Air War in Northern Laos, 1 April–30 November 1971," U.S. Air Force Project CHECO Report, 22 June 1973, USAFHRC.

19. Information from a retired intelligence officer who was in a position to have an accurate count of CIA personnel in Thailand and Laos. ("Contract wives" refers to the practice of hiring the wives of CIA personnel to perform clerical and other duties.) William Colby, *Lost Victory* (Chicago, 1989), 198, states: "The total number of CIA personnel who supported this effort was between 300 and 400." This number seems too high.

military operations in Laos. Godley, by all accounts, brought a great deal of interest and enthusiasm to the job. He presided over daily "operations meetings" at the embassy, lasting from 9 A.M. to 10:30 A.M. (or later), at which he received detailed briefings from military and intelligence personnel on developments in the war over the preceding twenty-four hours.[20]

Godley delegated responsibility for the tactical conduct of the war to his CIA station chief, B. Hugh Tovar. An experienced and respected intelligence officer who had served with the Office of Strategic Services during World War II and had been a member of a small OSS team that had operated in Laos at the end of the war, Tovar preferred to exert a general supervision over military affairs and allow his subordinates to handle the operational details.[21]

In conformity with Ambassador Unger's original organizational scheme, the primary CIA headquarters for the conduct of the war—in effect Tovar's "executive agent"—was not in Laos but in Thailand.[22] Located in a two-story block building adjacent to an aircraft parking ramp at Udorn Royal Thai Air Force Base, the 4802d Joint Liaison Detachment was the CIA's command center for military operations in Laos. In charge of the 4802d was Lloyd "Pat" Landry, a paramilitary specialist who had been involved in Laotian affairs for more than a decade. "As a boss," one junior officer recalled, "he had a reputation of being blunt and having the capability to make hard decisions and sticking to them."[23]

Landry's chief of operations was George C. Morton, a retired Green Beret colonel who earlier had "laid the foundations of the Special Forces effort in Vietnam."[24] Other CIA officers oversaw air operations, photo-

---

20. A profile of Godley appeared in the *New York Times,* 12 July 1973. See also the informative staff report of a visit to Laos by James G. Lowenstein and Richard M. Moose: U.S. Senate, Subcommittee on U.S. Security Agreements and Commitments Abroad of the Committee on Foreign Relations, *Laos: April 1971,* 92d Congress, 1st Session (Washington, 1971), 2.

21. Interview with B. Hugh Tovar, 13 March 1992; Arthur J. Dommen and George W. Dalley, "The OSS in Laos: The 1945 Raven Mission," *Journal of Southeast Asian Studies* 22 (September 1991): 327–46.

22. As noted by Senate staffers Lowenstein and Moose, following a visit to Southeast Asia in January 1972, Udorn Royal Thai Air Force Base was "the most important operational military nerve center in Thailand." U.S. Senate, Subcommittee on U.S. Security Agreements and Commitments Abroad of the Committee on Foreign Relations, *Thailand, Laos, and Cambodia: January 1972,* 92d Congress, 2d Session (Washington, 1972), 12. My portrait of CIA activities is drawn from interviews and correspondence with several retired intelligence officers.

23. James E. Parker, Jr., to the author, December 1992.

24. Shelby L. Stanton, *Green Berets at War: U.S. Army Special Forces in Southeast Asia, 1956–1975* (Novato, Calif., 1985), 48, 52–53, 62.

graphic and communications intelligence, and order-of-battle assessments, and coordinated military operations and requirements with 7/13 Air Force headquarters, also located at Udorn.[25] Finally, Landry had excellent rapport with General Vitoon Yasawatdi ("Dhep"), commander of "Headquarters 333," the Thai organization in charge of their forces in Laos.[26]

Lines of authority ran from Udorn to CIA regional headquarters in Laos at Pakse, Savannakhet, Long Tieng, Luang Prabang, and Nam Lieu. The most important of the five subunits was Long Tieng, the major logistical and operational base in Military Region II, and headquarters of Major General Vang Pao, Hmong tribal leader and commander of the Region.[27] Joseph R. Johnson, the CIA's chief of unit at Long Tieng, oversaw some twenty or so paramilitary and support personnel who advised Hmong and Thai units. He also directed the activities of Air America, a CIA-owned airline, and Continental Air Services, a contract air carrier. His chief of operations, Jerrold B. Daniels, who had the confidence of Vang Pao, was responsible for coordinating military activities in the Region, especially those relating to the Hmong. Major Jesse E. Scott commanded the U.S. Air Force's Air Operations Center at Long Tieng and (nominally) the ten U.S. Air Force forward air controllers, who used the radio call sign "Raven."[28]

The United States in 1971 was in the process of accelerating its withdrawal from Vietnam. President Nixon had proclaimed in 1969 that Asian boys should fight Asian wars. By the end of 1970, U.S. troop strength was down to 280,000, and declining rapidly. With regard to Laos—where Asian boys were fighting Asian wars—the Nixon administration adopted a defensive posture. Like Kennedy before him, Nixon wanted a neutral Laos that would serve as a buffer between pro-Western Thailand and the aggressive intentions of North Vietnam and China. While willing to approve the use of B-52s and support Thai "volunteers" in Laos, it was clear by 1971 that Nixon had no intention of making a major commitment of U.S. forces to assure Laotian neutrality.

Early in 1971, the Royal Lao government ordered General Vang Pao to seize as much territory as possible in Military Region II before con-

25. On U.S. Air Force activities in Laos, see Earl H. Tilford, Jr., *Crosswinds: The Air Force's Setup in Vietnam* (College Station, Texas, 1993).

26. General Vitoon Yasawatdi's activities are discussed in Rueng Yote Chantrakiri, *The Thoughts and Memories of the Man Known as Dhep 333* (Bangkok, 1992). I am indebted to the Office of the Vice President for Research at the University of Georgia for a grant to have this volume translated from the Thai by Kris Petcharawises.

27. On Vang Pao's background, see Keith Quincy, *Hmong: History of a People* (Cheney, Wash., 1988), 160–94.

28. V. H. Gallacher and Hugh N. Ahmann interview with Jesse E. Scott, 6 April 1973, USAFHRC. See also Christopher Robbins, *The Ravens* (New York, 1987).

gressional restraints reduced available U.S. air sorties to thirty-two per day after 1 July. Vang Pao launched a major offensive in June. Effectively using his air mobility and tactical air resources, the Hmong leader managed to drive the enemy from the PDJ for what proved to be the last time. In order to blunt the anticipated enemy dry season offensive, it was decided to establish five major artillery strong points on the PDJ. Manned and defended by Thai troops, these mutually supporting bases were intended to attract the enemy's attention. The North Vietnamese army, according to an optimistic scenario, would assault these fixed positions—and be destroyed by artillery fire and tactical air power.[29]

As the time neared for the expected enemy offensive, intelligence reports coming into the CIA operations center at Udorn grew ominous. In early November communications intelligence revealed that sixteen long-range 130-mm field guns were en route to northern Laos. Hanoi, the CIA learned, had appointed one of their senior army commanders—General Le Truong Tan—to direct the year's dry season offensive. Overhead photography revealed a growing number of troops and supplies moving along Route 6 toward the PDJ, including large covered trailers. Although B-52s and F-4 fighter bombers were targeted against the road, the traffic continued.[30]

Nonetheless, there was a general feeling of confidence that the enemy offensive could be stopped. James E. Parker, Jr., a newly arrived intelligence officer who had been assigned as desk officer for Military Region II, inspected the Thai artillery bases in early December and came away impressed. The firebases, with their 105-mm and 155-mm guns, were placed so that each base could be protected by artillery fire from two or three adjacent positions. Visiting the northernmost position, Parker received an optimistic appraisal of the situation from its Thai commander. The position, he said, was "impregnable," with its three inter-connected rings of firing positions, bunkers, well-fortified mortar pits, barbed and concertina wire, and mines. Local artillery, he boasted, was available within seconds; flareships, gunships, and tactical air support were on call.[31]

December 15 and 16 saw only light ground activity on the PDJ. On 17 December smoke enveloped the area during the daylight hours, cut-

29. William W. Lofgren and Richard R. Sexton, "Air War in Northern Laos, 1 April–30 November 1971," U.S. Air Force CHECO Report, 22 June 1973, USAFHRC; Hamilton Merritt, *Tragic Mountains*, 266–76.

30. Teletype report, "The 1971/1972 Communist Dry Season Offensive in Northern Laos," n.d. This document, most likely generated by the CIA in Laos ca. May 1972, is in the author's collection. See also Kenneth J. Conboy, "Vietnam and Laos: A Recent History of Military Cooperation," *Indochina Report*, 19 (April-June 1989): 1–15.

31. Parker to the author, December 1992.

ting short resupply flights to the Thai strong points. At 1835 hours that evening, the long-anticipated enemy offensive began. Using for the first time in Laos Soviet-made long-range 130-mm guns that far outranged the Thai artillery (sixteen miles versus nine miles), the North Vietnamese hit all Thai positions simultaneously. Tank-supported infantry then broke through the defensive rings around the bases. By the next morning, the northernmost position had fallen, and the other bases were under heavy pressure.[32]

As the enemy attack continued during 18 and 19 December, tactical air support—upon which the entire defensive scheme had been premised—was noticeable by its absence. With Vang Pao and the Thais pleading for air support, the CIA urged 7/13 Air Force at Udorn to supply the desperately needed sorties—all to no avail. Finally, Ambassador Godley contacted 7th Air Force headquarters in Saigon. He was told that all available U.S. aircraft were involved in search-and-rescue operations.[33]

On the afternoon of 18 December, an F-4 supporting the Thai positions on the PDJ was shot down by a MIG-21, the first air-to-air loss in Laos. Two other F-4s engaged the MIG as it fled toward the North Vietnamese border. Caught up in the chase, the F-4s ran out of fuel, and the four crew members ejected. The following day, another F-4 was brought down east of the PDJ by antiaircraft fire. The Air Force had launched a massive search and rescue operation for these downed crew members, which drew off the tactical air resources that otherwise would have gone into the battle on the PDJ.[34]

Time ran out for the Thai defenders. By the morning of 20 December, all artillery strong points had fallen. The surviving Thai troops headed south in disarray, pursued by the North Vietnamese army. Continental Air Services pilot Edward Dearborn, who had been airdropping supplies to the Thai positions, reported the scene: "By 1300 local, our efforts were confined to picking up the wounded and survivors of the fire bases. Most of them were working their way to LS-15 [Ban Na]. A pitiful sight from two weeks before. The majority were shell shocked and most were suffering from wounds, exposure, or shock in one form or another."[35]

32. The progress of the battle can be followed in the daily situation reports by Air America operations managers Thomas H. Sullivan and Jerome S. Connor, located in the Sullivan collection, Air America Archives, University of Texas at Dallas.

33. Tovar interview, 13 March 1992.

34. *New York Times*, 21 and 22 December 1971.

35. Edwin B. Dearborn, "Notes on PDJ Battle, December 17–20," 23 December 1971. Copy courtesy of Edwin B. Dearborn.

The North Vietnamese pushed into the mountainous terrain south of the PDJ and headed toward Long Tieng. While Hmong and Thai defenders strengthened their positions along Skyline Ridge, tactical airstrikes— once again available—slowed but could not stop the enemy advance.[36]

At 1530 hours on 31 December 1971, North Vietnamese gunners opened fire on Long Tieng. The shelling, which included rounds from the dreaded 130-mm guns, continued intermittently throughout the night, causing heavy damage to installations in the valley.

The ground assault against Skyline began a few days later. An estimated 19,000 North Vietnamese troops were thrown into the battle. They were opposed by a mixed force of some 10,000 Hmong, Thai, and Lao defenders. The North Vietnamese four-pronged offensive went well at first. The major attack came from the north, aimed at Skyline Ridge. In hard fighting, the enemy captured several key positions along the two-mile-long ridge, then moved antiaircraft batteries into position to restrict the flow of air supplies to the hard-pressed defenders. A prong from the south, preceded by sapper attacks, targeted a radio station and POL storage facilities in the valley, while attacks from the east and west completed the encirclement of Long Tieng. At the same time, North Vietnamese units took control of Sam Thong, the former headquarters of the USAID mission in northern Laos.

On 12 January 1972, Radio Pathet Lao announced that Long Tieng had fallen to "Lao Patriotic armed forces." Two days later, Hanoi's official military newspaper, *Quan Goi Nhan Dan,* published a detailed account of the "great victory." Nearly 1,000 enemy troops had been killed, it claimed; ten aircraft had been wrecked; and hundreds of weapons, including ten large guns, had been captured or destroyed. The loss of Long Tieng, *Quan Goi Nhan Dan* concluded, represented a turning point in the war: "Confusion now exists between Laos and U.S. authorities in Vientiane."[37]

Hanoi's victory announcement proved premature. In mid-January, the CIA brought in Thai reinforcements, together with several 1,200-man units of irregular troops from southern Laos, considered to be the government's elite force. By late January, the CIA-led Lao troops, in bitter— often hand-to-hand—fighting, had retaken Skyline from the North Vietnamese, at a cost of one-third to one-half of their effective strength. Thanks to their efforts, Long Tieng was placed at least temporarily out of the danger—if not out of range of the 130-mm guns.[38]

36. Major General Alton D. Slay, chief of staff for operations at 7th Air Force, End-of-Tour Report, USAFHRC, is more optimistic in appraising the important role of the Air Force.

37. *Quan Goi Nhan Dan*, 14 January 1972. The author is indebted to Lloyd Landry for a photocopy of the newspaper and translation.

38. *Thailand, Laos, and Cambodia: January 1972*, 18.

While the Air Force hunted the well camouflaged artillery pieces—and found several—the defenders of Long Tieng dug in deeper and waited for the next assault. It took nearly two months for the North Vietnamese—their supply lines harassed by B-52s, tactical air strikes, and Hmong ambushes—to accumulate sufficient material to stage the expected attack.

In mid-March 1972, the North Vietnamese army once again tried to push the defenders off Skyline. This time, the enemy planned to use heavy T-34 tanks, bringing them in along the road from Sam Thong. Michael E. Ingham, CIA officer in change of Thai forces in Military Region II, had learned of the enemy's intentions from a North Vietnamese prisoner. He had his men place antitank mines along the road in front of their main defensive position. As it turned out, North Vietnamese sappers removed most of the mines, except for the two closest to the Thai position. On 30 March two T-34 lead tanks hit these mines and were immobilized, effectively blocking the road to Long Tieng.[39]

Heavy fighting along Skyline Ridge continued into the last days of April, with key positions changing hands several times. Unable to obtain their objective, the North Vietnamese finally removed a division from the area and sent it to support the Easter offensive against South Vietnam. On 19 May President Nixon congratulated Ambassador Godley: "The Communist dry season [offensive] in Laos has been blunted this year, largely through the tireless efforts of your Mission. You have done a tremendous job under difficult conditions."[40]

Ambassador Godley certainly deserved President Nixon's accolades. His CIA-led forces had scored an impressive victory over a capable and determined enemy. For a time, U.S. officials believed that this military success might contribute to the creation of a neutral Laos. For example, CIA Director William Colby, in awarding an Intelligence Star to one of the case officers who directed the Lao irregular forces, commented in February 1974: "I think you made a major contribution not only to the battle, but also to the successful outcome in Laos. That was a very sticky period. And the situation at Long Tieng was considered a critical one." The recent conclusion of a ceasefire agreement and "steps toward achieving some kind of coalition government," Colby concluded, "is in good part a credit to your work."[41] Unfortunately, the coalition government proved only an brief interlude. The Communists soon took control of the country.

39. Michael E. Ingham to the author, 7 January 1993; *Pacific Stars and Stripes*, 2 April 1972.

40. A copy of Nixon's message is in the microfilm collection of Air America records in the author's possession.

41. Colby presentation to Elias P. Chavez, 8 February 1974. Copy of presentation courtesy of Elias P. Chavez.

The CIA, nonetheless, remained proud of its efforts in Laos. As CIA Director Richard Helms later observed: "This was a major operation for the agency. . . . It took manpower, it took specially-qualified manpower, it was dangerous, it was difficult." The CIA, he contended, "did a superb job."[42]

Helms had a point. Criticized following the Bay of Pigs fiasco in 1961 for its inability to conduct large-scale military operations, the CIA directed the war in Laos for more than a decade—and fought the North Vietnamese and Pathet Lao to a standstill. The cost—at least in American lives—had been small: eight CIA case officers were killed during the war, four in aircraft accidents and four as a result of enemy fire.[43]

Lao, Thai, and Hmong losses, of course, were much higher. The Hmong suffered most, both during and after the war. As Douglas S. Blaufarb, CIA station chief in Vientiane, 1964–66, has observed, whatever the Hmong gained by associating with the United States, "it certainly was not worth the high price they paid." But, Blaufarb wisely adds, criticism of the U.S. alliance with the Hmong involves the application of "a lavish hindsight without regard to the realities of the time it was undertaken."[44]

In any event, the anticommunist forces in Laos won the battle for Skyline Ridge. As in Vietnam, however, victory on the battlefield did not mean much in the end. It merely delayed the final outcome of the war.

42. Ted Gittinger interview with Richard Helms, 16 September 1981, Oral History Program, Lyndon Baines Johnson Presidential Library, Austin, Texas.

43. Two of the four intelligence officers who were killed in aircraft accidents—Louis O'Jibway and Edward Johnson—died when an Air America helicopter flew into the Mekong River on 20 August 1965, while en route from Nam Lieu, Laos, to Udorn, Thailand. In addition to the eight case officers, three CIA employees, serving as Air America crew members, were killed in the crash of a C-46 on 13 August 1961, and are memorialized by three stars, without names, in the "Book of Honor" in the lobby of CIA Headquarters.

44. Douglas Blaufarb, *Counterinsurgency Era* (New York, 1977), 168.

Fast-Movers and Herbicidal Spraying in Southeast Asia

Richard D. Duckworth

(Overleaf) An F–4 prepares to spray herbicide in its testing mission.

THE 366TH TACTICAL FIGHTER WING (TFW) WAS NOT AN EXPERIMENT BUT RATHER A COMBAT EVALUATION

(Right) A trio of UC–123s wing their way on a defoliation mission in 1966.

he fixed-wing aerial spraying of Agent Orange and other defoliation herbicides in Southeast Asia during the Vietnam War was controversial during that conflict and remains controversial today. At the time, however, this program was considered vital and much effort was expended, both in the field and in the laboratories back home, to see that it succeeded. For the most part, C/UC–123B/K Provider aircraft of the 12th Air Commando/Special Operations Squadron (SOS) were those involved in spraying herbicides under the designation of Project Ranch Hand. Not well known, though, is the role F–4D Phantom II aircraft of the 366th Tactical Fighter Wing (TFW) briefly played in 1969 in this effort. Also not well known are the intense deliberations at all command levels concerning the continued need for the F–4D or the UC–123 as aerial sprayers.

Why so little has been known or written about this unique "fast-mover" mission is a curious question that has bothered the author for years. What has been written comprises only two paragraphs in William A. Buckingham's *Operation Ranch Hand: The Air Force and Herbicides in Southeast Asia, 1961-1971* (Washington, 1982), and merely three sentences in Paul Cecil's *Herbicidal Warfare: The Ranch Hand Project in Vietnam* (New York, 1986). And both authors term these missions as "test," "research and development," or "experimental."

It has always been this author's contention, however, that the "fast-mover" spray program as flown by the 366th Tactical Fighter Wing (TFW) was not an experiment but rather a combat evaluation intended to provide data on employment and effectiveness under combat conditions. This mission was in direct response to an important Southeast Asia operational requirement.

Further substantiation of this program as a non-test combat evaluation can be gained from Gen. George S. Brown's response to an Aerospace Studies Institute query in August 1970 concerning the topic, "Use of Combat Theater as a Test Area." General Brown and his staff at Seventh Air Force replied that the combat theater definitely was not an area for system testing. They indicated that depicting the SEA theater in that light would give an aura of experimentation to combat operations that would be completely erroneous. Headquarters Seventh Air Force concluded that during the initial deployment stage, combat evaluation was conducted on new equipment to determine its operational suitability in

PROJECT RANCH HAND BEGAN INFORMALLY ON JANUARY 10, 1962

the actual combat environment, and that this evaluation *was not* merely in-theater testing. Since perfect environmental simulation facilities did not exist, it was understandable that some aspects of testing slipped into the combat evaluation phase during the introduction of new equipment to the theater. Still, all efforts were made not to burden the combat forces with even the hint of test activities in a combat zone.[1]

Project Ranch Hand began informally on January 10, 1962, when a C–123 sprayed less than 200 gallons of Purple herbicide on an area north of South Vietnam's Route 15, east of Saigon.[2] Ranch Hand's formal inauguration was January 13, with two missions spraying 960 gallons each, again along Route 15. On February 2, 1962, Ranch Hand lost a C–123B (tail number 56-4370) and its three man crew during a training mission. Capts. Fergus C. Groves, II, and Robert D. Larson, and SSgt. Milo B. Coghill became the first Air Force fatalities of the Vietnam War. The downed C–123 was also the first Air Force combat aircraft lost in Vietnam.[3] Before Ranch Hand's herbicide operations were terminated in 1971, the unit would lose ten C/UC–123s and twenty-six crewmen.[4]

Colonel Richard D. Duckworth, USAF (Ret.), is a retired bank vice president now doing estate/trust consulting. He frequently speaks and writes on the Agent Orange controversy. During the Vietnam War, he was an aircraft commander with the 12th SOS, then a staff officer at Seventh Air Force headquarters. Of his 5,000 flying hours, 100 were logged on combat missions over Laos, Cambodia, and South Vietnam. Before retiring in 1981 as Chief, Department of National Security Affairs at the Air War College, he attended the National War College and the Industrial College of the Armed Forces, and held positions on the faculties of the Air Force Academy and Pennsylvania State University.

6

[Above] A quartet of UC-123s defoliate a wide swath of South Vietnam containing an enemy base camp in 1966.

[Right] The left side of the river exhibits the effects of herbicide defoliation, while the right bank was unaffected.

RANCH HAND'S HERBICIDE OPERATIONS WERE TERMINATED IN 1971

263

THE UC–123,
DESPITE ITS
EXCELLENT
ABILITY TO
ABSORB
PUNISH-
MENT, WAS
TOO SLOW
AND VUL-
NERABLE

Virtually every Ranch Hand commander complained that the UC–123, despite its excellent ability to absorb punishment, was too slow and vulnerable to the increasingly sophisticated enemy weaponry.[5] In late 1968, Headquarters, Seventh Air Force (in Saigon) and Headquarters, USAF determined that if herbicide operations were to continue, a more efficient and faster delivery system was required, particularly in high-threat priority areas over and near the Ho Chi Minh Trail in Laos. It was in this area that Air Force, Navy, and Marine aircraft flew Commando Hunt (I, III, V, and VII) missions against North Vietnamese truck traffic, truck parks, lines of communications, storage, and supply areas. A triple canopy jungle hid much of the enemy's operations and movements from aerial reconnaissance.

For air attacks to be even remotely successful, as well as safe, it was assumed that the jungle had to be "fast-mover" defoliated without resorting to the costly heavy suppression tactics normally used to support high-threat spray missions. In early January 1969, Col. John W. Roberts, commander of the 366th TFW (the "Gunfighters") at Da Nang, was queried as to the feasibility of using F–4Ds on defoliation missions. He agreed with the proposal and was directed to

proceed immediately (if spray tanks could be devised) with an F–4D defoliation program. Roberts delegated the mission to his wing's 390th Tactical Fighter Squadron (TFS). Thus, from January through March 1969, this squadron (under operations orders codenamed "Trailbast") sprayed herbicides, not high explosives, both in-country and out (Laos), over targets where the threat from ground fire was believed to be "too high" for the use of the UC–123s.[6]

Between January 17 and March 29, 1969, the 390th flew nine missions using F–4Ds as high-speed spray planes. Two standard external wing tanks, after being modified internally and provided with nozzles, were determined to be the most practical dispensers. These TMU-28/A tanks each carried 278 gallons of herbicide. Normally, each tanks would carry 370 gallons of fuel, but in order to fill the nose and tail sections, the liquid had to be pumped under pressure causing the herbicide to foam. Accordingly, only the tank's center section was filled.[8]

On January 17, 1969, an F–4D (67-7531) flew a test mission over the South China Sea east of Da Nang successfully spraying colored water. Three days later, a second test sortie was flown at 24,000 feet on a simulated mission profile to confirm spraying capability using Blue herbicide.[9]

(Right) The underside of a
UC–123 rigged for defoliation missions.

THE JUNGLE
HAD TO BE
"FAST-
MOVER"
DEFOLIATED
WITHOUT
RESORTING
TO THE
COSTLY
HEAVY SUP-
PRESSION
TACTICS

8

264

(Above) Col. (later Brig. Gen.) John W. Roberts, on the right, Commander of the 366th Tactical Fighter Wing, and his testing teams.

A TEN-MILE-LONG AREA (16 KILO-METERS) COULD BE COVERED IN 70 SECONDS

The 390th flew seven combat herbicide missions between January 25 and March 29. Each mission consisted of three F–4Ds spraying high-threat priority targets in South Vietnam and Laos. The first combat mission (January 25) was over South Vietnam and the first Laos mission was flown January 29. Normal delivery for the spray missions was at 500 knots indicated airspeed (kias) at 100 to 200 feet above the trees. The delivery route would be marked by a forward air controller. A ten-mile-long area (16 kilometers) could be covered in 70 seconds, and it was assumed that with this brief exposure time, there would be no need for fighter escort, as there was for the UC–123s. The three F–4s would fly with the two wingmen ten degrees to the rear and about three plane-widths from the leader. At a distribution rate of 4.3 gallons per acre, this formation resulted in a spray pattern approximately 300 feet wide. At the same distribution rate and width, it would take one UC–123 four to five minutes to cover the same distance.[10]

The F–4D experienced some problems when used as a spray aircraft. On three of the missions

a tank either collapsed or failed. On the March 26 mission, an F–4D (65-0674) sustained heavy damage to the forward section of the right defoliation tank, the underside of the right wing, and the inboard side of the fuselage and right aileron. Fortunately, the crew brought their plane back safely. It was believed, but not fully determined, that a venturi suction effect around the tank spray nozzle caused the failures. Following these mishaps, several modifications to the tank were incorporated, including mounting a shut-off valve, operated by the conventional weapons release system, in the tank bottom aft of the center section, and welding a metal cowling around the valve opening to increase and improve the spray pattern.[11]

The last F–4 combat herbicide mission was flown over Laos on March 29. During this mission, the number 3 aircraft (66-8809) crashed during its run. Initially, it was suspected that another spray tank had failed, but the Phantom's pilot, Capt. Popendorf, who ejected and was rescued, stated that small arms or automatic weapons fire had struck the plane prior to his los-

The author stands next to his UC–123. Note the herbicide puddle behind the author.

FIND A WAY TO DELAY AND NOT LET THE AFSC MAJOR AND HIS TEAM BRING ANY ... HERBICIDE EQUIPMENT TO PUT ON THE GUNFIGHTER F–4S

ing control of the F–4. Not so lucky was his "backseater," 1st Lt. Frederick W. Hess. First listed as missing in action, he was subsequently declared killed in action. This crash brought the use of the F–4D as a spray plane to a tragic end.[12]

Ranch Hand defoliant spraying operations continued for another year. On April 15, 1970, the Department of Defense (DOD) ordered the Military Assistance Command, Vietnam (MACV), Army Chemical Corps (J3-09), and the 12th SOS to cease spraying Orange herbicide. With only a small quantity of White herbicide[13] (the substitute for Orange) remaining in Air Force stocks in Vietnam, and no mature crop targets available for Blue herbicide until July, the last defoliation spray missions were flown on May 9, 1970. The following day, the squadron began psychological warfare and flare-drop operations in support of the Cambodian incursion.[14]

The conclusion of defoliation missions by the Ranch Hand squadron did not end efforts to revive the use of the F–4Ds as "fast-mover" spray planes. In early July 1969, less than four months after the last, costly, F–4 spray mission, Headquarters USAF proposed reactivating the F–4 program using "certified" spray tanks developed by Air Force Systems Command (AFSC). This proposal (SEAOR 195 FY 70) led to a new Seventh Air Force Combat Requirements of Capability (Combat ROC 19-70) later that month. The ROC stated the need for a tactical fighter defoliant system to include a delivery altitude of approximately 100 feet, a speed of 400-500 kias, and the capability to deliver herbicide at thee gallons per acre on a single pass.[15]

I came upon the F–4D spray story while serving from February to July 1970 as, first, a UC–123 aircraft commander with the 12th SOS and, then, as the last Ranch Hand Herbicide Project Officer (TACPSO) in the Seventh Air Force's Tactical Air Control Center (TACC) at Tan Son Nhut. In late April 1970, a major in the Office for Technical Application for Southeast Asia (TAFSEA) of the Armament Development and Test Center (ADTC) at Eglin AFB, Florida, called me. He announced that, after working for nearly half a year, ADTC had developed "certified" TMU-28/B liquid agent spray tanks for high-speed defoliant dispensing. This AFSC agency believed they had developed a short-term solution to the Seventh Air Force ROC 19-70 requirement. These modified tanks, designated PAU-7/As, differed significantly from the tank used during the 1969 missions. The modifications to the TMU-28/B tanks consisted of: the addition of a butterfly valve in the ram air inlet and another valve in the herbicide outlet port; electrical and mechanical changes to permit the operation of the valves through the aircraft armament system; rubber tubing attached to the valve on the outlet port and extending the length of the spray boom; the clamping and bolting at the dissemination end of the tubing with an aluminum sleeve to lessen turbulence as the agent was dispensed through the spray boom. These modifications gave the PAU-7/A tank an on-off capability lacking in the previous configuration. The major and an AFSC team were ready to bring 16 of these tanks to Da Nang to restart the "fast-mover" spray program by conducting training and assisting in the initial employment of the PAU-7/As on defoliation missions. The major and an AFSC team were ready to bring sixteen of these tanks to Da Nang to restart the "fast-mover" spray program by conducting training and assisting in the initial employment of the PAU-7/As on defoliation missions.

Headquarters USAF approved the Southeast Asia portion of the evaluation, which was tentatively scheduled for June 1970, and would be conducted by the 366th TFW. When Brig. Gen. John Roberts (formerly the 366th's commander), the Director of TACC (TACD), was informed of the call from Eglin AFB, he reminded me that both he and Gen. George S. Brown, the Seventh Air Force leader and also Deputy Commander for Air MACV, were finishing their tours and would be leaving shortly. Roberts said jokingly that if I wanted to make a career in the Air Force, I had better find a way to delay and not let the AFSC major and his team bring any "fast-mover" herbicide equipment to put on the "Gunfighter" F–4D/Es while he was still in Southeast Asia.

At that time, a requested delay was the only proper course to follow. Orange defoliant had been banned just a week earlier and the on-going UC–123 missions were rapidly depleting the White herbicide. By early May, there would be no defoliant avaiable for the proposed PAU-7/A eval-

10

uation. Also, no more defoliant would be available in the foreseeable future, unless the DOD reversed its order to cease spraying Orange, or until new shipments of White arrived.

Certainly one of the main reasons for Gen. Roberts' change of attitude and his reluctance towards restarting this program was the cost in life and aircraft to the "Gunfighters" when he had been the wing commander in 1968-1969. After only twenty-three sorties and nine missions, the 366th had lost one crew member and had another severely injured in the F–4D shot down in Laos and had another aircraft out of commission due to spray tank "flutter" which caused severe damage to the aircraft. The general also knew that, due to increasing "Triple A" intensity and sophistication, "The Trail" was getting more and more hazardous by the day.

The November 1968 bombing halt of North Vietnam had enabled the enemy to move more anti-aircraft guns into Laos. From November 1968 to May 1970, the number of guns (some very large caliber) had jumped fourfold. The bulk of enemy fire was from 37mm cannons, and other automatic weapons and small arms fire, and it became so accurate and intense that some stretches of "The Trail" were considered too dangerous even for the higher-flying, night-operating AC–130 gunships.[16] F–4Ds, no matter what airspeed and at only 100-200 feet above the jungle canopy, could easily become cannon fodder. The "Gunfighter" F–4 loss on March 29, 1969, might be an omen of tragic events to come.

Gen. Brown no doubt felt the same as Gen. Roberts concerning the proposed F–4 mission. However, he was also greatly concerned and dis-turbed over the "dedicated air to the (Army)" aspect of the 12th SOS Ranch Hand aircraft. He told me several times that the UC–123s were Air Force aircraft controlled by the Seventh Air Force; they did not belong to the J3-09 Army Chemical Corps, as the commander of that organization had indicated on numerous occasions. Both Gen. Brown and the Seventh's previous commander, Gen. William M. Momyer, had expressed serious reservations concerning the command and control aspects of this "dedicated air" role of Seventh Air Force aircraft, be they C–7s, EC–47s, C/UC–123s or, especially, Strategic Air Command B–52s.[17]

On May 8, 1970, Seventh Air Force received a message announcing that the quarterly meeting of the DOD Joint Technical Coordinating Group, Defoliant/Anti-Crop Subcommittee would be held at Camp Smith, Hawaii, on June 4-5. To Seventh Air Force personnel, the meeting's timing and location appeared to be a rather convenient arrangement for MACV J3-09, since prior meetings had always been held in the Washington, D.C. area. A number of subjects were to be discussed, including restrictions on the use of Orange, the use of alternate defoliants, and the DOD position on the use of herbicides.[18]

Gens. Brown and Roberts and the Deputy Chief of Staff for Current Plans (DPLA), Col. Malcolm E. Ryan (TACP), my immediate supervisor, were very interested in what would be discussed at this meeting, and how any new proposals might affect Seventh Air Force. Instead of the Seventh Air Force Deputy Chief of Staff, Materiel, as specified in the message, they chose to send their TACC herbicide specialist from the

GEN. WILLIAM M. MOMYER HAD EXPRESSED SERIOUS RESERVATIONS CONCERNING THE COMMAND AND CONTROL ASPECTS OF THIS "DEDICATED AIR" ROLE OF SEVENTH AIR FORCE AIRCRAFT

HIS RELUCTANCE TOWARDS RESTARTING THIS PROGRAM WAS THE COST IN LIFE AND AIRCRAFT TO THE GUNFIGHTERS

The author in the cockpit of his UC–123.

267

CHRONOLOGY

January 10, 1962	First Ranch Hand C–123B spray mission flown in South Vietnam.
February 2, 1962	Ranch Hand C–123 crashes, killing its crew. This is the first USAF combat loss in Vietnam.
January 25, 1969	First F–4D combat spray mission flown over South Vietnam. First out-country mission flown four days later.
March 29, 1969	F–4D shot down down during spray mission over Laos. This loss ends the use of the F–4D "fast-mover" program.
April 15, 1970	DOD informs Air Force and Army to cease spraying Orange herbicide. Nearly 25,000 drums (1,400,000 gallons) still remain in South Vietnam.
May 9, 1970	12th SOS sprays out the last White herbicide in Air Force stocks, effectively ending the service's defoliant mission.
July 2, 1970	PACAF approves inactivation of 12th SOS. Squadron becomes "A" Flight, 310th TAS at Phan Rang.
July 17, 1970	COMUSMACV officially cancels all Air Force "fixed-wing" defoliation missions. Six C–123s continue to spray Blue on crops and two C–123s continue insecticide missions. U.S. Army authorized to continue spraying White and Blue around bases and LOCs.
July-October 1970	Units of the America1 Division perform unauthorized spraying of Orange.
October 1970	COMUSMACV orders all stocks of Orange consolidated in centralized location.
December 4, 1970	DOD cancels all future shipments of Blue to South Vietnam.
January 7, 1971	Final Ranch Hand crop mission. Six C–123s returned to airlift, two continue on insecticide mission.
May 1, 1971	Under a presidential directive, COMUSMACV ends all herbicide spraying.
June 1, 1971	Final Ranch Hand insecticide mission.
August 18, 1971	Washington again permits U.S. Army to spray chemical defoliants until Dec. 1, 1971. Only Blue and White in Army stocks used. No "fixed-wing" assets authorized. An extension later granted with no termination date. This continued until the departure of the last U.S. troops in 1973.
April 1972	1,370,000 gallons of Orange removed from South Vietnam and sent to Johnston Island. An additional 850,000 gallons are in open storage at Gulfport, MS.
September 3, 1977	All remaining stocks of Orange, including that from Gulfport, incinerated at sea west of Johnston Island. The Air Force estimated total cost of the storage and destruction of Orange at over $8 million in 1977 dollars.

Special Operations Branch (TACPSO). Thus, I became the first operational 12th SOS crew member to ever attend this type of gathering. I was allotted the final time slot on the last day for the Seventh's presentation, but I had also been well-prepared by Col. Ryan to inject Seventh Air Force positions and views as necessary throughout the two-day session. It did, in fact, become necessary to speak up often during the meetings.

Discussions on the "fast-mover" program took place early the first day of the meeting. Following a briefing on some new experimental high-speed tanks that AFSC had been working on, the subject of who would control F–4D spray missions surfaced. Col. Harold C. Kinne, who had been the MACV J3-09 during the initial F–4D spray missions and who was now at Headquarters, U.S. Army Pacific (USARPAC), stated that "if there was ever a need for this requirement [the "fast-mover" program], it was short-range and none exists now."[19]

Col. Bruce M. Whitesides, the present MACV J3-09, commented only that "there was a need for an operational re-evaluation" of the F–4 mission. Their reluctance to be enthusiastic about the "fast-movers" was understandable. Both Chemical Corps men knew that Seventh Air Force would totally direct and control the execution of the spraying program, from initial targeting through final fragmentary ordering of the sorties. There would be no "dedicated air" aspect, as had been the case with the UC–123s. I added that although Headquarters USAF showed much interest in this part of the herbicide program, Seventh Air Force had delayed introduction of the new F–4 spray tank until further advised because supplies of defoliants were now inadequate to support the introduction and the combat evaluation.

The next presenter, Dr. William F. Warren, HQ CINCPAC, J3-0S, remarked that CINCPAC was countering Gen. Brown's June 2 message requesting consideration toward the inactivation of the 12th SOS with a message of their own questioning this action in light of the proven effectiveness of herbicides on the enemy. His paper stressed the total effectiveness of crop destruction and its direct relationship on the enemy's capabilities. I countered that many other weapons, both Air Force and Army, also greatly contributed to the enemy's ineffectiveness.

Much of the rest of the day was taken up discussing the various herbicides and problems with their storage and destruction. Dr. Charles E. Minarik, the top herbicide scientist at Ft. Detrick, Maryland, spent some time describing the problems with dioxin, the trace contaminant in both Orange and Purple herbicides, commenting that "he could not positively state or rule out that dioxin in herbicides did not affect humans. Therefore, Orange herbicide was now prohibited from any use in the USA." Minarik went on to talk about the most important question of the meeting. He revealed that the Secretary of

THE MES-
SAGE WAS
THAT THERE
WOULD BE
NO REAL
LIFTING OF
THE
RESTRICTED
USE OF
ORANGE

Defense's office had released to him the gist of what to expect in a forthcoming DOD message then being formulated for Secretary of Defense Melvin Laird's signature. In essence, the message was that "there would be no real lifting of the restricted use of Orange, only that it could be used in very limited areas.... [and] these areas would be unpopulated and never near streams or water sources."

Since South Vietnam was a virtual watershed, only small-scale herbicide use would be authorized and then only on "mountaintops." Dr. Minarik and Cols. Kinne and Whitesides all stated that with this message, as far as they could see Ranch Hand was "de facto dead" and no further use of the UC–123s was envisioned. Why the Secretary's message had not yet been sent caused some debate, but it was believed that he was awaiting the results of an ecological meeting later in the week. Dr. Minarik seemed more worried about the future of the Ft. Detrick complex because they were losing many people. It appeared to me that many of the committee members would soon be out of business and were looking for new areas of employment.

The next morning Col. Whitesides made his presentation, which became almost a plea for help from those at the meeting to keep the herbicide operations going. He appeared desperate, which surprised most, if not all, of the participants. According to the colonel, Gen. Brown's message requesting inactivation of the 12th SOS had been "signed by the MACV chief of staff over his written objections." Noting that there were still 23 active spray projects, of which 13 were crop destruction, and 30 more priority projects were available, he lamented that the herbicide mission had no more dedicated aircraft. Continuing in the same vein, Whitesides complained about the recent stringent controls being applied by the U.S. Embassy in Saigon which required fresh staffing on all projects, new or old, thus increasing the time frame for approval of targets by three or four months.

Turning to me, he said that he could not understand Seventh Air Force's negative attitude toward the herbicide operations. I responded that the 12th SOS was now actively engaged in psywar and flare operations in Cambodia, and any new decision on the use of herbicides could complicate these missions or other future needs, particularly airlift, where there was a shortage of C–123s. I continued that the Seventh and the 12th SOS were presently surveying all projects submitted, but any further movement on these projects could not be done until receipt of directions from higher headquarters.

Col. Whitesides concluded his presentation by commending the professionalism of the 12th SOS. He indicated that he was recommending the squadron for a Presidential Unit Citation. This would become Ranch Hand's fourth and last such award for its operations in Southeast Asia. While I heartily applauded the Army's recognition of

COL.
WHITESIDES
... INDICATED
THAT HE
WAS RECOM-
MENDING
THE
SQUADRON
FOR A PRESI-
DENTIAL
UNIT
CITATION

the 12th SOS, I mentioned that the Ranch Hand personnel were only doing their mission, like all other Seventh Air Force tactical units.

My briefing later that morning concluded the presentations. I detailed some of the tactical difficulties encountered in combat herbicide operations, such as the need for and use of fighter escorts, the forward air controllers and the coordination required of them and the spray planes during the spray runs, radio and formation discipline, targeting, etc. Much of this information was new to the committee because there had never been an operational representative at previous meetings. I again pointed out that Air Force headquarters still had a profound interest in the herbicide program, as shown by the proposed reactivation of the 366th TFW's F–4D program. However, as stated earlier, J3-09 knew these aircraft would be under the full command and direct operational control of the Seventh Air Force TACC from targeting through the complete mission. The Army Chemical Corps would have no involvement in the "fast-mover" program.

Following this final day of meetings, I called Col. Ryan to give him my report. He said, "Well done," and hoped that I would enjoy my short leave in Hawaii before returning in mid-June to South Vietnam to complete my tour. I had literally reported my way out of a memorable job at TACPSO, because it now appeared there would be no need for a Ranch Hand Herbicide Specialist at Seventh Air Force. Shortly after returning, I was transferred to the Seventh's Directorate of Tactical Analysis as a Pilot Research Analyst.

Before transferring to my new duties, I had one final project to oversee as the Herbicide Project Officer. I was to coordinate with the 366th TFW and other Seventh Air Force organizations on the Seventh Air Force Operational Order (OPORD) 70-6, titled "PAU-7/A High Speed Defoliation Tank Evaluation." This OPORD originated within the Current Plans Division (TACP) of TACC and had been written by Col. Ryan and his planning staff. There still remained a chance that very limited "fixed-wing" defoliation missions would be approved, especially "out-country."

The OPORD's purpose was to provide for the introduction and combat evaluation of the PAU-7/A tank in the Southeast Asia combat environment. Under the heading, "Concept of Operations," the OPORD stated that the PAU-7/A tanks could provide Seventh Air Force with a high-speed defoliation capability to be used on high-threat priority targets designated too dangerous for the much slower UC–123Ks. Further, this capability would combine the advantage of speed with the increased potential to defoliate priority LOCs, storage areas, and truck parks (primarily along the Ho Chi Minh Trail in Laos) without the employment of costly heavy suppression tactics normally associated with this type of mission. This order was the direct result of the July 1969 Combat ROC 19-70 proposal to reactivate the F–4 defoliation program, despite the

WOULD THE
F–4D HAVE
REPLACED,
OR JUST
SUPPLE-
MENTED,
THE SLOW
UC–123 HAD
ANY ... DEFO-
LIATION
BEEN
APPROVED?

doubts of Gens. Brown and Roberts. The 18-page OPORD directed and instructed the combat evaluation of these high-speed tanks to determine their effectiveness over high-threat targets.[20]

Prior to my return from the Hawaii conference, Gen. Roberts left Southeast Asia. I felt I now could honor his "previous request" and could, without hesitation, assist in the coordination of the OPORD with the Seventh Air Force's organizations tasked to work it. Space for the signatures of Maj. Gen. Ernest C. Hardin, Jr., the Seventh Air Force deputy chief of staff, operations, and Gen. George S. Brown was provided on page 12 of the main order. To my knowledge, their signatures never appeared on this order, and I have retained the only known carbon copy of that OPORD. Brig. Gen. Walter T. Galligan had replaced Gen. Roberts as TACD on June 10, 1970. By late June, Gen. Hardin was heading Seventh Air Force in Gen. Brown's absence.

Gen. Hardin had already established a very close and friendly working relationship with Gen. Creighton W. Abrams, the MACV commander. Both men, as well as Gen. Brown, were not particularly enthusiastic about continuing the "fixed-wing" herbicidal program. Therefore, on July 17, 1970, even with the subtle pressure from Headquarters USAF to continue the "fast mover" spray program, it seemed appropriate to these field commanders to permanently discontinue any future "fixed-wing" large-scale Air Force defoliation mission in Southeast Asia. This left only minimal crop and insecticide missions for the deactivated 12th SOS and its remaining UC–123s at Phan Rang.[21]

Would the F–4D have replaced, or just supplemented, the slow UC–123 had any limited "fixed-wing" defoliation been approved? From my experience and the evidence presented, it appears to me that the F–4Ds would have replaced the UC–123s, especially out-country. This would have occurred, however, only if the Seventh Air Force

commander would have had complete command and operational control from targeting through fragging. The Army Chemical Corps J3-09 would not have been involved as it had been with Ranch Hand. In my view, the Air Force would have developed, refined, and retained the "fast-mover" capability for use against the North Vietnamese during the upcoming Commando Hunt V and VII interdiction operations.

As late as mid-1971, Air Force intelligence agencies were estimating that the labyrinth of routes and bypasses known as the Ho Chi Minh Trail encompassed approximately 3,500 kilometers of heavily defended, motorable roads. Actually, the enemy had more than 13,000 kilometers of roads and trails.[22] An article titled "Tonnage and Technology," in the Spring 1997 issue of Air Power History, highlighted the importance of the supply denial operations (Commando Hunts I, III, V, and VII) on the Ho Chi Minh Trail. The author stated that with all the technology, munitions, and money (over $3 billion spent on the Igloo White Sensor System alone) expended on the Trail, air power alone was unable to effectively cut this vital North Vietnamese supply artery.[23]

Even if the F–4D program could have successfully defoliated long segments of the Trail, Commando Hunts V and VII would probably have failed, and the air effort, although looking good statistically, would have been left wanting. We would have lost the battle of the Ho Chi Minh Trail—with or without "fast-mover" defoliation. However, we will never know if the F–4s would have replaced the UC–123s because the use of Air Force "fixed-wing" aircraft for herbicide spraying was overcome by events. These events were led by the official demise in mid-July 1970 of large-scale Air Force participation in defoliation type herbicidal warfare, although some defoliant spraying continued to be conducted by the Army.

On May 1, 1971, Gen. Abrams, using a presidential directive, ended all U.S. herbicide opera-

The UC–123, shown spraying at right, was more closely suited to the defoliation mission.

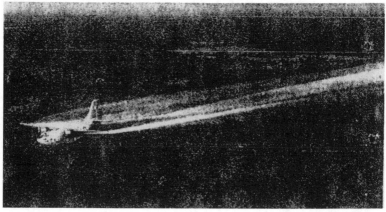

14

270

tions. In the ensuing months, however, ground troops suffered a number of casualties while trying to clean vegetation from wire entanglements and fields of fire. Washington relented and permitted chemical defoliation, using only Blue and White herbicides but no "fixed-wing" assets, to continue until December 1, 1971. As the expira-

tion date neared, the MACV commander asked for and received an extension with no termination date. This policy continued until the last U.S. troops departed South Vietnam in 1973. Their departure ended the extensive, lengthy, and disappointing U.S. military involvement in Southeast Asia.[24] ∎

NOTES

Acknowledgments: I would like to thank CMSgt. Thomas Raab, the 366th Wing historian, who supplied information that was unavailable in other Air Force sources. Lt. Col. Steve Topper, an old "Fox Four" pilot at Tenth Air Force headquarters in Fort Worth, Texas, was invaluable in locating sources and obtaining the information needed to tell the final and complete story of this unique Phantom spraying mission. Members of the staffs of the USAF Museum at Wright-Patterson AFB, Ohio, the Air Force Historical Research Agency and the Air University Library, the latter two located at Maxwell AFB, Alabama, were very helpful in guiding the author to various documents. A number of individuals at Air Combat Command headquarters, Langley AFB, Virginia, also provided me with useful information. Gen. John W. Roberts, USAF (Ret.), Maj. Gen. Malcolm E. Ryan, USAF (Ret.), and Col. Herman L. Gilster, USAF (Ret.), were immensely helpful in reviewing the final version of this article and providing their candid insights into both the Traildust "fastmovers" and the Ranch Hand aerial sprayers. Finally, William T. Y'Blood, a historian in the Air Force History Support Office, helped me to organize and articulate this story.

1. Gen. George S. Brown, "Query from Aerospace Studies Institute," Aug. 16, 1970. HQ 7AF Directorate of Tactical Analysis. This was a draft reply to Brig. Gen. Ginsburgh's request from Commander, Seventh Air Force for information on 20 topics (generally 4 to 6 subtopics under each topic). The author was the action officer for this project which was to substitute for Gen. Brown's End-of-Tour Report.
2. William A. Buckingham, Jr., *Operation Ranch Hand: The Air Force and Herbicides in Southeast Asia, 1961-1971.* (Washington, D.C.: Office of Air Force History, 1982), p. 33. The primary compounds in the various herbicides used in Vietnam were 2,4-D and 2,4,5-T. Two other compounds, picloram and cacodylic acid, were also used in combination with the primary ingredients in a couple of the herbicides. Purple contained 50 percent of 2,4-D and 50 percent of 2,4,5-T in two different forms. Orange contained the same 50/50 mix but was less expensive to manufacture and was more effective. Orange replaced Purple in 1965 as the main defoliant used in SEA. Over 60 percent of the nearly 20 million gallons of herbicides sprayed was Orange. (Buckingham, p. 199.)
3. *Ibid.*, p. 39; John Schlight, *A War Too Long: The USAF in Southeast Asia, 1961-1975.* (Washington, D.C.: Air Force History and Museums Program, 1996), p. 8.
4. The designation of the C–123s being used for herbicide spraying was changed to UC–123 in November 1965.
5. Paul Cecil, *Herbicidal Warfare: The Ranch Hand Project in Vietnam.* (New York: Praeger, 1986), p. 140 and footnote 4, p. 209.
6. Buckingham, pp. 151; Author's telephone conversation with Paul Cecil, Dec. 5, 1981.
7. Tank, Miscellaneous Unit-28. Several other types

of spray tanks were developed for use on F–4s. (John Lake, ed., *McDonnell F–4 Phantom: Spirit in the Skies.* (London/Washington: Aerospace Publishing/Airtime Publishing, 1992), p. 106.
8. Memo, CMSgt Raab to 10 AF/DOT (Lt Col Topper), subj: Ranch Hand F–4Ds and Air Crews (your request, 8 Jan 97), Feb. 3, 1997.
9. Blue was composed of 100 percent sodium salt of cacodylic acid. A desiccant or drying agent, it was primarily used on crops or other narrow leaf vegetation. Blue accounted for approximately 10 percent of the herbicides sprayed.
10. Cecil, p. 140; Memo, Raab to Topper, Feb. 3, 1997.
11. Memo, Raab to Topper, Feb. 3, 1997.
12. *Ibid.*
13. White was an 80 percent triisopropanolamine salt of 2,4-D and a 20 percent triisopropanolamine salt of picloram. White, which accounted for nearly 30 percent of the herbicides sprayed, was a water-based substitute for Orange. Orange was diluted with diesel fuel or kerosene to attain the correct droplet size and spray diffusion.
14. Author's personal records.
15. Seventh Air Force Operation Order 70-6, June 1970, pp. 2-7.
16. Darrel D. Whitcomb, "Tonnage and Technology: Air Power on the Ho Chi Minh Trail," *Air Power History*, Vol. 44, No. 1 (Spring 1997), pp. 9-10; Laurie R. Dick, "AC-130 Spectre Earns its Wings," *Vietnam*, Vol. 10, No. 1 (June 1997), p. 33.
17. Gen. George S. Brown, "Query from Aerospace Studies Institute," Aug. 16, 1970; Schlight, pp. 26-32.
18. Msg, SAAMA to OOAMA/OONNTB et al, 082150Z May 70, subj: Quarterly Meeting, DOD Joint Technical Coordinating Group, Defoliant/Anti-Crop Subcommittee.
19. Memo, Maj. Duckworth to Col. Ryan (TACP) and Lt. Col. Fox (DMS), subj: Trip Report to Defoliation/Anticrop Sub-Committee of DOD Joint Coordinating Group (Chemical/Biological) Meeting at Camp Smith, Hawaii, 3-5 Jun 70, Jun. 20, 1970. All subsequent quotations of this meeting are from this document.
20. OPORD 70-6, June 1970, pp. 1-8.
21. Buckingham, pp. 168, 205-6.
22. Herman L. Gilster, *The Air War in Southeast Asia: Case studies of Selected Campaigns.* (Maxwell AFB, Ala.: Air University Press, Oct. 1993), p. 16; Ray L. Bowers, "Air Operations in Southeast Asia: A Tentative Appraisal," in *Air Power and Warfare: Proceedings of the Eighth Military History Symposium*, USAF Academy, eds. Al Hurley and Robert Ehrhart, (Washington, D.C.: Office of Air Force History and USAF Academy, 1979), pp. 318-20; Michael MacLear, *The Ten Thousand Day War—Vietnam: 1945-1975.* (New York: St. Martin's Press, 1981), p. 209.
23. Whitcomb, pp. 6-17.
24. Roger P. Fox, *Air Base Defense in the Republic of Vietnam, 1961-1973.* (Washington, D.C.: Office of Air Force History, 1979), p. 78.

ONLY IF THE SEVENTH AIR FORCE COMMANDER WOULD HAVE HAD COMPLETE COMMAND AND OPERATIONAL CONTROL

271

Setup:
Why and How the U.S. Air Force Lost in Vietnam

EARL H. TILFORD, JR.

In his book *War Without Fronts: The American Experience in Vietnam*, Thomas C. Thayer makes the point that the Vietnam War was, first, an air war and, second, a ground war of attrition. To support his thesis, Thayer points out that the U.S. Air Force was the fastest to build up its forces, reaching nearly 90 percent of its peak strength by the end of 1966, and that it also remained in the theater the longest of any service, not closing down its Thailand-based headquarters until January 1976. Approximately half of the several hundreds of billions of dollars spent on the Vietnam War went to support Air Force, Navy, and Army aerial operations.[1] The air forces of the United States and its allies dropped nearly 8 million tons of bombs on Indochina, well over twice the tonnage dropped by the Allied powers in all of World War II. The U.S. Air Force, by its own accounting, dropped 6,162,000 of those tons.[2] For all this expenditure of effort, firepower, and resources—not to mention lives—the air war was occasionally pivotal but *it was never decisive.*

In April 1975, when 20 divisions of North Vietnamese troops were headed toward Saigon, with columns of tanks and trucks strung out along Route 1 and other major highways, a perfect situation existed for the effective use of air power. Fighter-bombers and B-52s could have decimated those forces and, perhaps (temporarily at least), averted doom for the Nguyen Van Thieu regime. But President Gerald R. Ford did not—indeed, could not—order those planes into action, except to cover

EARL H. TILFORD, JR. is associate professor of history at Troy State University in Montgomery and visiting professor of military history at the U.S. Air Force's Air Command and Staff College. He is the author of *A History of Air Force Search and Rescue Operations in Southeast Asia, 1961–1975* (1980) and *Setup: What the Air Force Did in Vietnam, and Why* (1991). Address for correspondence: Dr. Earl H. Tilford, Jr., 114 Diane Drive, Prattville, AL 36067.

ARMED FORCES & SOCIETY, Vol. 17 No. 3, 1991, pp. 327–342.

the final, ignominious withdrawal from Saigon. Fifteen years of costly warfare had divided and frustrated the American public and sapped its will. It was politically impossible for Ford to send American forces back into action for a cause that had been lost long before April 1975. The fact that Saigon was falling despite the United States having dropped 8 million tons of bombs contributed to Washington's inability to act to avert the final collapse of the Republic of Vietnam. Consequently, North Vietnamese units raised the Viet Cong flag over Ho Chi Minh City as a prelude to the creation of a unified, Communist Vietnam.

How Air Power Contributed to the Setup

There were no witch-hunts in America after 1975. President Ford, seeking national reconciliation after the tragedy of the Vietnam War and the turmoil of the Nixon presidency, urged the nation to look to the future. That was good enough for the U.S. Air Force, where there was a concerted effort "to put Vietnam behind us." Vietnam was declared an "aberration"—just as two decades before when then secretary of the Air Force Thomas K. Finletter dubbed the Korean War a unique diversion, never to be repeated, from the true course of strategic air power.[3] As in the mid-1950s, the post–Vietnam War Air Force returned to preparing to counter the Soviet threat in the more familiar environs of Europe and, to a lesser extent, the Pacific Rim. The Air Force, unlike the Army, failed to learn from the Vietnam War. Those lessons the Air Force did carry away revolved around tactics—especially those related to high-technology weapons like laser and electro-optically guided bombs. Throughout the Air Force, when addressing the lessons of Vietnam, its officers preferred to focus on Linebacker II, the 11-day aerial operation conducted over North Vietnam in December 1972, as a reaffirmation of traditional doctrines and strategies, thus avoiding the uncomfortable implications of failure.

While Linebacker II has attained near eschatological significance in Air Force mythology, what most airmen miss is the importance of the first Linebacker. In response to Hanoi's massive invasion of South Vietnam with conventional forces in spring 1972 (the Easter Offensive or the Nguyen Hue Offensive), President Nixon ordered American warplanes back into action over North Vietnam in Operation Linebacker. From 8 May through 23 October 1972, Air Force, Navy, and Marine Corps planes pounded railyards, petroleum-storage facilities, airfields, bridges, and roads throughout North Vietnam. Gone were many of the restrictions that had hampered aerial operations during Rolling Thunder, the bombing of North Vietnam from 2 March 1965 until 1 November 1968. Most significantly, the harbors at Haiphong and Dong Hoi were closed with aerially delivered mines; also, in the northwest and northeast, highways and railroads—vital transportation links to China in the rugged hill country north of Hanoi—were bombed successfully. The effect was to make it impossible for North Vietnam to import the military supplies needed to sustain its large forces inside South Vietnam, where the army of the Republic of Vietnam, with massive U.S. aerial support, contained the Communist offensive. It was Linebacker I that compelled Hanoi to negotiate seriously and to reach an agreement acceptable to Richard Nixon and Henry Kissinger, if not so acceptable to President Nguyen Van Thieu of South Vietnam.[4]

American airmen, especially those in the Air Force, *believe* in air power, and their faith is not diminished by the near certainty that American conventional air power could have obliterated North Vietnam in two weeks. The United States had tremendous advantages in military resources that seemingly dwarfed the capabilities of the Indochinese Communists. Although this disparity was enormous, it also led to the self-delusion that applied firepower, even in lesser doses, could substitute for strategy.

If, as Thayer suggests, the Vietnam War was, first and foremost, an air war, then the failure of the United States to achieve its admittedly tenuous, ill-defined, and limited goals is also a failure of air power. In other words—words that are an anathama to many in the Air Force— it lost. While the reasons for that are many and complex, Air Force professionals need to address five points that are peculiar to that service (although elements of them apply to other services as well), and two others that are generically inherent in air power.

History

Air-power enthusiasts tend to have a selective sense of history. The U.S. Air Force was—and is—a victim of its history. From the 1920s, air-power enthusiasts within the Army, however well-intentioned, engaged in subterfuge and intrigue to promote their case for an independent Air Force. Like an illegitimate child at a family reunion, the U.S. Air Force felt less than comfortable with its origins—all the more so since its primary reason for being was based on faith in the unproven doctrine of strategic bombing. Wedded to strategic bombing, the Air Force neglected other missions, particularly close air support, which tended to tie air assets to the needs of ground commanders. This aggravated interservice rivalries because, while the Air Force did not especially want the close-air-support mission, neither did it want the U.S. Army to coopt it and thereby procure combat airplanes. Interservice squabbling, which dominated and poisoned relationships among the armed services in the 1950s, were transplanted to Vietnam, where they had an adverse effect on operations, especially during the period between 1962 and 1965.[5]

Doctrine

Strategic bombing, flying to the enemy's heartland to lay waste to vital industrial centers, has dominated Air Force doctrine from the first Air Force Manual 1-series in 1953 to its latest published edition of AFM 1-1. This doctrine led Air Force leaders to believe that North Vietnam, a preindustrial, agricultural nation, could be subdued by the same kind of bombing that helped to defeat industrialized Nazi Germany and Imperial Japan. This faith in strategic bombing doctrine had the effect of blinding Air Force leaders to the true nature of the war, which was at its essence a revolutionary civil conflict, and not a struggle between industrialized powers. Consequently, American generals were unable to devise a plan applicable to the war at hand, forcing presidents John F. Kennedy and Lyndon Johnson to turn to their civilian advisers for military strategy. The unconventional nature of the war prior to 1968 especially confounded air-power proponents.

Technology

The strategic-bombing doctrine espoused by the Air Force fit well with the Eisenhower administration's policy of massive retaliation, itself driven more by economic than military reasons. Thus, the nation's newest service was able to gobble up the largest slice of each budget pie between 1954 and 1961. The B-52, the B-58, and the XB-70 were all at the leading edge of technology, as were the Century-series fighters obtained by the Tactical Air Command. This fascination with technology in the 1950s carried over to Vietnam in the 1960s, where the Air Force was ever in search of a technologically inspired "silver bullet" to end the war quickly. As early as 1963, airmen assigned to the first units sent to South Vietnam urged the deployment of F-100 single-seat fighter-bombers and B-57 twin-jet medium bombers, planes that they felt would quickly "finish this thing."[6] Cluster bombs, napalm, herbicide defoliants, sensors dropped along the Ho Chi Minh Trail to monitor traffic and aid in targeting, gunships, and electro-optically guided and laser-guided bombs all promised much, and while some delivered a great deal of destruction, in the end technologically sophisticated weapons proved no substitute for strategy. What technology did, however, was to help foster a managerial mindset.

Management

The managerial ethos, used effectively in marshalling forces during World War II, and institutionalized in the 1950s, took hold in the 1960s to turn the air war into a production-line affair. High-tech weapons demand effective and efficient management from initial research and development through procurement and deployment. In seeking efficiency, the tendency is to look for definable and objective criteria for assessing effectiveness in terms of productivity. The managerial ethos, implemented during the massive buildup of the Air Force in the 1950s, dominated the service in the 1960s. It promoted the objectivity of the quantifiable at the expense of the subjectivity of the creative but unpredictable. War, however, being inherently more subjective than objective, proved both unpredictable and, in its larger aspects, unmanageable.

That was especially true in Vietnam, where the art of unconventional warfare practiced by the enemy was not susceptible to the rigid approaches fostered by the Air Force's managerial elite. For the Air Force, the Vietnam War came to resemble production-line warfare, in which success was assessed through statistical compilations that became an end unto themselves. Statistics proved a poor substitute for strategy, and perceived successes fostered by the numbers game succeeded in providing only the illusion of victory. What it did was to fool many into thinking that air power was winning the war.

Decreased Intellectual Acumen

Imagination and innovation are inimical to managers intent upon efficiency and productivity. The intellectual quality of articles appearing in the *Air University Quarterly Review*, which along with its bimonthly successor the *Air University Review*, served as the Air Force's professional journals, steadily declined in the 1950s and 1960s. The decline in the sophistication of articles signed by higher-ranking officers, particularly general officers, was especially obvious. Early editions of *Air University Quarterly Review* contained articles rich in ideas—some flawed to be sure, but nevertheless vibrant. Generals and colonels proposed and debated emerging air-power concepts and articulated their own thoughts on doctrine, strategy, and other institutional issues.

However, by the mid-1950s this had virtually ceased. In part Secretary of Defense Louis Johnson's Consolidation Directive Number 1, issued in 1949, was to blame. It required that all information from the Pentagon be screened not only for security but also for policy and propriety. The impact was soon evident in the quality of articles published in the *Review*. Articles by general officers (often ghostwritten by their executive officers or aides) rarely—if ever—dealt with substantive issues in a provocative or innovative way. The trend continued until the *Air University Review* was compelled to seek articles written by civilian scholars, who were not subject to censorship by the public-affairs officers. Meanwhile, articles written by officers, especially generals, became increasingly insipid. Gen. Charles A. Gabriel's, "The Air Force: Where We Are and Where We Are Going," and Lt. Gen. James P. McCarthy's "SAC Looks to the Future," appearing in 1984 and 1986 issues of the *Review*, were representative of articles that, while they "tell the Air Force story," also confuse professional writing with public relations.[7]

Doctrinal thinking was hampered by Gen. Curtis E. LeMay's statement before Congress in 1961 that doctrine written in 1935 was still appropriate.[8] One result was that air-power leaders transferred strategic thinking to civilian think tanks like the Air Force-sponsored RAND Corporation. Consequently, when Presidents Kennedy and Johnson turned to their military leaders for a strategy to follow in Vietnam, the generals could not devise one appropriate to the war as perceived by the civilian leaders. Instead of understanding the dynamics of a limited war, air-power leaders sought to refight World War II, a conflict for which the doctrine of strategic bombardment was better suited. In Vietnam, the Air Force along with other services was rarely outfought, but like the other services, it was often *outthought*.

Generic Reasons

Two attributes of air power are generic and beyond the control of the Air Force. First, air power is awesome in its destructive potential, and that is both intimidating and, for airmen, intoxicating. Bombs and missiles, like bolts from Zeus, come from above. Since most Americans know little about air power, aerial warfare inherits many of the same awe-inspiring attributes of the gods. When the Vietnam War dragged on, many Americans looked to air power for a quick way to end the conflict. However, when they were disappointed, they turned rather quickly to an almost opposite point of view—that their Air Force was unleashing its cruel technology on a peaceful and peace-loving people. Hanoi's propaganda apparatus found it easy to promote images of schools, pagodas, churches, hospitals, and dikes obliterated by bombs.[9] When the public's perceptions about air power were skewed, an American strength was turned against itself.

Second, aerial warfare is inherently technical and difficult for most people to understand. While air-power leaders, especially those in the Air Force, had little understanding of the nature of the Vietnam War, civilian leaders at the highest level of the U.S. government had little grasp of the more technical aspects of bombing. Presidents Kennedy and Johnson, for a number of different reasons, were more inclined to seek advice from their civilian staffs than from their generals, even when it came to operational issues such as whether or not to bomb surface-to-air-missile sites.[10] Although these civilians were more politically astute than the generals, men such as Robert McNamara, McGeorge Bundy, and Walt Whitman Rostow were as ignorant of the technical aspects of bombing as Air Force generals seemed to be of its political implications. "The best and the brightest" generally believed air power could work miracles far beyond those attributed to it by the most ardent air-power enthusiasts. To the unschooled, it seemed that if x number of bombs could accomplish y result, 1/10th x would achieve a correspondingly smaller objective. Therefore limited bombing could achieve limited objectives.

Historians, political scientists, economists, and lawyers are not expected to be masters of the art of war. It is understandable that they would not comprehend the factors affecting circular error probable—the percentage of any number of bombs falling within a certain distance of the aiming point—and its relationship to force packaging. Air Force generals by and large understood CEP and force packaging very well, but they were not masters of the art of war because they were incapable of integrating the social, cultural, and political dimensions of the conflict with its military aspects. That was a key factor in structuring the setup that resulted in America's defeat.

The Danger of Unhealthy Myths

After the American Civil War, myths played a role in healing the war's wounds among defeated Southerners. The war had devastated the South, and its people knew the bitterness of total defeat as no Americans (except Native Americans) have before or since. White Southerners invented the myth of a noble cause, in which their glorious dead had perished fighting against tremendous odds. The myth had an element of truth to it, and because most Southerners understood that secession was not only a bad idea to begin with but also a dead issue, it was not, on balance, an unhealthy myth since it helped to heal the wounds of war.

Unhealthy myths are those that serve to excuse or delude. The stab-in-the-back thesis emerged in Germany after the First World War. It held that a combination of Jews, democrats, and Communists betrayed the cause, selling out the German nation and its army by forcing a surrender while the army was holding its own in the field. This myth, devised to cover the shortcomings of Kaiser Wilhelm II and Generals Hindenburg and Ludendorff—the commanders who lost the war—also deluded the nation and was a factor contributing to the failure of the Weimar Republic and the subsequent rise of Adolf Hitler and the Nazis. Likewise, in the post–Vietnam War Air Force, a number of unhealthy myths, including a version of the stab-in-the-back thesis, enforced a kind of institutional self-delusion.

The most-popular and most widely accepted Air Force Vietnam myth is that Linebacker II, the so-called "Christmas Bombing" of December 1972, "won" the war. A corollary to the myth holds that if air power had been used with equal resolve earlier, anytime between 1965 and 1969, the war could have been concluded sooner and on more favorable terms. This line of reasoning has contributed to an "our-hands-were-tied-behind-our-back" thesis similar to the Germany stab-in-the-back thesis that held sway in the German officer corps after World War I. The our-hands-were-tied thesis has dominated thinking about Vietnam in the Air Force because it blames the final outcome on a host of convenient villains: a pernicious press, antiwar activists, and perhaps most disturbingly on "interference" by politicians who "restrained" the military.

As with most myths, there are elements of truth to the one surrounding Linebacker II. Certainly the December 1972 bombing paved the way for a final agreement that allowed the United States to complete its withdrawal from South Vietnam. It also compelled Hanoi to release American prisoners of war. In the euphoria surrounding the signing of the Paris Accords, the withdrawal of the last American troops from the South, and the return of the POWs, there was the illusion of victory. The conclusion that air power delivered that victory appealed to the Air Force.

The Air Force Association led the way in trumpeting the perceived accomplishments of Linebacker II. Editorials in the February, March, and April 1973 editions of *Air Force Magazine*, the official organ of the Air Force Association, praised Linebacker II. Not only was it cast as a vindication of traditional tenets of strategic-bombing doctrine, but it also proved the enduring worth of the manned bomber.[11]

Bolstered by official policy pronouncements and by remarks of high-ranking officers, the myth of Linebacker II gained in prominence. The chairman of the Joint Chiefs of Staff during the Christmas bombings, Adm. Thomas H. Moorer, speaking before the Navy fighter pilots' annual Tail Hook Reunion in Las Vegas on 8 September 1973, stated "airpower, given its day in court after almost a decade of frustration, confirmed its effectiveness as an instrument of national policy in just nine and a half flying days."[12] Retired Air Force general T.R. Milton, lamenting the fall of Saigon in the June 1975 edition of *Air Force Magazine*, stated that the December 1972 bombing of North Vietnam was, "an object lesson in how the war might have been won, and won long ago, if only there had not been such political inhibition."[13] In his book *Airpower in Three Wars*, former 7th Air Force commander, Gen. William W. Momyer, prognosticating about future aerial campaigns, wrote, "An early Linebacker II campaign (with the enforcing threat of subsequent Linebackers) can be strategically decisive if its application is intense, continuous, and focused on the enemy's vital systems."[14] A decade after the end of the American involvement in Vietnam, Milton wrote, "The Christmas bombings of 1972 should have taken place in 1965."[15]

Returning prisoners of war strengthened the myth. Adm. James B. Stockdale wrote of the impact of the bombing, "One look at any Vietnamese officer's face told the whole story. It telegraphed accommodation, hopelessness, remorse, fear. The shock was there; our enemy's will was broken."[16] Brig. Gen. Robinson Risner wrote, "We could see a definite change in the attitude of the Vietnamese. Before they had been defiant . . . But it was a totally different situation with the B-52s."[17] Virtually all the repatriated POWs credited the Christmas bombing with their release. *Post hoc, ergo propter hoc.*

Many air-power enthusiasts shared the feelings of the POWs concerning Linebacker II. They also believed that had Linebacker II been conducted in 1965, the war might have ended then on terms more favorable to the United States and South Vietnam. Although appealing, there are many problems with this position. In 1965, the North Vietnamese would have had much to lose by ending the fighting. Their goals had not been realized, and Washington's demand that Hanoi stop supporting the National Liberation Front and remove its increasingly large number of troops from South Vietnam was unacceptable. Furthermore, the guerrilla war in the South probably would have continued because the Viet Cong, despite claims by Hanoi, was not yet fully controlled by the North Vietnamese.

Additionally, what many hands-tied theorists tend to forget is that by December 1972 America's goals had changed and American troops were headed home. Hanoi, on the other hand, had secured the right to keep a large army in South Vietnam. With time as their ally, the North Vietnamese figured that after the American withdrawal they would eventually win. In December 1972, with most of their military and political objectives won—or at least achievable—it made good sense for Hanoi to sign a peace agreement . . . one that President Nguyen Van Thieu of South Vietnam found absolutely abhorrent.[18] In the end, Linebacker II served very little tactical military purpose other than rearranging the rubble caused by the May through October bombings, dubbed Linebacker I. It was Linebacker I that had jeopardized Hanoi's designs on South Vietnam, not the Christmas bombings.

The Air Force has no monopoly on Vietnam myths. There were myths about air power held by people outside the Air Force that have been perpetuated by those intent on criticizing America's role in Vietnam. Again, Linebacker II looms prominently.

At the time, the press dubbed Linebacker II "the Christmas bombing," and some journalists compared it to firebomb raids on German and Japanese cities during World War II. When one wing of the Bach Mai Hospital was damaged, a cry went up not only from Hanoi but from many quarters of the world press. No one mentioned that the hospital was located close to a primary North Vietnamese fighter base. No one raised the possibility that the damage might have been caused by a stray bomb aimed at the base or suggested that a spent North Vietnamese surface-to-air missile might have fallen on it. Certainly no one made the point that the Air Force *could* have targeted the hospital (which it didn't) since the roof and grounds had been used by antiaircraft guns during Linebacker I.[19]

Indeed, Linebacker II has become as precious to the mythology of those who were in the antiwar movement as it has to many within the Air Force. H. Bruce Franklin, the John Cotton Dana professor of English and American Studies at Rutgers University, stated in a 1988 article in the *American Quarterly*, "During the Christmas bombing of North Vietnam, Hanoi alone was hit with 100,000 tons (of bombs)."[20] His source for this preposterous figure was antiwar activist Gloria Emerson's *Winners and Losers*. Following the footnote trail, one discovers that Emerson's source was an unnamed official in Hanoi.[21] Thus, "somebody in Hanoi said so" becomes sufficient documentation to support an article published in a respected and prestigious American scholarly publication.

Franklin is an avowed Marxist and self-proclaimed Maoist, but even mainstream scholars have occasionally accepted some of the more facile pronouncements concerning Linebacker II. George C. Herring, a highly respected historian and author of *America's Longest War*, used Hanoi's figure of 34 B-52s shot down during Linebacker II rather than the verifiable figure of 15, released by the Air Force.[22] Herring, however, uses correct figures in later editions.

There are other air-power-associated myths precious to the antiwar viewpoint. Nancy Zaroulis and Gerald Sullivan's monumental study of the peace movement, *Who Spoke Up? American Protest against the War in Vietnam, 1963–1975*, published in 1985, stated that "U.S. and South Vietnamese planes dropped *220 million* tons of bombs in the area (around Khe Sanh) during the seventy-seven day siege."[23] No source is cited. In fact the United States dropped 8 million tons of bombs in Indochina between 1962 and 1973, compared with a total of around 4 million tons dropped by all the warring nations in the Second World War.

Myths can be dangerous when they excuse failure or underpin ideology. At the least, as with the numbers reported by Franklin, Zaroulis, and Sullivan, myths promote biased and slanted versions of history. As with the myth that Linebacker II brought North Vietnam to its knees, myths can lead to self-delusion. When historians promote a particular ideological or political bias, their bias can perpetuate misunderstanding and ignorance. When soldiers adhere to myths to support institutional interests, they run risks with potentially greater and more violent consequences.

Victory does not foster the same compulsion for self-examination as defeat. With its institutional eyes fixed firmly on the perceived accomplishments of air power, as typified by Linebacker II, the Air Force returned to the Soviet threat, putting its recent unpleasant Vietnam experience behind it. The "party line" espoused by public affairs officers was comforting; when the last Air Force units pulled out of South Vietnam (not Thailand) in 1973, the Republic of Vietnam was still an independent nation. Whatever lessons the Air Force sought were tactically oriented and technologically applicable—for example, fighters need an internally mounted gun, outstanding maneuverability, and a bubble canopy for better vision. For too many airmen, the Air Force role in Vietnam nestled in their memories as an unbroken string of victories marred only by "political constraints that kept us from winning." It seemed indelicate to ask why a disproportionate number of Air Force heroes from the Vietnam War were airmen who had been shot down and held captive.

At best, America's war in Vietnam was morally ambiguous and not amenable to textbook solutions propounded by members of a bureaucratic technocracy. Perhaps that is why the study of the Vietnam War was slighted at the Air War College and the Air Command and Staff College, two of the professional military education (PME) schools at Air University, located at Maxwell Air Force Base, Alabama. From 1974 through 1979, the Air War College, the Air Force's premier PME school for specially selected senior officers, devoted only 2.5 hours of study to the Vietnam War in a case study entitled "TACAIR in Vietnam." Not surprisingly, it focused on the role of air power in Linebackers I and II. That block of instruction comprised 1.4 percent of the 172 hours devoted to studying "general purpose force employment." The same amount of time was allotted for studying air power during the six-day Arab-Israeli War of 1967.[24]

Air Command and Staff College, a 10-month long course for majors, offered its first elective on the Vietnam War in 1983, but that year it was cancelled because fewer than 10 officers (out of more than 500 attending the school) signed up. By contrast, courses on family financial planning, personal computers, and physical fitness were packed.[25]

Despite publication of some excellent official histories by officers assigned to the Office of Air Force History, no serving Air Force officer wrote a book comparable to the many fine books on Vietnam written by U.S. Army officers—until Maj. Mark Clodfelter's *The Limits of Air Power: The American Bombing of North Vietnam* (1989). The Air War College took a step in the right direction when it made the book mandatory reading. Still, it had taken nearly two decades for a serving Air Force officer to write a book critical of the way that service fought the war.[26]

Sadly, few Air Force officers in the 1970s and 1980s read history books. That fact was reflected in the service doctrine manuals, the Air Force's "officially sanctioned beliefs" about the way air power should be used. The current version (dated 1984) of Air Force Manual 1-1, *Basic Aerospace Doctrine*, lists the Strategic Aerospace Offensive as the Air Force's first mission and defines this as the ability "to neutralize or to destroy the enemy's war-sustaining capabilities or will to fight . . . through the systematic application of force to a selected series of vital targets."[27] The strategic planners and operations officers who devised the 94-targets list would have been comfortable with this manual. Incredibly, the manual for tactical operations, AFM 2-1, was not revised between 1969 and 1989.

In Vietnam, what confounded America's primary strength—air power—was that it was used in measured doses over time to pursue limited objectives. Air Power leaders, accustomed to thinking of warfare in terms of either a Warsaw Pact versus NATO scenario or a final nuclear face-off against the Soviet Union, could not devise a strategy appropriate to the war at hand under the conditions dictated by political leaders. Furthermore, the commitment of the North Vietnamese and their Viet Cong allies to objectives that were more total in nature provided them with the moral strength needed to outlast the United States. Given their willingness to fight for an exceedingly long time if necessary, the Vietnamese were able to turn America's advantage in military resources against itself. In the end. dropping 8 million tons of bombs was no substitute for a coherent strategy. Not only that, it subverted America's moral position, fostered national and international disapprobation, and eventually crippled America's ability to maintain its proxy-state regimes in Indochina. Despite the enormous expenditure of firepower, the level of violence employed was neither sufficient nor well-focused enough to secure a successful outcome. Short of the total obliteration of North Vietnam, something that was quite properly never considered by America's leadership, it is unlikely any level of aerial firepower short of an all-out nuclear attack would have sufficed. In the final analysis, however, the war was not America's to win or lose. It was South Vietnam's war. Perhaps the final tragedy was inevitable from the day that the United States created the Republic of Vietnam.

The ambiguities of the Vietnam War remain. What is more certain is that warfare is more than sortie generation and firepower on targets. It incorporates many factors, including some that are traditionally considered beyond the purview of the soldier, such as politics and economics. But geography, the weather, and the many aspects of culture— one's own as well as the enemy's—are factors that determine the way nations fight their wars. Above all, warfare, especially limited warfare, is an art. As such, it requires intellectual sophistication, mental dexterity, and the ability to think abstractly.

The setup may not yet be complete. Potential adversaries, in places as diverse as Central America, the Korean peninsula, and the Middle East, will bring their individual dynamic to the battlefield. If the Air Force is to perform successfully within the context of national objectives, its leaders must become masters of the art of war. As long as air power enthusiasts cling to Linebacker II as evidence to support the hallowed doctrine of strategic bombing, what history can teach them about Vietnam and air power will go unlearned.

Notes

1. Thomas C. Thayer, *War without Fronts: The American War in Vietnam* (Boulder, Colo.: Westview, 1985), 26 and 37.

2. Raphael Littauer and Norman Uphoff, eds., *The Air War in Indochina* (Boston: Beacon Press, 1971), 11; and Carl Berger, ed., *The United States Air Force in Southeast Asia: An Illustrated Account* (Washington, D.C.: Office of Air Force History, 1984), 135.

3. Thomas K. Finletter, is quoted in Robert F. Futrell, *Ideas, Concepts, Doctrine: A History of Basic Thinking in the United States Air Force, 1907–1964* (Maxwell Air Force Base, Ala.: Air University Press, 1974), 147.

4. See Mark Clodfelter, *The Limits of Air Power: The American Bombing of North Vietnam* (New York: Free Press, 1989), 166; and Melvin F. Porter, *Linebacker: Overview of the First 120 Days*, Project CHECO (Honolulu: Headquarters, Pacific Air Forces, 27 September 1973), 45–52 (in the Air Force Historical Research Center, Maxwell AFB, Ala., File No. K717.0414-42).

5. Air Force and U.S. Army squabbling over roles and missions was intense during the advisory period of American involvement, from 1962 to 1965. In 1963, the director of Air Force Plans, Headquarters, U.S. Air Force noted, "It may be improper to say that we are at war with the Army. However, we believe that if the Army efforts are successful, they may have a long term effect on the U.S. military posture that could be more important than the battle presently being waged with the Viet Cong." See Robert F. Futrell, *The United States Air Force in Southeast Asia: The Advisory Years to 1965* (Washington, D.C.: Office of Air Force History, 1983), 148.

6. (Lt. Col.) Charles E. Trumbo, Jr., interview with J. Grainger [Director of Plans, 2d Air Division] 13 July 1963, Air Force Historical Research Center, Maxwell Air Force Base, Alabama, File No. K526.54-2.

7. See: (Gen.) Charles A. Gabriel, "The Air Force: Where We Are and Where We Are Going?" *Air University Review* 35, 2 (January/February 1984): 2–10; and (Lt. Gen.) James P. McCarthy, "SAC Looks to the Future," *Air University Review* 38, 1 (January/March 1987): 13–23.

8. LeMay is quoted in Futrell, *Ideas, Concepts, Doctrine*, 405.

9. Many American scholars and journalists were duped by Hanoi's propaganda. For an excellent example, see Harrison E. Salisbury, *Behind Enemy Lines—Hanoi: December 23, 1966–January 7, 1967* (New York: Harper & Row, 1967); almost any page will do.

10. See *The Pentagon Papers: The Defense Department History of the United States Decision Making on Vietnam*, (Sen. Mike Gravel edition) vol. 4 (Boston: Beacon Press, 1975), 24; and John Morrocco, *The Vietnam Experience: Thunder from Above, Air War, 1941–1968* (Boston: Boston Publishing, 1984), 107.

11. See John L. Frisbee, "The Phoenix That Never Was," *Air Force Magazine* 56, 2 (February 1973): 4; John L. Frisbee, "Not with a Whimper, But a Bang," *Air Force Magazine* 56, 3 (March 1973): 5–6; and Martin W. Rostow, "The B-52's Message to Moscow," *Air Force Magazine* 56, 4 (April 1973): 2.

12. Moorer's remarks were reprinted in *Air Force Magazine* 56, 11 (November 1973): 2.

13. (Gen.) T.R. Milton, (U.S. Air Force, Ret.), "USAF and the Vietnam Experience," *Air Force Magazine* 58, 6 (June 1975): 56. The tendency to blame civilian political leaders for "tying the hands" of the military through imposing "political constraints" is pervasive in the American military, especially the Air Force. Air-power advocates

tend to separate military operations from political considerations. They need to consider that whenever air power, with its awesome implications for destruction, is factored into the equation, political considerations will be as well and that operational decisions have to be constantly recalculated to accommodate political realities. Among kinds of military operations, the use of air power carries the most political baggage.

14. (Gen.) William W. Momyer, (U.S. Air Force, Ret.), *Airpower in Three Wars* (Washington, D.C.: GPO, 1978), 339.

15. (Gen.) T.R. Milton, (U.S. Air Force, Ret.), "The Lessons of Vietnam," *Air Force Magazine* 66, 3 (March 1983): 110.

16. Jim and Sybil Stockdale, *In Love and War: The Story of a Family's Ordeal and Sacrifice during the Vietnam Years* (New York: Harper & Row, 1986), 432.

17. Robinson Risner, *The Passing of the Night: My Seven Years as a Prisoner of War of the North Vietnamese* (New York: Random House, 1973), 237. In the years after the end of the Vietnam War, the repatriated POWs were accorded the status of heroes – which indeed they were. However, their contention that the Christmas bombing had secured their release by "bringing the enemy to their knees" was accepted as an unassailable article of truth. No one, and quite understandably so, made the point that their perspectives on the war were narrowly confined to their prison cells, and that fear on the face of guards did not necessarily mean that Hanoi's leadership shared the same trepidation.

18. Nguyen Tien Hung and Jerrold L. Schecter, *The Palace File* (New York: Harper & Row, 1986), 196–204.

19. Hays Parks, "Linebacker and the Law of War," *Air University Review* 34, 2 (January/February 1983): 25.

20. H. Bruce Franklin, "How American Management Won the War in Vietnam," *American Quarterly* 40, 3 (Summer 1988) 423.

21. Gloria Emerson, *Winners and Losers: Battles, Retreats, Gains, Losses, and Ruins From a Long War* (New York: Random House, 1976), 42.

22. George C. Herring, *America's Longest War: The United States in Vietnam, 1950–1975* (New York: Random House, 1979), 248. Beginning with the 1986 edition, Herring uses the Department of Defense figure of 15 B-52s shot down during Linebacker II.

23. Nancy Zaroulis and Gerald Sullivan, *Who Spoke Up? American Protest against the War in Vietnam, 1963–1975* (New York: Holt, Rinehart, & Winston, 1984), 151. Zaroulis and Sullivan also state that 100,000 tons of bombs fell on North Vietnam during Linebacker II but claim it took only 5 days for the Air Force to drop that tonnage, not 11. No source is given (p. 396).

24. (Maj.) Suzanne Budd Gehri, *Study War Once More: Teaching Vietnam at Air University* (Maxwell Air Force Base, Ala.: Air University Press, 1985), 6. The Air War College did not begin offering a Vietnam War elective until 1987.

25. The author began offering electives on the Vietnam War at the Air Command and Staff College in 1983. Although the first class was cancelled, subsequent classes were filled.

26. Col. Jack Broughton, an F-105 pilot during Rolling Thunder, the air campaign against North Vietnam from March 1965 through October 1968, published *Thud Ridge* (Phil-

adelphia: Lippencott, 1969) immediately after his forced retirement. Broughton criticized the Johnson administration and Secretary of Defense Robert S. McNamara for their "interference" in operational matters. His second book about the air war, *Going Downtown: The War Against Hanoi and Washington* (New York: Orion, 1988), retains the "our hands were tied behind our back" thesis, but Broughton directs some of the blame at Air Force leaders for not understanding the nature of the Vietnam War. He is particularly hard on former Commander in Chief of the Strategic Air Command, Gen. Jack Ryan and Gen. John Vogt, who, some years after Broughton retired, became commander of 7th Air Force. Colonel Broughton waited until after his retirement before writing critically about the Air Force's role in Vietnam. Major Clodfelter—most courageously—wrote *The Limits of Air Power* while still serving in the Air Force.

27. AFM 1-1, *Basic Aerospace Doctrine*, 16 March 1984, 3-2.

Journal of Interdisciplinary History, xxix:2 (Autumn, 1998), 243–262.

Scott Sigmund Gartner

Differing Evaluations of Vietnamization

You know that an attack is "just a probe" only after it is over.

Tobias Wolff, *In Pharoah's Army: Memories of the Lost War*

Research on wartime behavior has grown substantially in recent years, analyzing domestic politics and war, battlefield effectiveness, war duration and expansion, and strategic choices. Critical to many of these studies is the notion that leaders evaluate the possible ramifications of policies and act on their assessments. Applying this type of analytical approach to the controversial Vietnam War decision of Vietnamization has important implications both for our understanding of this particular war and war in general.[1]

President Nixon's administration initiated Vietnamization in 1969 to alter how the war was fought in order to decrease us losses and shift the burden of fighting to the South Vietnamese. Although Vietnamization clearly led to the withdrawal of us troops, and a subsequent decrease in us casualties, there is no systematic analysis of the effectiveness of Vietnamization in obtaining two other military objectives that the Nixon administra-

Scott Sigmund Gartner is Associate Professor of Political Science, University of California, Davis. He is the author of *Strategic Assessment in War* (New Haven, 1997); co-author, with Marissa Edson Myers, of "Body Counts and 'Success' in the Vietnam and Korean Wars," *Journal of Interdisciplinary History,* XXV (1995), 377–395.

This research was funded in part by a grant from the National Science Foundation, SBER-9511527. The University of California, Davis, Institute of Governmental Affairs and Social Science Data Service, also provided assistance. The author would like to thank Bethany Barratt, Diane Felmlee, Christopher Gelpi, Robert Jackman, Michael Koch, Russell Leng, Randolph Siverson, Gary Segura, and James Spriggs for their helpful comments.

© 1998 by the Massachusetts Institute of Technology and the editors of *The Journal of Interdisciplinary History.*

1 For a discussion of war outcomes, see Allan Stam, *Win Lose or Draw* (Ann Arbor, 1996); Gartner and Randolph M. Siverson, "War Expansion and War Outcome," *Journal of Conflict Resolution,* XL (1996), 4–15. About battlefield effectiveness, see Dan Reiter and Stam, "Democracy and Battlefield Military Effectiveness," *ibid.,* XLII (1998), 259–277. For an example of the impact of duration, see Scott Bennett and Stam, "The Duration of Interstate Wars, 1816–1985," *American Political Science Review,* XC (1996), 239–257. For studies of war expansion, see Patrick Regan, "Conditions of Successful Third Party Intervention in Interstate Conflicts," *Journal of Conflict Resolution,* XL (1996), 336–359; Alastair Smith, "To Intervene

tion sought: (1) reducing the levels of lethality faced by American troops, and (2) changing the relationship between US and South Vietnamese forces in conducting the war. Assessment of these two goals is especially important given the conflicting conclusions reached by American wartime officials and subsequent historical accounts about the military impact of Vietnamization.

Employing a variety of statistical analyses of quantitative data—a primary source for American decision makers during the war—this article shows that Vietnamization had a more substantial impact on the fighting than historical accounts commonly recognize. Vietnamization affected the relationship between US and South Vietnamese forces fundamentally. Vietnamization did more than just lead to the withdrawal of troops from Vietnam; it changed the basic structure of the war. Most important, according to the measures that American decision makers preferred at the time, it was reasonable to conclude that Vietnamization was working.

This article has two goals. The first is to tell a story about the military consequences of Vietnamization that is not well known. To borrow Leng's words, the method deploys quantitative data to "come as close as possible to the detailed description . . . afforded by qualitative studies, without losing the advantages in reliability and replicability that come from operationally defined procedures." Quantitative data can manifest a pattern previously unnoticed by historical analysis in a way that facilitates replication and constructive critique.[2]

The second goal is to reconcile the evaluations of Vietnamization by contemporary American officials and later historical

---

or Not to Intervene: A Biased Decision," *ibid.*, XL (1996), 4–15. For examples of studies about the impact of strategy, see Gartner, *Strategic Assessment in War* (New Haven, 1997); Reiter, *Crucible of Beliefs: Learning, World Wars and Alliances* (Ithaca, 1996). For studies analyzing the nexus of domestic politics and war, see Gartner and Gary M. Segura, "War, Casualties, and Public Opinion," *Journal of Conflict Resolution*, XLII (1998), 278–300; *idem* and Michael Wilkening, "All Politics Are Local: Local Losses and Individual Attitudes Towards the Vietnam War," *ibid.*, XLI (1997), 669–694; Bruce Bueno de Mesquita and Siverson, "War and the Survival of Political Leaders: A Comparative Study of Regime Types and Political Accountability," *American Political Science Review*, LXXXIX (1995), 841–855; *idem* and Gary Woller, "War and the Fate of Regimes: A Comparative Analysis," *ibid.*, LXXXVI (1992), 638–646.

2 Russell J. Leng, *Interstate Crisis Behavior, 1916–1980: Realism Versus Reciprocity* (Cambridge 1993), 25.

accounts. The quantitative data on which many officials relied to evaluate policy effectiveness have remained largely unexamined by postwar scholars. Employing different criteria and sources of information, scholars and officials reached different conclusions.[3]

The claim is *not* that the quantitative data collected during the war were accurate, that they represented the sole means of evaluation, or that they were immune to manipulation in order to justify unpopular decisions. Nor is it that the United States "won" the war, or that Vietnamization was an unrecognized "success." Nonetheless, the operational data that influenced many decision makers testifies to facts about Vietnamization that the larger political issue of South Vietnam's defeat has obscured.

CONFLICTING EVALUATIONS OF VIETNAMIZATION   What did Vietnamization accomplish? For one thing, it allowed Nixon to continue an unpopular war and achieve a landslide reelection in 1972. Yet, on April 30, 1975, communist forces decisively defeated the Army of the Republic of Vietnam (ARVN) and toppled the South Vietnamese government. These most obvious, and conflicting, results of Vietnamization are reflected by the opposing evaluations of the policy's effectiveness in contemporary and historical accounts.

During the war, many American officials viewed Vietnamization positively. On April 17, 1971, Nixon declared, "Vietnamization has succeeded." The military shared this positive position. In a 1974 survey of all generals in the United States Army who had served in Vietnam, 58 percent agreed that the Vietnamization program was soundly conceived, and 36 percent conditionally agreed. Only 6 percent disagreed. In the same study, 73 percent of the generals stated that Vietnamization was so effective that it should have been implemented earlier.[4]

---

3 Studies that note the importance of quantitative indicators for those who made decisions concerning the Vietnam War include Alain C. Enthoven and K. Wayne Smith, *How Much Is Enough: Shaping the Defense Program, 1961–1969* (New York, 1971); Guenther Lewy, *America in Vietnam* (New York, 1978); Thomas C. Thayer, *War Without Fronts: The American Experience in Vietnam* (Boulder, 1985); James J. Wirtz, *The Tet Offensive: Intelligence Failure in War* (Ithaca, 1991); Deborah Avant, *Political Institutions and Military Change* (Ithaca, 1994); Gartner, *Strategic Assessment.*
4 Philip Davidson, *Vietnam at War: The History 1946–1975* (New York, 1988), 660; Douglas Kinnard, *The War Managers* (Wayne, N.J., 1977), 144, 145.

Others outside the government and the military echoed this view. In a 1970 Rand report on Vietnamization, Pauker, who had opposed US policies toward South Vietnam from 1955 to 1969, argued that the United States "may have accomplished a feat of political alchemy," making the government of South Vietnam politically viable. Herring wrote, "Vietnamization was in full swing by early 1970, and most observers agreed that significant gains had been made."[5]

As the war continued, evidence mounted that Vietnamization was having its effect. Many argued that North Vietnam launched the 1972 Easter Offensive—the first large-scale invasion of South Vietnam by the North Vietnamese Army (Tet, in the winter of 1968, had involved indigenous Vietcong guerrillas)—out of fear that "Vietnamization was succeeding" and that the government of South Vietnam was increasing its control over the countryside. Hence, the Offensive was meant to "cripple the Vietnamization effort." The ARVN's actions during the Easter Offensive strengthened this assessment. After the ARVN stopped the largest communist attack since Tet, US Defense Secretary Melvin Laird declared that the ARVN's military performance was "astonishingly successful." Despite general concerns about the poor leadership and widespread corruption in the ARVN, and regrets that Vietnamization had not been implemented earlier, a widespread view among generals, politicians, and scholars was that Vietnamization had altered conditions on the battlefield beyond the mere withdrawal of US troops.[6]

This perspective was shattered by events in the spring of 1975 and the rapid defeat of South Vietnam. The speed of the North Vietnamese conquest left little doubt that the ARVN and the government of South Vietnam were weaker than had been previously perceived. The manifestations of these weaknesses, which challenged the earlier claims of effectiveness, are evident in postwar evaluations of Vietnamization.

5   Ibid., 146; George Herring, America's Longest War: The United States and Vietnam: 1950–1975 (New York, 1979), 226.
6   Kinnard, War Managers, 148; George D. Moss, Vietnam: An American Ordeal (Englewood Cliffs, 1990), 331; Stanley Karnow, Vietnam: A History (New York, 1991), 657. Karnow also notes that Melvin Laird "had a vested interest in seeing Vietnamization work" and that Nixon was "privately glum" about the situation. Robert Pape suggests that it was the interaction between US airpower and the North Vietnamese Army strategy that lead to the United States' success in Bombing to Win: Airpower and Coercion in War (Ithaca, 1996).

Most postwar analysts emphatically deny the military accomplishments of Vietnamization. They considered Vietnamization a sham, designed largely to masquerade the unilateral withdrawal of US forces necessitated by the antiwar movement in the United States. Moss stated that Vietnamization "rested on a fantasy"—a failure that repeatedly "flunked" the test. Davidson called Nixon's claim that Vietnamization was having a positive impact "an Orwellian untruth of boggling proportion."[7]

ANALYZING THE IMPACT OF VIETNAMIZATION   The Nixon administration intended Vietnamization to alter the military nature of the Vietnam War by decreasing US casualties and preparing the ARVN to bear the brunt of the fighting. These military goals were intended to mesh with the political goal of creating a more popular and stable government in South Vietnam. Although many of the ideas behind Vietnamization originated with Lyndon Johnson's administration, the Nixon administration was responsible for expanding the conception and implementing the policy, as well as for coining the term.[8]

The effort to decrease US casualties was primarily a response to domestic dissent from the left, but it also touched on a concern of the right. Similar to the Republicans who supported Douglas MacArthur during the Korean War, members of the Nixon administration increasingly came to believe that a war of attrition against an Asian power was a mistake, because Asians were willing to tolerate higher casualties than the United States, or any other Western power, would. MacArthur wrote that countries like China and North Korea displayed "gross indifference to human loss." Likewise, John Foster Dulles expressed caution about getting involved in wars of attrition with Asian countries that were "glutted with manpower." The Nixon administration was eventually convinced that the North Vietnamese were insensitive to casualties. A conference chaired by Henry Kissinger in early 1969 determined that dramatic and deadly military actions "might not

7 Tom Wells, *The War Within: America's Battle Over Vietnam* (New York, 1994); James William Gibson, *The Perfect War: Techno-War in Vietnam* (Boston, 1986); Michael Maclear, *The Ten Thousand Day War, Vietnam: 1945–1974* (New York, 1981); Timothy J. Lomperis, *The War Everyone Lost—and Won* (Washington, D.C., 1984); Moss, *Vietnam*, 307, 337; Davidson, *Vietnam at War*, 660.
8 *Ibid.*, 601; Wells, *War Within*.

force concessions from Hanoi." In a widely circulated analysis of North Vietnamese documents that same year, McGarvey stated that North Vietnam "regards any cost in Communist lives as bearable so long as a sufficient number of casualties are inflicted on the enemy." Although official, racially attributed valuations of human life, such as that written by MacArthur, were rarer during the Vietnam war, similar concerns became popular in the Nixon administration.[9]

In April 1969, Kissinger ordered Richard Helms, William Rogers, and Laird to prepare "timetables for transferring combat roles to South Vietnamese forces, and restricting the US role to combat support and advisory missions." Vietnamization was born on July 1, 1969. Decision makers employed quantitative measures to assess its three central military objectives: (1) to decrease the rate of US losses; (2) to decrease the lethality, or risk of death, for Americans serving in Vietnam; and (3) to make the ARVN the primary combatant against the communists.[10]

OBJECTIVES 1 AND 2: REDUCING AMERICAN CASUALTIES   The new Nixon Administration wanted to decrease the salience of the war. One way to do so was to decrease lethality, and the risk of lethality, for the soldiers who remained in Vietnam. Nixon believed that American casualties eroded public support and later studies supported the notion. As Figure 1 shows, monthly American casualty figures fell dramatically after the implementation of Vietnamization. In this respect, Vietnamization had a significant impact.[11]

Although this decrease in US monthly casualties is well known, the second objective—decreasing the risk of death faced

---

9 Douglas MacArthur, *Reminiscences* (New York, 1964), 387; Robert J. Art and Kenneth N. Waltz, *The Use of Force* (Lanham, 1988), 100; Herring, *America's Longest War*, 250; John Mueller, "The Search for the 'Breaking Point' in Vietnam: The Statistics of a Deadly Quarrel," in Bruce Russett, Harvey Starr, and Richard J. Stoll (eds.), *Choices in World Politics: Sovereignty and Independence* (New York, 1989), 88. Popular works on Vietnam include a great deal of discussion about the role of race. See for example, Philip Caputo, *A Rumor of War* (New York, 1996).

10 Jeffrey T. Richelson (project director), *Presidential Directives on National Security: From Truman to Clinton* (Washington D.C., 1994), 284; Kinnard, *War Managers*.

11 Mueller, *War Presidents and Public Opinion* (New York, 1973); Gartner, Segura, and Wilkening, "All Politics Are Local"; Gartner and Segura, "War, Casualties and Public Opinion."

Fig. 1 Monthly Number of Americans Killed in Action during the Vietnam War

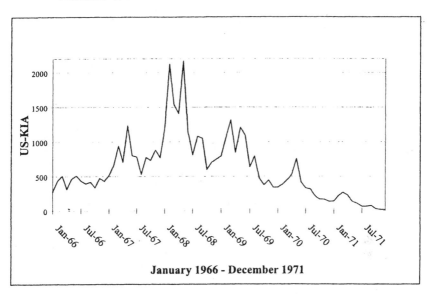

January 1966 - December 1971

by American troops—has been left unexamined. All else being equal, decreasing the number of troops at risk necessarily entails a reduction in the number of deaths. But was all else held equal? In particular, did Vietnamization alter the likelihood that an individual American serving in Vietnam would be killed?

After Vietnamization, the probability that an individual American in Vietnam would die in combat decreased significantly. The ratio of US-KIA (killed in action) to American troop levels—US-KIA/US-TROOP—as shown in Figure 2, drops after the implementation of Vietnamization. Note that this decrease occurred despite the rapid rate of withdrawal of US forces that accompanied Vietnamization. An analysis of variance (ANOVA) comparison of the value of the ratio before and after the implementation of Vietnamization generates an F value of 81.5 and a significance of .0001, strongly suggesting that the likelihood of an American soldier dying in Vietnam significantly decreased after Vietnamization. In other words, Vietnamization not only reduced the total number of deaths by shrinking the baseline of American soldiers at risk; it also altered the way that the war was fought. US soldiers

Fig. 2 Ratio of Monthly US–KIA and Troops Levels during the Vietnam War

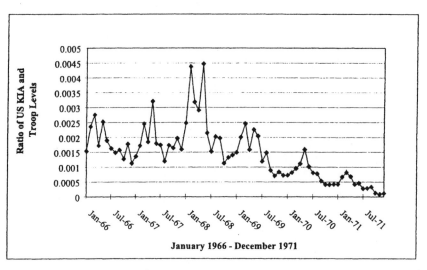

January 1966 - December 1971

were less likely to die in combat if they served after Vietnamization.

OBJECTIVE 3: CHANGING THE CONDUCT OF THE WAR   Vietnamization proposed to modernize and improve the South Vietnamese military so that it might take primary responsibility for the fighting, allowing US forces to switch roles from combatant to ARVN supporter. These changes were designed to alter the war's structure. Prior to Vietnamization, US forces conducted search and destroy operations against North Vietnamese and Viet Cong main force units. The ARVN operated separately, within the "shield" supposedly formed by the US efforts. Essentially, two wars were taking place, the main one—the US forces against the communists—and the minor one—the ARVN against the communists—with little coordination between the two.

As represented in Figure 3, Vietnamization attempted to implement a one-war situation, in which the beefed-up ARVN would fight the communists and the United States would support and advise it.[12]

12   Nguyen Duy Hinh, *Vietnamization and the Cease-Fire* (Washington, D.C., 1980).

Fig. 3 From Two Wars to One

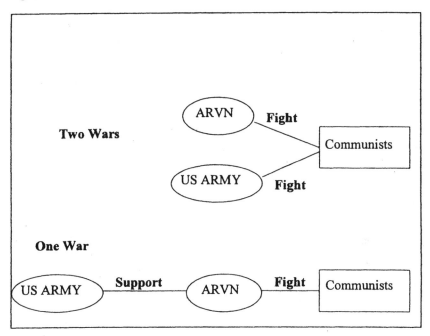

Such a shift should manifest measurable changes in the operational variables traced by US leaders during the war—for example, casualties, sorties, troop levels, and weapons captured. Note that variables such as ARVN casualties or US troop levels did not *cause* US casualties. Rather, they are visible indicators of the nonobservable factors that influenced how the war was fought.[13]

Prior to Vietnamization, when US and ARVN forces fought independently, units from both militaries might be involved in a battle and might incur casualties at a similar rate (although the respective absolute losses might vary, and smaller attacks might involve only units from one military). Since the communists frequently attacked in spring, casualties for both US and ARVN forces tended to increase during that season. Similarly, the Tet Offensive resulted in significantly higher casualties for both coun-

13 Avant, *Political Institutions;* Gartner and Melissa Edson Myers, "Body Counts and 'Success' in the Vietnam and Korean Wars," *Journal of Interdisciplinary History,* XXV (1995), 377–395; Thayer, *War Without Fronts;* Samuel Lipsman and Edward Doyle, *The Vietnam Experience: Fighting for Time* (Boston, 1983), 50; Hinh, *Vietnamization.*

tries. In the two-war scenario, communist attacks should reveal positive correlations in US and ARVN casualty rates.

The single-war scenario of Vietnamization, however, should show a counter-pressure on this positive relationship. Although communist attacks still inflicted casualties on both the ARVN and US armies, ARVN forces, not US forces, were often the primary combatants, allowing the US military to take a supporting role through artillery and air power. The US infantry, which incurred the most American casualties, would be deployed only when ARVN forces were either unavailable or insufficient to meet a threat. As Hinh stated, "whenever US units suspended combat activities and prepared to leave, the RVNAF [ARVN] immediately made an effort to take over and strove hard to maintain security and the continuance of the pacification effort." This alteration changed the correlation of such operational variables as US- and ARVN-KIA.[14]

Many of the factors that caused US-KIA prior to Vietnamization—for example, large-scale communist attacks that involved both US and ARVN troops—remained after Vietnamization, still causing US and ARVN deaths to be positively associated. Thus, even if Vietnamization was able to change the underlying structure of the war, US- and ARVN-KIA figures are not necessarily correlated negatively. But, if Vietnamization were effective, the relationship of US and ARVN fatalities should become significantly *less positively* correlated.

The analysis of the impact of Vietnamization on the structure of the war takes two forms: first, a bivariate ordinary-least-squares (OLS) regression between monthly US- and ARVN-KIA between January 1966 and December 1971, during which 93 percent of all US fatalities in the Vietnam War occurred. The results are shown in Table 1. ARVN-KIA is positively correlated with US-KIA. The coefficient of .28 is highly significant: For each ARVN death between 1966 and 1971, .28 Americans died. Put differently, slightly more than three ARVN soldiers died for each American soldier.[15]

In order to determine whether this relationship was constant throughout the war, Figure 4 shows the residuals (the difference between the predcicted and observed values) of the regression

14   *Ibid.,* 64.
15   The data in Table 1 were taken from "Unclassified Statistics on Southeast Asia," published by the Comptroller, Office of the Secretary of Defense, and reprinted in Raphael Littauer and Norman Uphoff (eds.), *The Air War in Indochina* (Boston, 1972), 267–272.

Table 1 US-KIA by Month in the Vietnam War—Bivariate Analysis

	MODEL I	
	COEFFICIENT	t
VARIABLE NAME	(STANDARD ERROR)	$(P > t)$
ARVN-KIA	.284	4.511
	(.063)	(.001)
Constant	136.547	1.186
	(115.131)	(.240)
$N = 72$	Adjusted $R^2 = .21$	

plotted over the seventy-two months analyzed. The residuals vary in a clear pattern, suggesting that a bivariate analysis of US- and ARVN-KIA provides a biased estimate. The positive residuals at the beginning of the war mean that the model underestimates US deaths, and the negative residuals toward the end of the war mean that the model overestimates them. The error term crosses the x axis (moving from under- to overestimating) at approximately the start of Vietnamization (July 1969), suggesting that the relationship between US- and ARVN-KIAS—and, thus, the manner in which the war was fought—systematically changed after Vietnamization. Although the pattern of the error term suggests that Vietnamization altered the structure of the war, systematic error terms are common in bivariate analyses, calling for a more sophisticated examination.[16]

The second analysis includes five modifications: First is a dummy variable to designate the time period after Vietnamization (VIETNAMIZATION), and second—since the question of whether the relationship between ARVN and US fatalities changed after the implementation of Vietnamization is crucial—an interactive term multiplying ARVN-KIA by VIETNAMIZATION. This term captures the independent effect of ARVN fatalities on US casualties following the implementation of Vietnamization.

Third, the analysis includes American troop levels to test whether the number of American troops was positively correlated (as Vietnamization proponents claimed, and earlier analysis indi-

---

16   All analyses were conducted in the statistical program, Stata. Tests are two-tailed.

Fig. 4 US- and ARVN-KIA Bivariate Residuals

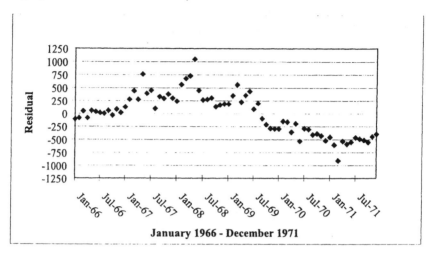

cated) with the rate of US-KIA after controlling for other factors. Since troop levels identify the population at risk, they help to form a baseline of possible US fatalities. The number of American troops in Vietnam is also important for controlling values of the error term that might occur because of extreme variations in the size of the American contingent there. Fourth, as suggested by Thayer, the analysis controls for seasonal effects.[17]

Finally, instead of OLS, a Cochrane-Orcutt regression was run because tests suggested that serial auto-correlation was a problem. In such time series data, unidentified factors at time *t* are likely to have a predictable influence on behavior at time *t* + *1*. Unless controlled for, serial auto-correlation can lead to an underestimation of the error term (and the incorrect inference that a coefficient is statistically significant). Unlike the systematic variance showed in the earlier plot of the residuals, however, serial auto-correlation does not create biased estimators. The Cochrane-Orcutt procedure, which attempts to control for the potential underestimation of the error term through the construction of an

17 The United States' Southeast Asia Casualties file contains casualties from 1957 (advisors) to 1990. After 1973, additions include those initially believed to be missing in action and later determined to be dead. Analysis of the entire period would not be appropriate since this study concentrates on decision making between 1965 and 1973.

error-correction factor called RHO, provides unbiased and more efficient results.

Model 2 is presented in equation 1:

$$US\text{-}KIA = \beta_1 ARVN\text{-}KIA + \beta_2 VIETNAMIZATION$$
$$+ \beta_3 ARVN\text{-}KIA \times VIETNAMIZATION + \beta_4 US\text{-}TROOP$$
$$+ \beta_5 SPRING + \beta_0 \qquad (1)$$

US-KIA is the monthly number of Americans killed in action; ARVN-KIA represents the monthly number of ARVN forces killed in action; VIETNAMIZATION is a dummy variable that is a one after July 1969 and a zero before; ARVN-KIA × VIETNAMIZATION is the interactive term ARVN-KIA times VIETNAMIZATION; US-TROOP represents the American troop strength measured biannually; SPRING is a seasonality control that captures the communist offensives that occurred regularly in March, April, and May; and β_0 represents the constant. Give the multiplicative nature of equation 1, when analyzed, it breaks down into two separate equations, one for pre-Vietnamization (2a) and the other for post-Vietnamization (2b):

$$US\text{-}KIA = \beta_1 ARVN\text{-}KIA + \beta_4 US\text{-}TROOP + \beta_5 SPRING + \beta_0 \quad (2a)$$

$$US\text{-}KIA = (\beta_1 + \beta_3)(ARVN\text{-}KIA) + \beta_4 US\text{-}TROOP + \beta_5 SPRING$$
$$+ (\beta_2 + \beta_0) \qquad (2b)$$

The results from the statistical analysis of equation 1 are shown in Table 2 as Model 2.[18]

The results strongly suggest that Vietnamization changed the way that the US and ARVN forces fought together. As expected, prior to Vietnamization, US-KIA and ARVN-KIA vary together positively. When the other factors are controlled for, the pre-Vietnamization effect of ARVN-KIA on US-KIA is .38, compared with a bivariate coefficient of .28 for the entire war. However, the

18   The closer the Durbin-Watson coefficient in Model 2 is to 2.0, the less evident are auto-correlation problems. See A. H. Studenmund, *Using Econometrics: A Practical Guide* (New York, 1992). The Durbin-Watson statistic for Model 2 (using a Cochrane-Orcutt technique) is 1.97, suggesting that auto-correlation is not a problem. The Durbin-Watson statistic on Model 2 run without the Cochrane-Orcutt technique is 1.05, strongly suggesting the presence of serial auto-correlation (results not shown). All of the equations exclude the presentation of error terms.

Table 2 US Killed in Action by Month during the Vietnam War— Multivariate Analysis

VARIABLE NAME	MODEL 2		MODEL 3	
	COEFFICIENT (STANDARD ERROR)	t $(P > t)$	COEFFICIENT (STANDARD ERROR)	t $(P > t)$
ARVN–KIA	.377 (.031)	12.165 (.001)	290 (.033)	8.75 (.001)
ARVN–KIA × VIETNAMIZATION	−.358 (.061)	−5.862 (.001)	—	—
VIETNAMIZATION	50.323 (122.805)	.410 (.683)	−575.662 (76.608)	−7.514 (.001)
SPRING	170.306 (44.727)	3.808 (.001)	120.000 (53.838)	2.229 (.029)
US–TROOP	.001 (.0003)	3.924 (.001)	.0096 (.0003)	2.935 (.005)
Constant	−211.588 (118.421)	−1.787 (.079)	−46.292 (148.128)	−.313 (.756)
RHO	0.48 (.105)	4.638 (.001)	.511 (.104)	4.930 (.001)
N = 71	Adjusted R^2 = .81		Adjusted R^2 = .70	

interactive variable, ARVN–KIA × VIETNAMIZATION, which represents the independent effect of ARVN combat deaths on US deaths after Vietnamization began, has a negative sign. Adding the two coefficients $(\beta_1 + \beta_3)$ reveals that the relationship between US and ARVN casualties after Vietnamization shifted dramatically, moving from its strong positive relationship (.38) to almost no relationship (.02)—a change of 94.7 percent. The coefficient shifted in the direction anticipated, given the change from two wars to one.[19]

As expected, the number of American troops in South Vietnam (US–TROOP), which specifies the population at risk for death in combat, is a significant, positive factor for explaining reduced US deaths. Yet, the independent variables explain variance in US–KIA beyond identification of the baseline population at risk. In addition to US–TROOP, the three variables, ARVN–KIA, ARVN–KIA × VIETNAMIZATION, and SPRING, are all statistically significant beyond the .001 level or better and move in the predicted direction. The

19 See Robert J. Friedrich, "In Defense of Multiplicative Terms in Multiple Regression Equations," *American Journal of Political Science*, XXVI (1982), 797–833, for a discussion of interactive terms in multiplicative models.

significantly positive effect of SPRING, which represents the annual communist spring attacks, demonstrates the seasonal effect identified by Thayer. As indicated by the significance of the other variables, however, SPRING does not remove the other results.[20]

In Model 2, the VIETNAMIZATION dummy term is not significant by itself. Instead, as predicted, the effect of VIETNAMIZATION on US-KIA is captured primarily by a change in the War's basic structure, which is represented by the interactive term ARVN-KIA × VIETNAMIZATION—which does not mean that VIETNAMIZATION is unimportant but that it works more powerfully when it interacts with ARVN-KIA than when alone. This point is evident in Model 3, which is identical to Model 2 except for its exclusion of the interactive term. The VIETNAMIZATION variable is powerful in Model 3, with, as expected, a large, negative coefficient and a strong *t*-statistic. The other variables, however, do not perform as well, and Model 3 does not explain as much of the variance as Model 2. Hence, although the VIETNAMIZATION variable is significant by itself, it captures more of the variance in US-KIA when it interacts with ARVN-KIA.

Figure 5 shows that Model 2's residuals are considerably smaller than those of Model 1. The residuals surround the *x*-axis more tightly, and they have considerably less systematic variance. The problems with the bivariate analysis are largely absent in the multivariate model. As would be expected in a model with more variables and an instrumental correction for auto-correlation, Model 2 explains more variance than Model 1.[21]

To reiterate, the variables ARVN-KIA, VIETNAMIZATION, SPRING, and US-TROOP did not *cause* US casualties. Rather, they represent observable indicators that attempt to measure less identifiable factors that might have resulted when the Americans and South Vietnamese switched to a one-war structure. In other words, this model does not identify the factors that determined US deaths; instead, it attempts to capture whether or not the environment in which those (unspecified) factors operated changed after the implementation of Vietnamization. However, evidence strongly suggests that these types of operational

20   Run by itself in a bivariate regression with US-KIA, US-TROOP explains only .02 percent of the variance of Americans killed in action. No other seasonal effects were found to have systematic effect on US-KIA. Results not shown.
21   RHO is the serial component of the error term.

Fig. 5 US- and ARVN-KIA Multivariate Residuals

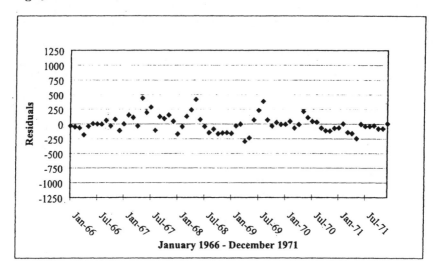

data influenced decision makers' assessments of the policy's effectiveness.

EVALUATING THE EVALUATIONS OF VIETNAMIZATION This analysis is the first to show that Vietnamization created an environment that significantly reduced the probability of an American soldier dying in Vietnam. That is, not only did the monthly rate at which Americans died in the war decrease; so did the probability that an individual US soldier would die. Vietnamization was also supposed to strengthen the ARVN enough to make it the main fighting opponent of the communists. On this score, the record is mixed. Scholars have shown that many of the problems that beset the ARVN prior to Vietnamization—namely, poor leadership and corruption—continued after it. Yet, during the war, operational measures employed by officials to assess the policy's effectiveness suggest that responsibility for fighting did indeed shift in the expected direction, as well as that American soldiers were less likely to die.

One reason for the serious divergence between contemporaneous and historical accounts of Vietnamization is that analysts have not examined whether official assessments of Vietnamization actually follow from the criteria and data that administration officials employed at the time. Since most postwar analysts focus

304

on the rapid defeat of the South Vietnamese in 1975, they tend to rely on events observable only after the war ended. In addition, their suspicions about the accuracy and the manipulation of the number-based data employed by government officials during the war have led them systematically to avoid these data in their own analyses, despite widespread recognition that these data were critical to decision makers.

The irony is that the Vietnam War is by far the best documented conflict in history, and the idea of measuring progress through figures was present in virtually all aspects of the American involvement in the conflict. Robert McNamara, Secretary of Defense from January 1961 until November 1967, wrote, "I insisted we try to measure progress. . . . I was convinced that, while we might not be able to track something as unambiguous as a front line, we could find variables that would indicate our success or failure." McNamara was not alone. Many American leaders trusted and depended upon the quantitative data that they collected during the Vietnam War. Donald Harrison, us national archivist, wrote, "The Vietnam War was the first war in military history to be run with the full-scale assistance of electronic data . . . collectively, this data provides evidence of what [information] was available to [the] decision makers." However, he also remarked, "[O]ne of the ironies of the historical analysis of the war in Vietnam has been an almost complete absence of computerized inquiry."[22]

Many of these wartime data, particularly the "body counts" of enemy casualties, appear to have been greatly exaggerated. Regardless of questions about their accuracy, if these data were instrumental in leaders' decisions, then they should enter into analyses of them. Quantitative data are vital to a full and complete understanding of the Vietnam War. According to Thayer, "Despite the problems the figures are useful and they must be addressed in any attempt to describe what happened in Vietnam." Without these data, studies of the Vietnam War present a partial picture of decision making.[23]

The lack of quantitative analysis of the Vietnam War intimates a larger problem: Scholars employing number-based ap-

22 Gartner and Myers, "Body Counts"; Mueller, "Search"; Robert S. McNamara, with Brian Van De Mark, *In Retrospect: The Tragedy and Lessons of Vietnam* (New York, 1995), 237; Samuel Adams, *War of Numbers: An Intelligence Memoir* (South Royalton, Vt., 1994), 76.
23 Kinnard, *War Managers;* Thayer, *War Without Fronts*, 30.

proaches have tended to concentrate on the initiation of conflict, whereas those who study wartime behavior have tended to employ qualitative historical approaches. Although a number of statistical analyses of wartime behavior have appeared recently, statistical analyses of individual wars and, in particular, the Vietnam War, remain rare. To rely exclusively on *ex post* phenomena and information unavailable to decision makers during the war is to ignore data that actually influenced views and events. Given the fundamentally different approaches taken by officials and scholars to assess the effectiveness of Vietnamization, it is not surprising that they have come to different conclusions.

Vietnamization was only one factor in a complex equation affecting the survival of the regime. It might have helped, for example, to delay the demise of the government of South Vietnam, but other factors influenced the eventual outcome. Trying to determine what was necessary for South Vietnam to win involves counterfactual analysis, which is particularly difficult for historical studies. As Overy states in his counterfactual analysis of World War II, the question of why the Allies won hardly ever arises because "Allied victory is taken for granted. . . . Explanations of Allied success contain a strong element of determinism. We now know the story so well that we do not consider the uncomfortable prospect that other outcomes might have been possible." Similarly, the defeat of South Vietnam has deterred scholars from examining the factors that influenced Vietnamization. When analyzed, Vietnamization turns out to be more than just a unilateral withdrawal.[24]

Studies based on information available after the Vietnam War are generally less supportive of Vietnamization than are assessments based on data available while the war was fought. These different sources of evaluative information represent conflicting methodological conceptualizations. Decision makers looked at whether the nature of the war was changing; post-war analysts traced the impact of Vietnamization on South Vietnam's defeat. It might be

24 Bueno de Mesquita, "Counterfactuals and International Affairs: Some Insights from Game Theory," in Phillip E. Tetlock and Aaron Belkin (eds.), *Counterfactual Thought Experiments in World Politics* (Princeton, 1996), 211–229; Barry Weingast, "Off-the-Path Behavior: A Game-Theoretic Approach to Counterfactuals and Its Implications for Political and Historical Analysis," *ibid.*, 230–246; James D. Fearon, "Counterfactuals and Hypothesis Testing in Political Science," *World Politics*, XLIII (1991), 169–195; Richard Overy, *Why the Allies Won* (London, 1995).

that the more Vietnamization succeeded, as measured at the time, the greater was the chance that the North Vietnamese would win the war, because the United States was turning the fighting over to a military force that could be defeated more easily. In other words, policymakers at the time might have interpreted statistics indicating progress in Vietnamization as progress in the war, when, in hindsight, the numbers demonstrate the growing vulnerability of South Vietnam to North Vietnamese military action.

There is no one way to evaluate Vietnamization. By telling a story about the impact of Vietnamization on the conduct of the war that has been largely overlooked, this article provides an explanation for why assessments of Vietnamization varied. Although many historians fail to take into account the figures that decision makers appear to have employed during the war, many social scientists similarly fail to include critical archival and historical information that places their statistical analyses in context.

US leaders might not have needed any empirical basis to form a positive assessment of Vietnamization; they simply might have lied about its effectiveness. The analysis in this article shows, however, that even without lying, wartime leaders who relied on quantitative operational measures and postwar scholars who relied on subsequent qualitative information probably would have drawn contradictory conclusions about the military impact of Vietnamization.

Another explanation for the discrepancy might be that political, not military, aspects of Vietnamization dominated leaders' assessments. This article examines only the military results of Vietnamization, not because they are more important than the political, but because Vietnamization altered the military situation in a way that is rarely addressed. Clearly, political goals such as decreasing US casualties and overall commitment to the war in deference to peace protests at home greatly influenced, and perhaps dominated, decisions regarding Vietnamization. Similarly, such important objectives as "winning the hearts and minds" of the South Vietnamese people and developing a more stable government in South Vietnam were critical to the prevention of a communist victory. But arguments that Vietnamization was primarily a political policy implicitly, or explicitly, make the case that it had little effect beyond withdrawing American troops and appeasing US domestic concerns. As this article shows, Vietnamization did much more than that.

Understanding the military impact of Vietnamization opens the door for the exploration of other important matters. For example, since the policy altered how the war was fought, but could not save the government of South Vietnam, what other factors influenced the outcome, and what criteria might have captured them? These types of questions are interesting only if the criteria that officials claimed to have influenced their decisions can be shown to support their views. If not, then why argue about what the appropriate criteria in this and future situations *should* be?

Lessons drawn from the Vietnam War have been critical for the practice of US national security. Fear of repeating the mistakes of Vietnam haunted the planning of the Gulf War. The lessons that the United States learned from the Vietnam War, such as winning quickly and avoiding quantitative measures of progress, still have currency. Given that these lessons have been drawn solely from nonquantitative and *ex post* studies, which capture important aspects of the war but systematically ignore other critical factors, relying on them so heavily might be ill-advised.[25]

Quantitative analyses employing *ex ante* data are not just useful for studying the Vietnam War; they are also useful for studying other wartime decision-making situations. This approach captures variables that were embedded in perceptions of policy at the time of its implementation, whereas "ex post measures do not properly depict an actor's decision-making environment." In addition, they permit the development of models about the viewpoints of decision makers that have predictive power.[26]

If decision makers employ number-based data, so must scholars. As the information age unfolds and militaries increasingly collect and rely on numbers, the study of wartime behavior must become increasingly oriented toward quantitative approaches. Failure in this regard will limit analysts' ability to understand how militaries conduct themselves in war.

25 Bob Woodward, *The Commanders* (New York, 1991); James Blackwell *Thunder in the Desert: The Strategy and Tactics of the Persian Gulf War* (New York, 1991); Colin Powell, with Joseph E. Persico, *My American Journey* (New York, 1995).

26 For a contrasting view of this uniqueness, see Gartner and Myers, "Body Counts"; Bueno de Mesquita, "Pride of Place: The Origins of German Hegemony," *World Politics*, XLIII (1991), 28–52; Stephen P. Nicholson and Ross A. Miller, "Prior Beliefs and Voter Turnout in the 1986 and 1988 Congressional Elections," *Political Research Quarterly*, L (1997), 199–213; Bueno de Mesquita, "Counterfactuals."

People's War in Vietnam

☆

John M. Gates

. . . the war in Vietnam was not a true insurgency but a thinly disguised aggression —Norman B. Hannah, 1975.

However the conflict began decades earlier, it has not ended as a bonafide civil war —Col. Robert D. Heinl, 1975.

It was not . . . a victory for people's revolutionary war but a straight forward conventional invasion and conquest
—Sir Robert Thompson, 1975.

There is great irony in the fact that the North Vietnamese finally won by purely conventional means, using precisely the kind of warfare at which the American army was best equipped to fight
—W. Scott Thompson & Col. Donaldson D. Frizzell, 1977.

There are still those who would attempt to fit it into the revolutionary war mold and who blame our defeat on our failure to implement counterinsurgency doctrine. This point of view requires an acceptance of the North Vietnamese contention that the war was a civil war, and that the North Vietnamese regular forces were an extension of the guerrilla effort, a point of view not borne out by the facts
—Col. Harry G. Summers, Jr., 1982.

In Vietnam, the guerrillas largely disappeared after they rose to mount a conventional attack, and the war then had to be won by the communists in conventional, almost American, terms —Timothy J. Lomperis, 1988.

T HE argument that in Vietnam the communists, often seen as "North" Vietnamese, triumphed in 1975 using "a conventional-war strategy" rather than engaging in a successful people's or revolutionary war is obviously not a new one, and it may even represent the predominant

The Journal of Military History 54 (July 1990): 325–44 © American Military Institute   ★ 32**5**

view of the war among senior American military officers and government officials. At first glance, the argument appears to be quite reasonable, buttressed by the credentials of the people making it, and it has great appeal to readers who may want to avoid interpretations implying that the United States lost the war in Vietnam because of its inability to combat a communist insurgency.[1]

In 1975 American television viewers saw the tanks of communist regular forces moving through the streets of Saigon and into the grounds of the Presidential Palace, a scene that has been rerun numerous times since its original filming. The powerful image of that particular footage, more reminiscent of World War II than the combat in Vietnam during the 1960s, lends support to the argument that people's war failed and that the war ended in a purely conventional attack. Also supporting such a view is the evidence, not widely recognized in the United States at the time, that local communist forces in South Vietnam suffered heavy casualties during the 1968 Tet Offensive. Data gathered in the last years of the war indicated that many Vietnamese, particularly in the South, were tired of war, and even the communists noticed that enthusiasm for their cause was waning. It is thus no surprise that with the passage of time the proposition that people's war failed in Vietnam and was replaced by a more successful conventional-war strategy has gained widespread acceptance.

One should be wary, however, of any argument that fits so well with the long-standing conventional-war bias of the American military or the desires of people who want to believe that the United States was not defeated in Vietnam. As persuasive and comforting as arguments about the failure of people's war, the conquest of South Vietnam by the North Vietnamese, or the communist adoption of a conventional-war strategy may seem, they should be viewed with great skepticism, for they tend to be rooted in serious conceptual errors.

People's War in Vietnam

In arguing the case that the war in Vietnam was primarily a conven-

---

1. For examples see Anthony T. Bouscaren, ed., *All Quiet on the Western Front: The Death of South Vietnam* (Old Greenwich, Conn.: Devin-Adair Co., 1977), particularly Robert D. Heinl, Sir Robert Thompson, and Norman B. Hannah, 64, 119, 148–49; W. Scott Thompson and Donaldson D. Frizzell, eds., *The Lessons of Vietnam* (New York: Crane, Russak, 1977), 279; and Harry G. Summers, Jr., *On Strategy: A Critical Analysis of the Vietnam War* (New York: Dell Pub. Co., 1984), 121–22; and Timothy J. Lomperis, "Giap's Dream, Westmoreland's Nightmare," *Parameters* 18 (June 1988): 30.

tional conflict, a number of authors have equated people's war with guerrilla warfare. They maintain that the inability of the communists to overthrow the Saigon government using guerrillas alone and the use of large numbers of regular troops in the final offensive of 1975 proves either the speciousness of the communist claim to have been fighting a people's war or the complete failure of people's war with the 1968 Tet Offensive. To understand people's war, however, one must view the phenomenon through the eyes of its practitioners, and the writings of well-known Vietnamese revolutionaries indicate clearly that the use of guerrillas was never the principal feature of the communist approach.

In Vietnamese communist writing, people's war is defined in terms of its participants and its goals, as well as its strategies and tactics. General Vo Nguyen Giap described it as "essentially *a peasant's war under the leadership of the working class,*" a view present also in the writing of Truong Chinh, another important leader of the Vietnamese communist movement.[2] Leadership resided in the communist party organization, as the representative of the working class, but the goal of mobilization was to create "a firm and wide national united front based on the worker-peasant alliance."[3]

For the Vietnamese communists, the political dimensions of people's war were particularly significant. Giap claimed that in fighting against the French, "the agrarian policy of the Party played a determining role," and he again referred to the importance of building "political forces" in a 1967 discussion of the war in the South.[4] Truong Chinh maintained that "military action can only succeed when politics are correct," adding that "conversely, politics cannot be fulfilled without the success of military action."[5] In their theoretical and historical writings, the Vietnamese communists placed such importance on the coordination of the military and political dimensions of people's war that Giap called it "a law of the revolutionary struggle in our country."[6]

As described by the communists, the process of people's war was always far more comprehensive than interpretations emphasizing guerrilla warfare acknowledge. Truong Chinh wrote of resistance that "must

---

2. Vo Nguyen Giap, *People's War, People's Army* (New York: Frederick A. Praeger, 1962), 27 (italics in original); and Truong Chinh, *Primer for Revolt* (New York: Frederick A. Praeger, 1963), 109.

3. Giap, *People's War*, 33.

4. Ibid., 31, and Vo Nguyen Giap, *"Big Victory, Great Task"* (New York: Frederick A. Praeger, 1968), 73.

5. Chinh, *Primer for Revolt*, 179.

6. Giap, *"Big Victory,"* 52.

be carried out in every field: military, economic, political and cultural," and Giap observed that "the fight against the enemy on all fronts—military, political, cultural, diplomatic, and so forth—is waged at the same time."[7] In his description of the people's war against the French, Giap noted that "parallel with the fight against the enemy, ... our Party implemented positive lines of action in every aspect, did its utmost to mobilise, educate and organize the masses, to increase production, practice economy, and build local armed and semi-armed forces."[8] To focus solely on the military elements of people's war is to miss the essential comprehensiveness of the approach.

Even when writing about the strictly military aspects of people's war the communists presented a picture of the phenomenon that is totally at odds with a fixation on guerrilla warfare. If any single strategic element predominated in the Vietnamese conception of people's war, it was protraction rather than the use of guerrillas. Ho Chi Minh observed in 1950 that "in military affairs time is of prime importance," and he ranked it "first among the three factors for victory, before the terrain conditions and the people's support."[9] Writing of "the imperatives of the people's war in Viet Nam" in 1961, General Giap placed "the *strategy of a long-term war*" first on his list, and earlier, during the war against the French, Truong Chinh observed that *"the guiding principle of the strategy of our whole resistance must be to prolong the war."*[10] As the latter told his compatriots, "only by wearing the enemy down, can we fulfill the strategic tasks of launching the general counter-offensive, annihilating the enemy and winning final victory."[11] Giap presented a similar view two decades later when he noted that "protracted resistance is an essential strategy of a people ... determined to defeat an enemy and aggressor having large and well-armed forces."[12]

Militarily, guerrilla warfare was only one element in a comprehensive approach, and the Vietnamese practitioners of people's war never viewed it as decisive. Giap noted that the war against the French had "several phases." Guerrilla warfare was important, "especially at the

---

7. Chinh, *Primer for Revolt,* 11, and Giap, ibid. See also Giap, *People's War,* 97.

8. Giap, *People's War,* 145.

9. "Instructions Given at the Conference Reviewing the Second Le Hong Phong Military Campaign," in Bernard B. Fall, ed., *Ho Chi Minh on Revolution: Selected Writings, 1920-1966* (New York: New American Library, 1968), 188.

10. Giap, *People's War,* 5-46, and Chinh, *Primer for Revolt,* 111 (italics in originals).

11. Ibid., 180

12. Giap, *"Big Victory,"* 55

outset," but with time "guerrilla warfare changed into mobile warfare." The communist military effort "passed from the stage of combats involving a section or company, to fairly large-scale campaigns bringing into action several divisions."[13] Giap saw the move from guerrilla war to mobile warfare as necessary "to annihilate big enemy manpower and liberate land," and he claimed that "to keep itself in life and develop, guerrilla warfare has necessarily to develop into mobile warfare." For him that progression was nothing less than "a general law."[14] Truong Chinh portrayed people's war in a similar way, calling it a "war of interlocking," in which "regular army, militia, and guerrilla forces combine and fight together." He too noted the need for guerrilla warfare to be "transformed into mobile warfare."[15]

In commenting on the war against the Republic of Vietnam and its American ally, Giap wrote of the coordination of "guerrilla, regional, and main-force units."[16] Similarly, in describing "the combined strength of people's war" in the final offensive of 1975, Generals Giap and Van Tien Dung noted a variety of techniques: *"military attacks by mobile strategic army columns as main striking forces, combining military struggle with political struggle and agitation among enemy troops, wiping out and disbanding large enemy units, completely liberating large strategic regions in the mountains, rural and urban areas, and winning total victory by means of a general offensive and uprising right in the 'capital city' of the puppet administration."*[17]

For the Vietnamese practitioners of people's war, guerrilla warfare was only one aspect of their military approach, with the military area itself being only one dimension of a much more comprehensive system of revolutionary warfare. In theory, the war moved through stages, from subversive activities that avoided direct confrontation with government military forces, to guerrilla war, and finally to mobile warfare in which regular forces predominated. In reality, however, Vietnam's communist revolutionaries were more pragmatic than implied by a theory of stages. The communists moved their strategic emphasis back and forth from stage to stage as events and circumstances warranted. At times all three stages of activity existed simultaneously. In both theory and practice,

13. Giap, *People's War*, 29–30.
14. Ibid., 106–7.
15. Chinh, *Primer for Revolt*, 139, 153.
16. Giap, *"Big Victory,"* 74.
17. Vo Nguyen Giap and Van Tien Dung, *How We Won the War* (Ypsilanti, Mich.: RECON Publications, 1976), 41 (italics in original).

people's war in Vietnam always encompassed much more than guerrilla warfare.

The Communist Movement in Vietnam

The role of the Democratic Republic of Vietnam (DRV or North Vietnam) in the people's war after 1954 is also frequently misunderstood by Americans. In part the problem is a function of the tendency of many Americans to see North Vietnam as a separate country bent on the conquest of its southern neighbor. Those same Americans have also tended to describe the 1975 offensive as an attack by "North" Vietnamese, implying that the leadership of the Vietnamese communist movement had regional rather than national roots.

In the eyes of Vietnam's communist leaders, however, the DRV was never a complete state, and their conception of Vietnam always included the territory governed by Saigon as well as that administered by Hanoi. General Giap characterized the North as "the liberated half of our country," seeing the DRV as "a firm base of action for the reunification of the country."[18] In 1956 Ho Chi Minh told the southern cadres regrouped above the demilitarized zone that the North was "the foundation, the root of the struggle for complete national liberation and reunification of the country." It was to become, he told them, "a strong base for our entire people's struggle."[19] Later, General Giap would refer to the North as "the vast rear of our army" and "the revolutionary base for the whole country."[20]

During the war against the French, Truong Chinh had noted Lenin's remark that "to wage a real war, we must have a strong and well organized rear," deeming it "very precious counsel for us in this long-term resistance war."[21] In the people's war for unification that followed the French withdrawal, the communists would not forget that "precious counsel." At the 1963 meeting of the Central Committee of the Vietnamese Worker's Party in Hanoi, the Third Party Congress recognized

18. Giap, *People's War*, 49, 34.

19. "Letter to the Cadres from South Vietnam Regrouped in the North" (19 June 1956), in Fall, *Ho Chi Minh on Revolution*, 272-73, 274.

20. Giap, *People's War*, 146. Although it denied the legitimacy of such views, the United States government recognized them, quoting passages from Giap and others in a section entitled "North Viet-Nam: Base for Conquest of the South" in Department of State Publication 7839, *Aggression from the North: The Record of North Viet-Nam's Campaign To Conquer South Viet-Nam* (Washington, D.C.: GPO, 1965), 20-21.

21. Chinh, *Primer for Revolt*, 211.

the special role of the DRV, saying the time had arrived "for the North to increase aid to the South" and "bring into play its role as the revolutionary base for the nation."[22]

Communist leaders did their best to maintain the fiction that the war in the South was being waged only "by the people and liberation forces of South Viet-Nam under the leadership of the National Front for Liberation," as Ho Chi Minh told a Western correspondent in 1965. Pham Van Dong had been equally disingenuous when he told Bernard Fall in 1962 that "the heroic South Vietnamese people will have to continue the struggle by their own means."[23] In the United States many opponents of the American war in Vietnam, including more than a few scholars, appear to have been deceived into accepting what George Kahin and John Lewis claimed was "the inescapable conclusion that the Liberation Front is not 'Hanoi's creation.'" They argued instead that the Front "has manifested independence and it is Southern."[24]

The fiction could not be maintained, however, and by 1967 General Giap would openly portray the war as a "revolutionary struggle" waged by "people throughout the country," both North and South. As he wrote at the time, "to protect the north, liberate the south, and proceed toward reunifying the country, the northern armed forces and people have stepped up and are stepping up the violent people's fight."[26] The United States government was correct in its claim that the communist guerrillas and cadres in the South, as well as the National Liberation Front, were operational elements of the DRV. Clearly people in the American antiwar movement often had difficulty distinguishing between reality and communist propaganda, but they did not have a monopoly on self-deception. Americans supporting the war failed to distinguish between reality and their own propaganda, failing to see that a sovereign and independent Republic of Vietnam (RVN) could only exist if the Saigon government and its American ally won the war. The RVN was not a state to be defended but a state to be created.

For Vietnam's communist leaders, a divided Vietnam was a Vietnam in agony, and as Wallace J. Thies observed, "DRV leaders such as Le Duan and Nguyen Chi Thanh were deeply and passionately committed to the goal of completing the revolution in South Vietnam. It was a

22. Thomas K. Latimer, "Hanoi's Leaders and Their South Vietnam Policies: 1954–1968" (unpublished doctoral thesis, Georgetown University, 1972), 154.

23. Fall, *Ho Chi Minh on Revolution*, 322.

24. George McTuran Kahin and John W. Lewis, *The United States in Vietnam*, rev. ed. (New York: Dell Pub. Co., 1969), 120

25. Giap, *"Big Victory,"* 47, 28.

goal they had been pursuing for virtually all of their adult lives."[26] Pham Van Dong attempted to convey the importance of national unification to the United States when he told Canadian diplomat Blair Seaborn in June 1964 that it was a *"drame, national, fondamental."* Seaborn reported his conversation to the United States government using the same French words to highlight the intensity of feeling among communist leaders when they viewed the unresolved crisis or *drame* created by the continuing division of Vietnam.[27]

Authors who write of "the partitioning of Vietnam at the 17th parallel as a result of the Geneva Accords of 1954" and call the communist triumph a "North Vietnamese victory," as one scholar has recently, need to give more careful attention to the available evidence.[28] The Geneva Accords created a situation in which two governments existed within Vietnam, but the Geneva documents did not "partition" the country. In 1954, neither communist nor anticommunist Vietnamese accepted the idea that their nation had been partitioned. As a U.S. National Intelligence Estimate noted in November 1954, "Partition at the 17th parallel is abhorred by all Vietnamese, who regard unity of the three regions of Vietnam as a prerequisite of nationhood."[29] Leaders of the rival governments in Hanoi and Saigon both viewed the seventeenth parallel dividing line as it was defined in the Geneva declaration: a "military demarcation line" that was "provisional and should not in any way be interpreted as constituting a political or territorial boundary."[30] The 1973 cease fire agreement recognized the provisional nature of the

26. Wallace J. Thies, *When Governments Collide: Coercion and Diplomacy in the Vietnam Conflict, 1964-1968* (Berkeley: University of California Press, 1983), 400.

27. George C. Herring, ed., *The Secret Diplomacy of the Vietnam War: The Negotiating Volumes of the Pentagon Papers* (Austin: University of Texas Press, 1983), 31.

28. Lomperis, "Giap's Dream," 25, 19.

29. "National Intelligence Estimate, 23 November 1954, Probable Developments in South Vietnam, Laos, and Cambodia Through July 1956," in United States State Department, *Foreign Relations of the United States, 1952-1954,* Volume XIII, *Indochina* (Washington, D.C.: GPO, 1982), Part 2, p. 2289. "The three regions of Vietnam" refers to the French subdivisions of Vietnam: Tonkin, Annam, and Cochin China. The Vietnamese referred to the three regions of their country simply as north, central, and south Vietnam. For early RVN statements on Vietnam as a single nation see Gareth Porter, ed. *Vietnam: The Definitive Documentation of Human Decisions* (New York: E. M. Coleman, 1979), 1: 581, 656.

30. "Final Declaration of the Geneva Conference on the Problem of Restoring Peace in Indochina, July 1954," in Gareth Porter, ed., *Vietnam: A History in Documents* (New York: New American Library, 1981), 160.

seventeenth parallel dividing line in exactly the same language.[31]

Communist leaders repeatedly claimed that only one, not two Vietnams existed, and initially noncommunist leaders in the South took the same position. Communist strength in the North precluded unification of Vietnam on terms acceptable to the United States and its Vietnamese allies in the South. As a result, American leaders created an illusory picture of the situation in Vietnam, portraying the conflict there as the result of the aggression of one sovereign state against another. In reality, it was a civil war between two Vietnamese parties, both of whom had originally claimed sovereignty over all of Vietnam. Although the United States often envisioned a solution to the Vietnam conflict similar to that achieved earlier in Korea, it could not create two sovereign states in Vietnam by rhetoric alone. The civil war would continue until the communists succeeded or were forced by the United States to abandon their goal of creating a revolutionary state in all Vietnam.

Significantly, the war in Vietnam was never a war of northerners against southerners. Before World War II, members of the Vietnamese communist party could be found throughout all of Vietnam. According to William Duiker, the Vietnamese Revolutionary Youth League, formed in 1925, "had sunk its roots in all regions of Vietnam,"[32] and Ho Chi Minh's August 1945 revolution was a nation-wide movement.[33] Not only was communist leadership in Vietnam national rather than regional from an early date, but it remained very stable throughout more than two decades of conflict. Except for a few readjustments after the death of Ho in 1969, it changed little from the 1950s to the mid-1970s.[34] Although the war in the South was directed by communists in Hanoi, that did not mean that the war was directed by "North Vietnamese." In fact, the group fighting to reunify the country was never composed solely of "North Vietnamese" or even led only by them.

Although biographical information on Vietnam's communist leaders is incomplete, the data that do exist support the conclusion that the

31. See Gareth Porter, *A Peace Denied: The United States, Vietnam and the Paris Agreement* (Bloomington: Indiana University Press, 1975), 322.

32. Willliam J. Duiker, *The Communist Road to Power in Vietnam* (Boulder: Westview Press, 1981), 25

33. The early years of Vietnamese communism are described fully in Huynh Kim Khanh, *Vietnamese Communism, 1925–1945* (Ithaca: Cornell University Press, 1982). See also Duiker, *Communist Road to Power,* Chapters 1–5.

34. "VWP-DRV Leadership, 1960–1973," Document No. 114, *Viet-Nam Documents and Research Notes* (Saigon: Joint United States Public Affairs Office, July 1973), 8.

people who controlled the DRV and the war to overthrow the government in South Vietnam came from all regions of the country. Both before and after Ho's death four of the eleven members of the politburo (36.4 percent) came from south of the seventeenth parallel, as did six of fourteen members of the politburo (42.9 percent) at the time of the communist triumph in 1975. In 1973, a majority of the nine-member Secretariat of the Vietnamese Workers Party (VWP) came from the South, as did half of the members whose place of birth can be determined (twenty of thirty-eight) elected to the Council of Ministers following the communist triumph.[35]

As a 1973 analysis of VWP leadership by the U.S. mission in Vietnam observed, one fact "that leaps out of the data about VWP Central Committee members is the large number of them, including Ho Chi Minh himself, who were born or were first active politically in Central Viet-Nam." The study noted that "a disproportionate number of the leaders of Vietnamese communism," including "leaders of the Party and government in the DRV, and of the People's Liberation Armed Forces and the People's Revolutionary Party in South Viet-Nam," were drawn from the "central provinces in both North and South Viet-Nam."[36] Individuals from central Vietnam constituted a majority in the Politburo and the VWP Secretariat during the war and in the Council of Ministers elected after it. Although the seat of the communist government that conquered the South resided in North Vietnam, its leadership was national, not regional.

The names of some of the individuals from south of the seventeenth parallel who held high positions in the communist leadership during the war are well known. One was Pham Van Dong, "probably Ho's closest associate since 1955," according to Bernard Fall,[37] and prime minister of the DRV during the war. Another was Le Duan, who served as secretary-general of the Vietnamese Workers Party and became the party's leader following Ho's death in 1969. The individual who assumed Ho's title as president, Ton Duc Tang, was also a southerner, as was vice-premier Pham Hung. Other southerners among the communist leadership, less well known to most Americans, included two central

35. Data compiled from ibid.; Central Intelligence Agency, *Reference Aid: Council of Ministers of the Socialist Republic of Vietnam* (Washington: Central Intelligence Agency, 1977); Borys Lewytzkj and Juliusz Stroynowski, eds., *Who's Who in the Socialist Countries* (New York: K. G. Saur Pub., 1978); and P. J. Honey, *Communism in North Vietnam: Its Role in the Sino-Soviet Dispute* (Cambridge, Mass.: MIT Press, 1963), Chapter 2.

36. "VWP-DRV Leadership," 3–4.

37. Fall, *Ho Chi Minh on Revolution*, 319.

committee members (Hoang Anh and Tran Quoc Hoan) and six leaders of the National Liberation Front and/or the People's Revolutionary Government in the South who also joined the government of the unified communist Vietnam after the war (Nguyen Thi Binh, Nguyen Van Hieu, Vo Van Kiet, Tran Luong, Huynh Tan Phat, and Tran Dai Nghia).[38]

Other communist southerners also gained widespread recognition. Colonel Bui Tin, a journalist who found himself the ranking regular officer at the Presidential Palace in Saigon, became prominent when he accepted the surrender there in April 1975, and General Tran Van Tra's history of the final offensive has become an important source for American scholars researching the war. Countless southerners also served in the ranks, not only as political cadres and guerrillas, but also as regulars. Knowledgeable authors recognize that southerners provided the vast majority of the combatants in the Viet Cong units that carried the major burden of the war before 1969, just as most authors now agree that communist leadership in Hanoi initiated and directed the war in the South from its inception.

The regular forces who moved down the Ho Chi Minh trail to participate in the large unit war against the Americans contained soldiers returning to the South as well as combatants from the North. Xuan Vu, for example, described the high morale of southerners in late 1965, "dying to go back . . . motivated by the idea of the great General Uprising."[39] Even the White Paper issued by the Department of State in 1965 provided evidence that the communists infiltrating the South were not northerners, although that was not the document's intention. Although the White Paper claimed that "as many as 75 percent" of the Viet Cong entering the South from January through August 1964 "were natives of North Viet-Nam," the eighteen cases given as specific examples consisted overwhelmingly of individuals born south of the seventeenth parallel. Southerners made up eight of the document's nine "individual case histories" and seven of an additional nine "brief case histories of typical Viet Cong" presented in an appendix.[40]

The conclusion from the available evidence seems clear: the communist movement in Vietnam was not directed by northerners, although the communist seat of power and government was in Hanoi, and the war that ended in 1975 was not a conquest of the South Vietnamese by the North Vietnamese. The war ended in a communist victory, but the

38. See Central Intelligence Agency, *Reference Aid* for confirmation.
39. David Chanoff and Doan Van Toai, *Portrait of the Enemy* (New York: Random House, 1986), 179.
40. *Aggression From the North,* 6-11, 33-37.

leaders of Vietnam's communist movement came from both sides of the seventeenth parallel, with the central region of the nation predominating. As historian Warren I. Cohen has observed, "if analysts persist in the notion that two separate nations existed in Vietnam in 1954, they will never understand the United States defeat there." The war between communist and anticommunist Vietnamese "was not a war of aggression by one nation against another. Separateness was something to be won on the battlefield by the secessionists, not proclaimed by others or imposed from outside."[41]

The 1975 Communist Offensive

Although the communist goal of unification under a revolutionary government was remarkably consistent, flexibility, rather than rigid commitment to guerrilla warfare or any other particular approach, was the hallmark of the people's war in Vietnam. Thomas K. Latimer highlighted that flexibility in his survey of the ongoing debate within the leadership of the Vietnamese Workers Party over the proper strategy in the struggle for unification. From 1954 to 1958, the communists undertook political organization and mobilization in the South while building socialism in the base area of the North and awaiting the collapse of the Ngo Dinh Diem government in Saigon. When that collapse did not take place, the communists adopted a more forceful approach, beginning with guerrilla warfare in 1959 and attempting to shift to mobile warfare in 1964. That move was thwarted by the United States, as was an attempt to gain a decisive victory early in 1968. The 1968 defeat led to the recognition by leaders of the party that they could "push the Americans out of South Vietnam by coordinating the political struggle with diplomacy."[42] Latimer viewed the strategic shift following the 1968 defeat, outlined in a May 1968 report authored by Truong Chinh, as "a half-step retreat."[43] At the time, the communist leadership reaffirmed the value of the protracted war model and focused their attention on the United States as the primary enemy to be negotiated or manipulated out of Vietnam. Political events within the United States made the achievement of that goal possible, but not before another communist move to mobile warfare was thwarted in 1972.

Given the flexibility inherent in the communist approach, none of

41. Warren I. Cohen, "Vietnam: New Light on the Nature of the War?" *International History Review* 9 (1987): 116.

42. Latimer, "Hanoi's Leaders," 235.

43. Ibid., 343.

the defeats proved decisive. Instead, the communists regrouped to make a successful bid for victory in 1975. As Latimer observed, "it was this ability to remain flexible, to fall back to a protracted war strategy, to beef up the political struggle aspect, as well as plunge ahead from time to time in an all-out military effort, which enabled the Vietnamese communists to sustain their 'revolution' in the south."[44] Another American scholar, Patrick J. McGarvey, had reached a similar conclusion even earlier. He predicted after the 1968 defeat that "Communist strategy will remain a dynamic one," in which "decisions will continue to be based on the realities of the battlefield." At about the same time Douglas Pike observed that "none of these means—diplomacy, proxy struggle, or direct military—is mutually exclusive."[45] Pike noted that the communist leadership in Vietnam "has no hesitation about abandoning one method or policy when another appears more promising."[46]

Just as people's war appeared to be nothing more than guerrilla warfare to some Americans, and the communist leadership appeared to be "North" Vietnamese, the communists seemed to have triumphed in 1975 by using a highly conventional approach. One author has even described the winning communist strategy as "an American one."[47] The Vietnamese communists' own descriptions of the final offensive, however, support a very different conclusion.

The local communist apparatus in the South suffered high casualties and resulting demoralization during the Tet Offensive of 1968 and from the Phoenix program implemented to help the Saigon government gain control over the countryside. Despite renewed organizational efforts of their own, the communists had not completely repaired the resulting damage to their movement by the time of the 1973 ceasefire agreement. In his study of the war in Long An province, Jeffrey Race noted that "the revolution movement in late 1970 was in a difficult position,"[48] a view confirmed by captured communist documents.[49]

44. Ibid., 195.

45. Patrick H. McGarvey, *Visions of Victory: Selected Vietnamese Communist Military Writings, 1964–1968* (Stanford: Hoover Institution on War, Revolution and Peace, 1969), 57.

46. Douglas Pike, *War, Peace, and the Viet Cong* (Cambridge, Mass.: MIT Press, 1969), 34–35.

47. Lomperis, "Giap's Dream," 19.

48. Jeffrey Race, *War Comes to Long An: Revolutionary Conflict in a Vietnamese Province* (Berkeley: University of California Press, 1972), 276

49. See, for example, "Directive 10/CT–71" and "Recapitulative Report on the Reorientation Courses Concerning the New Situation and Missions Conducted" in *Viet Nam Documents and Notes, Number 102, Part III* (Saigon: Joint United States Public Affairs Office, 1973).

In his memoir, General Tran Van Tra, commanding communist forces in the region surrounding Saigon, observed that as late as 1973 "all units were in disarray, there was a lack of manpower, . . . shortages." According to Tra, mid- and lower-level cadres, seeing the enemy "winning many new victories," concluded "that the revolution was in danger."[50] That did not mean, however, that the Viet Cong had been totally destroyed.

The estimate of relative strength that appears in Colonel William Le Gro's study, *Vietnam from Cease-Fire to Capitulation*, indicates that local forces of one kind or another, particularly outside of Military Region I, still made up a substantial portion of communist strength in South Vietnam. Although the Viet Cong constituted only 16.9 percent of total communist combat troops in January 1973, local forces provided more than 50 percent of the administrative and service personnel. In Military Region III, local forces supplied 20 percent of the combat troops and and 68.8 percent of the administrative and service personnel. In Military Region IV the percentages were 40.7 and 92.3 respectively.[51] The ARVN Chief of Staff for II Corps estimated that in 1975 communist regular units constituted no more than 46 percent of the forces he faced in his area.[52]

Such estimates indicate that Viet Cong strength after Tet had recovered far more than advocates of the conventional war thesis would have one believe, particularly in the heavily populated region of the Mekong Delta and the area surrounding Saigon. Furthermore, estimates such as Le Gro's are of military strength, and they do not appear to include the communist political infrastructure. Although the Viet Cong had been hurt at Tet and hard pressed afterward, they had not been destroyed.

The strength and value of local irregular forces would become apparent in 1975 when the communists began their final offensive. Although the American military has used irregular forces in mounting a conventional attack, it does not rely upon aid from guerrilla forces, popular militia, and political cadres in the enemy's homeland to facilitate and sustain the offensive movement of its regular forces. In Viet-

---

50. Tran Van Tra, *Vietnam: History of the Bulwark B2 Theatre*, Vol. 5, Concluding the 30-Years War (Ho Chi Minh City: Van Nghe Publishing House, 1982 in JPRS No. 82783—2 February 1983), 33.

51. William E. Le Gro, *Vietnam from Cease-Fire to Capitulation* (Washington, D.C.: U.S. Army Center of Military History, 1985), 28.

52. Stephen T. Hosmer, Konrad Kellen, and Brian M. Jenkins, *The Fall of South Vietnam: Statements of Vietnamese Military and Civilian Leaders* (New York: Crane, Russak, 1980), 168.

nam in 1975, however, communist regulars were not only dependent upon the aid received from irregulars, but their success was the result of years of unconventional warfare that had severely eroded the will and fighting ability of their anticommunist opponents. To call the communists' 1975 offensive "conventional" completely ignores both the events that had made the offensive possible and the role of irregular forces in supporting the final attack.

In assessing the successful campaign in the South, Generals Giap and Dung claimed that *"everywhere regional forces, militia, guerrillas and self-defense units* seized the opportunity to hit the enemy." They gave local forces credit for having "seized control in many places, wiped out or forced the withdrawal or surrender of thousands of garrisons, shattered the coercive machine of the enemy at the grassroots level, and smashed their 'popular defense' organizations." The result of that activity, they went on to say, was "better conditions for our regular units to concentrate their attacks on the main targets of the general offensive."[53] General Tran Van Tra described the 1975 offensive in a similar way, noting the use "of combined forces—both armed forces and the political forces of the people—in a widespread general offensive and uprising." Tra claimed that the communists "prepositioned" regular forces "in each area, in coordination with extensive local [forces] and militia" to create "an extremely potent revolutionary people's war."[54]

Communist descriptions of specific battles during the 1975 campaign also noted the involvement of guerrillas and other irregulars. According to General Tra, the successful attack on Phuoc Long province that preceded the 1975 offensive was the work of two "understrength" divisions, "in combination with the local forces," and he noted similar cooperation between local and regular forces in the Mekong Delta at the time of the general offensive.[55] Further north, according to General Dung, the liberation of Tam Ky and Tuan Duong, and the defeat of the Fourth and Fifth regiments of the ARVN Second Division on 24 and 25 March was the result of attacks by the Second Division of Zone 5 "in coordination with regional forces." He also gave credit for the liberation of the northern part of Quang Ngai province to "regional forces, in coordination with the masses."[56] Dung and an

53. Giap and Dung, *How We Won*, 41 (italics in original).

54. Tra, *Vietnam*, 151.

55. Ibid., 132, 147.

56. Van Tien Dung, *Our Great Spring Victory* (New York: Monthly Review Press, 1977), 105.

official history published in Hanoi both noted the coordination of regular units with attacks by guerrillas and other local forces in other battles in Zone 5, including the attack on Danang.[57] Interviews with RVN officials and military officers confirmed the important role played by communist irregulars, sustaining the conclusion that ARVN forces in III and IV Corps were so "hard pressed and tied down by local Communist forces" that they "could not be disengaged to form reserves to meet the fresh enemy divisions moving down from the north."[58]

Irregular forces were particularly active as the communist attack converged on Saigon. In 1972 communist forces in the Mekong Delta had not supported the offensive elsewhere, and RVN units from IV Corps had been used to reinforce III Corps. According to the ARVN Commander of the Capital Military District, however, in 1975 the communists "tied up those troops by the activities of the local Communist forces." Later those same local forces moved in captured vehicles into Long An province to threaten Route 4 and support the offensive against Saigon.[59]

General Dung also noted that in the provinces surrounding the city local forces at all levels increased in size and engaged in "continuous activities" that "tied down and drew off a number of enemy main-force units in IV Corps" and elsewhere, while "special action and sapper units" worked within the city.[60] Another communist history noted the way in which local forces helped to create "a staging area for our main-force units" by their attacks on "outposts, subsectors, and district capitals."[61] A specific example of such an attack, in which guerrillas surrounded an enemy post at Bo Keo, appeared in the diary of Tran Ham Ninh, aide to General Vo Van Thanh, commander of the column attacking Saigon from the south.[62]

According to General Dung, following the fall of Saigon, communists in the Mekong Delta and throughout the southern region "mounted a series of attacks under the direct leadership of the local party

57. Ibid., 109, and War Experiences Recapitulation Committee of the High-Level Military Institute, *Vietnam: The Anti-U.S. Resistance War for National Salvation 1954-1975: Military Events* (Hanoi: People's Army Publishing House, 1980 in JPRS 80968—3 June 1982), 173, 176-77.

58. Hosmer, Kellen, and Jenkins, *Fall of South Vietnam*, 231.

59. Ibid., 232.

60. Dung, *Great Spring Victory*, 249.

61. War Experiences Recapitulation Committee, *Vietnam*, 180.

62. Ninh's diary entries are in Tra, *Vietnam*, 178-85. The guerrillas surrounding Bo Keo are noted on 178.

branches." He claimed that by "coordinating these attacks with uprising by tens of thousands of the masses, they liberated all cities and towns, captured all big military bases, all district towns and subsectors, and all enemy outposts."[63] Although General Tra's claim that "the spirit of the masses were seething" and the statement in an official communist history that "in addition to the military attacks, millions of people arose" in the final days of the campaign are probably exaggerations,[64] the important work of communist cadres and irregulars in the 1975 offensive should not be underestimated.

In addition to the role that irregulars played in intelligence gathering, logistical support, and combat, communists at the local level engaged in significant political activity directly supporting the 1975 offensive. Giap and Dung observed that local political forces "carried out a campaign of agitation among enemy ranks to bring about their disintegration," helping to destroy the agencies of enemy political power and helping "set up revolutionary power in various locations."[65] General Tra claimed that during the offensive "many villages set up revolutionary administrations," and General Dung noted that by the time of the attack on Saigon "our political infrastructure existed in every section of town." Inside the city, he wrote, "there were dozens of members of the municipal party committee and cadres of equivalent rank, members of special war committees, hundreds of party members, thousands of members of various mass organizations, and tens of thousands of people who could be mobilized to take to the streets."[66]

The cadres and their followers not only took political power as the offensive proceeded and the Saigon government collapsed, but they acted in advance to undermine the morale of the enemy's armed forces. Tran Ham Ninh referred in his diary to "coordinating combat and the proselyting of enemy trooops," and according to General Dung, during the attack on Saigon people within the city "used megaphones to call on Saigon soldiers to take off their uniforms and lay down their guns." Such popular action, wrote Dung, "created a revolutionary atmosphere of vast strength on all the city's streets."[67]

To call the communist offensive in 1975 a conventional attack one must ignore the numerous references in communist sources regarding

63. Dung, *Great Spring Victory*, 249.

64. Tra, *Vietnam*, 162 and War Experiences Recapitulation Committee, *Vietnam*, 182.

65. Giap and Dung, *How We Won*, 42.

66. Tra, *Vietnam*, 196, and Dung, *Great Spring Victory*, 172.

67. Ninh in Tra, *Vietnam*, 182 and Dung, *Great Spring Victory*, 244.

the important contribution made by local forces and political cadres. One must also ignore statements in which Vietnamese communists specifically characterize the attack as one falling outside the traditional category of conventional war. General Tra, for example, maintained that the 1975 offensive was "not a plan to launch a general counteroffensive . . . as in a regular war." Instead, it embodied "parallel military and political efforts."[68] Gen. Dung described the campaign as one in which "our forms and methods of fighting and style of attack bore the spirit of the rules of revolutionary warfare in the South," and the March 1975 description of the attack provided by the Politburo in the midst of the campaign described it as a "general offensive and general uprising." By "coordinating offensives and uprisings" the communists saw themselves "striking from the outside in and from the inside out."[69]

In describing their defeat in interviews after the war, officials and officers of the RVN stressed their own failures in ways that also emphasized the unconventional aspects of the war. Their stories of panic, disorder, demoralization, defeatism, paralysis, and incompetence seemed to confirm the communist view that the war was won as much by political and diplomatic maneuvers as by military ones. According to the RVN respondents, the collapse of the South was caused more by internal problems that had developed over many years than by the weight of the final communist offensive. General Tran Van Don lamented the "incompetence on our military side," while another anonymous respondent spoke of "lazy, corrupted and unqualified generals." The Speaker of the House, Nguyen Ba Can, believed that by 1975 there existed a "pychological collapse that struck every South Vietnamese," seen, among other things, by the "widespread" draft dodging noted by Buu Vien and other officials. Despite strong communist pressure, leaders were "unwilling or afraid to take any initiative."[70] The problems described by the ARVN officers and government officials, including the abandonment of South Vietnam by the United States, were the results of years of protracted war and not a function of the final communist offensive. The 1975 attack was the *coup de grace* of a successful people's war rather than the *coup de main* depicted in many recent American accounts.

Although the 1975 communist offensive relied upon regular units attacking in very conventional ways, the descriptions of the offensive by

68. Tra, *Vietnam*, 94.
69. Dung, *Great Spring Victory*, 186, 133.
70. Hosmer, Kellen, and Jenkins, *Fall of South Vietnam*, 100, 75, 56, 119, 71.

the men who directed it and by those who tried to counter it indicate that the communists were definitely not engaging in conventional war as that term is normally understood in the United States. American conventional war doctrine does not anticipate reliance upon population within the enemy's territory for logistical and combat support. It does not rely upon guerrilla units to fix the enemy, establish clear lines of communication, and maintain security in the rear. And it certainly does not expect enemy morale to be undermined by political cadres within the very heart of the enemy's territory, cadres who will assume positions of political power as the offensive progresses. Yet all of these things happened in South Vietnam in 1975, and to call the offensive that orchestrated them a conventional attack, as that term is normally understood in the United States, is to misunderstand the reasons for communist success. As William Duiker has observed, "the fact that the 1975 campaign was primarily a military offensive should not obscure the fundamental reality that the Party's success over a generation was attributable, above all, to nonmilitary factors."[71]

Conclusions

Despite the evidence contradicting their views, some people will continue to believe that North Vietnamese communists conquered South Vietnam with a conventional strategy. At no time, however, was it a conventional war; from beginning to end it was a people's or revolutionary war in which both irregular and conventional forces played important roles. It was also not a war between North and South; it was always a conflict between Vietnamese communists from all parts of Vietnam and anticommunists, also from all parts of Vietnam but located geographically in the nation's southern half. Although the communist war effort was directed from Hanoi and depended on northern as well as southern resources, the war was fought and won in the South by the application of a strategy incorporating political and diplomatic as well as military struggle over a prolonged period of time. In short, it fit the model of people's war articulated by both Asian theorists and their Western interpreters. The conflict ended in 1975 after a communist offensive by regular units and local irregulars quickly demolished a dispirited opposition worn down by more than a decade of protracted war.

No matter how firmly individuals might wish to believe that the communist strategy of people's war failed in Vietnam or that commu-

71. Duiker, *Communist Road to Power,* 319.

nists from the North conquered the South in a conventional invasion, those views are not well supported by the evidence. To understand the war, one must first abandon the view that the conflict was a war of aggression, North against South, and recognize that the communist triumph was the result of the successful implementation of a strategy of people's war.

Recently, General Phillip B. Davidson concluded that "our defeat in Vietnam has taught us nothing."[72] If that pessimistic conclusion is true, then certainly some of the blame must rest with those who, over the years, have refused to recognize the true nature of the war.

72. Philip B. Davidson, *Vietnam at War: The History, 1946-1975* (Novato, Calif.: Presidio Press, 1988), 796, 811. In 1967-68 General Davidson served as General William Westmoreland's chief intelligence officer in Vietnam.

Acknowledgments

Chen, King C. "Hanoi's Three Decisions and the Escalation of the Vietnam War," *Political Science Quarterly* 90 (1975): 239–59. Reprinted with the permission of the author and The Academy of Political Science.

Kahin, George McT. "Political Polarization in South Vietnam: U.S. Policy in the Post-Diem Period," *Pacific Affairs* 52 (1979–80): 647–73. Reprinted with the permission of the University of British Columbia.

Mueller, John E. "The Search for the 'Breaking Point' in Vietnam: The Statistics of a Deadly Quarrel," *International Studies Quarterly* 24 (1980): 497–519. Reprinted with the permission of Blackwell Publishers.

Cannon, Michael W. "The Development of the American Theory of Limited War, 1945–63," *Armed Forces and Society* 19 (1992): 71–104. Reprinted with the permission of Transaction Publishers.

Badillo, Gilbert, and G. David Curry. "The Social Incidence of Vietnam Casualties: Social Class or Race?" *Armed Forces and Society* 2 (1976): 397–406. Reprinted with the permission of Transaction Publishers.

Savage, Paul L., and Richard A. Gabriel. "Cohesion and Disintegration in the American Army: An Alternative Perspective," *Armed Forces and Society* 2 (1976): 340–76. Reprinted with the permission of Transaction Publishers.

Carafano, James Jay. "West Point at War: Officer Attitudes and the Vietnam War, 1966–1972," *Journal of Popular Culture* 21 (1988): 25–35. Reprinted with the permission of the Popular Press.

Christy, Howard A . "Patrolling Hill 55: Hard Lessons in Retrospect," *The Marine Corp Gazette* 78 (1994): 76–83. Reprinted with the permission of the Marine Corp. Association.

Wunderlin, Clarence E., Jr. "Paradox of Power: Infiltration, Coastal Surveillance, and the United States Navy in Vietnam, 1965–68," *Journal of Military History* 53 (1989): 275–89. Reprinted with the permission of the Virginia Military Institute.

Brush, Peter. "The Significance of Local Communist Forces in Post-Tet Vietnam," *Journal of Third World Studies* 15 (1998): 67–78. Reprinted with the permission of the Association of Third World Studies Inc.

Kirkland, Faris R. "The Attack on Cap Mui Lay, Vietnam, July 1968," *Journal of Military History* 61 (1997): 735-60. Reprinted with the permission of the Virginia Military Institute.

Whitcomb, Darrel D. "Tonnage and Technology: Air Power on the Ho Chi Minh Trail," *Air Power History* 44 (1997): 6–17.

Leary, William M. "The CIA and the 'Secret War' in Laos: The Battle for Skyline Ridge, 1971–1972," *Journal of Military History* 59 (1995): 505–17. Reprinted with the permission of the Virginia Military Institute.

Duckworth, Richard D. "Fast-Movers and Herbicidal Spraying in Southeast Asia," *Air Power History* 45 (1998): 4–15.

Tilford, Earl H., Jr. "Setup: Why and How the U.S. Air Force Lost in Vietnam," *Armed Forces and Society* 17 (1991): 327–42. Reprinted with the permission of Transaction Publishers.

Gartner, Scott Sigmund. "Differing Evaluations of Vietnamization," *Journal of Interdisciplinary History* 29 (1998): 243–62. Reprinted from the *Journal of Interdisciplinary History* with the permission of the editors and The MIT Press, Cambridge, Massachusetts. Copyright 1998 by the Massachusetts Institute of Technology and the editors of the *Journal of Interdisciplinary History*.

Gates, John M. "People's War in Vietnam," *Journal of Military History* 54 (1990): 325–44. Reprinted with the permission of the Virginia Military Institute.

An environmentally friendly book printed and bound in England by www.printondemand-worldwide.com

PEFC Certified

This product is
from sustainably
managed forests
and controlled
sources

www.pefc.org

PEFC™
PEFC/16-33-415

FSC

Mixed Sources

Product group from well-managed
forests, and other controlled sources
www.fsc.org Cert no. TT-COC-002641
© 1996 Forest Stewardship Council

This book is made entirely of chain-of-custody materials

#0028 - - C0 - 229/152/18 - CB